Looking Back on the Vietnam War

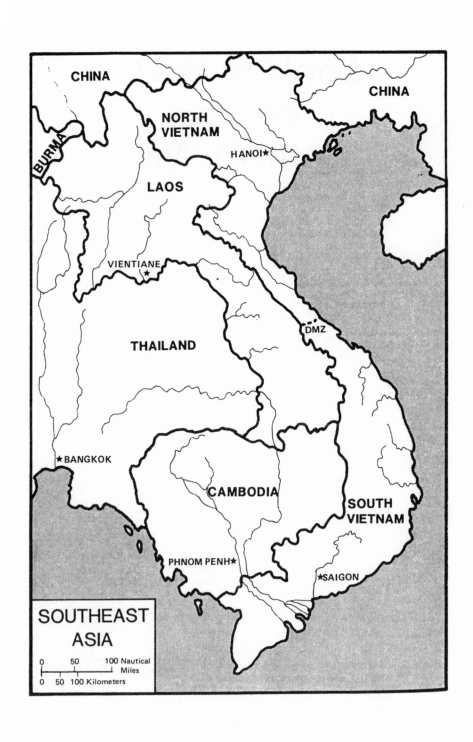

CHINA

NORTH
VIETNAM

BURMA

HANOI★

CHINA

LAOS

VIENTIANE
★

DMZ

THAILAND

★BANGKOK

CAMBODIA

SOUTH
VIETNAM

PHNOM PENH★

★SAIGON

SOUTHEAST
ASIA

0   50   100 Nautical
                    Miles
0   50 100 Kilometers

LOOKING BACK
ON THE
VIETNAM WAR

A 1990s Perspective on the
Decisions, Combat, and Legacies

EDITED BY
WILLIAM HEAD
AND
LAWRENCE E. GRINTER

Westport, Connecticut
London

Library of Congress Cataloging-in-Publication Data

Looking back on the Vietnam War : a 1990s perspective on the
  decisions, combat, and legacies / edited by William Head and
  Lawrence E. Grinter.
      p. cm.
    Includes bibliographical references and index.
    ISBN 0–275–94555–3 (pbk. : alk. paper)
    1. Vietnamese Conflict, 1961–1975—United States. I. Head,
  William. II. Grinter, Lawrence E.
  DS558.L66   1993b
  959.704'3373—dc20   92–39177

British Library Cataloguing in Publication Data is available.

A hardcover edition of *Looking Back on the Vietnam War: A
1990s Perspective on the Decisions, Combat, and Legacies* is
available from the Greenwood Press imprint of Greenwood
Publishing Group, Inc. (Contributions in Military Studies,
Number 142; ISBN: 0–313–28869–0)

Library of Congress Catalog Card Number: 92–39177
ISBN: 0–275–94555–3

First published in 1993

Praeger Publishers, 88 Post Road West, Westport, CT 06881
An imprint of Greenwood Publishing Group, Inc.

Printed in the United States of America

The paper used in this book complies with the
Permanent Paper Standard issued by the National
Information Standards Organization (Z39.48–1984).

10 9 8 7 6 5 4 3 2 1

Contents

Preface
William Head   vii

Abbreviations and Acronyms   ix

Introduction: The Vietnam War—A Look Back, A Look
Ahead
William Head   1

Part I: Background and Overview   **13**

1. Vietnam and Its Wars: A Historical Overview of U.S.
    Involvement
    William Head   15

2. The Global Dimensions and Legacies of a Brushfire War
    Marc Jason Gilbert   51

Part II: Decision Making and Policy Makers   **75**

3. The Johnson Administration's Conduct of Limited War in
    Vietnam
    George C. Herring   79

4. From the Tonkin Gulf to the Persian Gulf: The Devolution
    of the Senate's Role in War Making
    Caroline F. Ziemke   95

5. China and the Revisionist Thesis
    John W. Garver   105

Part III: The Air War   **119**

 6. Bombing Our Way Back Home: The Commando Hunt and
     Menu Campaigns of 1969–1973
     Earl H. Tilford, Jr.   123

 7. Of Demons, Storms, and Thunder: A Preliminary Look at
     Vietnam's Impact on the Persian Gulf Air Campaign
     Mark Clodfelter   145

 8. North Vietnamese Air Defenses During the Vietnam War
     Douglas Pike   161

Part IV: The Ground War   **173**

 9. If at First You Don't Succeed, Try to Rewrite History:
     Revisionism and the Vietnam War
     John M. Gates   177

10. Everything Is Perfect and Getting Better: The Myths and
     Measures of the American Ground War in Indochina, 1965–
     1968
     Larry E. Cable   191

Part V: Legacies   **225**

11. The Lessons and Ghosts of Vietnam
     Lorenzo M. Crowell   229

12. Reflections on the Vietnam War: The Views of a
     Vietnamese on Vietnamese-American Misconceptions
     Bui Diem   241

     Selected Bibliography   249

     Index   259

     About the Editors and Contributors   269

Preface

Now over two decades removed from the events that led to the major American intervention in the Second Indochina War (called the Vietnam War), the U.S. involvement still haunts Americans. In the most fundamental sense it is the only war this country ever lost, and it was one in which so much was expended by so many for such a questionable purpose. Why did American policy makers determine that South Vietnam, a nation with no industry and few natural resources of value, was worth defending against communism? Why did they draw the line in Southeast Asia? How could they determine that it was in America's interest to go half-way around the world and spend billions of dollars to defend the so-called "honor" of the free world? Once in Vietnam, why did America's seemingly omnipotent military power fail to bring to heel a Third World nation in a backwater of the world? This book examines a group of the salient factors that contributed to the outcome of the American war in Vietnam. These include decision making, the air war, and the ground war. In addition, the book examines some critical legacies that have impacted the United States since the end of the war.

This collection began as a body of research from a small group of scholars and seekers concerned about the Vietnam War and what it did to America, Vietnam, and the world. Over one hundred people met at Georgia Tech in February 1991 under the sponsorship of the Association of Third World Studies and the Georgia Tech School of International Affairs. Twenty-five widely recognized scholars presented and discussed every aspect of the war. Entitled "Vietnam: Impact and Legacy," the round table also included graduate students and nonacademics who lent a touch of new blood and perspective to the proceedings.

The conference took place in the midst of the American-Iraqi conflict in the Persian Gulf—a fact that even scholars of Vietnam, trying to remain objective and focused, could not ignore. In the end, it proved to be fortuitous since the Persian Gulf provided us with a foil that made our analysis of the Vietnam conflict all the more effective. These prominent scholars have reconsidered and revised their analyses especially for the use of fellow academics, students, and the general public. Of greatest importance is the fact that all of the chapters are based on new research and new sources. Many of the sources are from places like the Johnson Library, the Indochina Archives at the University of California, the National Archives, and the Air Force Historical Research Agency. Most have only been made available for research since 1990. This has led to some new and controversial conclusions by the authors—theories and conclusions only hinted at before but now supported by important new primary research. If for no other reason, this alone makes this book unique and significant.

This book is dedicated to those who still struggle to overcome ideological prejudice about the Vietnam War at both extremes and find, if not perfect truth, at least a possibility of future peace. It is also for those who suffer painful memories but refuse to turn away from reality in order to remind our posterity that Vietnam, like all wars, isn't about *Rambo* but about dying. It is for those who fought, who shed their blood, who served, who studied and protested, who anguished and suffered, and especially those on all sides who did not return home alive.

—William Head

Abbreviations and Acronyms

AA	Antiaircraft
AAA	Antiaircraft artillery
AAR	After Action Report
AF	Air Force
AFB	Air Force Base
AFM	Air Force Manual
AID	Agency for International Development
ARVN	Army of the Republic of Vietnam (South)
ASEAN	Association of Southeast Asian Nations
ATO	Air Tasking Order
AVF	All Volunteer Force
BDA	Battle Damage Assessment
CIA	Central Intelligence Agency
CINCPAC	Commander in Chief, Pacific Command
CINCPACAF	Commander in Chief, Pacific Air Forces
COMUSMACV	Commander, United States Military Assistance Command, Vietnam
CORDS	Civil Operations and Revolutionary Development Support
COSVN	Central Office for South Vietnam
CTZ	Central Zone
D.C.	District of Columbia (Washington)
DIA	Defense Intelligence Agency
DOD	Department of Defense

DMZ	Demilitarized Zone (17th Parallel)
DRV (DRVN)	Democratic Republic of Vietnam (North Vietnam)
EOTR	End of Tour Report
FANK	Forces Armec Nationale
GPO	Government Printing Office
GVN	Government of Vietnam
HandI	Harassment and Interdiction
I Corps	U.S. Army First Corps' South Vietnamese Area of Operations
II Corps	U.S. Army Second Corps' South Vietnamese Area of Operations
JCS	Joint Chiefs of Staff
KIA	Killed in Action
LOE	Letter of evaluation
MAAG	Military Assistance Advisory Group
MAC	Military Airlift Command (U.S.)
MACV	Military Assistance Command, Vietnam
MAF	Marine Amphibious Force
MLR	Main Line of Resistance
NASA	National Aeronautical and Space Administration
NCO	Noncommissioned officer
NLF	National Liberation Front
NVA	North Vietnamese Army (same as PAVN)
NVN	North Vietnam
OER	Officers' Effectiveness Report
OPlan	Operation Plan
OSS	Office of Strategic Services
PACAF	Pacific Air Forces (U.S.)
PAVN	People's Army of Vietnam (North) (same as NVA)
POL	Petroleum, oil, lubricants
PRVN	People's Republic of Vietnam (North Vietnam)
R&D	Research and development
R&R	Rest and relaxation
RTAFB	Royal Thai Air Force Base
RVN	Republic of Vietnam (South Vietnam)
SAC	Strategic Air Command (U.S.)
SAM	Surface-to-air missile
SAR	Search and rescue
SIOP	Single Integrated Operational Plan

SKS	Samozaryadnyi Karabin Simonova, Russian 7.62 Boevey 1943 carbine supplied to Vietminh and VC, 1945 to 1964
SOW	Special Operations Wing
SRV	Socialist Republic of Vietnam
STRICOM	Strike Command (U.S.)
SVN	South Vietnam
TAC	Tactical Air Command (U.S.)
TDY	Temporary duty
TFW	Tactical Fighter Wing (U.S.)
The "Trail"	The Ho Chi Minh Trail
UN	United Nations
UPT	Undergraduate Pilot Training
U.S.	United States
USA	United States Army
USAF	United States Air Force
USAID	United States Agency for International Development
USARV	United States Army, Vietnam
USIA	United States Information Agency
USIS	United States Information Service
USMC	United States Marine Corps
USN	United States Navy
VC	Viet Cong
Vietminh	Short name for 1940s/1950s Vietnamese Independence Faction (Viet Nam Doc Lap Dong Minh Hoi—League for the Independence of Vietnam formed 1941)
VNAF	Vietnamese Air Force (South)
VNCC	Vietnamese Commander in Chief
VWP	Vietnamese Workers' Party
War Zone A	A VC redoubt north of Saigon
War Zone B	A VC redoubt northeast of Saigon
War Zone C	A VC redoubt northwest of Saigon, roughly encompassing northwest Tay Ninh Province
War Zone D	A VC redoubt north-northwest of Saigon centered on the intersection of the borders of Bing Long, Phuoc Long, and Bin Buong Provinces
WIA	Wounded in Action

Looking Back
on the
Vietnam War

Introduction: The Vietnam War—A Look Back, A Look Ahead

William Head

In the movie *Apocalypse Now*, actor Robert Duvall portrays a fanatical Air Cavalry lieutenant colonel obsessed with surfing even in the midst of his helicopter gunship's attack on a Viet Cong–held village. His men fly into combat to the pulsating sounds of Wagner's "The Flight of the Valkyries" blaring over loudspeakers rigged to the choppers. They leave playing cards on the bodies of dead enemy soldiers. In the end, shirtless, wearing a blue cavalry hat from the nineteenth-century West, napalm bursting in the background, he turns to the movie's hero, played by Martin Sheen, and says, "I love it! I love the smell of napalm in the morning! It smells like . . . VICTORY!"

It may seem a skewed view to many, or simply a depiction of part of Stanley Kuberic's genre of 1970s moviemaking, but victory, such as the kind pictured in the movie, is what Vietnam means to most Americans today. From the standpoint of realism, it is more truthful than such things as *Rambo*, but beyond that, it is in a sense, as is the entire miasmic world of Hollywood Vietnam, embellished by the hypnotic battle scenes of *Apocalypse Now*, *Platoon*, and *Full Metal Jacket*, psychologically the reality that still stalks the American national psyche.

Vietnam has generated ghosts and demons so haunting and so psychologically debilitating that in the effort to exorcise these specters, to purge past failures, the United States and its leaders over the past decade have embraced a series of debatable military victories over fifth-rate troops in Third World countries. In an effort to reaffirm our national honor and our moral purpose, and restore our self-worth so tainted by the defeat in Vietnam, we have altered history, in literature and films, and overcelebrated military victories undertaken for dubious purposes.

But even with such victories, the old American pride engendered by overcoming a Great Depression, experiencing real victory in World War II, walking on the moon, and standing as the world's shining beacon of freedom, rings hollow. In reviewing the grand Persian Gulf welcome-home parade, Sydney Schanberg of *Newsday* noted,

I do not hear the spontaneous joy and revelry of a great nation celebrating a grand success. What I hear instead are people desperate for an uplift, depressed by the lingering weight of Vietnam, weary of the ills in our economy and our system of social care—and therefore wishing it all away with a giant circus of flyovers, bagpipes, tanks, majorettes, missiles, and tons of cascading confetti.[1]

Everybody loves a parade, but Vietnam has not gone away despite the parades given us by the Bush administration. The Vietnam debate should not end until it is extensively and honestly evaluated for its meaning. In fact, what President Bush did was make the need for such study all the greater by fallaciously comparing Vietnam to the Gulf War.

VIETNAM AND THE PERSIAN GULF WAR

One of the most discouraging misconceptions to arise from the Persian Gulf War was that it somehow was a vindication for Vietnam. President Bush, from the outset, established this tone for the general public. On the night of January 16, 1991, as he announced the opening of the air war against Iraq, he declared,

I instructed our military commanders to take every necessary step to prevail as quickly as possible, and with the greatest degree of protection possible for American and Allied service men and women. I've told the American people before that this will not be another Vietnam, and I repeat this here tonight. Our troops will have the best possible support in the entire world, and they will not be asked to fight with one arm tied behind their back.[2]

Such sentiments struck a popular cord, one to which most military commanders ascribed. This shouldn't be surprising since the vast majority had spent their formative years in Vietnam and had bitter memories of what they believed were the short-sighted war policies of Presidents Lyndon B. Johnson and Richard M. Nixon. In a series of October 1990 interviews with Chief of the Joint Chiefs of Staff (JCS), General Colin Powell, Lt. Gen. Walter E. Boomer, Commander of U.S. Marine forces in the Gulf, Admiral Frank B. Kelso II, Chief of Naval Operations, and General Carl E. Vuono, Army Chief of Staff, in *U.S. News & World Report* the latter summed up his comrades' feelings when he noted that, "The group of leaders who are in the key positions, we were all about the same rank during Vietnam days, majors and lieutenant colonels, and I think all of us were shaped by the low point in the military in the early 70's."[3]

In December 1990, General Powell once again alluded to military leadership's concern about the ghost of Vietnam. During a final inspection tour of the Gulf theater, the general declared that once diplomacy fails "you go in to win decisively, not to force people to the negotiating table.''[4] The statement was an obvious referral to what he believed was the mistaken policies of Vietnam.[4]

The American public embraced these same concerns and was also firmly convinced of the need to fight a different war in the Persian Gulf. Understandably, even Saddam Hussein attempted to take advantage of America's Vietnam phobia. During and after the fall hostage crisis, Hussein took every opportunity to warn the American public that a war with Iraq might be another long, bloody, and divisive struggle ''like Vietnam.''[5]

THE REALITIES OF THE VIETNAM WAR

Despite politically popular notions that a disloyal press, the antiwar movement, and civilian political restriction on the U.S. military cost the United States victory in Southeast Asia, most analysts agree that these Vietnam and Gulf wars, although comparisons can be made, were very different.

The most critical difference is that whereas the Vietnam conflict occurred at the height of the Cold War, the struggle in the Persian Gulf was the first major post–Cold War conflict. In Vietnam, U.S. political leaders always had to be concerned about widening the war into a global war with the Soviet Union and/ or the People's Republic of China (PRC). A Cold War mindset compelled the United States to pour hundreds of billions of dollars into a limited war effort in which nevertheless 58,000 Americans died, and 8 million tons of bombs fell. East-West rivalries motivated the USSR and PRC to supply a constant stream of arms, materiel, and spare parts to their client ally. From the standpoint of American air power, one of the most significant items the Soviets supplied North Vietnam in abundant quantities were surface-to-air missiles (SAMs), which wrought heavy losses on U.S. aircraft by forcing crews to fly into the teeth of a heavy antiaircraft artillery (AAA) defense.[6]

After initial allied air attacks destroyed almost all of Iraq's considerably more advanced SAMs, their antiaircraft capability was severely limited because air operations were conducted at high altitude. This was even more significant because during the Gulf War the Soviet Union, Iraq's primary supplier of these sophisticated weapons, was ostensibly part of the twenty-eight-nation coalition and did not provide replacements. China also stayed out of the Gulf, as did most of the other major arms suppliers, due, at least in part, to the UN embargo. Although Iraqi nighttime AAA fire was spectacular to see on the CNN evening news, its effectiveness was minimal compared to what the SAMs might have done.

Other critical differences between the two conflicts range from the obvious contrasts of weather, climate, and terrain to the technological advances that exceeded the predictions of even the most optimistic allied avionics advocates. From an air power standpoint, operations in Vietnam posed the most difficult challenges of jungle terrains and tropical climates. Accurate bombing, locating enemy targets, and wear and tear on aircraft were only a few of the difficulties

faced by U.S. air forces. On the other hand, in the Iraqi and Kuwaiti theaters—
Allied aircraft attrition notwithstanding—coalition air forces had one of the best
set of natural circumstances available in air war history. It is also worth men-
tioning that aircraft damage and fatigue problems unique to the area were ef-
fectually remedied by well-trained Air Force field repair teams used to training
exercises conducted in the Nevada desert.

New electronic warfare, avionics, and weapon system packages have made it
easier to fight an effective conventional air war. In addition, the structural toughness of modern jets is remarkable considering the numerous minor hits they can
withstand without crashing. Similar structural and engine damage would have
downed many of America's World War II, Korean, or Vietnam vintage aircraft.

In Part III on the air war, the reader is fortunate to have three articles written
by acknowledged experts on this important aspect of the conflict in Vietnam.
Earl H. Tilford, Jr., examines the post–Rolling Thunder campaigns in "Bombing
Our Way Back Home: The Commando Hunt and Menu Campaigns of 1969–
1973." Mark Clodfelter, the author of the acclaimed work, *The Limits of Air
Power*, examines the comparative nature of the Vietnam and Persian Gulf air
wars in his chapter, "Of Demons, Storms, and Thunder: A Preliminary Look
at Vietnam's Impact on the Persian Gulf Air Campaign." Douglas Pike, the
preeminent expert on the Viet Cong and People's Army of Vietnam, gives us a
rare look at "North Vietnamese Air Defenses During the Vietnam War." All
three authors provide important new research and analysis on the air war in
Vietnam. They make it clear that a comparison between the two wars is risky
business but an exercise worth undertaking to correct any misconceptions brought
about by overzealous air power proponents looking for a sponge to wipe away
the failures of the past.

VIETNAM AND THE GULF BY THE NUMBERS

By the end of allied operations in the Gulf on February 27, 1991, their air
forces had flown nearly 125,000 overall sorties, of which more than 110,000
were combat sorties, and they lost only fifty-one planes, thirty-eight of which
were combat aircraft (twenty-nine of those being American). The enormity of
this effort can be appreciated when compared to similar numbers from the air
war in Vietnam. From June 1965 to August 1973, B–52s flew 125,479 sorties,
while tactical aircraft few over 2 million sorties during the same time. However,
the United States flew more sorties and expended more bombs in six weeks in
the Persian Gulf War than during any single year in Vietnam.

During the Vietnam conflict two of the most significant air campaigns were
the Linebacker I (May 10–October 23) and II (December 18–29) campaigns of
1972. In the first, "155,548 tons of bombs fell on North Vietnam, one-fourth
the tonnage dropped during Rolling Thunder" (1965–1968). In the second, U.S.
Air Force B–52s flew 729 sorties dropping 15,237 tons of bombs. Over the six
months of the Linebacker campaigns, the number of bomber sorties and tons of

bombs dropped were essentially the same as in the six weeks of the Persian Gulf War. With the use of "smart bombs" and superior targeting technology by the Allies, tactical aircraft were far more proficient than similar attacks had been in Vietnam; fewer bombs did more damage per sortie in the Persian Gulf War than in Vietnam.[7]

The Gulf War, although waged against a Third World country, was a classic conventional war fought along the lines of strategies and tactics (i.e., the Air-Land Battle plan of NATO) developed in World War II, Korea, and the Arab–Israeli wars of the previous four decades. And America's military is very good at conventional combat. In all these wars air superiority, although it didn't win the war alone, proved an essential determining factor in the outcome. In Vietnam, despite U.S. air supremacy, the war couldn't be successfully prosecuted. This can at least in part be explained, as Douglas Pike does in his chapter on "North Vietnamese Air Defenses During the Vietnam War," by an analysis of the nature of the Vietnam conflict, which for the most part was not conventional. Even when it did finally become more characteristic of a conventional war, it did so at the choosing of the enemy and not the Americans.

According to Pike in his earlier work on the Viet Cong and People's Army of North Vietnam (PAVN), the Vietnamese Communist leaders conceptualized their struggle, or *dau tranh minh*, on two levels—one a sociopolitical and economic struggle (political or *dau tranh chinh tri*) and the other a military or armed struggle (armed or *dau tranh vu trang*). In this regard, they undertook action against the Allies in three ways: *dich van*, action among the enemy; *dan van*, action among the people; and *binh van*, action against the enemy.

Pike makes a powerful argument that American leadership never grasped the true reality of the war and characterizes U.S. strategic policy as "vincible ignorance," or "you know you do not know that you do not know it, but you don't care." Thus, the American attitude toward war has always been that it is an occasionally painful social necessity, while to the Communist Vietnamese it was a total commitment to struggle. Pike provides compelling evidence that the North Vietnamese Communists' resolution was almost inexhaustible and that they were willing and able to absorb large numbers of casualties. From the military standpoint this was largely due to the previously mentioned Soviet resupply of critical weapons. With these advantages they could, and did, carry on the war at both *dau tranh* levels, alternating one to the other as circumstances necessitated.[8]

George Herring, in his well-respected book *America's Longest War*, points out that the Indochina conflict to which U.S. leaders, beginning in the late 1950s, persistently committed themselves, had begun as an anticolonial civil conflict aimed at purging Vietnam of foreigners.[9] But Herring goes on to say, in "The Johnson Administration's Conduct of Limited War in Vietnam," that U.S. perceptions of the conflict changed, and thus so did American policies. Kennedy, and especially Johnson, tried to dictate what the character and nature of the struggle would be and how the results would be formed. Instead, as Herring and

Douglas Pike both argue, the enemy dictated the nature and results of the war in Indochina because, in the end, it meant more to them.

Regardless of one's approval or disapproval of the resulting Socialist Republic of Vietnam (SRV), the war in Vietnam was the outgrowth of what became known in the post–World War II era as a "peoples' revolution." It was fought on various diplomatic, political, propagandist, military, and even economic levels using numerous means and methods with varying success. The almost exclusive employment of conventional weapons, strategies, and policies by the United States, especially in the early days, could never have completely destroyed the Communists. Even if the United States had done as revisionists such as Admiral U.S. Grant Sharp have advocated, in hindsight—that is, bring the full brunt of military power to bear—there is no real evidence that this would have attained U.S. goals. As Herring notes, U.S. goals were ill-conceived and kept changing. Worst of all, as Ambassador Bui Diem points out in his chapter "Reflections on the Vietnam War: The Views of a Vietnamese on Vietnamese-American Misconceptions," in trying to help the South, American leaders undermined the South Vietnamese leadership structure, ultimately helping to eliminate—via lack of experience and training, as well as death, or loss of power through incessant coups—most of the talent necessary for the South to eventually protect and defend itself.[10]

This is easily contrasted with the circumstances in the Gulf conflict. Saddam Hussein, as President Bush suggested, compared more with Benito Mussolini or Adolf Hitler than Ho Chi Minh. Iraq's invasion of a weaker neighbor compares more with the German invasion of Poland in 1939 or the Italian invasion of Ethiopia in 1935 than any military action taken by the Vietminh, Viet Cong, or regular North Vietnamese Army (NVA) until 1975. In addition, Iraqi tactics more closely resembled those employed in World War I by both sides, or by the French at the Maginot Line in 1940, rather than NVA or Viet Cong insurgency tactics. As Pike, Herring, Cable, and Tilford point out in this book and elsewhere, Iraq had no military strategy worthy of the word, whereas the Communist Vietnamese strategies articulated through time were consistently superior to the strategies attempted by the Americans. The comparison goes even deeper when one compares the Germans' strategies of blitzkrieg and their end run through the Low Countries in 1940 with General Schwarzkopf's "Hail Mary" end run around the Iraqi forces in southern Kuwait.[11]

Both John M. Gates in "If at First You Don't Succeed, Try to Rewrite History: Revisionism and the Vietnam War" and Larry E. Cable in "Everything Is Perfect and Getting Better: The Myths and Measures of the American Ground War in Indochina, 1965–1968" focus on the land war in Vietnam and the unique differences in the Vietnamese ground campaigns. They both agree that the tactics used by the Vietnamese and the ones which should have been used by the Americans were completely foreign to the U.S. establishment, which was incapable of adjusting. In the Gulf War, the U.S. military fought using tactics it had developed to fight the Soviets in Europe. Fortunately for the Americans, the Iraqi Army was organized, trained, and equipped by the USSR. It was, in effect, a "lite" version of a stronger beer. It was also very poorly led.

THE U.S. MILITARY ORGANIZATION SINCE 1975

In many respects, the advances and improvements in the U.S. military since 1975 are not because of specific lessons from the war in Southeast Asia but because the character and opinions of present-day leaders were formed by that war: They were determined not to lose again. The growing professionalism of U.S. forces since the U.S. failure in Vietnam has been a positive trend. However, the failure of the United States to augment its standing military with anything approaching an adequate selective service listing to be used in wartime has created a potential crisis in U.S. force structure. The Gulf War did not fully demonstrate this because the war lasted such a short time. However, had it gone past a year and rotations of hundreds of thousands of forces been necessary, the Americans would have been unable to replace their standing forces on the front line with anything close to a trained or skilled force to carry on a protracted conflict. The questionable use and performance of too often ill-prepared Reserve and National Guard forces during the recent Middle Eastern conflict also points up the weakness of the AVF system which if not fully funded, supplied, and augmented will leave the United States poorly defended in a conflict with anything resembling a viable foe.

AIR POWER IS THE THING

Although it should be evident that Vietnam furnished little of specific military value to U.S. and Allied combat planners in the Persian Gulf, the policies developed after 1975 out of the aura of defeat, combined with basic common sense and professional expertise, led to a smashing American and Allied military victory in the Persian Gulf War. This was especially true with regard to air power. But Tilford's chapter warns that to simply proclaim that air power did nothing wrong in Vietnam and could have won the war if left to its own design is both naive and a disservice to the Air Force. It is a disservice that may be perpetrated, this time on a greater scale now that air power has performed so well in the Persian Gulf. It is a mistake derived from the sensitivity of defeat and now compounded by an apparently total victory.

In his book *Setup: What the Air Force Did in Vietnam and Why*, Tilford argues that the Vietnam-era Air Force was a bureaucratic technocracy where statistical indices of success became a substitute for strategy. The numbers from Vietnam were remarkable; indeed, the numbers from the Gulf War are also remarkable. For example, during the strategic airlift of August 17, 1990, to March 1, 1991, U.S. cargo transport aircraft flew 15,317 sorties carrying 519,458 tons of supplies, and 482,997 passengers. Altogether it was, in seven months, the greatest American airlift in total numbers since the eight-year effort of the U.S. airlift during the Vietnam conflict.[12] To quote General Hansford T. Johnson, Commander, U.S. Transport Command, "We moved more tons more miles in the first six weeks of Desert Shield than in 65 weeks of the Berlin Airlift."[13]

Ultimately, it was because of the innovation of airlift experts in the Air Force that this enormous effort was executed so capably. To get the job done, some C–141s arrived in Saudi Arabia without their paint scheme. Several KC–10 and KC–135R refuelers were temporarily converted into cargo haulers, and the Commercial Reserve Air Fleet (CRAF) was activated in August 1990 to assure the rapid deployment of adequate personnel and supplies to the Gulf region.[14] Of course, as many experts have noted, the buildup could never have proceeded effectively if Saddam Hussein had used his air force early on to harass transports or bomb Saudi airfields.

VIETNAM, THE GULF, AND DECISION MAKING

In the end, perhaps the one clear similarity between the Gulf War and Vietnam conflicts was the heavy-handed method of White House control over the powers of the government and military to make war. In examining President Bush's policy-making style and the role of his advisers, Robert Woodward's recent book *The Commanders* points out the many similarities in the civilian leadership and the contrast in the military leaders during the two wars.[15]

One good contrasting example in the present book is found in George C. Herring's chapter "The Johnson Administration's Conduct of Limited War in Vietnam," which examines the cobwebs of personalities and foibles that made up the decision-making processes used by President Johnson and his advisers during the Vietnam War.

One can also compare the declining role of Congress in Caroline F. Ziemke's chapter entitled "From the Tonkin Gulf to the Persian Gulf: The Devolution of the Senate's Role in War Making." It examines the Congress's patriotic but misguided desire to support President Johnson's Vietnam policies (especially during the Gulf of Tonkin Resolution). Ziemke effectively argues that as a result of the efforts by long-time hawks like Georgia Senator Richard B. Russell, the Congress unwittingly abdicated its constitutional authority to wage war to such an extent that, despite efforts to the contrary by senators like Sam Nunn, it was all but completely circumvented by President Bush during preparations for the Persian Gulf War.

Ziemke's work also inspires the thoughtful reader to ask, "What if the war had not gone so well?" "What ifs" are important in the historical scheme of things because events like war are so full of risk they should be fully analyzed. For example, what if the war had gone badly? What if Iraqi tanks had crossed into Saudi Arabia immediately after securing Kuwait? What if their air force had been used properly from the outset? What if the war had lasted for a year or two or three? What would have happened even if the war had gone "less well''—as it surely would have if Iraqi forces had operated properly? If any of these caveats had been factored in, the president and Congress surely would have come to blows. Would this have meant the curtailment of presidential power under the War Powers Act? Indeed, Ziemke's chapter makes us ask all these questions, especially from the perspective of the Vietnam conflict.

One aspect of the two wars that is not comparable is the influence of Robert McNamara. His complex personality and often curious relationship with President Johnson is the topic of several chapters. McNamara first wanted only to win in the South by destroying the NLF and strengthening any non-Communist regime by making it economically, militarily, and politically safe. But eventually McNamara became convinced of the North's direction in the war effort and spear-headed, if not master-minded, the Gulf of Tonkin process and the expansion of the U.S. role in Vietnam. Ultimately, this did not achieve the desired goal and, as Ambassador Bui Diem notes in his analytical chapter "Reflections on the Vietnam War: The Views of a Vietnamese on Vietnamese-American Misconceptions,'' in its desire to save non-Communist South Vietnam the U.S. intervention not only expanded the role of the North, the Soviets, and the Chinese, but it also disabled the very leaders and elements of the southern polity and military that might have, over a period of time, been able to create a viable alternative to the NLF.

John W. Garver in his chapter "China and the Revisionist Thesis'' expands the examination of the possibility of Chinese intervention in the war. He agrees with the revisionist thesis that Johnson refused to invade North Vietnam out of fear of a Korean-style intervention by the Chinese. However, unlike these historians, Garver argues that Johnson's concerns over increased Chinese and Soviet involvement were not only valid but would have resulted, ultimately, in more states such as Thailand and Burma falling to communism.

In the end, Johnson's policy in Vietnam was colored by his desire to maintain "guns and butter'' and to force the Vietnamese Communists (like the French under Laniel) to the peace table. The U.S. effort to increase the "quotient of pain'' on North Vietnam also created an overly optimistic view of the war in the American public's mind in late 1967. Not only did this contribute to a total loss of public confidence in the war after Tet, but it caused the U.S. leadership to totally misinterpret the nature of the war before and after the Tet offensive, and thus "vincibly ignorant'' U.S. leaders decided that the NLF and the North were the same! This ignored the reality that the NLF was independent in the 1950s and early 1960s. Moreover, while supplied increasingly by the North after the 1965 U.S. buildup, the NLF still acted on its own and not as Northern stooges until the rash acts of Tet all but destroyed them as a fighting organization.

Both chapters by Gates and Cable analyze often overlooked aspects of the late 1960s ground war and the policies thus made by U.S. leaders from a lack of proper knowledge of the situation. They also decry the recent trend by revisionist authors to look back and determine that if only the United States had fought a conventional war committing more men and materiel from the outset, we could have won. As John Gates notes, that's rewriting history. Worst of all, it fails to ask the question, "What would we have won?"

CONCLUSION

Only a reexamination of the truth of Vietnam can help the passage of time repair the stinging wounds of the Vietnam War and prevent popular and politically expedient misconceptions and misrepresentations from allowing the truth to be hidden and leave the wounds to continue to fester and the ghosts to continue to haunt our dreams of the future. This book pays particular attention to the legacies of the Vietnam War. Besides, Ambassador Diem's personal reflections on Vietnam in the section on legacies also includes Crowell's "The Lessons and Ghosts of Vietnam."

In the end, the entire book from its opening chapter through sections on decision making, the ground war, air war, and legacies provides "A Look Back, A Look Ahead."

NOTES

1. Sydney H. Schanberg, "Politics, Not Patriotism, Dominate Gulf War Parade," *Atlanta Constitution and Journal* (June 10, 1991): 3A.

2. Transcript, "Nationwide Television Broadcast of a Speech by President George Bush on the Beginning of the Air War in the Persian Gulf," 9:00 P.M. EST, January 16, 1991, in *Facts on File* 51, no. 2617 (January 17, 1991): 28.

3. "Lines in the Sand," *U.S. News & World Report* (October 1, 1990): 29–34. This theme is developed in popular and compelling revisionist books such as Adm. U. S. Grant Sharp, *Strategy for Defeat: Vietnam in Retrospect* (Novato, CA: Presidio Press, 1986). It blames the U.S. defeat on its political leaders who "lacked resolve." Sharp writes, "We could have achieved victory with relative ease, and without using nuclear weapons or invading North Vietnam. All we had to do to win was to use our existing air power—properly."

4. "You Go in to Win Decisively," *U.S. News & World Report* (December 24, 1990): 126.

5. Editorial, "Why Hussein Smells Victory," *U.S. News & World Report* (December 24, 1990): 67.

6. For further examination of this issue see George Herring, *America's Longest War* (New York: Wiley, 1979), 130–31, 147–51 [hereafter *America's Longest War*]; Mark Clodfelter, *The Limits of Air Power: The American Bombing of North Vietnam* (New York: The Free Press, 1989), 137, 188–93 [hereafter *Limits of Air Power*]; Carl Berger, ed., *The United States Air Force in Southeast Asia, 1961–1973: An Illustrated Account* (Washington, DC: Office of Air Force History, 1984), 70–79, 166–67, 219–21 [hereafter *USAF in SEA*]; Earl H. Tilford, Jr., *Setup: What the Air Force Did in Vietnam and Why* (Maxwell AFB, AL: Air Univ. Press, 1991). The best chapter for this issue is chapter 3 on Rolling Thunder, pp. 89–163. Those who read Herring's, Tilford's, and Clodfelter's

books, as well as Admiral Sharp's work (see note 3), will note that they disagree with Sharp on the potentially decisive nature of air power in Vietnam.

7. Berger, *USAF in SEA*, 166–67; Clodfelter, *Limits of Air Power*, 166, 194. For more on Linebacker see Clodfelter, *Limits of Air Power*, 156–72, 181–202; Briefing transcript, Pentagon spokesperson Peter Williams, January 27, 1991, sect. 1, p. 6. Note that the differences in sortie numbers from the different sources is due to helicopter sorties that were often not included. During the February 28, 1991, theater briefing, the Allied spokesperson placed the official number of sorties at 106,000 for forty-three days of combat; see *Facts on File*, 51, no. 2623 (February 28, 1991): 129. It should also be noted that sortie numbers from Vietnam also vary; see, for example, the *Washington Post* (January 31, 1991) article that placed the total Vietnam B–52 sorties mentioned above at 126,615. However, in reviewing USAF figures this number was the total of planned sorties. The above number is the number actually flown; see *Facts on File* 51, no. 2619 (January 31, 1991): 60.

8. For more on PAVN and VC strategies, see Douglas Pike, *PAVN: People's Army of North Vietnam* (Novato, CA: Presidio Press, 1986); ch. 1 and Conclusion express the above-mentioned thesis very effectively [hereafter *PAVN*]. See also Douglas Pike, *Vietcong: The Organization and Techniques of the National Liberation Front of South Vietnam* (Cambridge, MA: MIT Press, 1966): 85–105 [hereafter *Vietcong*].

9. Herring, *America's Longest War*, 43–107; Pike, *PAVN*, chs. 2–3, which examine, through exhaustive primary research, the civil and colonial nature of the struggle and how U.S. entry tried to change this but failed. This issue is also dealt with throughout Pike's *Vietcong*. Another more conservative work that generally agrees with the above thesis is David Chanoff and Van Toai Doan, *Portrait of the Enemy* (New York: Random House, 1986).

10. For a well-balanced account of problems experienced by South Vietnamese leaders and their problems with the U.S. presence, see Bui Diem and David Chanoff, *In the Jaws of History* (Boston: Houghton Mifflin, 1987).

11. Anthony Kemp, *The Maginot Line: Myth and Reality* (New York: Military Heritage Press, 1988): 84–92.

12. Message, U.S. Central Command to Military Airlift Command, Rpt., "Desert Storm Airlift Figures," Feb. 282134Z; MAC News Service, "CNC MAC Discusses the Past Year—Part I," *End of Year Report*, December 90 [hereafter "CNC MAC"]; John Berry, "How Much Is Enough," *Newsweek* (November 5, 1990): 16–17; SMSgt. Douglas I. Gilbert, "Logistics Lifeline: Sustaining Desert Shield," *Airman*, vol. 34, no. 11 (November 1990): 22–23.

13. "CNC MAC."

14. Four articles discoursing this massive airlift, the lessons of the past, and the solutions used in the Gulf War, are Major Donald E. Hamblin, "Distribution Priority System: Time for a Change?" *Air Force Journal of Logistics* 14, no. 4 (Fall 1990): 17–21 [hereafter *AFJL*]; Major Benjamin L. Dilla, "Logistics Support Limitations in the Vietnam War: Lessons for Today's Logisticians," *AFJL* 14, no. 4 (Fall 1990): 35–38; SSgt. James C. Mesco, "Airlifting Logistics: Warner Robins Air Logistics Center's Support of 'Desert Shield' Airlift Operations," *AFJL* 15, no. 3 (Summer 1991): 6–10; William Head, "Air Power in the Persian Gulf: An Initial Search for the Right Lessons," *AFJL* 16, no. 1 (Winter 1992): 10–19.

15. Robert Woodward, *The Commanders* (New York: Simon & Schuster, 1991).

Part I

Background and Overview

The first part of this book traverses the breadth of the Vietnam War from the opening historical overview by William Head to Marc Jason Gilbert's world view of the war. Head provides a straightforward historical look at Vietnamese history and ultimately how and why the United States became involved in what began as a French colonial problem and continued as a Vietnamese civil struggle with external intervention. By briefly reviewing the history of Vietnam, its colonial period and its successful expulsion of the French in 1954, Head seeks to explain U.S. involvement not as an unfortunate accident, but rather as a conscious decision made by American leaders based on assumptions about the responsibilities and omnipotence of U.S. power. He focuses on four climatic periods—the Geneva Convention of 1954, the assassination of Ngo Dinh Diem in 1963, the Tet Offensive of 1968, and the Paris Peace Accords of 1973—to explain how and why the United States entered the conflict and how and why they eventually withdrew.

Gilbert's chapter takes another approach by seeking to determine the world's view of the Vietnam War. This includes not only its opinions of American involvement but also the legacy the war left for the rest of the world. In doing so he artfully helps us understand the war not in the narrow American context but also in the broader context of world history.

Both chapters attempt to provide, each in different fashion, an overview of, and introduction for, the more specific topics to come later in the book.

1

Vietnam and Its Wars: A Historical Overview of U.S. Involvement

William Head

In *Vietnam Reconsidered*, editor Harrison E. Salisbury called the Vietnam War "the war that seems to have no ending, the war that lies heavy on our hearts and still awakens us in nightmare. . . . " He went on to ask, "How did it come about; what machine set it in motion; what passions fueled its escalation and left as residue in American lives such debts—human, political, moral, social, philosophical?"[1]

Over the past thirty odd years, thousands of poignant books and articles have been published seeking to fully comprehend the Vietnam War. Even in the time since 1984 when Salisbury and his colleagues completed their exhaustive review, dozens of conferences have been convened and studies published still seeking to discover the elusive truths of what has become the American enigma we call the Vietnam War. The war has been so pervasive in its effects on the recent history of American politics, economics, and society that in one almost Orwellian perspective the whole prior history of Vietnam and Indochina seems to be just a series of preludes to the tragic American-sponsored play acted out on that remote Southeast Asian stage from 1954 to 1975.

Of course, the history of Vietnam was not traced out for the benefit of any foreign culture such as that of the United States but for those who were born in, have lived in, were shaped by, and died in Vietnam. This is true of all nations, and in Vietnam today it continues to be true despite nearly one hundred years of French colonialism, four years of Japanese occupation, twenty years of American intervention, and nearly forty years of Communist socioeconomic control. And yet, in 90 percent or more of all the books and articles ever written about Indochina, the focus has been on America's unhappy two-decade sojourn in what most Westerners still see as a remote part of the world. Even in popularly acclaimed works like Stanley Karnow's *Vietnam: A History*, companion to the PBS television documentary, and Frances FitzGerald's *Fire in the Lake*, the lengthy background chapters on Vietnamese history and French colonialism seem designed to provide a perspective from which to understand American involvement in the 1950s, 1960s, and 1970s.[2]

This is true, at least in part, because most of the history of Indochina has been written by Westerners for Westerners. Moreover, the leaders of the Vietminh, Viet Cong (National Liberation Front/NLF), Communists, and/or Socialist Republic of Vietnam have traditionally restricted Western access to their records and documents regarding the post–World War II era. In turn, they themselves have done little in the way of writing anything objective or scholarly about their own history. As a result, the only two scholars who have done much on the North Vietnamese Communists or the Viet Cong are Jean Lacouture, who wrote an overly sympathetic biography of Ho Chi Minh entitled *Ho Chi Minh: A Political Biography*, and Douglas Pike, whose *Viet Cong* and *PAVN: People's Army of North Vietnam* remain the only worthwhile and objective studies of the Vietnamese Communist military.[3]

In many ways the twenty years U.S. forces spent in Vietnam were not only the most important in Vietnamese history (certainly its modern history), but also some of the most significant in U.S. and world history as well, since it was on this small peninsula that the two greatest military powers in the world confronted each other—albeit indirectly—for two decades. From the Vietnamese standpoint, facing down the greatest power on earth certainly rates as one of the most important events in its history. As for America, it may well have been the beginning of the end of its dominant role in the world—Pax Americana.

Thus, I think it is worth looking at the Vietnam War and America's role in that war at least one more time. This is exactly what *Looking Back on the Vietnam War* does. Certainly, the legacies of the past sixteen years have been profound, and even in light of the misplaced public euphoria over the Persian Gulf War, the Vietnam conflict still has a powerful grip on our national psyche. This is one legacy that George C. Herring, in ''The Johnson Administration's Conduct of Limited War in Vietnam,'' and Lorenzo M. Crowell, in ''The Lessons and Ghosts of Vietnam,'' will examine later in this book.

LOOKING BACK

Before looking forward, however, to the legacies of Vietnam in the 1990s, it is worthwhile to look once again at the events surrounding America's role in the Indochinese conflict. It seems to me that U.S. involvement was marked by four periods, each highlighted by one or more specific events.

The first era was the post–Geneva Conference period in the late 1950s and early 1960s when the United States assumed the French anti-Communist mantle. This was when America began to provide material aid and advisers to support the southern, conservative, Catholic regime of Ngo Dinh Diem (1956–1963).

The second period, following the assassinations of Diem and President John F. Kennedy in November 1963, was highlighted by the Gulf of Tonkin incident, the ensuing congressional resolution (August–September 1964), and the presidential commitment of 270,000 (eventually 560,000) troops to support a ground war in Vietnam in 1965.

The third critical phase came in late 1967 and early 1968 when the Communists launched their infamous Tet Offensive and the siege of Khe Sanh. This was, in retrospect, the climax of the war. Ironically, what from a purely military point of view was a great victory for U.S. forces proved to be a political disaster. Even though the Viet Cong were destroyed as an effective fighting force, the collapse of U.S. public support for the American commitment led not only to the curtailment of plans for an invasion of the North by U.S. troops, but also to the cessation of American bombing of the North, and the end of the political career of President Lyndon Johnson. In short, what the years of NLF insurgency could not do, U.S. public opinion, fueled by pre-Tet miscalculations and misinformation from the Johnson administration, seemingly did overnight—led to a protracted withdrawal of U.S. forces from Vietnam.

The last stage was highlighted by the Paris Peace Accords of January 27, 1973, and the fall of Saigon on May 1, 1975.

INDOCHINA BEFORE THE AMERICANS

For over a thousand years, from 111 B.C. to A.D. 939, the northern portions of Vietnam and mainland Southeast Asia were part the Chinese Empire. After that, the three regions of what is today Vietnam—Tonkin (north), Annam (central coast), and Cochin China (south)—became tributary states of China until the French took over control in the mid–nineteenth century. Even though the Vietnamese enjoyed some modicum of political autonomy under the Chinese, members of the ruling classes erected their governmental and cultural order on Confucian patterns.[4]

Arrival of the French

French traders and Catholic missionaries first reached China and Indochina in the seventeenth century. The seeds for French political usurpation were sewn from the middle of the next century through the 1850s. In China, during the first half of the nineteenth century, the growing presence of English, French, Russian, and later American and Japanese merchants, missionaries, soldiers, and gunboats slowly eroded the power and sovereignty of the Ch'ing Dynasty, and these same countries moved to acquire colonies from China's former tributaries. The French, using local collaborators and puppet officials, gradually took control of the entire Indochina peninsula.[5]

In 1855, Napoleon III sent a mission to negotiate a treaty with the Vietnamese leaders of the Nguyen Dynasty (established in 1802) in their capital of Hue. The purpose of the mission was ostensibly to end the persecution of French and Spanish priests and local Christians. When the negotiators failed to settle the outstanding issues, the French and Spanish sent a fleet to force the treaty on the

Vietnamese. By 1862, Saigon had been occupied by French ground forces and ceded to France. Over the next twenty years the French gradually took control of all of Indochina. By 1883, they had troops in Hanoi and Haiphong and declared a protectorate over Vietnam. Despite Chinese resistance, which led to a brief war in 1884–1885, neither China nor Vietnam were in a position to withstand the French onslaught. In 1885, China recognized the French treaties that had been forced upon Vietnam, thus allowing its former tributary to officially become part of France's colonial empire.[6]

For the first time in the history of Vietnam and Indochina, the entire region was unified. In Vietnam, the Nguyen Dynasty was not destroyed by the French but instead did France's bidding through a compliant emperor. Although the French were more tolerant of educated natives than other western colonials, they did not abide native nationalism. Even so, those Vietnamese who were French-educated soon found it hard to reconcile such French revolutionary ideals as liberty, equality, and fraternity with the iron-handed treatment of native Indochinese in general. Thus, the French failed, as did the Japanese and Americans later, to win anything resembling broad native support. This was particularly true among those educated professionals who opposed the alien European rule and thus also the puppet monarchy. In this way, the French, through the method of their rule, sowed the seeds of their own failure.[7]

French Rule

Historians agree that the Vietnamese were the most rebellious of the colonial peoples in Indochina. At first, most Vietnamese nationalists such as Phan Boi Chau and scholars at the University of Hanoi sought reformist avenues such as autonomy under a constitutional monarchy. The French authorities, however, ignored these voices of moderate reform and thus opened the door to more extreme nationalists such as Ho Chi Minh. While in his late twenties Ho had gone to France to study. It was just after World War I that he took part in the organization of the French Communist party. He subsequently studied Communist guerrilla tactics and Marxist economic theories in Moscow and by 1925 was in China working with the Communist faction (CCP) of the Kuomintang under the Comintern agent Michael Borodin. His hopes for a general Asian Communist offensive were soon dashed when Chiang Kai-shek purged the CCP in Shanghai in April 1927. In 1930, he united several dissident groups to form the Communist Party of Indochina. However, several Communist-sponsored peasant uprisings were brutally crushed by the French over the next two years. Ho was imprisoned from 1931 to 1933 in Hong Kong, and by the end of the decade it seemed as though the Communists, nationalists, and leftists in Indochina had been destroyed forever.[8]

World War II and Nationalist Revival

The advent of World War II and the passage of French authority from the Third Republic to the pro-Axis Vichy government soon revived Vietnamese nationalism. As noted by Paul Clyde and Burton Beers in their book *The Far East*, "Japan's occupation of Southeast Asia, 1941–1945, was an immediate source of this new nationalistic vitality."[9] From early 1942 until September 1945, the Vietminh or League for the Independence of Vietnam, a nationalist coalition group led by two Marxists Ho Chi Minh as Secretary-General and Vo Nguyen Giap as commander of their guerrilla army, fought the Japanese to a standstill, even creating a "liberated zone" in northern Tonkin.

In the spring of 1945 the Japanese had seized control of Vietnam from the Vichy French and established a puppet Vietnamese government under Emperor Bao Dai, who had been a figure in the old Nguyen Dynasty. But, by the end of the war in September even Bao Dai recognized the viability and popularity of the Vietminh and thus willfully abdicated in favor of the Democratic Republic of Vietnam led by Ho Chi Minh.[10]

As Stanley Karnow puts it, "Hanoi awoke to a festive day on September 2, 1945." During the ceremonies, Ho Chi Minh "climbed onto a wooden platform and, speaking into a simple microphone in his reedy rural accent, he asserted Vietnam's independence. . . . " The words he used, as Karnow notes, were not unfamiliar to most in the audience: " 'We hold the truth that all men are created equal, that they are endowed by their Creator with certain unalienable rights, among them life, liberty, and the pursuit of happiness.' "[11]

The Yankee Doodle character of the proceedings didn't end there. Because the Vietminh had no official Vietnamese national anthem, they borrowed the "Star Spangled Banner" for their parade and ran up, alongside their own, an American flag, borrowed from a group of OSS agents led by Colonels Peter Dewey and Archimedes Patti, who were present at the ceremonies. Both Ho Chi Minh and General Vo Nguyen Giap heaped words of praise on the United States and its revolutionary heritage of freedom, equality, and justice for all.[12] As George Herring writes in *America's Longest War: The United States and Vietnam, 1950–1975*, "The prominent role played by Americans at the birth of modern Vietnam appears in retrospect one of history's most bitter ironies."[13]

Ho's unabashed reference to American independence was no accident. On the one hand, he did sincerely appreciate the fact that an OSS medic (part of the Deer Team mission), Paul Hoagland, had saved him from malaria and dysentery in early 1945; but Ho was a pragmatic man who never really trusted American motives in Southeast Asia. Nonetheless, despite having had earlier appeals to President Woodrow Wilson ignored a generation earlier, he hoped to appeal again to the United States, this time as an equal partner in the great antifascist alliance of World War II. He hoped for material aid to rebuild his war torn country and for U.S. influence which might prevent the French from trying to regain control over Indochina.[14]

The First Indochina War (France versus the Vietminh)

When the war ended, it seemed to Allied leaders a simple matter for the Free French to reassume administrative control over Indochina. At Potsdam, however,

Allied leaders commissioned the Nationalist Chinese to occupy the northern half of Vietnam while the British occupied the south. Although the transition in the south went smoothly, the fact that the Chinese had tolerated Ho's government in the north meant that the French met organized resistance as they returned to Hanoi in early 1946. Lacking support from either the United States or Chinese Nationalists, Ho, cognizant of superior French power, tried to negotiate with them. Even though the French, in an agreement signed on March 16, 1946, recognized Ho's government as a free state with the right to have its own army, they insisted that Ho's Democratic Republic become part of an Indochinese Federation within a French "Union." It soon became clear that despite this agreement France's true design was the complete restoration of their colonial authority throughout the peninsula. By November 1946, the French had established a rival regime in Cochin China which, supported by large numbers of French air and naval forces, attacked Ho's by now totally Communist forces in the North. Thus began the first Indochina War, which would last for over seven years.[15]

By 1950, the situation had intensified due to local and world events. In 1949, the French formally sponsored the establishment of a new non-Communist regime in Saigon under the leadership of former Emperor Bao Dai. The Soviet blockade of Berlin from April 1948 to May 1949, the detonation of an atomic weapon by the Soviets in September 1949, and the institution of the Communist People's Republic of China (PRC), under the leadership of Communist Party Chairman, Mao Tse-tung, in October all heightened the growing tensions that evolved into the Cold War.

This culminated in the Soviet-sponsored North Korean invasion of South Korea in June 1950. The result in Vietnam was that the Chinese and Soviets soon recognized Ho's Democratic Republic and provided the Vietminh with material support, while the United States and Great Britain recognized the French regime in the South and sometime later began supplying aid to the French military effort against the Vietminh. Both the administrations of Democratic President Harry S Truman (1945–1953) and Republican Dwight D. Eisenhower (1953–1961) supported the French in Vietnam because they seemed to be fighting the spread of Asian communism.[16]

By 1950, the French military campaigns in Indochina had cost over $1.5 billion, and with economic problems at home making the war less popular with each passing day the French had to find some alternative or face the unthinkable— withdraw. With the start of the Korean War, U.S. leaders were more convinced than ever of the need to support the French, and in late 1950 they sent $133 million in military aid and large quantities of surplus arms to keep the French fighting. They followed that over the next two years with $50 million in technical aid and in excess of $500 million in total aid. Little changed when Eisenhower became president. In fact, at the insistence of his secretary of state, John Foster Dulles, the new administration sent an additional $400,000 in aid in 1953.[17] Arthur Schlesinger noted, "by 1954, according to French figures, the United

States was paying 78.25 percent (490 billion old francs) of the French cost of the war; the French were paying 21.75 percent (136 billion old francs)."[18]

Indeed, the United States had, if not in body, already committed its mind and soul to guaranteeing a non-Communist Indochina in the 1950s. In an effort to justify this massive economic commitment, Eisenhower declared during a press conference in early 1954 that the prospect of a Vietminh victory was like having "a row of dominoes set up; . . . you knock over the first one, and what will happen to the last one is that it will go over very quickly."[19] Thus the domino theory became part of the American popular political lexicon.

Dien Bien Phu

With the backing of U.S. funding, the French sustained what seemed to be the upper hand on the battlefields of the war with the Vietminh. They controlled most of the cities and major towns; however, their hold on the countryside was weak. French forces, enjoying superior firepower, frequently drove deep into Vietminh territory only to have the enemy return when they withdrew to begin an offensive in another area.

General Henri Nevarre became the new French commander in May 1953 and soon concocted a plan that presupposed that the only way to defeat the enemy was to draw him into a pitched and conventional battle. To do so, he decided to draw all his scattered forces into a single unit at a position so susceptible to Vietminh attack that the enemy would be drawn in and destroyed by superior French weaponry. Although supported by an additional $385 million in U.S. aid, the French military also faced a French government, under Premier Joseph Laniel, which suffered from public and economic pressure to end its commitments overseas, and which was beset by the notion that the best that could be attained from the protracted war with the Communists was a stalemate.[20]

The site of this climactic battle was a small village in the far northwestern part of Vietnam named Dien Bien Phu. The French were correct about the Vietminh's willingness to attack, but they totally underestimated the fervor of their enemy as well as its ability to concentrate large numbers of artillery, and the willingness of its commander, General Giap, to expend the lives of his men. Despite a heroic French defense, which included units of the French Foreign Legion, and massive air drops, the French, after fifty-five days of resistance, were forced to surrender to Giap on May 7, 1954.[21]

THE ORIGINS OF AMERICAN INVOLVEMENT IN THE VIETNAM CONFLICT

The Geneva Conference

The fall of Dien Bien Phu was not only a major military setback, but to a greater extent it was a political defeat of enormous proportions. In France, it led to the downfall of the Laniel government, to be replaced by that of Premier Pierre Mendes-France. Seeking a quick, peaceful, and face-saving solution, Mendes-France, working with Dulles, soon was able to convene a conference of world powers in Geneva, Switzerland, to settle the independence of Indochina.

Prior to the first meeting the French leader announced that the French would withdraw by July 21, 1954. This forced a sense of urgency on the conferees. Among those present were the French, Americans, Soviets, Chinese, Vietminh, representatives of the government of Emperor Bao Dai, Laotians, Cambodians, and British. The resultant Geneva Accords, signed on July 21, pledged to respect the independence and sovereignty of Vietnam, Laos, and Cambodia; temporarily accept the 17th parallel as a dividing line between North and South Vietnam; prohibit the introduction of foreign forces into Indochina; solve all issues and supervise all settlements through an international control commission; and to hold elections in Vietnam by 1956, in order to unify the country under one government. These elections were never held due, in part, to U.S. and South Vietnamese abstinence in signing the final agreement.[22]

It should be noted that in the years that followed, the United States would be accused of undermining the accords by supporting a separate nonelected government in the South under Prime Minister Ngo Dinh Diem. However, the United States clearly had three strong counterarguments to disavow such a charge. First, they did not sign the accords because they felt that the election would not be fair and that most people in the South did not want them in the first place. This is at least borne out by the fact that southern leaders vehemently resisted signing the accord as well and, in fact, dubbed July 21st "National Shame Day." Second, the United States based its support of elections on UN supervision for which the accords never provided. Last, it is clear that even Ho Chi Minh was not thrilled by the solution. In fact, he later admitted that it suited the needs of his erstwhile Communist brothers (the Soviet Union and PRC) more than it did the People's Democratic Republic of Vietnam. It was also, with provision for regrouping zones (Communists in the North and non-Communists in the South), more significant in defining terms that would allow for a peaceful and orderly French withdrawal than creating a blueprint for the future of the region. In the end, the only clear reality that resulted from Geneva was that Vietnam would not be unified anytime in the near future and the war would continue for a long time.[23]

Ngo Dinh Diem and SEATO

Following the Geneva settlement, U.S. Secretary of State John Foster Dulles initiated a conference in Manila, the Philippines, in September 1954, which resulted in the creation of the Southeast Asia Treaty Organization (SEATO). Patterned on the successful U.S.–sponsored North Atlantic Treaty Organization (NATO), the members included the United States, Great Britain, Australia, New Zealand, France, the Philippines, Pakistan, and later, under "special protocol terms," Laos, Cambodia, and the Republic of Vietnam (South Vietnam).

Although Dulles hoped that SEATO would mirror NATO's success in stemming Soviet communism in Europe, the fact was that since "SEATO had no military forces of its own and no explicit pledges of support for its purposes," it was, as some observers described, a "pale reflection" of NATO. These deficiencies were also exacerbated by the fact that important neutralist states like India, Burma, Indonesia, and Ceylon did not join. The reality of SEATO's weakness in fact pushed the United States to act unilaterally to solidify the non-Communist regime in South Vietnam after the Geneva settlement. Thus, in October, the Eisenhower administration took the first fateful step toward American involvement in the Vietnamese struggle when the president formally committed U.S. military aid to Bao Dai's Prime Minister Ngo Dinh Diem.[24]

Even though the president's letter to Diem technically promised "economic assistance to assist the Government of Viet-Nam in developing and maintaining a strong, viable state, capable of resisting attempted subversion of aggression through military means," most of the aid delivered was actually used for military purposes.[25] More important, as Arthur Schlesinger declared in 1966, "In subsequent years both the SEATO treaty and the 1954 Eisenhower letter to Diem have been cited as not justifying but *requiring* every action the United States has taken since in Vietnam, including sending in several hundred thousand combat troops eleven years later."[26]

In later years, Eisenhower denied that SEATO and his letter committed the United States to the kind of involvement that Johnson ultimately undertook. In 1965, the former president argued that he and Dulles had "contemplated only economic and political support for the Saigon government." As Schlesinger notes, however, by its implications "the Eisenhower letter and, to a lesser degree, the special protocol to the SEATO treaty did draw a line across Southeast Asia." They were not a legally binding set of documents, and they certainly did not compel the United States in any way to intervene militarily in South Vietnam, but "they did in a political way involve the United States in holding that line." Ironically, Schlesinger says, "no vital strategic interest required that it [the line] be drawn where it was. But it was drawn in South Vietnam, for better or worse; a vital American interest was thus created where none had existed before . . . which ended by carrying the United States into the fourth largest war of its history."[27]

America's Growing Commitment to South Vietnam: Diem versus the NLF

Between 1955 and 1960, while the Lao Dong or Communist Party of the North—under the leadership of Ho Chi Minh as president, General Giap as minister of defense and army commander-in-chief, Pham Van Dong as premier and foreign minister, and Truong Chinh as leader of the National Assembly—drew up a constitution and formalized, through elections and coercion, its one-party dictatorship, the South was beset by factional struggles for power among various splinter groups such as the Binh Xuyen, Hoa Hao, Caodaists, and Catholics. In the end, two brothers, Ngo Dinh Diem and Ngo Dinh Nhu, from a powerful Roman Catholic family, emerged to form in October 1955 the Republic of Vietnam. Diem became its president.[28]

Over the next eight years, with U.S. economic and military support, the South was ruled in an authoritarian manner. Diem himself embodied an older generation of Vietnamese nationalists who spoke French, had acquired wealth, and were generally Roman Catholic. This group had no desire to change the basic structure of traditional Vietnamese society. As a result, Diem's regime became increasingly characterized by "manhunts, political re-education camps, and the 're-groupment' of the population [which] caused spreading discontent and then armed resistance on the countryside."[29] Not only did they crush their non-Communist opposition, but 90 percent of those Communist cadres which had been developed in the South after the Vietminh had moved north in 1954.

Yet, try as he might, Diem could not wipe out the opposition through such authoritarian methods. Although in the early days Hanoi had little to do with the southern Communists, or "Viet Cong" as Diem called them, his persecution of all rival groups eventually forced many former nationalists to side with the Communists in order to oppose Diem.[30] In the long run, Diem's failure to observe the Buddhist, Confucian, and rural traditions of the vast majority of the people in his area of control led to a growing resentment among the common people, especially since he was supported by foreigners (the United States).[31]

By 1958, the civil violence and insurrection in the South had intensified, as had northern support of the Viet Cong, even though it was not until September 1960 that the Lao Dong officially recognized the recently created National Liberation Front (NLF)—the political wing of the southern Communist insurrectionists. Ho Chi Minh declared that this was now the time for the liberation of the South from the imperial grip of the United States in order to finally complete the unification of the Vietnamese state. Over the next five years, as many as 2,000 newly equipped and trained Communist guerrillas, the vast majority of whom had originally been from the South, infiltrated back south to carry out the called for uprising.[32]

However, as Stanley Karnow argues, "to label the National Liberation Front as simply a satellite of Ho Chi Minh's regime, as American spokesmen were to do, was to miss a key point. For there were serious divergences between the northern and southern Communists in a society as pluralistic as Vietnam, and perhaps they could have been exploited." This is borne out, says Karnow, by the fact that, "following the reunification of Vietnam in 1975, the southerners became increasingly antagonized by northern carpetbaggers—an indication that Vietnamese regionalism was strong."[33]

Douglas Pike, the preeminent scholar on the Viet Cong, notes that from 1959 to 1962 the Viet Cong's military effort changed "from a loose, disparate collection of dissident groups, often with nothing more in common than hostility for the Diem government, into a tightly knit movement.'' Pike further points out that this new manifestation was designed to

restructure the social order of the village and train the villagers to control themselves. This was the NLF's one undeviating thrust from the start. Not the killing of ARVN [Army of the Republic of Vietnam] soldiers, not the occupation of real estate, not the preparation for some great pitched battle at an Armageddon or a Dien Bien Phu, but organization in depth of the rural population through the instrument of self-control.[34]

At the same time, it is important not to create a fanciful image of the Viet Cong. As Arthur Schlesinger contends, ''they did not simply represent a movement of rural organization and uplift. They extended their power as much by the fear they incited as by the hope they inspired.''[35] Indeed, Pike describes the world of the NLF and those it influenced as ''a muzzy, myth-filled world of blacks and whites, good and evil, a simplistic world quite out of character with the one to which the Vietnamese are accustomed.'' Says Pike, it was a world where ''one felt, . . . tomorrow's society, the beginning of 1984, where peace is war, slavery is freedom, the nonorganization is the organization.''[36]

The Kennedy Years

By the beginning of 1961, Viet Cong attacks in the South had become more brazen and successful. This was bad enough in itself, but when added to the fact that southern forces were clearly not trained to fight the right kind of war, the prospects for the future were certainly grim. Moreover, as Frances FitzGerald notes, the Confucian ideal provided that good rulers ruled well, and thus legitimacy of any political regime in Vietnam, as in China, depended on success, since heaven smiled on good rulers and gave them victory and the people peace and prosperity. This was then the traditional basis for the struggle, and as FitzGerald says, ''Confucian logic was, in a sense, pure pragmatism applied over a vast distance in time.''

Both sides accepted this notion, the only difference being that the NLF leaders (many of whom, like Nguyen Huu Tho, were not Communists) ''successfully assimilated the Western conceptual framework and translated it into a form of intellectual organization that their less-educated compatriots could understand.'' It is therefore easy to understand, as FitzGerald argues, why this ''world where there is no clear air of abstraction, no 'principles' and no 'theories,' cannot but seem 'muzzy' and 'myth-filled' to Westerners.''[37]

The year 1961 also marked a change in U.S. political leadership with the inauguration of Democratic president John F. Kennedy, who at least seemed to understand better the insurgency nature of the conflict and the need not only for a military victory, but socioeconomic, political, and psychological victories as well. From the outset he spurned the idea of a northern strategy and/or the use of large numbers of U.S. combat soldiers. Even so, by 1963, the administration's frustration with Diem's lack of popular support and growing protests by Buddhist monks led even Kennedy to increasingly frame his policies in military terms.[38]

The Overthrow of Diem and Nhu

The climax of the opening phase of America's involvement in Vietnam came with a series of events both in Vietnam and America between May and November 1963. On May 8, Diem forbade the Buddhists to fly flags to celebrate Buddha's 2527th birthday. This was followed on August 21 by government raids on Buddhist pagodas in Saigon and Hue which resulted in the deaths of over 50 and 4,000 arrests. Nationalist opposition leaders in the South soon used these events to turn an increasing number of students and professionals against the Diem regime.

Diem's actions had not only narrowed his political base but caused President Kennedy to cut some aid to the South Vietnamese government in October despite previous reassurances of continuing U.S. support in September. The result was a military coup on November 1–2, which had at least the tacit approval of the U.S. Ambassador, Henry Cabot Lodge, and the Central Intelligence Agency (CIA). The president himself no doubt had some knowledge of the move against Diem and his brother Nhu. The coup, which was originally designed to exile the two men, wound up as a shootout which led to the brutal murders of the Ngo brothers in the back of an armored personnel carrier. Ironically, only three weeks later President Kennedy also lay dead from an assassin's bullet in Dallas.[39]

Over the next several months, between late 1963 and the summer of 1965, only the imposing presence of American prestige, economic support, and growing military power kept South Vietnam afloat. Even so, nine administrations, mostly made up of military strongmen, tried and failed to create in the South some semblance of a legitimate government. However, with Lyndon Baines Johnson now the American president, the war would soon take on a new character, one that would commit Americans to win the war that U.S. civilian and military officials like General William Westmoreland, and later even Secretary of Defense Robert McNamara, believed those in the South could not win for themselves.[40]

THE GULF OF TONKIN: PHASE II OF AMERICA'S INVOLVEMENT IN VIETNAM

During the 1964 election, Arizona Republican Senator Barry Goldwater advocated an aggressive northern strategy that called for bombing of North Vietnam's cities and invasion if necessary. President Johnson constantly rejected such a policy. On October 21, 1964, just over two weeks before the U.S. election, he made what is, in retrospect, one of the most ironic statements in U.S. history: "We are not going to send American boys nine or ten thousand miles away from home to do what Asian boys ought to be doing for themselves.''[41] However, even as he reassured the American public of the limited nature of the U.S. military commitment, events had occurred and plans were underway that had already changed the future of the U.S. role.

The Gulf of Tonkin Resolution

On August 4, 1964, President Johnson, in a national address, revealed that the U.S. destroyer *Maddox*, on "routine patrol in international waters near the Gulf of Tonkin," had been attacked by four North Vietnamese torpedo boats, two days earlier. Based on this and another unspecified attack on unnamed U.S. ships the next day, the president announced that U.S. aircraft from the carrier U.S.S. *Ticonderoga* had attacked the patrol boat's bases as well as oil storage depots in the area near the great port city of Haiphong. This was at that time the first air attack on the North by U.S. air forces, but it would certainly not be the last.

What was not generally known at the time was that the *Maddox* and *C. Turner Joy* had been carrying out electronic eavesdropping and reconnaissance missions inside North Vietnamese waters. In hindsight, this may not have made much difference. At the same time the president made his announcement; he also asked the Congress for special powers to more effectively prosecute the conflict in Southeast Asia. Within hours, the Congress had passed what became known as the "Gulf of Tonkin resolutions," allowing the president to "take all necessary measures to repel any armed attack against the forces of the United States and to prevent further aggression." It further allowed the president, without congressional approval, to determine "to take all necessary steps, including the use of armed forces, to assist any member or protocol state of the Southeast Asia Collective Defense Treaty requesting assistance in defense of its freedom."[42] Shepherded through the Congress by Arkansas's Democratic Senator J. William Fulbright (later an outspoken opponent), the House voted for the resolution 416–0 and the Senate 88–2, with only Senators Ernest Gruning (Rep.–Alaska) and Wayne Morse (Rep.–Oregon) dissenting.[43]

Even though the president now had a blank check to carry out his policy in Vietnam, the elections temporarily interfered with further expansion of the American role. However, as the president's National Security Council began meetings in January and February 1965 on how to continue its commitment to Vietnam, a second event occurred that led the president to use the full power of U.S. military force.[44]

On February 6, 1965, Viet Cong guerrillas infiltrated the American compound at Pleiku and blew up the officers' quarters in Quinhon..As a result, the president initiated a series of moves that eventually built up U.S. combat troops to 550,000 by 1968.[45] A few months later, General Maxwell Taylor admitted to some confidants in the media that "If Quinhon and Pleiku hadn't happened, we would have had to create them." As reporter Morley Safer said years later, "One can fairly conclude that the president's determination to hang the coonskin on the wall had reached something approaching an obsession; and good soldiers and decent diplomats were obliged to share that obsession or get out."[46]

The Buildup and the Air War

Events moved rapidly on the ground and in the air. In March 1965, U.S. Marines landed on the Vietnamese coast to take up defensive positions guarding the air base at Da Nang. The next month they began offensive operations to clear the area of Viet Cong. In June, with a buildup totaling nearly 150,000 men, U.S. Army and Marine personnel were authorized to undertake any offensive they deemed necessary to support the government and military of South Vietnam. Finally, in July, the president approved General William C. Westmoreland's request for an additional forty-two battalions in order to begin offensive operations.[47]

Of significance is the fact that most of the combat troops, especially Marines, who first went to Vietnam were very confident and dedicated. As one Marine lieutenant, Philip Caputo, put it in his compelling work, *A Rumor of War*, as "we marched into the rice paddies on that damp March afternoon, we carried along with our packs and rifles, the implicit conviction that the Viet Cong would be quickly beaten."[48]

Of equal significance was the decision to commit U.S. Air Force, Navy, and Marine air power to a protracted air campaign known as Rolling Thunder. Using numerous tactical aircraft such as the Air Force's F–4 Phantoms and F–105 Thunderchiefs, U.S. air forces spent millions of tons of bombs and flew millions of sorties against positions in North Vietnam. Officially, Rolling Thunder lasted from February 1965 to April 1972, although it was interrupted from March to November 1968. In fact, the major force of this operation, which has generally been recognized as a strategic and planning failure, was really only a shell of itself after March 31, 1968, when President Johnson stopped the campaign in a futile effort to initiate serious negotiations to end the war. In the end, Rolling Thunder cost 918 aircraft and the lives of 818 pilots.[49]

Overall, there were dozens of air campaigns, such as Commando Hunt, carried out near the Laotian border, and the B–52 campaigns of Linebacker I and II in 1972. North and South, in Laos, in Cambodia, throughout Indochina, U.S. air power, using every variety of aircraft at its disposal, flew nearly 5 million combat sorties. These included: attacks by AC–47, AC–119K, AC–130, and Army helicopter gunships; cargo/transport missions by C–7s, C–123s, and C–130s; Strategic Airlift operations by C–141s and later C–5s; day and night raids along the Ho Chi Minh Trail by B–57 Canberras; defoliation missions using Agent Orange and 1,000-pound bombs; tactical attacks by dozens of Air Force, Navy, and Marine fighters; and hundreds of thousands of classic bombing raids by B–52s.[50]

Earl Tilford says in his book *Setup*, "Other than possibly boosting the morale of a few South Vietnamese generals, Rolling Thunder failed to achieve its principal objectives."[51] With the limited successes of the Linebacker and other more focused campaigns, the same could be said for the entire air war. Although the nearly 25,000 Air Force and 10,000 Navy and Marine personnel fought bravely, in the end the entire air war was not only ineffective but created the very situation it sought to prevent. It changed the scope of the war after 1965 by involving the North to a much greater extent. It also gave the enemy a propaganda tool which it used to great effect. Lastly, it changed the entire U.S. pretext for the war from one designed to secure a non-Communist South Vietnam out of a southern civil war to defeating a northern-led invasion.

Not only did the air war confuse the voting and concerned population of the United States, but eventually it gave those who doubted the validity of the war a focus to demonstrate the inconsistencies of the general American policy in Vietnam. Worst of all, it demonstrated the muddled planning of American political and military leadership and their clouded perspective on the entire situation in Indochina. In short, the air war was the best example of America's "vincible ignorance."

A New Government in South Vietnam

By June 1965, the Allies felt secure enough to hold what were, in retrospect, relatively open and fair general elections for a new non-Communist government in the South. The new premier was a Buddhist, swashbuckling former chief of South Vietnam's Air Force, General Nguyen Cao Ky. Even though this government was later ousted in a relatively bloodless change of power, Ky soon reappeared in early 1967, a vice-president of a new government headed by former Army chief, Nguyen Van Thieu. Thieu would lead the South from 1967 to the fall of Saigon in 1975, having been reelected in 1971.[52]

The number of American troops grew steadily, and by August 1965 they totaled 125,000, and by the end of the next year 400,000. The buildup reached a climax in mid–1968 when U.S. ground forces totaled over 550,000 men and women with an additional 21,000 Air Force personnel.[53] Of course, the buildup and the bombing also widened the war, a fact that U.S. military leaders accepted since they also believed that it would also shorten the conflict.

Military leaders, like General William Westmoreland, were the major advocates of the buildup and of a conventional military solution (that included invasion of the North) of the conflict. However, as Arthur Schlesinger notes, "far from discouraging external assistance to North Vietnam, our bombing made Russian and Chinese aid to Hanoi a matter of Communist competition and honor."[54]

Today, promilitary, right-wing apologists, or "revisionists" as they've been dubbed by the majority of scholars in the field—especially by former soldiers such as retired Army General William C. Westmoreland in his book *A Soldier Reports* and Admiral U.S. Grant Sharp in *Strategy for Defeat: Vietnam in Ret-*

rospect—have tirelessly argued that a few more bombs and soldiers in a conventional war would have yielded the results the United States sought.

This has been countered emphatically and persistently by scholars such as
John M.Gates and Larry E. Cable whose arguments in the present book, "If at
First You Don't Succeed, Try to Rewrite History" and "Everything Is Perfect
and Getting Better," respectively, exemplify their belief that such reappraisals
cloud the critical issues of the Vietnam conflict and wrongly places blame for
the defeat on a handful of foolish civilian leaders and the suspect "liberal"
media. In his exhaustive survey of the ground war, *Conflict of Myths*, Cable
asserts very convincingly that such "what if" arguments circumvent the need
to take a hard look at the shortcomings of the U.S. military, especially its leaders,
during Vietnam. It is, in his opinion, time to stop shifting blame and make an
honest analysis of why U.S. military strategy failed so miserably in Vietnam.[55]

Of course, it should also be asked of those generals from that era who now
say such and such should have been done, why didn't they push their ideas then?
Clearly, if generals under and around McNamara and Johnson *really* believed
the administration's policies were wrong, they didn't say so at the time.[56] The
answer is simply that the highest and most influential generals of that time were
politicians first and not soldiers like Colin Powell today who, although politically
artful, is a soldier first.[57] Moreover, Lyndon Johnson aggressively suppressed
dissent in his administration.

As noted earlier, Douglas Pike characterized the U.S. strategic policy as
"vincible ignorance," or "you know you do not know that you do not know
it, but you don't care."[58] Frances FitzGerald expanded on this problem by arguing
"that even those Americans responsible for the conduct of the war knew relatively
little about their enemy, for within the NLF politics was all: it was at the time
the foundation of military strategy and its goal. For the NLF military victories
were not only less important than political victories, but strictly meaningless
considered in isolation from them."[59]

Instead of ending the war, U.S. intervention only made it bigger and longer.
The indecisive nature of both administration goals and military strategies, as
well as popular misconceptions brought on by official misinformation and ignorance of the situation, led to an Orwellian world within the American military
organization and hierarchy. This is clearly framed by Morley Safer in "How to
Lose a War: A Response from a Broadcaster," when he reveals that on August
20, 1967, Lieutenant General Creighton Abrams, at the behest of his commander,
General Westmoreland, cabled the Joint Chiefs, explaining that Military Assistance Command, Vietnam (MACV) wanted to reduce enemy troop numbers
120,000 to 130,000 by the end of the year. But, as Safer recalls, this goal was
not attained by combat but instead by a "secret weapon . . . the press handout.
Just take them off the books." The reason for such a prefabrication? To prevent
the U.S. news media from creating the "erroneous and gloomy" notion that the
United States wasn't winning the war. Later, Paul Walsh of the CIA wrote that

this manipulation of numbers ''was one of the greatest snow jobs since Potemkin constructed his village.''[60]

Indeed, one of the greatest casualties of America's involvement in Indochina was the harm done to its integrity. Today, following the Persian Gulf War, the trend continues as the redefinition of U.S. social values in *1984* terms spirals aimlessly forward in a dedicated effort to reclaim the illusions of past glory and to exorcise the demons and ghosts of Vietnam.

Safer concludes by quoting Winston Churchill's recollections of the deceptions and trickery used by the Allies to keep the secrets of D-Day: ''In wartime, truth is so precious that she should always be attended by a bodyguard of lies.'' However, notes Safer, ''The lies were designed to beguile and confuse Hitler and the German high command. In Vietnam there was a bodyguard of lies as well. But from whom was it keeping the truth?''[61]

Ironically, in this effort to manage public opinion, both the military and the administration became the victims of their own distortions. In late 1967, the public was repeatedly told by dozens of officials that the war was almost over because the Viet Cong were all but destroyed. The public believed the reports. Indeed, the officials who were altering the numbers had done such a good job they too came to believe their own stories. But when possibly one hundred thousand Viet Cong and People's Army of North Vietnam (PAVN) troops struck during the Tet Offensive and at Khe Sanh, destroying nearly every shred of government popular credibility, the U.S. public reaction all but ended this country's involvement in Vietnam. To be sure, Tet was the climactic battle of the second Indochina War.

PHASE III: THE AMERICAN CLIMAX: TET AND KHE SANH

To quote George Herring, ''By the end of 1967, Vietnam was wrecking the Johnson presidency. The consensus the President had so carefully woven in 1964 was in tatters, the nation more divided than at any time since the Civil War.''[62] Nonetheless, in the words of Maxwell Taylor, Johnson determined to ''stick it out'' and moved to bolster sagging U.S. public morale and support for the war with a public relations campaign vigorously rebutting critics and assuring the American people that victory was just around the corner.[63] In November 1967, Westmoreland was brought home, supposedly to high-level meetings. In reality, he came to make a series of appearances reassuring everyone of the inevitability of an American victory. The president in an address to Congress declared, ''We have reached an important point where the end begins to come into view.'' He even went so far as to intimate that some U.S. troops might soon be brought home.[64] During a White House dinner for the prime minister of Singapore the president, in what proved to be a painfully ironic comment, declared that ''you have a phrase in your part of the world that puts our determination very well. You call it 'riding the tiger.' You rode the tiger. We shall!''[65]

Indeed, during Tet, the lunar new year of the dragon, U.S. policy would soon be swallowed by the tiger it was riding. In a bold and risky change of strategy, NLF and North Vietnamese leaders, acting in conjunction, conceived a plan to attack all the regional and provincial capitals in the South at once. In turn, this uprising would act as both a diversion and spearhead for an attack by PAVN regulars, orchestrated by General Giap himself, against the northwestern outpost of Khe Sanh.

At 2:45 A.M. on January 30, 1968, a suicide squad of nineteen Viet Cong guerrillas blasted their way into the U.S. Embassy compound in Saigon. They held their positions for over six hours, finally being overpowered at 9:15 A.M. All were either killed or severely wounded. Over the next several weeks the U.S. and South Vietnamese militaries found themselves fighting tens of thousands on their own home ground. So well entrenched were the enemy soldiers that Allied leadership had to commit tanks, gunships, and bombers to a massive counteroffensive. The resulting destruction was enormous.[66]

The Battle for Hue

Although thousands of VC and PAVN forces swarmed over South Vietnam and hundreds of battles and skirmishes were fought, usually with great loss of life and destruction of property, the one battle that more than any other symbolized the entire Tet Offensive was the fight for the northern city of Hue. An ancient capital of imperial Vietnam and a city filled with Buddhist shrines, classic art, and historic architecture, it was a Vietnamese treasure—until it was all but razed to the ground.

Between 7,500 and 8,000 Communist troops invaded Hue eventually seizing control of the ancient Annamese imperial citadel in the heart of the city. Whereas in most cases during Tet the Communist forces were quickly driven off after the shock of the initial attack, Hue became the exception. It took three bloody weeks to retake the city. The U.S. and South Vietnamese troops lost nearly 500 killed, the Communists between 3,500 and 5,000 killed. Hundreds of thousands of refugees clogged the roads to the South attempting to flee the holocaust. In the aftermath, 2,800 bodies, mostly civilians, many government officials, were found in mass graves in and around the city, the product of VC and PAVN executions. This number was soon added to by the disappearance of another 2,000 citizens of the ancient city.[67]

Khe Sanh

Even before the battle for the cities began, PAVN regulars had undertaken a series of assaults against several U.S. positions throughout South Vietnam. In October and November 1967, they attacked the Con Thien Marine base, the towns of Loc Ninh and Song Be near Saigon and Dak To in the Central Highlands. These assaults were quickly repelled by American reinforcements sent by General Westmoreland. But despite heavy losses, Communist troops succeeded in scattering U.S. forces all over South Vietnam. In later years General Giap asserted that this was all part of a diversion to keep the United States pinned down while the planned Tet assaults were being prepared. If so, this phase of the general offensive worked to perfection. At the center of this part of the diversion was Khe Sanh, a U.S. Marine base along the Laotian border.[68]

Robert Pisor in his probing monograph *The End of The Line: The Siege of Khe Sanh*, describes the scene as follows:

The cold chill of his steel helmet came right through the plastic liner, and Captain Bill Dabney's shoulders shivered for a moment before he willed them still. The Marines of India Company filed past, stumbling, grumbling in the gloom. It was five o'clock in the morning in the northern mountains of South Vietnam.

Dabney stood on the crest of a gnarled thumb of a mountain called Hill 881 South. From this height he could see the bone-shaped scar of an Army Special Forces camp at Ling Vei, the church steeples of Khe Sanh Village, the smokey hamlets of the mountain tribesman known as Bru, the airstrip and bunkers of the Khe Sanh Combat Base—and even the thick-walled villas of French planters where wrinkled, brown women sorted coffee beans and gracious ladies served creme de menthe on the patio.

All around lay a phantasmagorical landscape, the kind of place where trolls might live. An awesome, sheer-sided mountain of stone called Co Roc guarded the gateway to Laos, the land of mystery and green mountains that flowed gently around Dabney's hill to the south. Tiger Peak loomed large in the hazy far distance, a barrier near the boundary of North Vietnam. Down on the plateau, confusing tangles of thorn and vine and low brush gave way to incredibly dense stands of twelve-foot-high elephant grass. Plummeting mountain streams frothed white against house-sized boulders on the hillsides. Across the valleys, silent waterfalls flashed like sunlit diamonds in the deep, green, velvet lushness of the jungle.[69]

It was to this fantasyland that General Westmoreland, convinced that General Giap's commitment of two crack PAVN divisions portended another Dien Bien Phu, sent 6,000 Marines to defend the garrison. The siege officially lasted from November 1, 1967, to April 1, 1968, even though it was not until April 9 that elements of the U.S. First Air Cavalry Division fighting their way up Highway Route 9 finally linked up with the defenders of Khe Sanh. To guarantee that the results of Dien Bien Phu would not be repeated, the United States supported the Khe Sanh defenders with massive air resupply and B–52 raids which dropped 100,000 tons of bombs on the five-square-mile battlefield. The battle became such an obsession for the president that he had a terrain map set up in the basement of the White House so he could be kept abreast of every movement. In the end, Khe Sanh held out and the PAVN eventually withdrew. However, actual effects of the siege remain, in many respects, very confusing.[70]

The results of Khe Sanh and the Tet Offensive must be examined in the context of military terms and U.S. popular opinion. At Khe Sanh the official count determined that 205 Marines were killed in action. However, as Robert Pisor notes, this was "a completely false number." Interviews with those present, such as Chaplain Ray W. Stubbe, place the number closer to 475. This number does not include those U.S. servicemen killed in collateral actions, nor does it include the hundreds of casualties suffered by South Vietnamese and Montagnard defenders of the Green Beret Special Forces compound on the southwest perimeter of the combat base. It also doesn't take into account the nearly 5,000 Bru who died in the battles in and around their villages. Finally, it does not take into account the 97 American and 33 ARVN troops killed in the final relief efforts.

What of the casualties for the PAVN? General Westmoreland's staff, taking into account the days of B–52 strikes on the surrounding hills, estimated enemy loses at 10,000 to 15,000. However, the official body count on site was 1,602. Even this total was in question. Marine Captain Bill Dabney later declared that, "Most body counts were pure, unadulterated bullshit. Generals manipulated a 'good kill' by flip-flopping numbers, and a certain dishonesty was bred. All of us knew that the staff wasn't coming out to count bodies in front of our lines."[71]

As for the Tet Offensive, official numbers place enemy battle deaths at 40,000 to 45,000, U.S. killed at 1,100, South Vietnamese 2,300, and civilian dead at 12,500. However, Communist casualties were questionable in this case as well. At a White House military briefing in March 1968, UN Ambassador Arthur Goldberg, recalling that U.S. figures determined that they suffered about one death for every seven wounded soldiers, asked the briefing officer how this compared to enemy figures. The officer replied it ran about three and one-half to one, which meant they suffered 160,000 to 175,000 wounded. But, replied Goldberg, "that is impossible," since that "meant the enemy had no more effective forces left on the battlefield! A long and devastating silence followed."[72]

Such exaggerations notwithstanding, Khe Sanh and Tet had devastating results on both Communist military forces and on U.S. morale. As George Herring writes, "As with much of the war, there was a great deal of destruction and suffering, but no clearcut winner or loser." Indeed, the assessment of the battle results cannot be measured only in terms of numbers. Clearly, although the PAVN and Viet Cong did suffer large casualties, the damage to the cities of South Vietnam poised a terrible threat to the already weak authority of the southern government. As Herring says, "The destruction visited upon the cities heaped formidable new problems on a government that had shown limited capacity to deal with the routine." Not only did it harm the infrastructure of Vietnam, portending a costly rebuilding campaign, but it meant that the fledgling pacification program just then beginning to garner some legitimacy in the countryside had to be suspended in order to rebuild the urban destruction.

In fact, as later events heightened the impact of Tet, the damage to the cities would prove the death kneel for the entire program. On the other hand, the Communists had not succeeded either—the NLF had undertaken what, in retrospect, proved a rash act, and had been all but destroyed as a fighting force. Looking back, it is obvious that from that time forward the PAVN would have to do the bulk of the fighting. On the other hand, the goal of Tet was not achieved either. "The North Vietnamese and Viet Cong did not force the collapse of South Vietnam. They were unable to establish any firm positions in the urban areas, and the South Vietnamese people did not rise up to welcome them as 'liberators.' "[73]

Defeat on the Home Front

What PAVN and Viet Cong arms could not do on the battle front, the reaction of American public and media opinion did. As Herring argues, "If, as most authorities agree, the North Vietnamese designed the Tet Offensive in large part for its impact on the United States, they succeeded, for it sent instant shock waves across the nation." Such respected newscasters as Walter Cronkite asked "What the hell is going on? I thought we were winning the war !" Art Buchwald compared the so-called victory to General Custer having the Sioux on the run.[74]

However, as Frances FitzGerald argues:

The curious aspect of the American public reaction to the Tet offensive was that it reflected neither the judgment of the American officials in Saigon nor the true change in the military situation in South Vietnam. "The whole campaign was a go-for-broke proposition," declared General Westmoreland shortly after the initial assault. . . . In a sense the enemy had delivered himself into the hands of the Allied troops. . . . As the succeeding year was to show, the Tet offensive seriously depleted the NLF main force units and wiped out a sizable proportion of its most experienced cadres, driving the southern movement for the first time into almost total dependency on the north. By all indices available to the American military, the Tet offensive was a major defeat for the enemy.[75]

As expected, congressional opponents of the war became more vocal than ever. But this was soon followed by criticism from legislators who were previously considered supporters. FitzGerald says, "Even the most 'hawkish' of the congressmen registered this disenchantment." Within the cabinet, advisers like Dean Rusk, McGeorge Bundy, and especially new Secretary of Defense Clark Clifford began to register doubts about the U.S. commitment. Add to this the successes of antiwar rival Democratic presidential candidates like Eugene McCarthy and later Robert Kennedy, and the pressure on the president to end U.S. involvement and initiate negotiations grew.[76]

Ironically, it was at this very crucial moment, in mid-March, that General Westmoreland, now confident of total victory, asked for 206,000 more U.S. troops to "cut the Ho Chi Minh trail, to invade the enemy sanctuaries in Cambodia, and to carry out an 'Inchon-type' landing in North Vietnam, encircling the enemy troops at the DMZ." It was the policy he had recommended all along and one he believed, with the Tet victory, Washington would finally accept. Pentagon leaders were inclined to support the request at a total of about 100,000 men, but the president, confronted with the possibility of having to call up inactive reserves on the heels of the public outcry following Tet, created an Executive Task Force to investigate the proposal. Headed by Clark Clifford, formerly one of the most outspoken supporters of the war, the task force recommended that the president not only send no more soldiers but that some attempt be made to open negotiations by halting U.S. bombing of the North.[77]

Johnson formally rejected Westmoreland's request on March 22, 1968. Eventually, he did deploy an additional 13,500 men to support the emergency situation still in effect in late March and early April.[78] As FitzGerald notes:

Johnson's decision did not reflect a "failure of nerve" among the American people, as certain U.S. officers would later claim. It reflected the American judgment on the administration's original war aims. And that judgment was much the same as the one the French had made on their own war aims in Vietnam some fifteen years previously. "The French people," wrote Michel Debre at the end of 1953, "feel that the war is out of their control and in the hands of destiny. . . . They have the impression that France does not know what she wants and that we are fighting aimlessly without a clear objective. What is painful is not so much the fact of fighting and accepting the sacrifices it is that we are apparently fighting without any goal." Only those responsible for the conduct of the war in Vietnam—those who had witnessed the devastation of the cities, the bodies piled on the streets and the crowds of refugees—did not appear to reflect upon these larger questions.[79]

On March 31, 1968, Johnson shocked the nation during a televised address when he not only announced a cessation of the bombing and efforts to begin negotiations, but that in order to concentrate on these new peace efforts he would not seek the presidential nomination of the Democratic party. It was an inglorious end to Johnson's presidency. The man who wanted to be remembered as the greatest domestic presidential leader in U.S. history instead would be remembered as his country's only president defeated in war. The remainder of that year was full of frustrations and further setbacks for the president. Although negotiations began in Paris on May 13, they quickly became deadlocked over what bombing cessation meant and if a general ceasefire could be obtained. Throughout the second half of 1968, these and other issues continued to stagnate efforts at peace. In addition, the presidential campaign soon became a full-scale attack on U.S. policies in Vietnam.

The early frontrunner for the Democratic nomination was Robert Kennedy whose outspoken antiwar advocacy was cut short by an assassin's bullet on June 4, 1968, following a smashing victory in the California primary. As a result, the nomination easily fell to Vice-President Hubert Humphrey, who although personally uncomfortable with the war, supported it out of loyalty to President Johnson. Even long-time "hawk" Richard Nixon, the Republican candidate, focused on a platform that advocated continuing peace efforts and turning the war over to the Vietnamese.

The low point of the campaign came in Chicago during the Democratic National Convention. The nationally televised event soon took on an air of violence when clearly peaceful antiwar demonstrations on August 29, 1968, were stopped by police using billy clubs, tear gas, dogs, and fire hoses. Thousands were arrested, and hundreds severely injured. Worst of all, it all was aired on prime-time national television. Perhaps due in part to this trauma, and certainly due to the effective anti–Great Society campaign of southern rights candidate George Wallace, who syphoned off traditional Southern Democratic support, Humphrey lost a painfully close election to Nixon in November. Now it was up to a new president and a new party—the Republicans—to solve the puzzle of the U.S. commitment to Vietnam.[80]

PHASE IV: THE PARIS PEACE ACCORDS AND THE DEFEAT OF SOUTH VIETNAM

The period from 1969 to 1973 was highlighted by events on the home front which served to reinforce public desire for withdrawal, while in Vietnam U.S. policy followed a dual approach—one part designed to continue support for the southern government of President Nguyen Van Thieu and the second part designed to withdraw U.S. troops and turn the war over to the ARVN—known as Vietnamization. This second part of President Nixon's policy was characterized by dramatic swings in strategy which at one point sought out northern leaders for negotiations and at another expanded the war through an invasion into Cambodia and B–52 raids over Hanoi in 1972. In the end, this policy only prolonged the inevitable conclusion derived from the climactic battle of the Tet Offensive.[81]

Domestic Unrest

The years 1969–1971 witnessed a continuation of the demonstrations and civil unrest begun at the Democratic National Convention the year before. On August 15–17, 1969, 400,000 mostly young people attended a rock concert in Bethel, New York, known as Woodstock. The theme of this historic event was peace, brotherhood, and an end to the war in Vietnam. At the same time the public soon discovered that a U.S. Army unit, commanded by a first lieutenant named William Calley, had murdered 200 Vietnamese in March 1968 near a little village named My Lai. The subsequent court martial and furor surrounding the "My Lai massacre" appalled most Americans and made them more certain than ever that the United States had no business in Indochina. Calley was convicted on twenty-two counts of murder in the summer of 1971 and sentenced to life in prison. It proved a hard pill for the public and the military to swallow. Even though he was later pardoned, Calley's deed, although in retrospect not altogether out of character with other war atrocities, did a great deal to stain the honor of the country and the Army.[82]

Even before the Calley case had a chance to fade into the back pages of the newspapers, the *New York Times* began publication of a series of secret Pentagon documents expropriated by a former Pentagon official, Daniel J. Ellsberg. The documents shocked the nation once again. They exposed all the half-truths of the decision makers from both the Johnson and Nixon years. From the prefabrications of the Gulf of Tonkin incident to the less than candid reasons for the Nixon decision to invade Cambodia, the *Pentagon Papers*, as they became known, read like a seedy spy novel. The only difference was this story was real.[83]

Nixon-Kissinger Foreign Policy

At the same time unrest was growing in the United States, it seemed that the Nixon administration's foreign policy continually underwrote the growing unrest with its constant fluctuation between Vietnamization and expansion of the conflict. Unknown to the public, in June and July 1969, Nixon had exchanged a series of letters with Ho Chi Minh through a mutual French acquaintance, Jean Sainteny. The letters led to a secret meeting in Paris between Nixon's National Security Advisor, Henry Kissinger, and North Vietnamese representative Xuan Thuy designed to bring about a ceasefire and negotiations.

Unfortunately, Ho died in September and the peace feelers temporarily went for naught. However, Kissinger did not give up, and by February 1970 new contacts had been made. On February 21, he held the first unofficial meetings with the official North Vietnamese negotiator Le Duc Tho in Paris. This meeting would eventually lead to more contacts with Hanoi and was only part of a general easing of east-west tensions popularly known as détente. By the spring of 1971, secret meetings between Kissinger and Chou En-lai of the People's Republic of China (PRC) and later Leonid Brezhnev, leader of the Soviet Union, led to announcements in July 1971 of presidential trips to the PRC and Soviet Union in 1972.[84]

In the midst of such diplomatic inroads in the spring of 1970, the president made a decision to invade Cambodia to destroy PAVN base camps and cut the Ho Chi Minh Trail supply route to South Vietnam. In March 1970, Nixon announced that the United States would continue its Vietnamization program by withdrawing 150,000 troops by year's end. At the same time the Cambodian government of neutralist Prince Norodom Sihanouk was overthrown by the pro-Western Prime Minister Lon Nol, ending U.S. fears that an incursion into Cambodia would be a violation of neutral rights.

In a risky move, the president decided to gamble that such an invasion would not expand the war and give cause to the PAVN to attack the Phnom Penh government and cause an antiwar backlash in the U.S. Nixon announced the invasion on April 30, declaring it was to stop Communist aggression into the South. The results were questionable in their benefit. The Allies killed 2,000 PAVN, cleared 1,600 acres and 8,000 enemy bunkers, captured thousands of small arms, large caches of ammunition, and effectively cut the Ho Chi Minh Trail for several months. However, since the PAVN had already begun shifting its infiltration to direct routes through the DMZ and the United States was now beset with another floundering non-Communist government to protect in Vietnam, the gains were not long-lasting.

In fact, Nixon's fears preceding the invasion soon came true, particularly at home where the protest exceeded anyone's wildest imagination. By the end of the summer, 415 college campuses had erupted in demonstrations and many had to be closed down. Two of the most violent protests came at Jackson State University in Mississippi and Kent State University in Ohio. At Jackson State University, state police killed two students and wounded nine during protests on May 2, 1970. Two days later, in what became the most famous of these protests, thirteen student protesters were gunned down by Ohio National Guard units, and four died.[85]

Nixon's efforts to curb the public outcry consumed much of his attention through the rest of 1970 and even into the early days of 1971. However, new contacts with the North Vietnamese began to bear fruit, and the announcement on July 15, 1971, of the president's historic trip to China soon began to calm the turbulent water at home. But here again the rollercoaster policy continued. No sooner had the president triumphantly completed his February 21–28, 1972, trip to China and announced a trip to Moscow in May to sign the SALT treaty, than negotiations with the North Vietnamese began to bog down once again.[86]

Angered by what he perceived to be lack of sincerity and deceit on the part of northern negotiators, and determined to bolster the sagging Thieu regime, the president ordered massive B–52 raids over civilian and military targets in North Vietnam. These raids, known as Linebacker I, lasted from May 10, 1972, to October 23, 1972. In addition, in May and June, U.S. naval and air units mined Haiphong harbor to interrupt ocean-going resupply of military stores to the North. Indeed, these raids proved the president's resolve to end the war on his terms and not to be intimidated by critics at home or abroad. In the end, events seemed to support Nixon's bold moves. In spite of early threats to cancel the May Moscow meeting, Communist Party Chairman Leonid Brezhnev met with Nixon and Kissinger, signing the SALT treaty on May 26. By October, the Hanoi leadership had made important new concessions, which ended the bombing and reinitiated serious talks in Paris. It seemed by the end of November everything was going Nixon's way. Not only was his foreign policy winning, but he'd won a landslide reelection against George McGovern of South Dakota.[87]

THE FINAL STEPS TOWARD AMERICAN WITHDRAWAL: THE PARIS ACCORDS

Yet, in the midst of his triumph, the seeds for Nixon's undoing had already been sown by his own supporters. The Watergate break-in, submerged by the election campaign, would by the middle of the following year begin the decline and fall of the Nixon presidency. Stories by *Washington Post* reporters Bob Woodward and Carl Bernstein, congressional hearings, justice department investigations, and legal prosecutions slowly revealed a trail of corruption and cover-up leading from the Committee to Reelect the President (CREEP) all the way to the president himself. Hampered by this growing scandal in December 1972, the president was still far enough removed from the impending scandal to once again use his bombers to force further concessions from the North Vietnamese. Linebacker II, or the Christmas bombings, lasted from December 18 to 29, 1972, killing by northern estimates 2,500 who were mostly civilians. It also brought the Linebacker total to about 1,000 sorties and 25,000 tons of bombs dropped.[88]

Whether the bombing forced the enemy back to the Paris negotiations, as Nixon later claimed, is hard to say, but negotiations did resume on January 8, 1973, and on January 27 Le Duc Tho and Henry Kissinger signed the Paris Peace Accords. The signing came only after last-minute maneuvers by American diplomats in Saigon convinced President Thieu not to sabotage the treaty. Promises of massive U.S. aid and efforts to gain a peaceful settlement with the North convinced Thieu to go along with the treaty. As it turned out, the South Vietnamese had good reason to fear the results of the Paris Accords. With the final U.S. withdrawals that followed in 1973 and 1974, the South soon found itself all but abandoned. This was particularly true after the Watergate scandal forced President Nixon to resign on August 9, 1974, in favor of his new Vice-President Gerald R. Ford of Michigan. The Accords, in retrospect, marked not only the final act of the American involvement in the Vietnamese tragedy, but the beginning of the end for South Vietnam.[89]

THE DOMINOES COME TUMBLING DOWN

By 1975, Congress, determined to reclaim at least some of its war-making powers, had restricted the aid that the president could send to the Thieu government. The North finally enjoyed an advantage in military firepower, in addition to all the other intangible strengths it had always held.

The final military action began on March 10–12, 1975, when PAVN forces took Ban Me Thuot in the Central Highlands. Within twenty-four hours, they had captured Pleiku and Kontum. Communist leaders now realized they had within their grasp total victory and thus launched a full-scale offensive directly south. On April 21, the last major ARVN stronghold guarding Saigon, Xuan Loc, fell to PAVN mechanized forces. Ten days later, on May 1, 1975, May Day in the Communist world, PAVN tanks rolled into Saigon and ran up the northern flag over the presidential palace. The world stood awestruck.

In the days preceding the fall of Saigon, now renamed Ho Chi Minh City, hundreds of thousands of Americans and former South Vietnamese military and government officials had fled in an effort to avoid the impending Communist retribution. In the meantime, the Cambodian capital of Phnom Penh had already fallen to a fanatical Communist faction known as the Khmer Rouge, led by a bloodthirsty radical named Pol Pot. Soon Laos would also be overrun by another pro-Communist faction known as the Pathet Lao.

It seemed to many that the domino theory had been fulfilled. All of Indochina was now Communist. The Southeast Asia battleground that nearly 60,000 Americans and close to a half million South Vietnamese, as well as thousands of Cambodians and Laotians had died to defend from ''aggression'' and ''the worldwide Communist menace'' was gone. Following twenty-five years on the heels of the fall of China to communism it was a bitter pill for Americans to swallow. The fact that the United States was not powerful enough to establish its will in a small Third World jungle country like Vietnam was an enormous blow to America's ego and prestige.[90]

LEGACIES

The legacies of Vietnam are still part of the American national mentality eighteen years after the end of the conflict. Within weeks of the fall of Cambodia, the U.S. vessel *Mayaguez* was seized by Cambodian gunboats and held for several days. President Gerald Ford, still smarting from the Vietnam humiliation in mid-May 1975, made what turned out to be a rash, but understandably bold, decision to send U.S. Marines to retake the ship. It proved a bloody expedition. Forty-one Marines died as well as several dozen Cambodian defenders. The ship was retaken at a high price considering the fact that earlier the previous day Cambodian officials had already agreed to release the ship. Nonetheless, Ford's decision was hailed publicly and by Congress as a great victory that restored some American pride and reputation.[91]

The Cambodian mission was only the first in a series of questionable foreign policy adventures that have been undertaken by U.S. leaders since 1975, most designed and proclaimed to be different from Vietnam. America's desire to avoid another Vietnam has led the United States into misadventures in Central America, disasters in the Middle East, and hollow victories in Grenada, Panama, and the Persian Gulf. Worst of all, it has left the United States unable to effectively oppose such truly evil regimes as those in Cambodia and Laos. Pol Pot's erstwhile regime was responsible for the death of between 1 and 2 million of Cambodia's population of 7 million. The world came to know the tragic little country as ''the killing fields.''

In Indochina itself, the fall of Saigon did not spell an end to war and bloodshed. Before the end of the 1970s Vietnam had fought a costly border war with its former ally China and invaded and taken over Cambodia. The irony of both conflicts is obvious, especially the latter. The fact that Vietnam was now the aggressor and occupier of another country, a Communist brother, not only drained its economy for maintenance of its military of over 1 million men, but it has damaged its standing in the Communist world and with its regional neighbors. Moreover, it has prevented closer contacts with the one country that could most effectively help rebuild its economy—the United States. Vietnamese soldiers in the guise of civilian aid personnel still occupy Cambodia. This, coupled with the genocidal program of the Laotian government against the Hmong, the Vietnamese persecution of the Bru, Montagnard, and other minorities, and the tragic episodes of the boat people fleeing the area, have left a legacy of conflict and death for many of the people of Indochina.

Perhaps the most symbolic legacy of the entire American experience in Vietnam was and is the fact that the greatest heroes have been the long-suffering prisoners of war who spent years in such brutal prisons as the "Hanoi Hilton."[92] Even today, Americans remain grimly determined to recover all the POWs and those missing in action (MIAs). In a sense, the POWs who survived because of their dogged determination were the heroes to come out of America's protracted involvement in Indochina, and thus they are symbolic of just how complete a defeat America sustained there.

One would be hard-pressed to better sum up the entire morass of America's war in Vietnam than George Herring's comments in *America's Longest War*. Although published in 1979, it has a prophetic ring which, in light of recent U.S. military adventures, reaffirms the need to continue to study the Vietnam War as honestly as possible. In Herring's words:

A successful American adjustment to the new conditions requires the shedding of old approaches, most notably of the traditional oscillation between crusades to reform the world and angry withdrawal from it. To carry the "Never Again" syndrome to its logical conclusion and turn away from an ungrateful and hostile world could be calamitous. To regard Vietnam as an aberration, a unique experience from which nothing can be learned, would invite further frustration. To adapt to the new era, the United States must recognize its vulnerability, accept the limits to its power, and accommodate itself to many situations it does not like. Americans must understand that they will not be able to dictate solutions to world problems or to achieve all of their goals. Like it or not, Vietnam marked the end of an era in world history and of American foreign policy, an era marked by constructive achievements but blemished by ultimate, although not irreparable, failure.[93]

The search for the truth of the Vietnam War is a search for the truth of our own national character and for our role in future world affairs. Indeed, the process of debate continues and should not end. It has evolved into a new era, away from the egotistical and emotional diatribes of the past, into a more professional and honest examination of all the aspects of that conflict. However, we still have a long way to go.

NOTES

1. Harrison E. Salisbury, "Introduction," in Harrison E. Salisbury, ed., *Vietnam Reconsidered: Lessons from a War* (New York: Harper & Row, 1984), 1 [hereafter *Vietnam Reconsidered*].

2. Stanley Karnow, *Vietnam: A History* (New York: Viking, 1983), 47–205 [hereafter *Vietnam*]; covers Indochinese history and French colonialism up to French withdrawal

in 1954. See also Frances FitzGerald, *Fire in the Lake* (New York: Vintage, 1972), 3–95 [hereafter *Fire in the Lake*].

3. See Jean Lacouture, *Ho Chi Minh: A Political Biography*, trans. by Peter Wiles (New York: Vintage, 1968); Douglas Pike, *Vietcong: The Organization and Techniques of the National Liberation Front of South Vietnam* (Cambridge, MA: MIT Press, 1966) [hereafter cited as *Vietcong*]; Douglas Pike, *PAVN: People's Army of North Vietnam* (Novato, CA: Presidio Press, 1986) [hereafter cited as *PAVN*].

4. Paul Clyde and Burton Beers, *The Far East: A History of Western Impacts and Eastern Responses, 1830–1975*, 6th ed. (Englewood Cliffs, NJ: Prentice-Hall, 1975), 193, 392 [hereafter *Far East*]. For more on Indochina before U.S. intervention, see Brian Harrison, *Southeast Asia: A Short History*, 3rd ed. (Englewood Cliffs, NJ: Prentice-Hall, 1966). For an account of the origins of French intervention, see John F. Cady, *The Roots of French Imperialism in Asia* (Ithaca, NY: Cornell Univ. Press, 1954).

5. Clyde and Beers, *The Far East*, 193; Karnow, *Vietnam*, 47–70.

6. Clyde and Beers, *The Far East*, 193–94; Karnow, 71–88.

7. Clyde and Beers, *The Far East*, 393–94; Karnow, 89–120.

8. Clyde and Beers, *The Far East*, 394; Karnow, 120–27; Thomas D. Boettcher, *Vietnam: The Valor and the Sorrow* (Boston: Little, Brown, 1985), 7–29 [hereafter *Valor and Sorrow*].

9. Clyde and Beers, *The Far East*, 395.

10. Ibid.; Karnow, *Vietnam*, 136–37, 140–43, 150–52; Boettcher, *Valor and Sorrow*, 31–63. For detailed accounts of the nationalist movement, its leaders, the success of the Vietminh organization, and the significance of World War II in destroying the antinationalist forces in Vietnam, see Huynh Kim Khanh, ''The Vietnamese August Revolution Reinterpreted,'' *Journal of Asian Studies* (Spring 1971): 761–82; William J. Duiker, ''Phan Boi Chau: Asian Revolutionary in a Changing World,'' *Journal of Asian Studies* (Fall 1971): 77–88.

11. Karnow, *Vietnam*, 135; Arthur M. Schlesinger, Jr., *The Bitter Heritage: Vietnam and American Democracy, 1941–1966* (Greenwich, CT: Fawcett, 1967), 23 [hereafter *Bitter Heritage*].

12. R. Harris Smith, *O.S.S.: The Secret History of America's First Central Intelligence Agency* (Berkeley, CA: Univ. of California Press, 1972), 354–55 [hereafter *O.S.S.*]. Chapter 10, ''Mission to Indochina,'' provides an inside look at the complicated situation that existed in the area during and just after WWII—especially with regard to America's role in those days. See also George Herring, *America's Longest War: The United States and Vietnam, 1950–1975* (New York: Wiley, 1979), 1 [hereafter *America's Longest War*]; Ellen Hammer, *The Struggle for Indochina, 1940–1955* (Stanford, CA: Stanford Univ. Press, 1966), 11–53, 94–105 [hereafter *Struggle for Indochina*].

13. Herring, *America's Longest War*, 1. R. Harris Smith also focuses on another irony: In late 1945, OSS officer and later director of Time-Life Films, Major Frank White was invited to talk to Ho who, in turn, asked Major White to deliver a message of goodwill to President Truman and to urge the United States to support Vietnamese independence. That night, after the interview, Ho invited White to a reception at the presidential palace where numerous high-ranking British, French, Chinese, and Vietminh officials were present. As it turned out, White was seated next to Ho himself. White later, in a letter to Smith dated March 9, 1971, recalled that: '' 'The dinner was a horror. The French confined themselves to the barest minimum of conversation and scarcely spoke to the Chinese, who quickly became drunk. . . . At one point I spoke to Ho very quietly. I think, Mr. President, there is some resentment over the seating arrangement at this table. I

meant, of course, my place next to him.' The wiry little Communist looked up at the OSS Major. His subdued reply still rings with tragic irony after the events of the past twenty-five years. 'Yes,' he said, 'I can see that, but who else could I talk to?' '' See Smith, *O.S.S.*, 360.

14. Smith, *O.S.S.*, 332–33; Karnow, *Vietnam*, 138–39.

15. Karnow, *Vietnam*, 153–60; Clyde and Beers, *The Far East*, 494; Herring, *America's Longest War*, 2–8; Schlesinger, *Bitter Heritage*, 24; Boettcher, *Valor and Sorrow*, 65–109; Hammer, *Struggle for Indochina*, 148–202.

16. Karnow, *Vietnam*, 169–75; Clyde and Beers, *The Far East*, 495–96; Herring, *America's Longest War*, 9–16. For more on Truman's policy in Indochina, see Richard Freeland, *The Truman Doctrine and the Origins of McCarthyism: Foreign Policy, Domestic Politics, and Internal Security, 1946–1948* (New York: Knopf, 1975), 343–44; Robert M. Blum, *Drawing the Line: The Origins of the American Containment Policy in East Asia* (New York: Norton, 1982), 106–24, 206–11; William Head, "The China Policy of the Truman Administration and the Debate Over Recognition of the People's Republic of China, 1949," in William F. Levantrosser, ed., *Harry S. Truman: The Man from Independence* (Westport, CT: Greenwood, 1986), 89–108. For more on the attitudes of President Harry S Truman, Secretary of State Dean Acheson, and other leading members of Truman's administration, see Robert Blum, "Ho Chi Minh and the United States, 1944–1946," in U.S. Senate, Committee on Foreign Relations, *The United States and Vietnam, 1944–1947* (Washington, DC: Government Printing Office [GPO], 1972). Page 13 has one painfully ironic twist—a letter that Ho sent to Truman suggesting that the United States set up a naval base at Camranh Bay under an independent Vietnamese government to guarantee the security of the region from foreign aggression. For the test of this note, see Neil Sheehan, Hedrick Smith, E. W. Kenworthy, and Fox Butterworth, *The Pentagon Papers* (New York: Bantam, 1971), Document 1, "Report of Ho's Appeal to U.S. in '46 to Support Independence," 26–27 [hereafter *Pentagon Papers*]. For another first-hand view of the situation from 1947 to 1952, see Dean Acheson, *Present at the Creation* (New York: Norton, 1969), 675–77. These pages cover key decisions reluctantly made by the Truman White House in favor of supporting the French in 1952.

17. Herring, *America's Longest War*, 16–25; Clyde and Beers, *The Far East*, 500; Boettcher, *Valor and Sorrow*, 111–32.

18. Schlesinger, *Bitter Heritage*, 24; Sheehan et al., *Pentagon Papers*, 1–10; Documents 2–3, 27–35.

19. Schlesinger, *Bitter Heritage*, 25; *Dwight D. Eisenhower, Public Papers, 1954* (Washington, DC: GPO, 1955), 382–84.

20. Herring, *America's Longest War*, 23–30; Clyde and Beers, *The Far East*, 496; Karnow, *Vietnam*, 181–93. For more on the French efforts to set up a Southern government under Emperor Bao Dai, see Robert Shaplen, *The Lost Revolution: The United States in Vietnam, 1946–1966* (New York: Harper & Row, 1966), 64; Ellen Hammer, "The Bao Dai Experiment," *Pacific Affairs* 23 (March 1950): 158.

21. Herring, *America's Longest War*, 31–38; Clyde and Beers, *The Far East*, 496; Karnow, *Vietnam*, 194–98; Sheehan et al., *Pentagon Papers*, 10–13, Documents 5–7, 35–40.

22. Herring, *America's Longest War*, 38–42; Clyde and Beers, *The Far East*, 496; Karnow, *Vietnam*, 199–205; Sheehan et al., *Pentagon Papers*, 13–18, Documents 8–14, 40–53.

23. Clyde and Beers, *The Far East*, 496–97ff. For more on the Geneva Conference and the Accords, see John T. McAlister, Jr., *Vietnam: The Origins of Revolution* (New

York: Knopf, 1969), 351–52; George McTurnan Kahin and John W. Lewis, *The United States in Vietnam* (New York: Dial, 1967; rev. ed., New York: Dell, 1969), 43–63; Robert F. Randle, *Geneva, 1954: The Settlement of the Indochinese War* (New York: Harper & Row, 1969), 569–72; Milton Sacks, "Background to the Vietnam War: An Introduction," *Studies on the Soviet Union*, vol. 6 (1966), 1–7. For a well-researched book, but one with a less-useful Marxist interpretation, see Thomas Hodgkin, *Vietnam: The Revolutionary Path* (New York: St. Martin's, 1981).

24. Clyde and Beers, *The Far East*, 500–501; Schlesinger, *Bitter Heritage*, 28–29; Herring, *America's Longest War*, 43–46; Karnow, *Vietnam*, 213–22; Boettcher, *Valor and Sorrow*, 134–43.

25. Schlesinger, *Bitter Heritage*, 29; Sheehan et al., *Pentagon Papers*, 19–25, Document 15.

26. Schlesinger, *Bitter Heritage*, 29.

27. Ibid., 30–31. Schlesinger wrote his book in 1966. Thus, at the time it was only America's fourth largest war. By the end of the Vietnam War it even exceeded Korea in terms of U.S. casualties, expended ordinances, cost, troops committed, etc., making it America's third largest war.

28. Herring, *America's Longest War*, 43–57; Clyde and Beers, *The Far East*, 498; Karnow, *Vietnam*, 213–24.

29. Schlesinger, *Bitter Heritage*, 35.

30. Ibid.; Herring, *America's Longest War*, 58–66; Sheehan et al., *Pentagon Papers*, 67–73.

31. FitzGerald, *Fire in the Lake*, 190–95; Sheehan et al., *Pentagon Papers*, 74–78.

32. Karnow, *Vietnam*, 225–39; Herring, *America's Longest War*, 67–72; Schlesinger, *Bitter Heritage*, 35–36.

33. Karnow, *Vietnam*, 239.

34. Pike, *Vietcong*, 111. As a whole, chapter 6, which deals with NLF organization, is the best nine pages anywhere on the subject.

35. Schlesinger, *Bitter Heritage*, 36.

36. Pike, *Vietcong*, 379, 383.

37. FitzGerald, *Fire in the Lake*, 24–25, 199. For a good and brief overview of the Kennedy years, see Sheehan et al., *Pentagon Papers*, 79–114.

38. Schlesinger, *Bitter Heritage*, 38–42; Herring, *America's Longest War*, 73–104; Karnow, *Vietnam*, 248–69; Boettcher, *Valor and Sorrow*, 153–90. For a view of the inner workings of the Kennedy administration's foreign policy machinery, see Sheehan et al., *Pentagon Papers*, 115–57, Documents, 16–32.

39. Schlesinger, *Bitter Heritage*, 43–44; Herring, *America's Longest War*, 103–7; Karnow, *Vietnam*, 279–311; Boettcher, *Valor and Sorrow*, 191–99; FitzGerald, *Fire in the Lake*, 180–83; Clyde and Beers, *The Far East*, 502–3; Sheehan et al., *Pentagon Papers*, 158–90, Documents 33–60, 191–233.

40. Herring, *America's Longest War*, 109–22; Karnow, *Vietnam*, 319–48; Boettcher, *Valor and Sorrow*, 200–202.

41. Schlesinger, *Bitter Heritage*, 44–45.

42. Clyde and Beers, *The Far East*, 503. For a complete text of the actual resolution, see *United States Department of State, Bulletin*, vol. V (August 24, 1964), 268. For details on the attack, see Karnow, *Vietnam*, 267–72.

43. For details on the congressional and administration maneuvering as well as the immediate results of the final vote, see Herring, *America's Longest War*, 122–26;

Boettcher, *Valor and Sorrow*, 202–3; Karnow, *Vietnam*, 367–77. For more details on the internal workings of the Johnson White House during the first eight months of 1964, see Sheehan et al., *Pentagon Papers*, 234–70, Documents 61–73, 271–306.

44. Karnow, *Vietnam*, 401–10. For the most balanced version—an account of almost hourly detail—regarding the NSC meetings and decisions of early 1965, see Larry Berman, *Planning a Tragedy: The Americanization of the War in Vietnam* (New York: Norton, 1982). Another work that focuses on the broader scope of events leading up to the NSC meetings which committed U.S. troops to Vietnam as well as the meetings and their immediate aftermath, see Henry Graff, *The Tuesday Cabinet* (Englewood Cliffs, NJ: Prentice-Hall, 1970), 37–40. These pages deal with Johnson's final decision to expand the U.S. ground commitment.

45. Karnow, *Vietnam*, 412–14; Herring, *America's Longest War*, 129–32. For President Johnson's own reflections on the Vietnam conflict and why he made his decisions, see the very slanted and defensive book, Lyndon B. Johnson, *The Vantage Point: Perspectives of the Presidency, 1963–1969* (New York: Holt, Rinehart, & Winston, 1971). The best source for the Johnson presidency is *The Public Papers of Lyndon Baines Johnson, 1963–1969* (Washington, DC: GPO, 1964–1971). For an account of the Johnson administration's decision to bomb the North and expand the ground war, see Sheehan et al., *Pentagon Papers*, 307–44, Documents 74–89, 345–81.

46. Morley Safer, "How to Lose a War: A Response from a Broadcaster," in Salisbury, *Vietnam Reconsidered*, 160–61 [hereafter "How to Lose a War"].

47. Herring, *America's Longest War*, 134–46; Karnow, *Vietnam*, 413–73 cover the escalation of the U.S. ground and air commitment in Vietnam from 1965 to 1967. An excellent and well-balanced official account of the USMC in Vietnam is Jack Shulimson, *U.S. Marines in Vietnam, 1966* (Washington, DC: History and Museum Division, U.S. Marine Corps, 1982).

48. Philip Caputo, *A Rumor of War* (New York: Ballantine, 1977), xii.

49. For complete survey coverage of the entire air war, see Boettcher, *Valor and Sorrow*, 205–71. The official U.S. statistics on the casualties of Rolling Thunder are on page 239.

50. There are a number of outstanding works on the air war. These include official accounts such as John Schlight, *The War in South Vietnam: The Years of Offensive, 1965–1968* (Washington, DC: Office of Air Force History, 1988); and Carl Berger, ed., *The United States Air Force in Southeast Asia, 1961–1973: An Illustrated Account* (Washington, DC: Office of Air Force History, 1984). For the more accepted scholarly interpretation of the air war, the two books that provide the most exhaustive and thorough research, as well as candid and sincere analysis, are Mark Clodfelter, *The Limits of Air Power: The American Bombing of North Vietnam* (New York: Free Press, 1989) [hereafter *Limits of Air Power*]; and Earl H. Tilford, Jr., *Setup: What the Air Force Did in Vietnam and Why* (Maxwell AFB, AL: Air Univ. Press, 1991) [hereafter *Setup*]. On the other side is another well-constructed work book by Admiral U. S. Grant Sharp, *Strategy for Defeat: Vietnam in Retrospect* (Novato, CA: Presidio Press, 1986) [hereafter *Strategy for Defeat*], which argues that if Linebacker-style raids had begun in 1965, instead of 1972, the war could have been won with airpower alone. One of the most balanced accounts of air power in the Indochina war deals with gunships and their development by Jack S. Ballard, *The United States Air Force in Southeast Asia: Development and Employment of Fixed-Wing Gunships, 1962–1972* (Washington, DC: Office of Air Force History, 1982). For a very slanted antiwar analysis of the overall military policies of the

United States at this time which pays a great deal of attention to the air war, see Robert L. Gallucci, *Neither Peace Nor Honor: The Politics of American Military Policy in Vietnam* (Baltimore: Penguin, 1975), 70–80.

51. Tilford, *Setup*, 154.

52. Clyde and Beers, *The Far East*, 503; Herring, *America's Longest War*, 138, 156–63, 238–40.

53. Schlesinger, *Bitter Heritage*, 46–47; Herring, *America's Longest War*, 133–40; Boettcher, *Valor and Sorrow*, 290–98; Sheehan et al., *Pentagon Papers*, 382–417, Documents 90–105, 418–58.

54. Schlesinger, *Bitter Heritage*, 55. For a view of the buildup and the decisions to increase the U.S. combat role in Vietnam, summer 1965–December 1966, see Sheehan et al., *Pentagon Papers*, 459–85, Documents 106–17, 486–509.

55. For the components of the controversy, see Admiral U. S. Grant Sharp, *Strategy for Defeat*; William Westmoreland, *A Soldier Reports* (New York: Doubleday, 1976); Larry Cable, *Conflict of Myths: The Development of American Counterinsurgency Doctrine and the Vietnam War* (New York: New York Univ. Press, 1986).

56. For an entertaining analysis of Johnson's relationship with his generals and advisers, see Robert Halberstam, *The Best and the Brightest* (Greenwich, CT: Fawcett, rev. ed., 1973).

57. Robert Woodward, *The Commanders* (New York: Random House, 1991).

58. For a complete analysis of this concept, see Pike, *PAVN*, ch. 1 and Conclusion. Another more conservative work which generally agrees with Pike's theory is David Chanoff and Van Toai Doan, *Portrait of the Enemy* (New York: Random House, 1986).

59. FitzGerald, *Fire in the Lake*, 189.

60. Safer, ''How to Lose a War''; Salisbury, *Vietnam Reconsidered*, 161–62.

61. Ibid., 163.

62. Herring, *America's Longest War*, 180.

63. Ibid., 181. For a look at the events leading up to the Tet Offensive, see Sheehan et al., *Pentagon Papers*, 510–41, Documents 118–30, 542–88. One of the most influential and optimistic reports prior to the Tet Offensive was Admiral Sharp's report on the air war dated January 1, 1968, in Sheehan et al., *Pentagon Papers*, Document 131, 613–15.

64. Sheehan et al., *Pentagon Papers*, 182; Richard P. Stebbins, *The United States in World Affairs, 1967* (New York: New York Univ. Press, 1968), 68 [hereafter *U.S. in World Affairs*].

65. Herring, *America's Longest War*, 182; original quote in Stebbins, *U.S. in World Affairs*, 397–98.

66. Herring, *America's Longest War*, 183–85; FitzGerald, *Fire in the Lake*, 518–21; Sheehan et al., *Pentagon Papers*, 589–96, Document 132, 615–21.

67. Herring, *America's Longest War*, 186–87; Karnow, *Vietnam*, 523–38; Boettcher, *Valor and Sorrow*, 333–46.

68. Herring, *America's Longest War*, 185.

69. Robert Pisor, *The End of the Line: The Siege of Khe Sanh* (New York: Norton, 1982), 15 [hereafter *Khe Sanh*].

70. Herring, *America's Longest War*, 185–86; Boettcher, *Valor and Sorrow*, 347–70.

71. Pisor, *Khe Sanh*, 258–61.

72. Ibid., 262–63.

73. Herring, *America's Longest War*, 188; Sheehan et al., *Pentagon Papers*, 596–601, Document 132, 618–21.

74. Herring, *America's Longest War*, 188–89. Original quotes in Donald Oberdorfer, *Tet!* (Garden City, NY: Doubleday, 1971), 158, and *Washington Post* (6 Feb. 1968), respectively.

75. FitzGerald, *Fire in the Lake*, 527.

76. Ibid., 525–26.

77. Ibid., 532–33; Herring, *America's Longest War*, 191–200; Boettcher, *Valor and Sorrow*, 370–382; Sheehan et al., *Pentagon Papers*, 597–601, Document 133, 621–22.

78. Herring, *America's Longest War*, 200–204; Sheehan et al., *Pentagon Papers*, 610–11, Document 134, 622.

79. FitzGerald, *Fire in the Lake*, 533.

80. Herring, *America's Longest War*, 204–16; Boettcher, *Valor and Sorrow*, 405–44; Karnow, *Vietnam*, 540–66; Sheehan et al., *Pentagon Papers*, 611–12, Document 134, 623.

81. For a personal view of Nixon's policy in Vietnam, see Richard M. Nixon, *R.N.: The Memoirs of Richard M. Nixon* (New York: Grosset & Dunlap, 1978). Sadly, what ought to be a valuable source of information is not, because the former president spends too much time defending his record and trying to explain away Watergate by blaming everyone from his adviser and political associates to the media for his own failures. A much better source of information for the Nixon years is *The Public Papers of Richard Nixon, 1969–1974* (Washington, DC: GPO, 1970–1976).

82. Herring, *America's Longest War*, 212, 236.

83. Ibid., 236. The original version of these secret documents was first published in book form as New York Times, *The Pentagon Papers* (New York: Bantam Books, 1971). Many other versions with different interpretations and added documents have been published since.

84. Herring, *America's Longest War*, 224; Boettcher, *Valor and Sorrow*, 452; Karnow, *Vietnam*, 623–25. For more on Kissinger's views on the Vietnam War, see Henry Kissinger, *Years of Upheaval* (Boston: Little, Brown, 1982).

85. Herring, *America's Longest War*, 228–34; Boettcher, *Valor and Sorrow*, 450–52; Karnow, *Vietnam*, 611.

86. Clyde and Beers, *The Far East*, 520; Thomas G. Paterson, J. Garry Clifford, and Kenneth J. Hagen, *American Foreign Policy: A History, Since 1900* (Lexington, MA: D. C. Heath, 1983), 570–74 [hereafter *American Foreign Policy*].

87. Paterson et al., *American Foreign Policy*, 579–81; Karnow, *Vietnam*, 623–50; Herring, *America's Longest War*, 241–43. For details on Linebacker I, see Tilford, *Setup*, 228–54; Clodfelter, *Limits of Air Power*, 150–76.

88. Clodfelter, *Limits of Air Power*, 182–202; Karnow, *Vietnam*, 650–54; Tilford, *Setup*, 253–65, 284–97. A good official history of Linebacker II is James R. McCarthy and George B. Allison, *Linebacker II: A View from the Rock* (Washington, DC: Office of Air Force History, 1979).

89. Karnow, *Vietnam*, 661; Boettcher, *Valor and Sorrow*, 446; Herring, *America's Longest War*, 242–49. For President Ford's personal viewpoints on Vietnam and other issues during his presidency, see Gerald R. Ford, *A Time to Heal: The Autobiography of Gerald R. Ford* (New York: Harper & Row, 1979).

90. Karnow, *Vietnam*, 660–70; Herring, *America's Longest War*, 255–61.
91. Paterson et al., *American Foreign Policy*, 608–609.
92. Karnow, *Vietnam*, 654–56.
93. Herring, *America's Longest War*, 272.

2

The Global Dimensions and Legacies of a Brushfire War

Marc Jason Gilbert

Few of the global conflicts that have plagued mankind in the last 200 years are as firmly rooted in the processes of modern world history than the American war in Vietnam.[1] The origins, conduct and aftermath of this war are related to some of the modern era's most significant themes: nationalism, imperialism, decolonization, communism, East-West and North-South confrontation, genocide, and *peristroika*. Yet, the global reach of the Vietnam War beyond its Cold War context is little understood in the United States. Although most Americans do know of Vietnam's place in America's effort to restrict the spread of communism in Asia, few are aware that this war was but the second of four related wars in twentieth-century Indochina[2] whose cumulative impact on world history transcends the involvement of the United States in the region.[3]

Such knowledge is hard to come by. Perhaps because the war ended in defeat, America's leaders have found it politic to either ignore or oversimplify the origins and wider ramifications of America's Vietnam War. In the aftermath of Operation Desert Storm, hardly a comparable event, President Bush and other makers of public opinion quickly sought to consign the ''specter of Vietnam'' to the trash heap of American history.[4]

If the Vietnam wars have any current significance in the minds of most Americans beyond a concern for the continued sufferings of their victims, they are largely seen as an example of how not to wage limited or low-intensity conflicts. Yet, although these terms are appropriate in the context of military analysis, they are not very useful for understanding and assessing the legacy of a struggle that has ancient roots, claimed thousands of lives in many countries, lasted for generations in Asia and for a generation in America, affected the course of Southeast Asian and international affairs, altered the shape of American foreign policy and domestic politics, and added new peoples to the American melting pot. The significance of such misidentification lies beyond semantics, for the failure to grasp the wider, global dimensions of the American war in Vietnam

and incorporate it into the historical memory of all Americans is to deprive it
of much of its meaning and misconstrue its lessons.

THE LEGACIES OF WAR AND EMPIRE IN SOUTHEAST ASIA

When the United States took serious notice of Southeast Asian affairs immediately after World War II, its interest was drawn to the region by war—a
global conflict that had evolved locally into an anticolonial revolutionary struggle
in a Cold War setting. Yet, it is clear that Vietnamese society was shaped by
earlier conflicts of longer duration and possibly greater impact than the modern
conflicts that so greatly contributed to its final form. War attended the birth of
the Vietnamese people who, alone among the many peoples of ancient southern
China, were able to sustain an identity distinct from Han civilization.[5] Though
compelled to adopt Chinese administrative and even cultural norms, Vietnam
retained much of its indigenous sociocultural identity, rendering it a striking
example of cultural fusion and premodern state formation. Centuries of war of
liberation waged against the imperialism of the "Greater Dragon" to the north
influenced the shape of Vietnamese national identity and the martial strategy,
dau tranh,[6] which the Vietnamese would later employ against Western adver-
saries.

Whereas its relations with China shaped its abhorrence of foreign rule, Vietnam's own efforts to acquire hegemony over its neighbors in the Mekong River
basin helped foster a martial ethos and chauvinism that so often accompanies
nation-building and wars of conquest. Vietnam's imperial pride not only contributed to the xenophobia and race hatred that characterized Vietnam's struggles
with the equally ethnocentric West, but poisoned Cambodian–Vietnamese relations and thereby contributed to the "war after the war": even today, Vietnamese advisers refer to their Cambodian allies in language more closely
approximating European discourse regarding inferior subject races than that cus-
tomarily employed when addressing Asian brothers-in-arms.[7]

The French, who were present at the creation of the last Vietnamese dynasty
in the late eighteenth and early nineteenth centuries, were well aware of the
warlike past, the pride, and the prejudices not only of the Vietnamese, but also
of the neighboring Cambodians and Laotians. French interest in the political
culture of Indochina, however, was largely limited to those aspects that they
could exploit so as to strengthen their hold over the region's economies.

In this attitude, as in most other respects, the French were not unique among
contemporary European empire-builders. The nature and impact of their rule in
Vietnam was, in fact, so normative that colonial Vietnam is now cited as a case
study of the fate of non-European nations in a world reshaped by European
expansionism. Both the imperial ideology of Jules Ferry, the prime minister
responsible for the final phase of the French conquest of Indochina, and the
policies of French proconsul Paul Domier, who rationalized French rule in the

region, are considered archetypes of modern imperialism and colonial administration. French efforts to privatize land ownership and commercialize agriculture in Vietnam merely followed the pattern of European imperial political
economy from Kenya to New Caledonia. The French were also not alone among
European empire-builders either in sanctioning a plantation system that valued
profits above human life or in seeking to profit from the expansion of the international drug trade at the expense of their subject-peoples.[8]

The Vietnamese response to European imperialism was also in keeping with
contemporary global trends. The peasant revolts in Vietnam, which were aimed
at restoring the traditional patterns of land tenure and labor that French empire-
builders sought to destroy, possessed many of the characteristics of similar efforts
in other parts of the European imperium: all were short-lived and all were futile
in the short term.[9]

The pattern of response from the Vietnamese elite to the French conquest was
also similar to that of their peers in other societies facing the Western challenge.
Though the Nguyen emperors were aware of the fate meted out by Europeans
to the *nawabs* and emperors of Mogul India, they made the fatal mistake of
using traditional forms of statecraft with an opponent whose power and barbarity
conformed to no Asian norms. Like their counterparts elsewhere in Asia, some
educated Vietnamese joined the peasants in armed resistance to the French. Other
members of the intelligensia sought to conquer the conqueror by embracing the
cultural values and political ideologies of the West. The remainder either held
themselves aloof from politics and the new colonial society, or took full advantage
of the opportunities for advancement colonialism offered the clever and well
placed. The latter, like others of the *comparador* class in India and Africa, either
served in the lower echelons of the imperial bureaucracy or became economic
middlemen.[10]

Those Vietnamese who sought to ride the Western currents of nationalism,
liberalism, socialism, and communism arrived at many of the same ideological
destinations as their Afro-Asian colleagues. Moderate constitutionalist parties
emerged in Vietnam, India, China, and throughout Africa at approximately the
same time. The reform-minded Brahmo and Arya Samaj religious movements
in India had much in common with Vietnam's *Cao Dai* and the *Hoa Hao*,
whereas the National Front of Subhas Chandra Bose championed in India the
mystical ultranationalism that was favored by its Vietnamese contemporary, the
Dai Viet. Though no Vietnamese moderate was as successful as Gandhi in
transforming indigenous political modalities into vehicles for modern political
change, India had a worthy counterpart to Ho Chi Minh in M. N. Roy, the
Communist *bête noire* of British Indian imperial officials.[11]

Despite the drama associated with the self-immolation of Buddhist monks in
Vietnam, the politicization of religious sects in colonial and postcolonial societies
was not confined to Vietnam or to Buddhism. Contemporary Buddhism in Burma
and Sri Lanka, Islam in Indonesia, and Catholicism in Latin America have also
served as vehicles of social and political protest.[12] Indeed, the convictions that

led Ho Chi Minh to embrace the secular religion of Marxism did not differ appreciably from those that led so many Third World leaders to take the socialist or Communist path: ardent nationalism, equally ardent anti-imperialism and the belief that alliance with the Communist bloc and socialism were essential for national liberation and the achievement of balanced economic growth.

VIETNAM IN A WORLD TURNED UPSIDE DOWN

Despite the rise of reformist and revolutionary movements in Southeast Asia and elsewhere in the late nineteenth- and early twentieth-century world, it is entirely possible that the European colonial order would have long remained immune to serious challenge were it not for the global thrust of economic dislocation and warfare that came to characterize twentieth-century world history. The First World War and the Great Depression ushered in a new age of revolution that weakened the world's superpowers, undermined the established order in colonial societies, and thus created an opening for dissident elements. The appeals for national self-determination made by Ho Chi Minh and by the Egyptian Delegation (*Wafd*) during the peace negotiations at the Palace of Versailles, and the fate of the uprisings in Vietnam, the Philippines, and El Salvador during the 1930s, are evidence of the global wave of revolution and repression facilitated by World War I and the subsequent global economic crisis.

The Second World War swept away those vestiges of colonial invincibility that had survived the Western Front and the Great Depression. It also provided unprecedented opportunities for Communists to gain control of anticolonial movements throughout Asia and the Third World. In Southeast Asia, the catalyst was Japan. Just as the French, in their failed wars against the British for global domination, helped usher the American Republic into existence, Japan's failed effort to replace American, British, French, and Dutch influence in Asia in the 1940s paved the way for the independence of Indonesia and Malaysia, and the triumph of Communist forces in China and Vietnam.[13]

VIETNAM, THE COLD WAR, AND WORLD COMMUNISM

Much of Vietnam's troubled history after World War II can be associated with France's desire to exploit the Cold War in its effort to thwart the process of decolonization in Indochina, a process the war had accelerated elsewhere in Southeast Asia. Cold War politics in Europe and Asia not only occasioned sizable American support for French colonialism in Indochina, but also tied the Vietnamese Communists closer to their self-serving allies, the Soviet Union and China.[14] The place of Vietnam in both the Cold War and in world communism was assured by Ho Chi Minh's activities in France, Moscow, and China in the 1920s and 1930s; by Ho's masterful use of "national front" tactics in Vietnam; and by Vietnamese support of Communist movements in Cambodia and Laos.[15]

Vietnam's place in the apparent final phase of Marxist-Leninism is best illustrated by the course of Vietnamese communism in the era of Gorbachev and Tiananmen Square. During the First and Second Indochina Wars, necessity had often been the mother of experiments in economic liberalization in North Vietnam. However, in the closing years of the latter struggle, the demands of total war had led to a great degree of centralization. Victory reenforced the Communist leadership's faith in both the value of a command economy and in democratic centralism. In the years immediately following the Vietnam War, these same leaders were hoisted on their own petard as their political and economic programs impeded the course of recovery already threatened by continued Western hostility. As they did in the 1950s, the hardliners in Hanoi ultimately looked to Beijing for their model, and they liked what they saw. Economic and political reform in Vietnam, as in China, was to be tolerated only within the framework of the Communist party.[16]

The ultimate fate of communism in Vietnam remains uncertain. The Politburo in Hanoi is now facing the kind of challenges to the Communist monopoly of power that undermined the confidence even of veteran *apparachiks* in Eastern Europe. Within the last eighteen months, Nguyen Khac Vien, Vietnam's foremost historian, and Bui Tinh, editor of the Vietnamese Communist party organ *Nhan Dan*, have called for the wholesale retirement of the party's elder statesmen in order to speed the restructuring (*doi moi*) of the Vietnamese economy. A senior Politburo member, Tran Xuan Bach, subsequently advocated the need for faster political change in the wake of the events then underway in Eastern Europe and the Soviet Union. He also warned his colleagues of the dangers inherent in separating political reform from economic liberalism. Under these assaults, the official party line has embraced the notion of "command capitalism," but the recent expulsion of Bui Tinh and Tran Xuan Bach from their posts, and the effort of the Vietnamese government to make common cause with China and North Korea in the defense of what remains of Marxism in Asia, indicates that, if the once bright flame of Asian communism is expiring, its Vietnamese alcolytes intend, at the very least, to rage against the dying light.[17]

THE VIETNAM WAR AND INTERNATIONAL AFFAIRS

While the origins and aftermath of the American war in Vietnam are related to powerful regional and global historical forces, the war itself altered global affairs. Scholars focusing on the war's impact on international relations have demonstrated that the war marked a turning point for the member states of the Association of Southeast Asian Nations, as well as for the South Korean and Japanese economies.[18] They have shown that the wars in Vietnam occasioned a bitter period in Australian social history, an active phase of India's foreign relations, and a hypocritical episode in Canadian diplomacy.[19] They have also established that the war opened new chapters in the histories of refugee communities[20] and genocide,[21] and constituted a challenge to well-established precedents in international law.[22]

Progress is being made toward the completion of studies that will assess the validity of the parallels that have been drawn between American policy and European imperialism in Asia, between the Vietnamese and American revolutions, and between insurgencies past and present in Vietnam, Malaya, the Philippines, Central America, and Vietnam.[23] The first major postwar study that places in comparative perspective the Vietnam and Algerian wars has already appeared, and it will be followed hopefully by examinations of the impact of the Vietnam conflict on the crises in Indonesia and the Dominican Republic that occurred after the first large-scale commitment of American ground forces in South Vietnam.[24]

In the future, we will no doubt see explorations of the role of the "boat people" as a pawn in Anglo-Chinese and Sino-American diplomacy and of the role of Cambodian refugees as a factor in the final phases of the Cambodian conflict. Perhaps such research will so broaden our perspective that the partition of Vietnam in 1954 may one day be regarded not as an anomaly produced by the Cold War, but viewed alongside the partitions of Ireland, India, Palestine, and, ultimately perhaps, South Africa, as an example of the methods twentieth-century leaders have employed when dealing with competing ideologies or unreconcilable peoples within the context of decolonization.

Although opposition to American intervention in Vietnam, Laos, and Cambodia constitutes one of the Vietnam War's most significant international elements, it will be some time before most Americans view the antiwar movement in its proper global perspective. The American public at large and far too many American scholars have not yet grasped the fact that the American antiwar movement was deeply rooted not only in the pacifism of the Old Left, but in the anticolonialist elements of the New Left movement which swept through the world's political and intellectual communities during the Vietnam War.

To the internationalists of the New Left in both Europe and America, the American war in Vietnam did not merely constitute a struggle between communism and capitalism (the New Left deplored both), but was part of a larger struggle pitting the creative forces arising from the revolution of the weak and oppressed against the destructive hierarchies of hegemonistic societies. The Vietnam War, in their eyes, appeared to be a battle of the flea against the leviathan, of the hoe against the tank, and of the village smith against the military-industrial complex. The more radical of those steeped in New Left ideology ultimately came to idealize the Vietnamese revolutionaries as the harbingers of a global revolution of the Third World against its oppressors in the Western and Eastern blocs.

Ignorant of this aspect of the antiwar movement, most Americans were and remain baffled by the behavior of those antiwar leaders, American and European, who condemned wartime atrocities attributed to American forces in Southeast Asia, but who refused to speak out against atrocities committed by the Viet Cong. Yet, to those who subscribed to the ideology of the New Left, condemning the crimes committed by America's enemy in Vietnam was tantamount to the commission of one of the worst offenses committed by the "haves" against the "have nots"—that of blaming the victim.[25] Critics of the antiwar movement may discuss such concerns as mere cant, but a valid assessment of that movement cannot be made unless it is placed in its international context.

THE GLOBAL LEGACIES OF VIETNAM-ERA MILITARY POLICY

While most Americans realize that their country's rise to world dominance and its commitment to a policy of Communist containment figured in the decision to invest American moral and material assets in Indochina, few appreciate the degree to which their own history as an emerging global superpower, and even its military strategy, was linked to, and would later influence the affairs of, Southeast Asia. Yet, the Asian dimension of American intervention in Southeast Asia is clear. America's first Southeast Asian conflict began with the decision to thwart Filipino nationalism and seize control of the Philippines as part of the spoils of the Spanish-American War, a war that marked the emergence of America as a global, imperial, and Asian power. The policies employed by the U.S. Army to pacify and maintain order in the Philippines later influenced American military operations in Vietnam: The real-life model for Graham Greene's *The Quiet American*, Edward Lansdale, was appointed as the architect of American nation-building and counterinsurgency in Vietnam on the strength of his success in helping to quell the *Huk* Rebellion in the Philippines.[26]

The success of Britain's Robert Thompson in subduing a Communist-backed insurgency in another Asian country under Western influence, Malaya, made him yet another much sought-after adviser to American policy in Vietnam, even though Thompson himself warned against the wholesale application of the "lessons" of the Malayan Emergency to Vietnam. According to Larry E. Cable, the lessons learned from military operations in Korea, yet another Asian country of interest to the United States, also shaped American policy in Vietnam. Cable has demonstrated that because the U.S. Army dismissed the guerrilla war in South Vietnam as but the prelude to a Korean-style cross-border invasion, it failed to understand the complexities of a new type of warfare employed by its Vietnamese opponents, a people's war of national liberation fought in conjunction with *dau tranh*, the ancient Vietnamese war-fighting strategy.[27]

As Larry E. Cable, John M. Gates, and Douglas Pike point out elsewhere in this volume, it was in large part due to America's failure to properly interpret its own experience of counterinsurgency in Asia and understand the meaning of new developments in insurgent warfare in that region that the American will to fight was broken. Also U.S. forces were compelled to withdraw from Vietnam prior to the cross-border invasion that the Vietnamese had long planned to occur under just such favorable conditions.

Yet, rather than accept the lesson that they had been out-thought, if not out-fought, some American military analysts claim that the final Communist offensive proves that they were correct in their original assessment. They are reluctant to advocate the updating of the United States Army's counterinsurgency tactics, which they consider—as they did in the Vietnam era—a mere sideshow, diverting the American military from its real mission: the set-piece conventional battle. Even so, the Pentagon has recently made an effort to better integrate low-intensity warfare into its training programs. But it has yet to fully translate this training into operational policy—no doubt because it has failed to fully fathom the nature of armed struggle in Vietnam, or to closely examine why armed struggle has taken such different courses in Cambodia, Laos, the Philippines, Indonesia, and Central America.

The implications of this failure are enormous. The countries the United States advises in the conduct of counterinsurgency, such as El Salvador and the Philippines, or which look to the United States for their counterinsurgency model, such as Turkey, are today preoccupied with the same big-unit, high-mobility and high-technology organizational patterns that the United States pursued in Vietnam, and they rely on strategies emphasizing free-fire zones, search and destroy operations, and strategic hamlets which are the hallmark of a counterinsurgency policy applied by the advocates of industrial warfare. Our allies are also determined, as was the United States in Vietnam, to view the root cause of unrest in their countries as external, rather than internal in origin, and are also prone to view the solution to such unrest in primarily military, rather than political, terms.[28]

The U.S. Air Force also misapplied the lessons of modern global warfare so as to contribute to the American failure in Indochina. Like the U.S. Army, it has distorted the realities of that defeat in such a way as to obscure the important lessons to be learned about the application of air power in the resolution of modern international conflict, and it has directly or indirectly encouraged other nations to pursue the same march of folly.

As Earl H. Tilford, Jr., reminds us in chapter 6 of this volume, the U.S. Air Force has historically sought to place strategic bombing at the forefront of American defense planning and has done so, in part, to secure its continued existence as a separate branch of military service. As part of this effort, the Air Force distorted the record of strategic bombing in the Second World War, suggesting that strategic bombing short of annihilation could enhance rather than diminish an enemy's will to resist, as the "blitz" on London suggested. Although in Vietnam the Air Force was obliged to act in a theater of operations that denied it the option of inflicting total annihilation, its institutional values forced it to continue to tout strategic bombing as the war's winning weapon. When air power failed to fulfill its promise, air power enthusiasts fabricated a myth, the miracle of Operation Linebacker II, to excuse the Air Force's failure to develop a doctrine of victory suited to Vietnam. They argued that, had America's politicians permitted the Air Force to pursue targets as freely in 1965–1970 as it did in December of 1972 during the second Linebacker campaign, it could have forced Hanoi to the conference table in the late 1960s as, they allege, it did in January 1973.

Tilford has demonstrated that this argument is ahistorical and inaccurate. The treaty which the air offensive of December 1972 allegedly forced Hanoi to sign in January 1973 left the Communists in so commanding a position in South Vietnam that victory was but a question of time. This casts doubt on the assumption that Hanoi would have entirely abandoned its effort to unite the country in the face of an earlier application of Linebacker II techniques, for certain defeat, not the dawn of victory, would have then been in the offing. Further, the threat of a Chinese or Russian intervention that had restricted target selection during Operating Rolling Thunder between 1965 and 1968 had receded by the time of Operation Linebacker II, rendering a comparison of the two campaigns not only counterfactual, but moot.[29]

It is unlikely, however, that Tilford's voice will be heard by those who cherish the air power enthusiasts' version of the Vietnam "stab-in-the-back" thesis. The devotees of air supremacy are so immune to historical argument that they now insist that Operation Desert Storm vindicates their interpretation of the meaning of Operation Linebacker II. Any attempt to refute such a claim must run afoul of David Patraeus's well-known pre–Gulf War admonition that we should avoid the "literal application of lessons extracted from Vietnam, or any other past event, to present or future problems without due regard for the specific circumstances that surround those problems."[30] Yet, a moment's indulgence in such risky business suggests that the record of Operation Desert Storm contradicts the assertions of Linebacker II myth-builders. Much to the disgust of veteran pilots such as John Buchanan and Dick Rutan, targeting in Vietnam had more to do with bureaucracy than battle: Too many on the Air Force management team valued numbers of sorties or targets destroyed over the significance or effectiveness of these strikes, thus confusing targeting with warmaking and bomb releases with the successful articulation of force.[31]

This mistake was repeated in Iraq, where all the self-congratulatory battle-damage estimates flaunted by the Air Force could not entirely conceal that it had failed to locate or destroy Iraq's superguns, nuclear and biological manufacturing facilities, and the bulk of its Scuds. Such failures can be attributed, at least in part, to an Air Force doctrine and spending policy unchanged since the beginning of the Vietnam era: The last SR–71 aircraft that might have detected these targets was retired five months prior to Desert Storm because "it didn't fit in with SAC's financially hungry nuclear fleet of bombers and missiles."[32]

Further, in Iraq, as in Vietnam, the Air Force, and, indeed, the U.S. Army and U.S. Marine Corps, were prevented from dealing a knockout blow against an enemy's infrastructure and its forces in the field. Kuwait was liberated with the same uncommon skill and valor the American military displayed in Vietnam,[33] but once again, the beaten foe was left with enough resources to continue to terrorize its own people and plan other schemes of conquest. On this occasion, however, America's military might was restrained not by the agents blamed by Air Force apologists for tying the hands of American pilots in Indochina (interfering and timid White House officials, dovish newsmen, and traitorous leaders of public opinion), but by a determined president whose aggressive policy was endorsed by Congress, the media, and the American public. President Bush's handling of the war's end-game phase in Iraq would seem to indicate, as did Johnson's and Nixon's management of the Vietnam conflict, that so long as the late twentieth-century battlefield is the nation-state, and combat occurs in regions of interest to the community of nations, the practice of total war and the achievement of total victory are mere chimeras, no matter how hawkish and undivided a great power's leadership and society might be.

Thus, the real lesson of both Linebacker II and Desert Storm air operations would appear to be that war is merely the continuation of political intercourse by other means, not a substitute for politics, domestic or international. Though this lesson is as old as Sun Tzu and as familiar as Clausewitz, it appears to be so difficult to assimilate that we can expect the myths surrounding Operation Linebacker II to continue to influence not only American defense policy, but the defense policies of other nations, such as Libya and Iraq, which have good reason to believe what the American champions of air power have claimed ever since the "Christmas Bombing" campaign of twenty years ago: that national strength and victory in battle belongs to those with the will and ability to project weapons of mass destruction well beyond their own frontiers. Countries like Libya and Iraq, which have as yet failed to acquire this capability, will no doubt continue to employ Vietnam's proven, if primitive, means to counter the application of such power against them: the boxed close-perimeter defense once known only to American pilots "going downtown" in the former North Vietnam, but which is now familiar to the millions around the world who viewed Cable News Network's videotape of antiaircraft fire over Baghdad.[34]

The leaders of less-developed countries are not the only ones who have sought to pursue some of the "lessons" American military policy makers have derived from the Vietnam War. The Red Army in Afghanistan followed the very course America's military apologists recommended in the wake of their country's defeat in Indochina. When the policies of the Russo-Afghan equivalent of Ngo Dinh Diem, President Amin, led to instability in an ally already threatened by a foreign-backed insurgency, the Soviets eschewed incremental escalation in favor of swift and relentless war. Yet, though the Soviet military rarely had their hands tied by officials in Moscow and faced no divisive antiwar movement at home, they were not much more successful in the Hindu Kush than America was in the jungles of Vietnam, and for largely the same reasons.

Like the Vietminh, the Afghan insurgents refused to be destroyed in a set-piece battle, or permit the attrition of their force in the defense of terrain, thereby confronting their Soviet opponents with the same unbreakable military deadlock their Vietnamese counterparts imposed on their Western foes: a stalemate that could not be resolved by internal political settlement due to the incompatible ideologies of the indigenous combatants. Faced with the continuation of a war that had tarnished their image in the world, and no light at the end of the tunnel, the Soviets, like the Americans, withdrew from their Asian battlefield to leave the ultimate outcome in the hands of indigenous leaders. Whether the nations of the world, including the United States, choose to acknowledge it or not, there are military lessons of global import to be learned from the Vietnam and Russo-Afghan wars: "conventional armies lose unconventional wars, and the massive application of firepower is no substitute for a theory of victory."[35]

The Soviet Union's Afghan policy did succeed in universalizing one tragic aspect of combat on the world's periphery: Veterans of the Russo-Afghan War returned to no more welcome and even less economic and medical assistance than that which greeted Americans returning from Vietnam. Fortunately, when Soviet and American veterans of the world's most bitter brushfire wars met in the late 1980s to share their experiences of unconventional warfare, understaffed veterans hospitals, and posttraumatic stress disorder, they not only helped comfort one another, but kept alive concerns about the needs of veterans that were being forgotten in the rush to effect reductions in public spending during the 1980s.[36]

Still, it should be noted that, in the opinion of John Wheeler, the former director of the federal Vietnam Veterans Leadership Program, if American casualties in the Gulf War had been high, those wounded would have had to "suffer the same conditions in veterans hospitals that brought so much pain in the Vietnam era: underbudgeting, too few nurses, overburdened doctors, red tape, and a feeling of abandonment by their country."[37]

If the global economy demands further cuts in public sector spending internationally, it is possible that American and Soviet veterans may join their restive counterparts in South Korea and, ultimately, in Vietnam itself, in an international effort to secure better treatment of a generation of "winter soldiers" who have already spent far too much time out in the cold.

There is at least one aspect of the global legacy of the war in Vietnam as revealed by Operation Desert Storm, which suggests that the lessons of that war can be integrated at both the policy-making and operational levels of international diplomacy and warfare. The Vietnam War taught American military commanders that the best war-fighting strategies could be undone by the mere appearance of illegality. They learned that, no matter how justifiable they might seem on the ground, events such as those that occurred at My Lai could greatly undermine not merely a campaign, but an entire war effort.

As a result of the Vietnam experience, the Department of Defense instituted new practices, such as mandatory instruction in the Law of War, for all commanders, and sought to expand the role of military lawyers to include participation in operations as well as in the drafting of contingency plans. The fruits of these changes were reaped during Operation Desert Storm. The chairman of the Joint Chiefs of Staff, General Colin Powell, told Steven Keeva of the American Bar Association that not only did the American military benefit from observing the Law of War during this campaign, but it was discovered that "lawyers proved invaluable in the decision-making process."[38]

Such words may well be anathema to the old guard, who, like Falstaff, think that lawyers are best positioned in front of, rather than behind, weapons of war. The record of Operation Desert Storm suggests, however, that legal personnel offered extremely valuable advice on many questions, including the shooting down of Scud missiles over neutral territory and the launching of attacks upon Scud launchers under conditions in which they could not be distinguished from nearby civilian road traffic.

Vietnam veteran General H. Norman Schwarzkopf, who was advised throughout the conflict in the Persian Gulf by staff judge advocate Colonel Raymond Rupert, has made no secret of his opinion that the military lawyer is "absolutely indispensable to military operations." As the spread of the rule of law appears to be keeping pace with the spread of liberal democracy in the wake of the Soviet collapse, it is possible to conclude with Keeva that "it appears likely that the Law of War and the lawyer's role in interpreting it will remain a major concern for the military in the coming years."[39]

It is, of course, an error to think that only Western military policy in Southeast Asia has bequeathed a legacy to the world. As mentioned above, Vietnamese air defense techniques are now employed throughout the Third World. Of possibly greater import is its lessons for the application of a "people's war." There is a lively debate among American military scholars over the significance of the Vietnamese example of a "people's war," but while scholars dispute its value, guerrillas in the Philippines have employed it with some success.

Similarly, although the genocidal policies and agrarian utopianism of the Khmer Rouge is regarded in the West as barbaric, the movement itself remains alive in Cambodia and its tactics and ideals are pursued with some vigor in Peru by the Shining Path (*Sendero Luminoso*), whose revolutionary goals will be achieved only after the Peruvian people "cross over the river of blood."[40] Further, although some American scholars might conclude that the theory of the general uprising may have been discredited by the experience of the Tet Offensive in 1968, others regard that campaign as the turning point of the war and many true believers from Palestine to El Salvador have since lived and died in the belief that a disciplined guerrilla force can lead a populace to take arms against a sea of troubles, and by opposing, end them.[41]

THE GLOBAL LEGACIES OF VIETNAM-ERA AMERICAN DIPLOMACY

Operation Desert Storm has raised a further pertinent aspect of the international dimensions of the American policy. From the start of the conflict between the French and the Vietminh in Indochina, America's leaders were haunted by the specter of a repetition of the West's policy of appeasement toward Nazi aggression. Presidents Truman, Eisenhower, Kennedy, and Johnson all had evoked the specter of Munich when rallying support to stop insurgency in South Vietnam. Such rhetoric encouraged Americans to view those who opposed the French and later the Diem regime as little more than Communist mercenaries fighting in the

cause of Soviet global domination. It also obscured the complexities of Vietnamese political culture, which permitted both Communist and non-Communist
to wear the mantle of patriotism. American diplomatic discourse thus facilitated
the repetition of the French error of underestimating the importance of the indigenous social structures, cultural loyalties, and military traditions forged by
2,000 years of almost continuous struggle waged by and among the states of
Southeast Asia.

Many of the world's leaders, a large number of American intellectuals, and
leaders of public opinion in the Third World viewed the application of the Munich
analogy to Vietnam as a device designed to conceal the West's effort to secure
its own neocolonial interests. This response contributed to the erosion of domestic
and international support which ultimately hobbled America's war effort and
sullied its reputation as a responsible superpower.

Yet, as William Safire has noted, the United States drew on the same rhetoric
to rally international opinion against Saddam Hussein's aggression in Kuwait.[42]
On this occasion, the evocation of the Munich analogy achieved much better
results in Europe and at home, but it received no better reception in the Arab
or Third Worlds. The latter audiences, while deploring Hussein's sack of Kuwait,
viewed the American and European effort to discredit Hussein by comparing
him to Hitler much the same as they viewed America's effort to equate Ho Chi
Minh with Stalin during the Vietnam era: as a smokescreen for Western self-
aggrandizement, if not blatant colonialism.[43] After all, many Indians and Arabs
consider these totalitarians as important figures due the threat they posed to
Western European colonialism in South, Southeast, and Southwest Asia.[44]

The most far-reaching lesson of the American war in Vietnam may thus be
that if America is to win the battle for the hearts and minds of the inhabitants
of the world's most troubled regions, it will have to become more aware of both
the global forces that have shaped their history as well as its own.[45] Should such
sensitivity succeed in contributing to a new style of American diplomatic discourse, those Americans who gave their lives in Vietnam will not have died as
much in vain, and fewer Americans in the future are likely to be asked to make
such a sacrifice.

Although scholars argue whether or not the Vietnam War heralded a decline
in America's ability to function as a world power,[46] they generally agree that
the shuttle diplomacy pursued by Kissinger and Nixon to extricate America from
Vietnam marked the emergence of today's multipolar world. There is little doubt
that the war altered the pattern of American international relations and thereby
the wider pattern of global affairs. The war not only alienated public opinion in
Europe, but placed further strains on the always uneasy Western Alliance.[47]

Paul Kennedy argues that the Vietnam War also inhibited the ability of the
United States to exploit the Sino-Soviet split, established a pattern in its relations
with Latin American nations characterized by military support for undemocratic
regimes, and left the United States adrift in the United Nations, where "the
American delegate appeared increasingly beleaguered and isolated." Kennedy

also argues that the war gave rise to an open discussion "over the regions of the globe which the United States would or *would not* fight in the future [which] disturbed existing allies, doubtless encouraged its foes, and caused wobbling neutrals to consider reinsuring themselves with the other side."[48] Thus, Vietnam may have altered the pattern of international relations in a manner detrimental to the long-term interests of the United States.

Kennedy's analysis suggests that the debate over the "Vietnam Syndrome" has had an impact upon the pattern of global affairs. That it will continue to do so is clear from Operation Desert Storm, the very action which President Bush, as referenced above, saw as the harbinger of a New Order, one without any Vietnam Syndrome, insofar as this term was taken to mean a reluctance to intervene militarily overseas (a definition hotly disputed by those who argue that its defeat in Vietnam ultimately made the United States more, not less, prone to act militarily abroad).[49]

The president believed his conduct of Operation Desert Storm rid the United States of its Southeast Asian albatross by eschewing half-measures, setting clear goals, and waging war until those goals were achieved. Many Iraqi Shi'ites and Kurds may, with reason, disagree with the president's assessment. They could argue that the United States failed to unseat Saddem Hussein because the specter of Vietnam raised fears of an Iraqi quagmire. Is this, they might ask, an America untroubled by fears of land wars in Asia? Is this not the same America that declined to take martial action in response to the revolution in Iran and the Russian invasion of Afghanistan in the aftermath of the Vietnam War?[50]

Some Haitians may ask similar questions about American resolve to act forcefully in the cause of peace and democracy in the decades after Vietnam. Yet, the course of recent congressional hearings on America's war on drugs suggest that if the Vietnam Syndrome still acts as a check upon American military activity abroad, it can function in a way acceptable to hawks and doves, past and present, and in a manner reassuring to a troubled world not quite ready to settle into a new and roseate new world order. The focus of these hearings was American antinarcotics policy in Peru, whose government, as mentioned above, now faces an escalating challenge from the Shining Path movement.

According to the Bush administration, this movement is so closely tied to the drug trade that "to confront drug trafficking in Peru is to confront *Sendero*." To address this problem, the Bush administration sought to strengthen the hands of federal agents in Peru by requesting an increase in American military assistance to the Peruvian government. Peru's counterinsurgency tactics so closely mirror the human rights violations of the Shining Path that Congress had in the past blocked military aid to that country, but administration officials have sought to remind congressmen of the naiveté of those of their predecessors who cut off aid to Cambodia in the belief that the Khmer Rouge could not be worse than the Lon Nol regime. It was the administration's contention that, despite the often deplorable actions of Peruvian armed forces, the Shining Path was by far the greater of the two evils.

The administration's request, however, troubled congressmen such as Robert C. Torricelli, who see "United States narcotics agents as 'sitting ducks' in somebody else's war." Torricelli, chairman of the House Western Hemisphere Subcommittee, advised Bernard W. Aronson, Assistant Secretary of State for Inter-American Affairs, that "perhaps we should be involved in the effort to defeat the Shining Path. Perhaps we should not. But the one thing we must avoid is getting involved through the back door. We have been down that road before."[51]

Most world leaders recognize that timidity in a great power poses as great a threat to global security and stability as overaggressiveness. Yet, if President Bush's reluctance to enter into the domestic affairs of Iraq, and Torricelli's admonitions about the grounds for intervention in Peruvian affairs, are symptoms of a Vietnam Syndrome, many in the international community may argue that they need more, not less, of the disease.

RACE AND GENDER ON THE GLOBAL BATTLEFRONT

The issue of race was a major element of the debate over the Vietnam War at home and abroad. Many Americans came to oppose the war because of concerns raised by the image of what folksinger Phil Ochs called "White Boots Marching in a Yellow Land" and the harsh reality of African Americans battling racism "in country" and at home. Until recently, however, the issue of race and the Vietnam War cannot be said to have received much serious attention in the United States. The literature of the African-American experience in Vietnam War is merely adequate.[52]

There are no major studies of the Hispanic-American and the American Indian experience,[53] and a program featuring the bitter recollections of Asian Americans who served in Vietnam broadcast on National Public Radio in the fall of 1991 was the first major media exploration of this subject.[54]

There is a danger in such a lacuna for a country that, within the lifetimes of most of those living today, may, if current trends continue, be populated by a majority of people of color. This danger was highlighted by the storm of protest sparked by the decision of the producers of the reality-based film *Bat–21* (1988) to make an end-of-credit reference to the ultimate fate of the real-life model of the white officer portrayed in the film by Gene Hackman, but make no mention of the African-American character played by Danny Glover. The protesters gave short shirft to the producers' subsequent defense that they could make no reference to the life of the African-American character because he was drawn from a composite of many individuals involved in the rescue operation described in the film. The protesters saw in this explanation only further proof of the American film community's lack of sensitivity to the issue of race in Vietnam. How, they asked, did the producers expect a public, not familiar with the true story, to react to a biographical reference to a major character portrayed by a white featured player and no reference to the principle character portrayed by his African-American costar?[55]

The broader significance of this issue was demonstrated by the even stronger protest from minority groups about the manpower allocations for Operation Desert Storm, when the matter of the high ratio of combat deaths among African Americans in Vietnam, which attracted international as well as national attention at the time, resurfaced with a vengeance.[56]

Operation Desert Storm also reopened the debate over women in the combat zone which many Americans thought the Vietnam War had settled. By emphatically revealing that modern warfare rarely possesses well-defined front lines, the American war in Vietnam should have led to a thorough reassessment of the role of women in combat zones and in combat. A debate did ensue, but the issue remained unresolved, as the controversy over the combat activities of female personnel in Operation Just Cause revealed. As a result, America wasted time, energy, and the value services of women in the American military until the debate was yet again rendered moot by the bravery and sacrifice of American women in the field during Operation Desert Storm.[57]

Yet, although we have at least begun to address the issues of gender raised by the Vietnam War, and real effort is currently underway to evaluate the impact of the Vietnam conflict on the women on the home front of that war in America,[58] we still have failed as a society to address the impact of the Vietnam War on Vietnamese women, or to use the war as a springboard for the discussion of the role of women in twentieth-century warfare.

At a recent symposium on the teaching of the Vietnam War sponsored by the National Endowment for the Humanities, the majority of male professors laughed in derision when a female colleague suggested some time be devoted to a discussion of the war from a woman's perspective. The Vietnam War was an important chapter in both the history of race relations and of women at war. It can teach America a great deal about race and gender relations, and thereby strengthen America's position as a world leader in freedom and equality, but not if the lessons of that war remain shrouded by insensitivity or outright prejudice.

WORLD LITERATURE AND FILM

From Nguyen Du's early nineteenth-century epic, *The Tale of Kieu*,[59] to Le Ly Haslip's 1993 post-Vietnam memoir, *When Heaven and Earth Changed Places*,[60] Vietnam has greatly contributed to the literature of the strife-torn and oppressed. From the Western-influenced individualist style that emphasized the alienation of the self to the triumph of social realism that identified death on the battlefield as the highest form of self-realization, Vietnamese prose and poetry reflects the transition from a traditional to a colonial to a modern society that many people have made in the modern era.[61]

The aftermath of the wars in Indochina, as described in the literature of the

Cambodian holocaust and of Vietnam's political reeducation camps, has provided the world with major contributions to the comparative literature of genocide and political repression.[62] Marguerite Duras's *The Sea Wall* (1950), Graham Greene's *The Quiet American* (1955), William J. Lederer and Eugene Burdick's *The Ugly American* (1958), and Tranh Van Dinh's *Blue Dragon, White Tiger: A Tet Story* (1983) do not merely expose Western imperial pretensions. They also lend insight into how, when cultures clash, the best of intentions can pave the way to hell even in as small and as beautiful a place as Vietnam. This theme is underscored by Philip Caputo's *Rumor of War* (filmed by Richard T. Heffron in 1980), Gustav Hasford's *The Dog Soldiers* (filmed by Stanley Kubrick as *Full Metal Jacket* in 1987), Tim O'Brien's *Going After Cacciato* (1979), and Chfong-hyo An's *White Badge: A Novel of Korea* (1989). It will, however, be as discourses on the human condition and on the universal experience of coming of age that these works will be remembered by future generations.

As might be expected, the French, with their extensive filmography of the First Indochina War, were among the first to address the American war in such now well-known films as *The Anderson Platoon* (1966) and *Live for Life* (1967). Less known, however, is the Vietnam cinema of other nations, such as Britain's *Tell Me Lies* (1968), Germany's *The American Soldiers* (1970), Japan's *Summer Soldiers* (1972), the U.S.–Chile coproduction, *Self-Portrait* (1973), and Australia's *The Odd Angry Shot* (1979). Many of these films exhibit the same failings as the antipodal *Rambo: First Blood, Part II* (1985) and *Platoon* (1986) in that they perpetuate stereotypical and ideologically constructed images of the Vietnam experience.

Like their American counterparts, however, they do reflect the place of the war in contemporary popular culture. This is particularly true of the new Vietnam War cinema in South Korea, where democratization is "slowly giving South Koreans the chance to explore the difficult path they have taken to their current prosperity." One of the soldiers in the forthcoming film of An's novel *White Badge: A Novel of Korea* concludes that, "The blood money we had to earn at the price of our lives fueled the modernization and development of the country. And owing to our contribution, the Republic of Korea, or at least the higher echelon of it, made a gigantic stride into the world market. Lives for sale. National mercenaries."[63]

It is likely that the potential of such films to deliver more universal and complex messages will increase with the passage of time and healing. Both *White Badge* and *In Country* (1989), with their examinations of memory and the process of coming of age, are a welcome addition to a filmography that is dominated by productions in which the American Vietnam veteran is portrayed as a drug-addicted psychopathic killer. In the future, we may see the battlefield internalized and the enemy an agent that acts to spur self-evaluation and the examination of larger truths. The scene is certainly set for American filmmakers to exploit the coming normalization of relations with Vietnam in such a way as to contribute, rather than to detract from, the new spirit of internationalism that is currently sweeping much, if not all, human society. Should they do so, they will find themselves on a parallel course with their Vietnamese colleagues.

Although the Vietnamese cinema has produced its share of self-aggrandizing war films, Vietnamese filmmakers have also been able to view that conflict as merely one of the many trials that have beset the Vietnamese people during their long history—trials that are traditionally blamed more on malign forces of fate than evil human agency.[64] Perhaps enough time has not yet passed for filmmakers drawn from the combatant nations to make a record of the Vietnam War for their own societies or for the larger human community that possesses the humane vision of Ken Burns's *The Civil War* (1991), but if or when they do, they will speed the healing from a war whose wounds still fester in the body politic of both Vietnam and America and whose larger meaning for the world the cinema has more often obscured than revealed.

CONCLUSION

The American war in Vietnam was an important episode both in the long history of the Vietnamese people and in the history of the so-called "American Century," but its origins, conduct, and legacy are closely tied to those ideas and events that have influenced the larger course of modern history. Accordingly, the war's legacies are as broad as its roots in the human experience are deep. Its legacies speak to us in the near universal language of revolution and reaction, national vindication and betrayal, Marxism rampant and in retreat. They remind us that no nation has a monopoly on the cultural exceptionalism that fuels the arrogance of power and sustains its apocalyptic companions: imperialism, military aggression, ideological rigidity, ethnocentrism, and internal social disintegration. The cry of Vietnam, as described by a Vietnamese poet, is the cry of all those who experience wars which pit culture against culture or brother against brother, whose conduct threatens the very ideals in whose defense it is fought and whose resolution leaves both victor and vanquished morally adrift.[65]

Recent events in Asia, Africa, and in Eastern Europe suggest that we can expect more, rather than fewer, such conflicts as this century draws to a close. Until the day they are banished from sight and memory, the American war in Vietnam will remain a window into the forces that shape modern world history.

NOTES

1. World War II is arguably the single most influential global event of the first half of this century, but its causes and legacies, from fascism to decolonization, also figure in the causes and legacies of the wars in Vietnam.

2. This chapter is intended to focus on the global dimensions of the American war in Vietnam, interpreted here to include U.S. actions in support of French colonialism and anticommunism (1945–1954), as adviser to the Republic of South Vietnam (1954–1963), and during the period from the Gulf of Tonkin Resolution (1964) to the collapse

of the Saigon regime (1975). The overall impact of Southeast Asia, ancient and modern, on world history has been explored by this writer in "Broadening the Horizons of a Course on the Vietnam War," in Marc Jason Gilbert, ed., *The Vietnam War: Teaching Approaches and Resources* (Westport, CT: Greenwood, 1991), 79–113.

3. The generation of Vietnamese that fought against the French and Americans understand that these conflicts are called the First and Second Indochina Wars in the West. They maintain, however, that their struggle against the Japanese occupation and "the war after the war" with China in 1979 are equally significant for their history.

4. "President Bush said the specter of Vietnam has been buried forever in the desert sands of the Arabian peninsula. But amid such signs of euphoria, there were warnings that a military victory, no matter how overwhelming, against a country with an economic output the size of Kentucky's, and a population less than a third of the size of Vietnam's, does not herald a new day." See the *New York Times* (March 4, 1991): 1A, 17A.

5. Most nations of Southeast Asia were at one time or another threatened by Chinese expansionism. Several were forced to acknowledge Chinese claims that they were tributary states. However, of these states only Vietnam survived.

6. This strategy favored a simultaneous and mutually supportive two-pronged assault on an adversary, one tailored to defeat its forces in the field and the other to defeat its war-making capacity at the level of politics and diplomacy.

7. The emergence of Southeast Asia and Vietnam in Asian and world history can be traced, for example, in David G. Marr and A. C. Milner, eds., *Southeast Asia in the Ninth to Fourteenth Centuries* (Canberra: Research School of Pacific Studies, the Australian National Univ., 1986); Anthony Reid, *Southeast Asia in the Age of Commerce, Vol. 1, The Lands Below the Winds* (New Haven, CT: Yale Univ. Press, 1988). The origins of the Vietnamese state is traced in Keith W. Taylor, *The Birth of Vietnam* (Berkeley: Univ. of California Press, 1983). The political culture of Vietnam is the subject of Ralph Smith, *An International History of the Vietnam War*, 4 vols. (London: Macmillan, 1983–1990).

8. See John F. Cady, *The Roots of French Imperialism in Asia* (Ithaca, NY: Cornell Univ. Press, 1954); Milton E. Osborne, *The French Presence in Cochin China and Cambodia: Rule and Response, 1859–1905* (Ithaca, NY: Cornell Univ. Press, 1969); Ngo Vinh Long, *Before the Revolution: The Vietnamese Peasants under the French* (Cambridge, MA: Harvard Univ. Press, 1973); Troung Buu Lam, *Patterns of Vietnamese Response to Foreign Intervention, 1858–1900* (New Haven, CT: Southeast Asia Studies, Yale Univ. Press, 1967).

9. The resistance to European imperialism may be traced in Michael Adas, *Prophets of Rebellion: Millenarian Protest Movements Against the European Colonial Order* (Chapel Hill: Univ. of North Carolina Press, 1979); Samuel Popkin, *The Rational Peasant* (Berkeley: Univ. of California Press, 1979); J. M. Pluvier, *Southeast Asia from Colonialism to Independence* (New York: Oxford Univ. Press, 1974); and James Scott, *The Moral Economy of the Peasant: Rebellion and Subsistence in Southeast Asia* (New Haven, CT: Yale Univ. Press, 1976).

10. See Joseph Buttinger's two-volume study, *A Dragon Embattled: A History of Colonial and Post-Colonial Vietnam*, 2 vols. (New York: Praeger, 1967). See also William Duiker, *The Rise of Nationalism in Vietnam* (Ithaca, NY: Cornell Univ. Press, 1976); David G. Marr, *Vietnamese Anti-Colonialism on Trial* (Berkeley: Univ. of California Press, 1971) and idem, *Vietnamese Nationalism on Trial* (Berkeley: Univ. of California Press, 1981).

11. See Sibnarayan Ray, ed., *Selected Works of M. N. Roy*, 3 vols. (New York: Oxford Univ. Press, 1991).

12. See Donald Eugene Smith, *Religion, Politics, and Social Change in the Third World* (New York: The Free Press, 1971).

13. See William Duiker, *Vietnam: Nation in Revolution* (Boulder, CO: Westview, 1983), 33–49.

14. For Sino-Vietnamese and Soviet-Vietnamese relations, see King C. Chen, *China and Vietnam, 1938–1954* (Princeton, NJ: Princeton Univ. Press, 1969); William Duiker, *China and Vietnam: The Roots of Conflict* (Berkeley: Institute of East Asian Studies, Univ. of California Press, 1986); idem, *China and Vietnam and the Struggle for Indochina* in a series by Joseph Zasloff, ed., *Postwar Indochina: Old Enemies, New Allies* (Washington, DC: Foreign Service Institute, U.S. Department of State, 1988) [hereafter *Postwar Indochina*]; Douglas Pike, *Vietnam and the USSR: Anatomy of an Alliance* (Boulder, CO: Westview, 1987); W. R. Smyser, *The Independent Vietnamese: Vietnamese Communism Between Russia and China, 1956–1969* (Athens: Ohio Univ. Center for International Studies, 1980).

15. William S. Turley, ed., *Vietnamese Communism in Comparative Perspective* (Boulder, CO: Westview, 1980) and William Duiker, *The Communist Road to Power in Vietnam* (Boulder, CO: Westview, 1981) attempt to place Vietnamese communism in global perspective. Laos and Cambodia have made their own unique contributions to world communism. The rise to power of the Communists in Cambodia is the focus of Ben Kiernan, *How Pol Pot Came to Power: The Rise and Demise of Democratic Kampuchea* (London: Verso, 1985) and Michael Vickery, *Cambodia: 1975–82* (Boston: South End, 1984). The best overviews of communism in Laos are Arthur J. Dominen, *Laos: Keystone of Indochina* (Boulder, CO: Westview, 1985) and MacAlister Brown and Joseph J. Zasloff, *Apprentice Revolutionaries: The Communist Movement in Laos, 1930–1985* (Palo Alto, CA: Stanford Univ. Press, 1986).

16. See James Olson and Randy Roberts, *Where the Domino Fell: America and Vietnam, 1945–1990* (New York: St. Martin's, 1990), 274–78; Stephan T. Johnson, "Vietnam's Politics and Economy in Mid–1987," in Zasloff, *Postwar Indochina*, 3–36.

17. See the *New York Times* (December 29, 1990): 1A; (March 4, 1991): 4A; (March 5, 1991): 5A; (April 1, 1991): 1A; the *International Herald Tribune* (August 29, 1991): 4.

18. See James R. Rush, "ASEAN's Neighborhood," in Zasloff, *Postwar Indochina*, 193–223; Thomas Havens, *Fire Across the Seas: The Vietnam War and Japan, 1965–1975* (Princeton, NJ: Princeton Univ. Press, 1987).

19. See Douglas A. Ross, "Canada, Peacemaking, and the Vietnam War: Where Did Ottawa Go Wrong?" in Elizabeth Jane Errington and B.J.C. McKercher, eds., *The Vietnam War as History* (New York: Praeger, 1990). Damodar R. SarDesai's work, *Vietnam: Struggle for National Identity*, 2nd ed. (Boulder, CO: Westview, 1991) discusses India's role in Vietnamese affairs.

20. See Valerie O'Connor, *The Indochina Refugee Dilemma* (Baton Rouge: Louisiana State Univ. Press, 1990); David Haines, ed., *Refugees as Immigrants: Cambodians, Laotians and Vietnamese in America* (Totowa, NJ: Rowman and Littlefield, 1989).

21. Ervin Staub, *The Roots of Evil: The Origins of Genocide and Other Group Violence* (New York: Cambridge Univ. Press, 1989).

22. Richard Falk, *The Vietnam War and International War*, 4 vols. (Princeton, NJ:

Princeton Univ. Press, 1968–1976); Peter D. Trooboff, ed., *Law and Responsibility in Warfare: The Vietnam Experience* (Chapel Hill: Univ. of North Carolina Press, 1975).

23. See Lawrence Grinter and Peter M. Dunn, eds., *The American War in Vietnam: Lessons, Legacies, and Implications for Future Conflicts* (Westport, CT: Greenwood, 1987).

24. See David L. Schalk, *War and the Ivory Tower: Algeria and Vietnam* (New York: Oxford Univ. Press, 1991).

25. These elements of the international dimension of the antiwar movement are vividly described in Robert V. Daniels, *The Year of the Heroic Guerrilla: World Revolution and Counterrevolution in 1968* (New York: Basic Books, 1989). See also Charles DeBenedetti, *An American Ordeal: The Antiwar Movement of the Vietnam Era* (Syracuse, NY: Syracuse Univ. Press, 1990); Richard Flacks, *Making History: The American Left and the American Mind* (New York: Beacon, 1988); Todd Gitlin, *The Sixties: Years of Hope, Days of Rage* (New York: Bantam, 1987).

26. See Cecil Currey, *Edward Lansdale: The Unquiet American* (Boston: Houghton Mifflin, 1988).

27. Ibid.; Larry E. Cable *Conflict of Myths: The Development of American Counterinsurgency Doctrine and the Vietnam War* (New York: New York Univ. Press, 1986); John Gates, *Schoolbooks and Krags* (Westport, CT: Greenwood, 1973); Robert Jackson, *The Malayan Emergency: The Commonwealth Wars, 1948–1966* (New York: Routledge, 1990); Brian Linn, *The United States Army and Counterinsurgency in the Philippine War, 1899–1902* (Chapel Hill: Univ. of North Carolina Press, 1989); Richard Stubbs, *Hearts and Minds in Guerrilla Warfare: The Malayan Emergency, 1948–1960* (Singapore: Oxford Univ. Press, 1989).

28. See John D. Waghelstein, "Counterinsurgency Doctrine and Low-Intensity Conflict in the Post-Vietnam Era," Peter M. Dunn and Lawrence E. Grinter, "Lessons, Legacies, and Implications of Vietnam," in Grinter and Dunn, eds., *The American War in Vietnam*, 127–37, 139–47, respectively. See also John M. Gates, "Vietnam: The Debate Continues," *Parameters* 15 (Spring 1985): 77–83; Lawrence E. Grinter, *Realities of Revolutionary Violence in Southeast Asia: Challenges and Responses* (Maxwell AFB, AL: CADRE Paper Series, Air Univ. Press, 1990). It is only recently that the Philippine government has abandoned a search for a military solution to insurgency and begun to "win the hearts and minds" in rebel areas through socioeconomic reforms.

29. See Earl H. Tilford, Jr., *Setup: What the Air Force Did in Vietnam and Why* (Maxwell AFB, AL: Air Univ. Press, 1991).

30. David Patraeus, "Lessons of History and Lessons of Vietnam," in Lloyd Mathews and Dale E. Brown, eds., *Assessing the Vietnam War* (McLean, VA: Pergamon-Brassey, 1987), 181.

31. See the recollections of Buchanan and Rutan in Harry Maurer, *Strange Ground: An Oral History of Americans in Vietnam, 1945–1975* (New York: Avon, 1989), 365–93. See also Tilford, *Setup.*

32. See Richard H. Graham (former 9th SRW Wing Commander), "SR–71 Lacked Priority," *Aviation Week and Space Technology* (February 25, 1991): 72.

33. It is worth recalling that "the failure to direct operational efforts toward a valid strategic goal is, by definition, strategic failure and tactical and operational brilliance which fails to serve a viable policy objective is at best irrelevant." See John F. Guilmartin, Jr., "Bombing the Ho Chi Minh Trail: A Preliminary Analysis of the Effects of Air Interdiction," *Air Power History* 38, no. 4 (Winter 1991): 3–18.

34. See "Iraqi Gunners Fire in 'Boxes' to Maintain Air Defense," *Aviation Week and Space Technology* (January 28, 1991): 24.

35. See Gennady Bocharov, *Russian Roulette: Afghanistan Through Russian Eyes* (New York: Harper Collins, 1990); Russell Watson, "Lessons of Afghanistan: Conventional Armies Lose Unconventional Wars," *Newsweek* 113, no. 2 (February 20, 1989): 26; the *New York Times* (January 8, 1988): 1A.

36. See Peter P. Mahoney, "The Wounds of Two Wars," *New York Times Magazine* 138 (June 11, 1989): 60; Ben Shepard, "Vietnam Vets and the Soviet Experience," *History Today* 39 (July 1989): 10; "Our Mutual Tragedy," *Time* 133 (June 5, 1989): 49.

37. John Wheeler, 'Toting Up the Cost of the Gulf War," *Atlanta Constitution and Journal* (February 23, 1991): 19A.

38. Steven Keeva, "Lawyers in the War Room," *ABA Journal* 77 (December 1991): 52.

39. Ibid., 59.

40. Barbara Crosette, "In Peru's Shining Path, U.S. Sees Road to Ruin," *New York Times* (March 18, 1992): 17A.

41. For Tet as a failure, see George Donaldson Moss, *Vietnam: An American Ordeal* (Englewood Cliffs, NJ: Prentice-Hall, 1990); Herbert Y. Schandler, *The Unmaking of a President: Lyndon Johnson and Vietnam* (Princeton, NJ: Princeton Univ. Press, 1977). Dan Oberdorfer, however, casts doubt on the very figures Moss and Schandler use to support their arguments in Dan Oberdorfer, *Tet!* (New York: Avon, 1972), 279–80.

42. William Safire, "Don Your Aggressive Battle Words," *International Herald Tribune* (August 27, 1990): 14.

43. See Fouad Ajami, "History Reflected in a Cracked Mirror," *U.S. News & World Report* 109 (August 27, 1990): 18; Edward Said, "A Tragic Convergence," *New York Times* (January 1, 1991): 29A.

44. See Thomas Friedman "A Dreamlike Landscape, A Dreamlike Reality," *New York Times* (October 28, 1990): 3E.

45. The United States must resist the temptation to dismiss Islamic fundamentalism as an Iranian heresy—its roots are in macrohistorical developments, such as the frustration of Arab and African nationalism and the failure of modernization to provide prosperity for the masses in the developing world.

46. The most recent and detailed analysis of the impact of the war is Anthony S. Campagna, *The Economic Consequences of the Vietnam War* (New York: Praeger, 1991). See also A. D. Horne, ed., *The Wounded Generation: America After Vietnam* (Englewood Cliffs, NJ: Prentice-Hall, 1981); Robert Warren Stevens, *Vain Hopes, Grim Realities: The Economic Consequences of the Vietnam War* (New York: New Viewpoints, 1976); John Wheeler, *Touched with Fire: The Future of the Vietnam Generation* (New York: Avon, 1985).

47. See Robert O'Neil, "The Vietnam War and the Western Alliance," in John Schlight, ed., *Second Indochina War Symposium: Papers and Commentary* (Washington, DC: Army Center of Military History, 1986), 229–44.

48. Paul Kennedy, *The Rise and Fall of the Great Powers: Economic Change and Military Conflict, 1500–2000* (New York: Random House, 1987), 404–9. See also Ole R. Holsti and James N. Rosenau, *American Leadership in World Affairs: Vietnam and the Breakdown of Consensus* (Winchester, MA: Unwin Hyman, 1984); Paul M. Kattenberg, *The Vietnam Trauma in American Foreign Policy, 1945–1975* (Boston: Beacon,

1980); Anthony Lake, *The Legacy of Vietnam: The War, American Society and the Future of American Foreign Policy* (New York: Council on Foreign Relations, 1976).

49. See Kattenberg, "Reflections on Vietnam: Of Revisionism and Lessons Yet to Be Learned," Mathews and Brown, eds., *Assessing the Vietnam War*, 159–70.

50. See William Safire, "Duty to Intervene," *New York Times* (April 15, 1991): 15A.

51. Crosette, "In Peru's Shining Path, U.S. Sees Road to Ruin," 17A.

52. Gerald Gill, who published one of the first portrayals of the experience of black Americans in the war, cites virtually the entire corpus of scholarship on this subject in his essay, "Black Soldiers' Perspectives on the War," in Walter Capps, ed., *A Vietnam Reader* (New York: Routledge, 1991), 173–85.

53. Ibid., 186–90, 191–204.

54. See Gilbert, *The Vietnam War: Teaching Approaches and Resources*, 29, 140, 176–77, 187–88, 217.

55. This writer, though aware of William C. Anderson's story of the rescue of Lt. Col. Iceal Hambleton, reacted with a start when the end-credit reference to Hambleton appeared at the end of the film. He was not alone—a murmur of anger rippled through the racially mixed audience in the theater at the showing he attended.

56. See "The Killing Fields Aren't Level," *New York Times* (January 28, 1991): 22A; Arch Puddington, "Black Leaders v. Desert Storm," *Commentary* 91 (May 1991): 28.

57. See "Fire When Ready, Ma'am: The Invasion Re-opens the Debate on Women in Combat," *Time* 135 (January 15, 1990): 29.

58. See Susan Jeffords, *The Remasculinization of America: Gender and the War* (Bloomington: Indiana Univ. Press, 1989); Barthy Bird, *Home Front: Women and Vietnam* (Berkeley, CA: Shameless Hussey, 1986).

59. Nguyen Du, *The Tale of Kieu*, trans. Huynh Sanh Thong (New Haven, CT: Yale Univ. Press, 1967).

60. Le Ly Haslip with Jay Wirts, *When Heaven and Earth Changed Places* (New York: Doubleday, 1989).

61. See Nguyen Ngoc Bich, Burton Raffel, and W. S. Merwin, *A Thousand Years of Vietnamese Poetry* (New York: Knopf, 1975); Nguyen Khac Vien and Hu Ngoc, *Vietnamese Literature* (Hanoi: Red River Publishing House, 1982).

62. See Someth May, *Cambodian Witness: The Autobiography of Someth May* (London: Faber and Faber, 1986); Doan Van Toai and David Chanoff, *The Vietnamese Gulag: A Revolution Betrayed* (New York: Simon & Schuster, 1986).

63. James Sterngold, "South Korea's Vietnam Veterans Begin to Be Heard," *New York Times* (May 10, 1992): 6A.

64. The plot of the Vietnamese film *Free Fire Zone* centers on an American assault helicopter pilot as the nemesis of a peasant family. When, in the film's denouement, the Vietnamese hero kills the pilot, the pilot's wallet falls open, revealing a picture of the American's family.

65. See Thich Nhat Hanh and Vo-Dinh, *The Cry of Vietnam* (Santa Barbara, CA: Unicorn, 1968).

Part II

Decision Making and Policy Makers

Douglas Pike in his book *PAVN: The People's Army of North Vietnam* describes U.S. policy in Vietnam as "vincible ignorance," or "you know you do not know that you do not know it, but you don't care." Indeed, one is reminded of these words throughout this following section on "Decision Making and Policy Makers." The one commonality in all these chapters is their new research and the additional insight that this research provides the reader and researchers. The decision-making processes and policy makers of the Vietnam era remain a complex group of dilemmas and personalities.

The preeminent scholar of American foreign relations with Vietnam, George C. Herring, begins this section with a probing examination of President Lyndon Johnson and the role of such advisers and generals as Maxwell Taylor, George Ball, William Westmoreland, Dean Rusk, and Robert McNamara. Drawing on a wealth of new research from the Johnson Library, Herring has reached deep into the inner circle of the Johnson White House, as well as into the personality and persona of the president, to recreate the internal decision-making apparatus, process, and underlying currents that went into making up the Johnson foreign policy in Vietnam.[1]

Like other analysts of Johnson, such as David Halberstam and Larry Berman, we witness an executive branch and military hierarchy dominated by one man—Lyndon Johnson. Obsessed by a desire to win in Vietnam and to build a Great Society at home—guns and butter—he was unable, or unwilling, either to focus the wealth of intelligence information he had on the enemy, or to properly utilize the abundance of analytical talent present in his advisers, to form a workable and effective policy or strategy in Vietnam. Herring paints the picture of a troubled man so incapable of accepting honest disagreement and criticism of his policies that he ignored and discouraged warnings of disaster for the country and himself in Vietnam. Indeed, the man who Herring describes fits well the colorful president that Robert Halberstam says once characterized a loyal adviser as a man who would "kiss my ass in Macy's main window at high noon and tell me it smelled like roses."[2]

Johnson not only cowed those in his cabinet, the White House, and the military, but also the Congress. Caroline F. Ziemke of the Institute for Defense Analyses, again drawing from new research materials, examines this awkward and reluctant relationship between Johnson and Congress. Focusing on the career of Georgia Senator Richard B. Russell, she traces his role and that of other so-called "Hawks" in ramming the Gulf of Tonkin Resolution down the throats of Congress and the public. In doing so she notes that, too late, Russell and others realized that they'd made a mistake, not only in committing the United States to an untenable conflict, but in giving away their constitutional right to make war.

Ziemke goes on to demonstrate the risk of this failure by the Congress to safeguard its heritage when she also reevaluates the way President Bush all but ignored the Congress in going to war in the Persian Gulf, further eroding the congressional prerogative to authorize war.

The last chapter in this section is by analyst and historian John W. Garver of the Georgia Institute of Technology. Unlike the other chapters that deal with decisions for war, Garver deals with the Johnson administration's decision to limit the war to Vietnam rather than risk Chinese and perhaps Soviet intervention. He begins by restating the thesis of revisionists, such as Harry Summers, that the United States lost the war because it failed to employ a rapid buildup designed to invade North Vietnam and Laos in 1965–1966 and thus cut off the source of supply to the Viet Cong allowing the South Vietnamese a chance to win the war in the South.

Summers argues that this came about because Johnson, recalling the Chinese invasion of Korea in November 1950, feared a repeat in Indochina if the United States invaded the North. Garver agrees that this was true, but unlike Summers who says it was a false fear, Garver makes a powerful case that a Chinese invasion in the midsixties was very likely if U.S. troops had invaded North Vietnam. Moreover, argues Garver, an invasion of North Vietnam would not have been as easy as the revisionists argue. According to Garver the failure of the 1979 Chinese invasion provides ample evidence of the tenacity of northern forces. He also provides indications that the Soviet Union, at the height of the Cold War, almost surely would have increased its support of both North Vietnam and China, expanding the struggle and ultimately melding a stronger Communist alliance among the three even after the war. Worst of all, says Garver, an increased Chinese and Soviet presence very well might have created a larger Communist threat in Thailand, Burma, Malaya, and Singapore.

Indeed, there are no hard and fast answers to the questions raised by these complex series of events. However, from Herring's view inside the Johnson-Kennedy White House to Ziemke's examination of the consequences of blind congressional support of a president and Garver's examination of a president's reluctance to use the full power of his military provide compelling theses through their research and logic. Considering the continuing controversy over culpability of these leaders and the results of their decisions, these three chapters provide important new insights and refreshing reappraisals in the ever expanding search for the veracity of Vietnam.

NOTES

1. Much of the original research and theme was first used by Herring in his previously published Harmon Memorial Lecture presented at the United States Air Force Academy, Colorado, on the evening of October 12, 1990. The Department of History at the Academy had graciously allowed Dr. Herring to restate his thesis in this new discussion, "The Johnson Administration's Conduct of Limited War in Vietnam."

2. For more on the personalities in the Johnson White House see David Halberstam, *The Best and the Brightest* (Greenwich, CT: Fawcett, rev. ed., 1973). For a more specific look at the decision-making style of the Johnson administration see Larry Berman, *Planning a Tragedy: The Americanization of the War in Vietnam* (New York: Norton, 1982).

The Johnson Administration's Conduct of Limited War in Vietnam

George C. Herring

This chapter focuses on the Johnson administration's conduct of the war in Vietnam. There is much that can be learned by looking at how the war was fought and explaining why it was fought as it was, without reference to alternative strategies, without presuming that it could have been won or was inevitably lost. Two crucial areas will be examined: the formulation of and subsequent nondebate over strategy, and the Johnson administration's efforts to manage public opinion. Such analysis should do much to help explain why the war was fought as it was and why it took the direction it did.

Limited war requires the most sophisticated strategy, precisely formulated in terms of ends and means, with particular attention paid to keeping costs at acceptable levels. What stands out about the Johnson administration's handling of Vietnam is that in what may have been the most complex war ever fought by the United States, there was never any systematic discussion at the highest levels of government of the fundamental issue of just *how* the war should be fought. The crucial discussions of June and July 1965 focused on the numbers of troops that would be provided rather than on how and for what ends they would be used. And this was the only such discussion until the Communist Tet Offensive forced the issue in March 1968.

Why was this so? Simple overconfidence may be the most obvious explanation. Americans could not conceive that the United States would be unable to impose its will on what Lyndon Johnson once referred to as that "raggedy-ass little fourth-rate country." There was no need to think in terms of strategy!

I suspect that the explanation goes much deeper than that. Although he worked at the role of commander-in-chief, personally picking bombing targets, agonizing over the fate of airmen, and building a scale-model of Khe Sanh in the White House situation room, unlike Polk, Lincoln, or Franklin Roosevelt, Johnson never took control of his war. Perhaps the weakest of American commanders-in-chiefs, he permitted himself to be preoccupied with other matters—the "Great

Society'' and the legislative process he understood best and loved. In contrast to Lincoln, Roosevelt, and even Truman, Johnson had little interest in military affairs and no illusions of military expertise. He was fond of quoting his political mentor, Sam Rayburn, to the effect that ''if we start making the military decisions, I wonder why we paid to send them to West Point''—perhaps a rationalization for his own ignorance and lack of security.[1]

President Johnson thus provided his advisers little direction and indeed at crucial points gave little hint of his thinking. National Security Adviser McGeorge Bundy literally pleaded with him in November 1965 to make clear his positions on the big issues so that Secretary of Defense Robert McNamara could be certain he was running the war ''the right way for the right reasons in your view.'' By late 1967, private citizen Bundy's pleading had taken on a tone of urgency, warning Johnson that he must wrest control of the war from the military and ''take command of a contest that is more political in character than any in our history except the Civil War. . . . ''[2]

McNamara himself might have filled the strategic void left by Johnson, but he was no more willing to take control than the president. In some ways an outstanding secretary of defense, McNamara was not an effective minister of war. Conceding his ignorance of military matters, he refused to interfere in what he saw as the military's bailiwick, leaving it to them to set the strategic agenda. When asked on one occasion why he did not tell his military subordinates what to do, and reminded that Churchill had not hesitated to do so, he responded that he was no Churchill.[3] Thus, as Stephen Peter Rosen observes, Johnson and McNamara refused to do what the civilian leadership must do: ''they did not define a clear . . . mission for the military and did not establish a clear limit to the resources to be allocated for that mission.''[4]

Instead, Johnson and McNamara saw their primary task as maintaining tight operational control over the military. This derived in part from the profound civil-military tension of the 1960s and from the conflict that raged beneath the surface during the Bay of Pigs debacle and the Cuban missile crisis. In addition, Johnson brought to the White House a southern populist's suspicion of the military. Suspecting that the generals and admirals needed war to boost their reputations, he was determined to keep a close rein on them.[5] The result in Vietnam was a day-to-day intrusion into the tactical conduct of the war on a quite unprecedented scale. The larger result, Rosen concludes, was an unhappy combination of ''high-level indecision and micromanagement.''[6]

Inasmuch as McNamara and Johnson's civilian advisers thought strategically, they did so in terms of the limited war theories in vogue at the time. Strategy was primarily a matter of sending signals to foes, communicating resolve, using military force in a calibrated way to deter enemies, or bargain toward a settlement. The Kennedy administration's successful handling of the Cuban missile crisis seems to have reinforced in the minds of U.S. officials the value of such an approach. ''There is no longer any such thing as strategy, only crisis management,'' McNamara exclaimed in the aftermath of Kennedy's facedown of Khrushchev.[7]

He could not have been more wrong, of course, and the reliance on limited war theory had unfortunate consequences. It diverted attention from real strategy and caused the problem of how to win the war in South Vietnam to be neglected. And when Hanoi refused to respond as bargaining theory said it would, the United States was left with no strategy at all.

Civil-military tensions further complicated the formulation of strategy. From the start, there were profound differences among top military leaders and between military and civilians as to how—or at least at what level—the war should be fought. Perhaps tragically, these differences were never addressed, much less resolved. Indeed, the decision-making process seems to have been rigged to stifle controversy. As a result, some questions were raised but not answered; others were not even raised. The sort of full-scale debate that might have led to a reconsideration of the U.S. commitment or to a more precise formulation of strategy did not take place. And the tensions and divisions that were left unresolved would provide the basis for bitter conflict when the steps taken in July 1965 did not produce the desired results.

During the July 1965 discussions on escalation in Vietnam, Johnson kept a tight rein on the decision-making process. Distrustful of the military, wary of the implications of their proposals for escalation, fearful of their possible influence with conservatives in Congress, he kept the Joint Chiefs of Staff (JCS) at arms length, giving them enough to keep them on board but conceding them little real input.

On both sides, deep divisions on strategy were subordinated to maintaining the appearance of unity. The Joint Chiefs were themselves deeply divided on how the war should be fought. But in the summer of 1965 and indeed after, they compromised their differences and developed unified positions to prevent McNamara from conquering them by exploiting their divisions.

Perhaps regrettably, the even deeper divisions between the civilians and the military did not surface. If the military had perceived Johnson's steadfast determination to limit U.S. escalation, they might have been more wary of going to war. The Joint Chiefs seem to have perceived more accurately than the civilians what would be required in Vietnam. Perhaps if Johnson had been more aware of their estimates and reservations he might have been more cautious.

In fact, the July 1965 discussions comprised an elaborate civil-military cat-and-mouse game, with the nation the ultimate loser. Fearful of the domestic and international implications of the all-out war proposed by the Joint Chiefs, Johnson kept them on short rein and rejected, without permitting any discussion, several of the proposals they felt essential for the prosecution of the war. On the other hand, aware of the JCS's position and eager to keep them on board, the president did not set firm limits or dictate strategy. He gave them enough to suggest that they might get more later.

The JCS did not deliberately deceive Johnson as to what might be required in Vietnam. On the crucial question of North Vietnamese resistance, they probably miscalculated as badly as he did. Perhaps to prevent him from accepting George Ball's arguments for withdrawal, however, they seem to have downplayed the difficulties the United States would face, and they quietly acquiesced in his refusal to mobilize the reserves. They seem to have assumed that once the United States was committed in Vietnam they could maneuver the president into giving them what they wanted by what JCS chairman General Earle Wheeler called a "foot-in-the-door approach."[8]

An equally crippling form of bureaucratic gridlock persisted throughout the period 1965–1967. Far more than has been recognized and far more than was revealed in the *Pentagon Papers*, no one in the Johnson administration really liked the way the war was being fought or the results that were being obtained. What is even more striking, however, is that despite the rampant dissatisfaction, there was no change in strategy or even systematic discussion of a change. Again, the system seems to have been rigged to prevent debate and adaptation.

From July 1965 onward, there were sharp differences over strategy within the administration. The running battle over the bombing, especially between McNamara and the Joint Chiefs, is well known.[9] But there was also widespread and steadily growing dissatisfaction with General Westmoreland's ground strategy. From the outset, the Marines strongly objected to the Army's determination to fight guerrillas by staging decisive battles "along the Tannenberg design."[10] More significantly, within the Army itself there was growing concern about Westmoreland's conduct of the war. Army Chief of Staff Harold Johnson increasingly questioned the wastefulness of search-and-destroy operations, as did Vice-Chief of Staff Creighton Abrams and some of Westmoreland's top field officers.[11]

Divisions within the military, of course, paled compared to the growing conflict between the military and civilians. The military bristled at Johnson's refusal to mobilize the reserves and protested the micromanagement of the war. "The idea," Marine General Victor "Brute" Krulak complained in 1967, seemed to be "to take more and more items of less and less significance to higher and higher levels so that more and more decisions on smaller and smaller matters may be made by fewer and fewer people."[12] For their part, the civilians worried about relentless military pressure for escalation of the war and increasingly pressed for cutbacks or even stoppage of the bombing, a ceiling on the number of ground troops, and a shift to a less costly and wasteful ground strategy.[13]

Despite these divisions, there was no change of strategy or even discussion of a change in strategy. One reason for this was the hallowed tradition of autonomy of the field commander. Although greatly concerned with the cost and consequences of Westmoreland's strategy, Army Chief of Staff Johnson deferred to his field commander. "I would deplore and oppose any intervention from the Washington level to impose limitations on further firepower application," he reassured Westmoreland. He would do more than suggest that it might be "prudent" to "undertake a very careful examination of the problem."[14]

More important was the leadership style of the commander-in-chief. President Johnson's entirely political approach to running the war—his consensus-oriented modus operandi—effectively stifled debate. On such issues as bombing targets and bombing pauses, troop levels and troop use, he kept dissent under control by making concessions to each side without giving any all it wanted.[15]

The president and his top advisers also imposed rigid standards of loyalty on a divided administration. Johnson's "Macy's window at high noon" brand of loyalty has been made legendary by David Halberstam.[16] McNamara and Dean Rusk shared his perverted notions of team play. In-house devil's advocate George Ball later recalled that McNamara treated his dissenting memos rather like "poisonous snakes," and considered them "next to treason." It is now clear, moreover, that when McNamara himself became a dissenter it was an excruciating experience for him.[17]

Finally, and most important, there is what might be called the "MacArthur syndrome"—the fear among civilians and military officials alike of a repetition of the illustrious general's challenge to civilian authority. Johnson lived in mortal terror of a military revolt and did everything in his power to avert it. "General, I have a lot riding on you," he blurted out to Westmoreland in 1966. "I hope you don't pull a MacArthur on me."[18] Themselves learning from Korea, the military carefully refrained from anything approaching a direct challenge to civilian authority. General Wheeler's approach emphasized rather short-term acquiescence and silence. Hopeful of getting strategic license by gradually breaking down the restrictions imposed by the White House, he encouraged General Westmoreland to continue to push escalation and to accept half a loaf to get his "foot in the door." He even instructed him to keep his subordinates quiet. If escalation were to occur following reports of military dissatisfaction, it might be concluded that the military was "riding roughshod" over civilians. Officers must understand the "absolute necessity for every military man to keep his mouth shut and get on with the war."[19]

Johnson and his top advisers thus squelched any form of dissent. In the summer of 1966, for example, Ambassador Henry Cabot Lodge and Marine Commandant General Wallace Greene conspired to challenge Westmoreland's conduct of the ground war. In a deep backgrounder (background report) in Saigon, Greene affirmed that with the existing strategy, it would take 750,000 men, five years, and at least partial mobilization to win the war. The reaction Greene later recalled, was "immediate" and "explosive." An "agitated" and as usual "profane" Lyndon Johnson demanded over long-distance telephone to know "What in the God-damn hell" he had meant by his statement and forced him to issue a retraction.[20]

Even in the spring of 1967, with McNamara now in open revolt against the war's conduct, and civilians and military officers deeply divided, there was no change in strategy or even discussion of a change in strategy. Characteristically, Johnson avoided a confrontation between the position of McNamara and that of the military. There was no discussion of the issues at the top levels. He delayed a decision for months, and when he finally decided he did so on a piecemeal basis, carefully avoiding discussion of the larger issues.[21]

Ironically—and significantly—the debate that could not take place within the administration took place in Congress in August 1967 in hearings before the Senate Preparedness Subcommittee—the Stennis committee. The original intent of the hearings was to ''get McNamara'' and force the president to escalate the war, and the JCS mounted the closest thing to a MacArthur-like challenge to the president's conduct of the war. Ironically, McNamara saw the hearings designed to get him as an opportunity to combat pressures for expanding the war without violating his own standards of loyalty to the president. In a strange, almost surreal way, the Stennis committee became a forum for the debate that could not take place within the inner councils of government.[22]

The debate nearly brought out into the open those issues that had smoldered beneath the surface for months. McNamara's testimony on August 25, 1967, against the air war, provoked a *near* revolt on the part of the Joint Chiefs. On that very night, according to Mark Perry, General Wheeler called an emergency meeting and asked his colleagues to join him in resigning en masse the following morning. They agreed. By the next morning, however, the chairman had second thoughts. ''We can't do it,'' he reportedly said. ''It's mutiny!'' In any event, he added, ''If we resign they'll just get someone else. And we'll be forgotten.''[23]

The Stennis hearings represented what Johnson had most feared—division within his administration and a military revolt backed by right-wingers in Congress. Remarkably, he was able to contain it. Publicly, he dealt with the problem by denying its existence. There were ''no quarrels, no antagonisms'' within his official family, he insisted. ''I have never known a period when I thought there was more harmony, more general agreement, and a more cooperative attitude.'' Administration officials followed to the letter the script written by their director. Years later McNamara admitted that he went through hell on the Stennis hearings. Yet at a White House meeting he praised General Wheeler for a ''helluva good job'' before the Stennis committee and observed that the small differences between himself and the JCS were ''largely worked out.'' Wheeler publicly dismissed rumors that the JCS had contemplated resignation with a terse: ''Bull shit!''[24]

To the end of his presidency, Lyndon Johnson continued to deny that there had been differences in his administration, and no one could have written a better epitaph for a hopelessly flawed decision-making process than its architect, the man who had imposed his own peculiar brand of loyalty on a bitterly divided government. ''There have been no divisions in this government,'' he proudly proclaimed in November 1967. ''We may have been wrong, but we have not been divided.''[25] It was a strange observation, reflecting a curiously distorted sense of priorities. And it was not true. The administration was both wrong *and* divided, and the fact that the divisions could not be worked out or even addressed may have contributed to the wrong policies, at huge costs to the men themselves—and especially to the nation.

By the time the divisions over strategy became acute in late 1967, Johnson's attention was drawn inexorably to the impending collapse of his support at home. Vietnam makes it abundantly clear that one of the central problems of waging limited war is maintaining public support without arousing public emotion. One of the most interesting and least-studied areas of the war is the Johnson administration's efforts to do precisely this. It should be emphasized: Vietnam was not fundamentally a public relations' problem, and a more vigorous and effective public relations campaign would not have changed the outcome. Still, what stands out quite starkly from an examination of the documents is the small, indeed insignificant, role played by public opinion in the decisions for war in July 1965 and the limited efforts made by the administration between 1965 and 1967 to mobilize public support for the war.

In examining the extensive White House files for June and July 1965, one is immediately struck by the almost negligible attention given to domestic opinion in the discussions leading to Johnson's decisions for war. At a meeting of July 21, George Ball, the foremost opponent of escalation, resorted to the obvious analogy, using charts from the Korean War to warn that public support could not be taken for granted. Admonishing that the war would become protracted, Ball reminded the group that as casualties had increased in Korea, public support had dropped.[26] A long war, he also predicted, would generate powerful pressures to strike directly at North Vietnam, risking dangerous escalation.

No one responded to Ball's admonition, but on those few other occasions when the issue came up the tone was generally optimistic. At another point in the same meeting, McGeorge Bundy observed that the nation "seemed in the mood to accept grim news." In another meeting, Marine Commandant Greene predicted that the nation would support the commitment of as many as 500,000 men for as long as five years.[27]

The issue also got a brief and revealing hearing at a meeting on July 27. Assuming George Ball's usual role of devil's advocate, Johnson asked his advisers if Congress and the public would go along with 600,000 troops and billions of dollars being sent 10,000 miles away. Only Secretary of the Army Stanley Resor responded, laconically observing that the polls showed that people were "basically behind our commitment." But, Johnson persisted, "if you make a commitment to jump off a building and you find out how high it is, you may want to withdraw that commitment," a remarkably prescient observation. No one responded, however, and nothing more was said. His mind apparently made up, Johnson dropped a crucial question and went on to something else.[28]

Why this absence of discussion of an issue that turned out to be so important? The answer, in one word, seems to have been complacency. After World War II, within the larger confines of the Cold War consensus, the executive branch had developed to a fine art the knack of analyzing and manipulating public opinion. Postwar administrations were never free from criticism, but in no case was a major foreign policy initiative frustrated by lack of public support. Perhaps because of this record of success, the administration assumed that the American people would tolerate large-scale involvement in Vietnam.[29]

The administration seems to have dismissed the Korean analogy because it felt it could get what it wanted without the travail and agony of Korea. Johnson and his advisers acted, Bill Moyers later conceded, in the expectation that "reason and mutual concessions" would prevail, and that Hanoi could be enticed or intimidated into negotiation and a drawn-out war could thus be avoided.[30] Thus, a fatal miscalculation about Hanoi's response to U.S. escalation may have been behind an equally fatal miscalculation about the longevity of public support.

The administration totally missed the significance of the budding peace movement. Rusk compared the campus protest of the spring of 1965 to the 1938 Oxford Union debate, observing that most of those who "took the pledge" later served in the war. Bundy later admitted, "We simply hadn't estimated the kinds of new forces that were loose in the land."[31]

Equally striking is how little the administration did in the first years of the war to mobilize public support. Administration officials in July 1965 had proposed a "full scenario" of actions to prepare the nation for war. Presidential aides suggested the creation of a citizens committee like the Committee for the Marshall Plan. White House adviser Horace Busby urged Johnson to go out and rally the public in the mode of a Churchill.[32]

Johnson rejected all such proposals. He undoubtedly feared that a public debate on Vietnam would jeopardize the Great Society legislation then pending in Congress, and he did not want to risk what he later called "the woman I really loved" for "that bitch of a war on the other side of the world."[33]

The president also feared that mobilizing the nation for war would set loose irresistible pressures for escalation and victory that might provoke the larger war with the Soviet Union and China that the commitment in Vietnam was designed to deter in the first place. As Rusk later put it, "In a nuclear world it is just too dangerous for an entire people to get too angry and we deliberately tried to do in cold blood what perhaps can only be done in hot blood. . . ."[34]

For McNamara, the person who gave practical application to the limited war theory, Vietnam was the prototype for the way war must be fought in the nuclear age. "The greatest contribution Vietnam is making," he observed early in the war, "is developing an ability in the United States to fight a limited war . . . without arousing the public ire," almost a necessity, he added, "since this is the kind of war we'll likely be facing for the next fifty years."[35]

Johnson thus gambled that without taking exceptional measures he could hold public support long enough to achieve his goals in Vietnam. The United States therefore went to war in July 1965 in a way uniquely quiet and underplayed.

With the exception of several hastily arranged, typically Johnsonian public relations blitzes, the administration persisted in this low-key approach for nearly two years. Complacent about public support and fearful of the implications of mobilizing the public, the administration in the first months "privatized" responsibility for selling the war, leaving to the Young Democrats, the Democratic National Committee, and the American Friends of Vietnam the responsibility for educating the public. The White House dealt with the budding peace movement by ignoring it, going out of its way in late 1965 to avoid "any impression of an overly worried reaction" to major demonstrations.[36]

Administration officials also responded to growing criticism in a way that was typically Johnsonian. If Ronald Reagan was the teflon president, to whom nothing stuck, Johnson—to a large degree by choice—was the flypaper president, to whom everything stuck. A compulsive reader, viewer, talker, and listener, he was at first intent on and then obsessed with answering every accusation, responding to every charge. When General Matthew Ridgway came out against the war, the president ordered General Harold Johnson to get statements of support from *two* World War II generals—Omar Bradley and "Lightning Joe" Collins.[37] Reams of paper were devoted to proving how wrong critic Walter Lippmann had been on so many occasions. Thousands of man-hours were wasted by harried White House staffers compiling dossiers on critics, especially the despised Kennedy brothers.[38]

It was the summer of 1967 before the administration belatedly recognized that it was losing the war at home. An increasingly frustrated president complained bitterly about his inability to get across his message: "It is hell when a president has to spend half his time keeping his own people juiced up."[39]

Johnson and his advisers were particularly worried about public perceptions, fed by the press, that the war had degenerated into a stalemate.[40] The president groped for some magic formula to reverse the spread of disillusionment, on one occasion longing for "some colorful general like MacArthur with his shirt neck open" who could dismiss as "pure communist propaganda" the talk of a stalemate and go to Saigon and do battle with the press."[41] "A miasma of trouble hangs over everything," Lady Bird Johnson confided to her diary. "The temperament of our people seems to be, 'you must get excited, get passionate, fight it and get it over with, or we must pull out.' It is unbearably hard to fight a limited war."[42]

Writing to Johnson in late 1967, Undersecretary of State Nicholas Katzenbach raised the perplexing question: "Can the tortoise of progress in Vietnam stay ahead of the hare of dissent at home?"[43] Katzenbach's Aesopian analogy suggests the extent to which by late 1967 the two strands of this paper had come together. And it made clear the dilemma faced by Lyndon Johnson. To stave off collapse of the home front, progress must be demonstrated in Vietnam; yet real progress might not be possible without clear indications of firm public support at home.

By late 1967, Katzenbach and other civilian advisers pressed Johnson to resolve the dilemma by doing what he had thus far adamantly refused to do— address directly the issue of how the war was being fought. A now blatantly dissident McNamara, civilians in the State Department and in the Pentagon, and establishment figures outside of government, all urged the president to check dissent at home by changing strategy in Vietnam. They pressed for cutting back or stopping the bombing. More important, they insisted that Westmoreland's costly and inconclusive strategy must be abandoned. They proposed shifting to a "clear and hold strategy" that might stabilize the war at a politically acceptable level and save South Vietnam without risking a wider war. They also pushed an incipient form of what would later be called Vietnamization, urging that greater military responsibility be shifted to the South Vietnamese.[44]

Speechwriter Harry McPherson and private citizen McGeorge Bundy got closer to the central flaws of Johnson's exercise of presidential powers in wartime. Bundy warned the president that since the principal battleground was now "domestic opinion," he, as commander-in-chief, had both the "right and duty to visibly take command of a contest that is more political in character than any in our history except the Civil War (where Lincoln interfered much more than you have)."[45]

Johnson was not moved by the appeals of his advisers. He was unsympathetic to repeated JCS appeals for expansion of the air and ground wars. But he doubted that McNamara's bombing halt would work. "How do we get this conclusion?" he scrawled on a memo where the secretary had predicted that stopping the bombing would lead to peace talks.[46] As before, he refused to make the hard decisions, and he refused to take control of the war. He "resolved" the strategic questions politically without addressing the strategic issues. He kicked McNamara downstairs to the World Bank and tossed the JCS a bone in the form of a few new bombing targets. In regard to ground operations, he would go no further than privately commit himself to review Westmoreland's search-and-destroy strategy at some undetermined point in the future.[47]

To resolve the dilemma posed by Katzenbach, Johnson chose to try to slow down the runaway rabbit of dissent at home rather than speed up or shift the direction of the turtle of progress in Vietnam. Thus, in the fall of 1967, he did what he had previously refused to do—he mounted a large-scale, multifaceted public relations program to rally support for the war. Believing that his major problem was a widespread and growing public perception that the war was a stalemate, he designed much of this campaign to persuade an increasingly skeptical public that the United States was in fact winning the war. Thus, he ordered the embassy and military command to "search urgently for occasions to present sound evidence of progress in Vietnam." U.S. officials dutifully responded by producing reams of statistics to show a steady rise in enemy body counts and the number of villages pacified.[48]

This fateful campaign backfired a few months later when the North Vietnamese Tet Offensive seemed to put the lie to its major premise, entrenching ever more deeply popular notions that the best the United States could attain was a stalemate. Tet also forced Johnson to come face-to-face with his strategic failure. After nearly two months of top-level deliberations focusing for the first time on crucial issues of how the war was being fought, he instituted some of the measures originally proposed by his civilian advisers in late 1967. Johnson's intervention came too late and did not go far enough to end the war, however, and he passed on to his successor a far more complex and intractable problem than he had inherited.

If we return to the initial question in this chapter—why was the Vietnam War fought as it was?—we see that, certainly, Johnson put his own indelible mark on the war. The reluctance to provide precise direction and define a mission and explicit limits; the unwillingness to tolerate any form of intragovernmental dissent or permit a much-needed internal debate on strategic issues; the highly politicized approach that gave everybody something and nobody much and that emphasized consensus above everything else—all these were products of a thoroughly political and profoundly insecure man, a man especially ill at ease among military issues and military people.

The determination to co-opt advisers and deceive the public rather than face them candidly and directly was also typically, if not uniquely, Johnsonian, as was the increasing personalization of the domestic debate. Johnson repeatedly denied that Vietnam was his war. It was "America's war," he insisted, and "If I drop dead tomorrow, [it] will still be with you." In one sense, of course, he was right. But in terms of the way the war was fought, Vietnam was far more his than he was prepared to admit or perhaps even recognized.[49]

Limited war theory also significantly influenced the way the war was fought. Korea, and especially the Truman-MacArthur controversy, stimulated a veritable cult of limited war in the 1950s and 1960s, the major conclusion of which was that in a nuclear age where total war was unthinkable, limited war was essential.

Johnson's civilian advisers were all deeply imbued with limited war theory, and it determined in many crucial ways their handling of Vietnam. They lived with the awesome responsibility of preventing nuclear configuration, and they were thus committed to fighting the war in "cold blood" and maintaining tight operational control over the military. They also operated under the mistaken assumption that limited war was more an exercise in crisis management than war itself. They were persuaded that gradual escalation offered the means to achieve their limited goals without provoking the larger war they so feared. And in the end, their notions turned out to be badly flawed.

It would be a serious mistake, however, to attribute America's failure in Vietnam entirely to President Lyndon Johnson's eccentricities and the false dogmas of limited war theory. The intractable problems in Vietnam were equally important. And a considerable part of the problem lies in the inherent difficulty of fighting limited war. Such wars, Stephen Peter Rosen has observed, are by their very nature *"strange* wars."[50] They combine political, military, and diplomatic dimensions in a most complicated way. Waging them requires rare intellectual ability, political acumen, and moral courage. Johnson and his advisers went into the war blindly confident that they knew how to fight limited war, and only when the strategy of escalation proved bankrupt and the American people unwilling to fight in cold blood did they realize their tragic and costly blunder. Deeply entangled in a war they did not understand and could find no way to win, they struggled merely to put a label on what they were doing. "All-out limited war," William Bundy later called it; "a war that is not a war" some military officers complained. Harry McPherson phrased it in the form of a question. "What the hell do you say? How do you half-lead a country into war?"[51]

The search for labels suggests the fundamental and perhaps intractable difficulties of limited war, and we must recognize in retrospect that there was no easy answer to the question raised by McPherson. The key military problem, Rosen contends, is "how to adapt, quickly and successfully, to the peculiar and unfamiliar battlefield conditions in which our armed forces are fighting."[52]

That this was not done in Vietnam may reflect the limited vision of the political and military leaders of the time. But it will not be easily done elsewhere. Nor is there any clear-cut answer to the dilemma of domestic opinion. Fighting in cold blood did not work in Vietnam, but there is no assurance that a declaration of war or partial mobilization would have been the answer either. In the Cold War context of 1965, Johnson and Rusk's reservations about the dangers of a declaration of war seemed well taken. Congressional sanctions in 1812 and 1848 did nothing to stop rampant and at times crippling domestic opposition. However much we might deplore the limitations of Johnson's leadership and the folly of limited war theory, even in the post–Cold War world we would be wise to heed the caveat in Lady Bird Johnson's 1967 lament: "It *is* unbearably hard to fight a limited war."[53]

NOTES

1. Andrew Goodpaster, oral history interview, Lyndon Baines Johnson Library, Austin, Texas.

2. Bundy to Johnson, November 5, 1965, Lyndon Baines Johnson Papers, National Security File, Bundy Memoranda, Box 5; Bundy to Johnson, November 10, 1967, Johnson Papers, Diary Backup, Box 81. Both Lyndon Baines Johnson Library, Austin, Texas.

3. Henry Brandon, *Anatomy of Error: The Inside Story of the Asian War on the Potomac, 1954–1969* (Boston: Gambit Press, 1969), 164; David Halberstam, *The Best and the Brightest* (New York: Random House, 1972), 248, 633 [hereafter *Best and Brightest*].

4. Stephen Peter Rosen, "Vietnam and the American Theory of Limited War," *International Security* 7 (Fall 1982): 96 [hereafter "Vietnam"].

5. For Johnson's populist observations on the military, see Doris Kearns, *Lyndon Johnson and the American Dream* (New York: Harper & Row, 1976), 262, [hereafter *Johnson and the American Dream*].

6. Rosen, "Vietnam," 96.

7. Ibid., 90–99. McNamara is quoted in James G. Nathan, "The Tragic Enshrinement of Toughness," in Thomas G. Paterson, ed., *Major Problems in American Foreign Policy*, Vol. II: *Since 1914* (New York: Harper & Row, 1984), 569.

8. Some of the Joint Chiefs later claimed that they gave Johnson accurate estimates of what would be required. See Hanson Baldwin, oral history interview, U.S. Naval Institute Library, Annapolis, Maryland, 710–11; Wallace Greene to Baldwin, September

25, 1975, ibid.; Greene handwritten notes, Wallace Greene Papers, Marine Corps Historical Center, Washington, D.C. For JCS disappointment at Johnson's refusal to mobilize the reserves, see Hanson Baldwin, "Military Disappointment," *New York Times* (July 29, 1965). For JCS minimizing of the difficulties, see record of LBJ meeting with JCS, July 22, 1965, and record of meeting in cabinet room, July 22, 1965, both in Johnson Papers, Meeting Notes File, Box 1, Lyndon Baines Johnson Library, Austin, Texas. Wheeler's "foot-in-the-door" strategy is articulated in Wheeler to Westmoreland, June 2, 1966, Backchannel Messages, Westmoreland and CBS Litigation Files, Record Group 407, Box 20, Federal Records Center, Suitland, Maryland.

9. See especially Mark Clodfelter, *The Limits of Air Power: The American Bombing of North Vietnam* (New York: Free Press, 1989), particularly Chapters 3 and 4.

10. Krulak to Wallace M. Greene, July 19, 1965, Victor Krulak Papers, Box 1, Marine Corps Historical Center, Washington, D.C.

11. Mark Perry, *Four Stars* (Boston: Houghton Mifflin, 1989), 156–58. Charles F. Bower IV, "The Westmoreland 'Alternate Strategy' of 1967–1968," unpublished paper in possession of the author, argues that as early as March 1967, Westmoreland himself was profoundly dissatisfied with the attrition strategy and "proposed an alternate strategy for Vietnam which implicitly recognized the weaknesses of attrition."

12. Krulak to Robert Cushman, May 25, 1967, Krulak Papers, Box 1, Marine Corps Historical Center, Washington, D.C.

13. Neil Sheehan et al., *The Pentagon Papers as Published by the New York Times* (New York: Bantam, 1971), 530–37 [hereafter *Pentagon Papers*].

14. Gen. Harold Johnson cable to Gen. William Westmoreland, October 20, 1967, Backchannel Messages, Westmoreland and CBS Litigation Files, Box 20, Federal Records Center, Suitland, Maryland.

15. Johnson developed this technique into a fine art, of course, and it was his primary *modus operandi* in dealing with his various advisers, but the tendency itself is all too common in Vietnam policy making and indeed in the American political system. For the way in which Richard Nixon operated in similar fashion, see George C. Herring, "The Nixon Strategy in Vietnam," in Peter Braestrup, ed., *Vietnam as History: Ten Years After the Paris Peace Accords* (Washington, DC: Univ. Press of America, 1984), 51–58.

16. "I don't want loyalty. I want *loyalty*," Halberstam reports him saying, "I want him to kiss my ass in Macy's window at high noon and tell me it smells like roses." See Halberstam, *Best and the Brightest*, 434.

17. George Ball, oral history interview, Lyndon Baines Johnson Library, Austin, Texas. McNamara's disillusionment with the war seems to have begun much earlier and to have run much deeper than most scholars have assumed. See, for example, Averell Harriman memoranda of conversations with McNamara, May 14, 28, 30, August 22, 31, November 26, 1966, all in W. Averell Harriman Papers, Box 486, Manuscript Division, Library of Congress; Harriman memorandum of conversation with McNamara, October 10, in W. Averell Harriman Papers, Box 520, Manuscript Division, Library of Congress. See also Paul Hendrickson, "Divided Against Himself," *Washington Post Magazine* (June 12, 1988): 20–31.

18. Paul Miles interview with Westmoreland, January 7, 1971, Paul Miles Papers, U.S. Military History Institute, Carlisle Barracks, Pennsylvania; Westmoreland historical briefing, July 12, 1967, William C. Westmoreland Papers, Box 29, U.S. Army Military History Institute, Carlisle Barracks, Pennsylvania.

19. Wheeler to Westmoreland, June 2, 1966, to Westmoreland and Sharp, February 13, 1967, to Sharp and Westmoreland, March 6, 1967, Backchannel Messages, Westmoreland and CBS Litigation File, Boxes 15–17, Federal Records Center, Suitland, Maryland.

20. Leonard Chapman, oral history interview, Marine Corps Historical Center, Washington, DC; New York *Herald-Tribune*, August 22, 23, 1966; Letter, Greene to the author, May 9, 1988.

21. Sheehan et al., *Pentagon Papers*, 539.

22. Robert Ginsburgh memorandum for the record, August 14, 1967, Johnson Papers, National Security File, Name File-Col. Ginsburgh, Box 3, Lyndon Baines Johnson Library, Austin, Texas.

23. Perry, *Four Stars*, 163–64. Perry's source for the story is an unnamed "former JCS flag rank officer." His account has been confirmed by a senior officer close to one of the deceased members of the JCS, but denied by General Wallace Greene and Admiral Thomas Moorer. Actually, rumors of a possible resignation en masse first surfaced at the time McNamara's departure was announced in late 1967 and were heatedly denied by administration officials. See *New York Times*, November 29, December 2, 4, 1967.

24. *Public Papers of the Presidents of the United States: Lyndon Baines Johnson, 1967* (Washington, DC: Government Printing Office, 1968), II, 816–17; McNamara deposition for Westmoreland trial, copy in Lyndon Baines Johnson Library, 113, 176, 322; record of meeting, LBJ, McNamara, Wheeler, Rusk, and Rostow, August 19, 1967, Johnson Papers, Meeting Notes File, Box 1, Lyndon Baines Johnson Library, Austin, Texas; *Washington Post*, December 29, 1967.

25. Tom Johnson notes on NSC meetings, November 29, 1967, Johnson Papers, Tom Johnson Notes on Meetings, Box 1, Lyndon Baines Johnson Library, Austin, Texas.

26. George W. Ball, *The Past Has Another Pattern* (New York: Norton, 1982), 400; Larry Berman, *Planning A Tragedy: The Americanization of the War in Vietnam* (New York: Norton, 1982), 109 [hereafter *Planning A Tragedy*]; notes on meeting, July 21, 1965, Johnson Papers, Meeting Notes File, Box 1, Lyndon Baines Johnson Library, Austin, Texas.

27. See previous note numbers 20 and 23.

28. Berman, *Planning A Tragedy*, 119.

29. See especially Richard Barnet, *Roots of War* (Baltimore: S&S Trade, 1973), 266–306; Michael Leigh, *Mobilizing Consent: Public Opinion and American Foreign Policy* (Westport, CT: Greenwood, 1976), 99–106.

30. Bill Moyers, "One Thing We Learned," *Foreign Affairs* 46 (July 1968), 662. A number of senior advisers interviewed by a Rand analyst in 1983 could not recall Ball's presentation at the July 21 meeting. Rusk later discounted Ball's estimates of casualties; McNamara claimed not to have seen his charts. David Di Leo, "Rethinking Containment: George Ball's Vietnam Dissent," unpublished manuscript in possession of author, 275.

31. Memorandum of conversation, Rusk and Harold Holt, April 28, 1965, "Asia and the Pacific: National Security Files, 1963–1969" (Frederick, MD, 1988), Reel 1, Frame 152; quoted in William Conrad Gibbons, "The 1965 Decision to Send U.S. Ground Forces to Vietnam," paper given at the International Studies Association, April 16, 1987.

32. Record of meeting, July 19, 1965, Johnson Papers, National Security File, Country File, Vietnam, Box 15; Busby to LBJ, July 21, 1965, Johnson Papers, Busby Files, Box 3, Lyndon Baines Johnson Library, Austin, Texas: Kathleen J. Turner, *Lyndon Johnson's Dual War: Vietnam and the Press* (Chicago: Univ. of Chicago Press, 1985), 149.

33. Kearns, *Johnson and the American Dream*, 251.

34. Rusk's statement is in Michael Charlton and Anthony Moncrief, *Many Reasons Why: The American Involvement in Vietnam*, 2nd ed. (New York: Hill & Wang, 1989), 115 [hereafter *Many Reasons Why*].

35. Quoted in Barbara Tuchman, *The March of Folly* (New York: Knopf, 1984), 326.

36. Chester Cooper memorandum, September 10, 1965, Johnson Papers, National Security File, Country File, Vietnam, Box 22, Lyndon Baines Johnson Library, Austin, Texas; Moyers memorandum, n.d., ibid., Box 194; Benjamin Read to Bromley Smith, August 10, 1965, ibid., Box 21; Melvin Small, *Johnson, Nixon and the Doves* (New Brunswick, NJ: Rutgers Univ. Press, 1988), 46–48.

37. Harold Johnson memorandum for the record, July 20, 1966, Harold Johnson Papers, Box 127, U.S. Military History Institute Library, Carlisle Barracks, Pennsylvania.

38. Walt Rostow to LBJ, May 9, 1966, Johnson Papers, Walt Rostow memoranda, Volume II, Lyndon Baines Johnson Library, Austin, Texas; Bill Moyers to Arthur Krock, September 15, 1966, Moyers' Office Files, ibid.

39. Notes on meeting with Robert Thompson, August 21, 1967, George Christian Files, Box 3, Lyndon Baines Johnson Library, Austin, Texas.

40. Earle Wheeler cables to William Westmoreland, August 2, 30, 1967, and William Westmoreland to U. S. Grant Sharp and Wheeler, August 3, 12, 1967, Background Messages, Westmoreland and CBS Litigation File, Box 20. Also, see Tom Johnson notes on LBJ meeting with Jim Lucas, August 14, 1967, Johnson Papers, Johnson Notes, Box 1, Lyndon Baines Johnson Library, Austin, Texas.

41. Notes on meeting, August 19, 1967, Johnson Papers, Meeting Notes File, Box 1, Lyndon Baines Johnson Library, Austin, Texas.

42. Lady Bird Johnson diary entry, January 5, 1967, Lady Bird Johnson, *A White House Diary* (New York: Holt, Rinehart, and Winston, 1970), 469.

43. Quoted in Larry Berman, *Lyndon Johnson's War: The Road to Stalemate in Vietnam* (New York: Norton, 1989), 106 [hereafter *Johnson's War*].

44. McNamara to LBJ, November 1, 1967, Johnson Papers, National Security File, Country File, Vietnam, Box 75, Lyndon Baines Johnson Library, Austin, Texas; Jim Jones notes on meeting, November 2, 1967, Johnson Papers, Meeting Notes File, Box 2, ibid.; Bundy to Johnson, November 10, 1967, Johnson Papers, Diary Backup File, Box 81, ibid.; William Depuy to Westmoreland, October 19, 1967, William Depuy Papers, Folder WXYZ (67), U.S. Army Military History Institute, Carlisle Barracks, Pennsylvania; "Carnegie Endowment Proposals," December 5, 1967, Matthew B. Ridgway Papers, Box 34A, ibid.; Katzenbach to Johnson, November 16, 1967, Johnson Papers, Box 75, Lyndon Baines Johnson Library, Austin, Texas, quoted in Berman, *Johnson's War*, 106–7.

45. McPherson to Johnson, October 27, 1967, Harry McPherson Office Files, Box 53, Lyndon Baines Johnson Library, Austin, Texas; Bundy to LBJ, November 10, 1967, Johnson Papers, Diary Backup, Box 81, ibid.

46. Handwritten notes on McNamara memorandum to LBJ, November 1, 1967, Johnson Papers, National Security File, Country File, Vietnam, Box 75, Lyndon Baines Johnson Library, Austin, Texas.

47. Johnson memorandum for the record, December 18, 1967, in Lyndon B. Johnson, *The Vantage Point* (New York: Holt, Rinehart, and Winston, 1971), 800–801.

48. Rostow to Ellsworth Bunker, September 27, 1967, Johnson Papers, DSDUF, Box

4, Lyndon Baines Johnson Library, Austin, Texas; Eugene Locke to LBJ, October 7, 1967, Johnson Papers, National Security File, Country File, Vietnam, Box 99, ibid.

49. Quoted in Berman, *Johnson's War*, i.

50. Rosen, "Vietnam," 83.

51. Bundy is quoted in Charlton and Moncrief, *Many Reasons Why*, 120; the military officers are quoted in Hanson Baldwin "Magaziner," December 16, 1965, Baldwin Papers, Box 27, Lyndon Baines Johnson Library, Austin, Texas; McPherson is quoted in Walter LeFeber, *America, Russia, and the Cold War*, 5th ed. (New York: Knopf, 1985), 254.

52. Rosen, "Vietnam," 83.

53. See note 43.

4

From the Tonkin Gulf to the Persian Gulf: The Devolution of the Senate's Role in War Making

Caroline F. Ziemke

In its entire history, the United States has fought only five declared wars: the War of 1812, the Mexican War, the Spanish-American War, World War I, and World War II. In all but one—the War of 1812—presidents presented hostilities as *faits accompli*; yet in all but the last two wars, congressional debate was heated and final votes were close. Numerous other military operations abroad have been initiated without declaration of war, legitimated instead by either specific congressional authorizations or ratified treaties. In most of those cases—most notably the quasi-war with France (1797–1800), the Tripolitan War (1801–1805), and the 1916 incursion into Mexico—it was congressional debate. This post–World War II trend amounts to a devolution of congressional war-making authority. The intended benefit was to strengthen U.S. foreign policy in the face of a mortal threat by demonstrating unity—or at least the appearance thereof. If that had to come at the price of the decline of some constitutional authority, then so be it. In Vietnam, however, the result was not a stronger position, but an ill-considered and divisive war.

This chapter focuses on the Senate's role in war making through the experiences of three of its members: Senators Richard B. Russell, J. William Fulbright, and Sam Nunn. The careers of these three legislators illustrate in microcosm the devolution of the Senate's war powers during the Cold War era. All three senators wielded considerable power in the Senate: Russell and Nunn as chairmen of the Senate Armed Services Committee; Fulbright as chairman of the Foreign Relations Committee. Perhaps more notably, all three can be fairly described as conservatives. Nunn shared Russell's consistently promilitary, pronational defense position; and only Fulbright could accurately be described as a dove. All three—Russell and Fulbright during Vietnam, and Nunn during the Persian Gulf crisis—strongly supported the initial executive aims in committing U.S. military power, but urged caution, arguing that less violent and costly means might serve U.S. interests as well or better than war.

The turf battle between the executive and legislative branches over war powers began before the ink was dry on the Constitution. In *The Federalist* No. 4, John Jay explained the motive behind vesting war-making powers in the legislative rather than the executive branch. "Absolute monarchs," he wrote, "will often make war when [their] nations are to get nothing by it, but for purposes and objects merely personal," which "will often lead [them] to engage in wars not sanctified by justice or the voice and interests of their people."[1]

The founding fathers sought to eliminate "imperial wars" by dividing the war powers between the executive and legislative branches. As Alexander Hamilton explained in *The Federalist* No. 69: "The President is to be the commander-in-chief. . . . In this respect his authority would be nominally the same with that of the king of Great Britain. . . . " In fact, however, it constituted "nothing more than the supreme command and direction of the military and naval forces, as first general and admiral of the Confederacy." The power of the British king, in contrast, extended to declaring war and raising and regulating of fleets and armies, powers that the U.S. Constitution afforded specifically to the legislature.[2]

It has been the natural tendency of the executive branch to use the commander-in-chief clause to expand presidential prerogatives. Through a series of emergency blanket authorizations—such as the Civil War "Food and Fodder Act" and the emergency economic powers granted to the executive branch during World War I—Congress willingly and, at the time appropriately, contributed to the process. As a rule, however, the executive did not cede such expanded authority back to Congress in peacetime, and many such wartime authorizations remain on the books today, ready to be revived at a stroke of the presidential pen.

The years leading up to World War II saw an unprecedented peacetime expansion of executive authority that was built largely on such prior authorizations—some dating back to the Civil War. In his effort to prepare the military and the economy for the approaching war in the face of a stubbornly isolationist Congress, President Franklin D. Roosevelt, provided a role model for the executive wars of the post–World War II era. Congress, more concerned with policy than constitutional implications, did little to resist. When it approved the Lend-Lease Act in March 1941, it effectively abdicated most of its last remaining prerogative—allocations. The courts, which energetically shot down FDR's similar attempts to usurp authority in domestic policy, shied away from the war powers question, dismissing it as a political rather than a constitutional problem. By December 8, 1941, the congressional declaration of war merely recognized a *fait accompli*.[3]

As a wartime—or near-wartime—expedient, Roosevelt's actions were laudable, but in too many instances those temporary wartime prerogatives became permanent peacetime habits. The extraordinary executive power Roosevelt amassed in pursuit of a large-scale war in defense of truly vital U.S. interests established the precedent for a long string of more controversial executive wars, police actions, and interventions during the post–World War II era.[4]

Senator Fulbright once described the years between 1940 and the Vietnam War as the "era of perpetual crisis." Because of the advent of nuclear weapons and the rise of East-West tension, the end of World War II brought neither real peace nor lasting security. Apparently intimidated by the enormity of the United States's new superpower responsibilities and the awesome potential of nuclear weapons, Congress elected not to reassert its proper constitutional authority over war making and ceded an ever greater share of its prerogatives in that area to the executive. Bipartisan foreign policy—based on the assumption that vocal opposition to administration policy in wartime amounted to providing aid and comfort to the enemy—became peacetime dogma.

Congress contributed to the dilution of its constitutional authority through two principal vehicles: authorization after the fact, as in the Korean War; and open-ended, blanket authorizations like the Middle East and Formosa Straits resolutions of the Eisenhower years. Both trends reinforced the Rooseveltian precedents, allowed successive administrations to vastly increase the scope of U.S. military commitments, and paved the way for the commitment of U.S. combat forces to a civil war in remote Southeast Asia.

From the very beginning, Senator Richard Russell expressed misgivings concerning American involvement in Vietnam. In 1953, when Assistant Secretary of State Thurston Morton informed him that the United States had sent its first 400 military advisers to South Vietnam, Russell replied that "I think you are opening up a trial today that will be costly in blood and treasure to the country and . . . where there are 200 or 300 in Vietnam today there will be thousands there tomorrow."[5] He doubted, first, whether U.S. interests in the area were vital, and, second, whether—vital or not—they were achievable by military means. Despite such deep-felt doubt, however, he did not open the issue to hearings—nor did any of his Senate colleagues. They avoided getting involved in such "messy subjects" that would do them no good politically.[6] The executive branch, as it would do so often in the coming crisis, interpreted congressional inaction as tacit approval and quietly, but steadily, increased the level of American political and military involvement in Southeast Asia.

Russell's open skepticism concerning U.S involvement in Vietnam did force the Johnson administration to delay its request for blanket authorization to conduct military operations in Vietnam.[7] In August 1964, North Vietnam gave the administration the excuse it sought to submit a resolution to Congress that was patterned after the 1954 Formosa and 1957 Middle East resolutions. The Armed Services and Foreign Relations committees approved the Tonkin Gulf Resolution after cursory hearings and with only one dissenting vote. On August 7, the Senate passed Joint Resolution 1145, better known as the Tonkin Gulf Resolution, with only two dissenting votes. The only mark the Senate left on the resolution was the so-called "Russell Amendment," which specifically provided for the resolution's termination through concurrent resolutions of Congress in the event that the executive branch was significantly to exceed the legislative mandate.

Russell expressed concern that "the portents of this resolution are great"; but he felt confident that "no reasonable and objective observer would assume a desire on our part to escalate the war or to broaden its scope." Moreover, he argued that the resolution did no more than express congressional approval of the Johnson administration's retaliatory actions, and reinforce the U.S. determination to take the necessary steps to defend its interests wherever they are endangered. Naively, perhaps, he reassured his fellow senators that the Tonkin Gulf Resolution did not alter the constitutional separation of war powers.[8]

As the United States slid deeper into the Vietnam War, Russell felt even more torn between his still deeply felt misgivings about the war and American goals, and his sense of loyalty to U.S. servicemen. Although he never conceded that U.S. forces belonged in Vietnam, Russell firmly believed that once the nation sent its military forces to fight and die there, those forces deserved the nation's full support. During his last years, Russell faced off against his old friend J. William Fulbright and resisted the Senate's repeated attempts to exercise its last unimpaired prerogative—the power of the purse—and force the Johnson, and later the Nixon, administration out of Vietnam by terminating appropriations. He repeatedly chided his colleagues that, if they were serious about ending the war, they should abandon their lofty ideological polemics and take courageous and concrete action by repealing the Tonkin Gulf Resolution.[9]

Russell was, from the beginning, a strict constructionist who believed that the U.S. Constitution provided a proper solution to almost any national crisis. "The survival of our government," he once lectured General Douglas MacArthur, "depends as much upon the delicate system of checks and balances designed by the founding fathers as upon our armies, our navies, and our fleets of airplanes."[10] But in light of the Cold War, Russell shared the view of most of his Senate colleagues that the United States should address the rest of the world with one voice—that there was no place for even loyal opposition in the dangerous postwar world. Russell never came to terms with the conflict between his strict constructionism and his dedication to a bipartisan foreign policy; as a result, he could never bring himself to express openly his "loyal opposition" and take the leadership role that might have allowed him to alter the course of a policy in Southeast Asia that he knew spelled disaster.

Senators J. William Fulbright and Richard Russell came from similar political cultures: both were conservative Southerners, staunch segregationists, and strict constructionists. Both were also old friends and political cronies of President Lyndon Johnson and both saw those friendships crumble under the pressure of the Vietnam War. After the Johnson administration's decision to escalate U.S. involvement in Vietnam to a full-fledged ground war, however, the two parted company. Where Russell chose to close ranks and "support the flag," Fulbright took upon himself the role of "loyal opposition" and openly and consistently criticized administration policy, ultimately leading the congressional effort to reassert its constitutional war-making prerogatives.

Fulbright shared Russell's early apprehension with the prospect of committing

American prestige to the defense of South Vietnam but, ironically, not his concern over executive encroachment into congressional war powers. In fact, in the fall of 1961 *Cornell Law Quarterly*, Fulbright argued that perhaps it was time for the United States to "overhaul" its "basic constitutional machinery," adding that he wondered "whether the time has not arrived, or indeed already passed, when we must give the executive a measure of power in the conduct of foreign affairs that we have hitherto jealously withheld."[11]

Fulbright cosponsored and skillfully steered the Tonkin Gulf Resolution through the Senate. Unlike Russell, he seemed fully cognizant of the resolution's inherent potential to expand American involvement. In fact, he admitted in debate that although the resolution was intended to deal primarily with North Vietnamese aggression against U.S. forces and fulfill U.S. obligations under the SEATO Treaty, and although he personally felt another ground war in Asia would be inadvisable, he did not know what the limits of the resolution were. A skeptical John Sherman Cooper pressed Fulbright as to the scope of the advance presidential authority, asking whether "if the President decided that it was necessary to use such force as could lead to war, we will give that authority by this resolution." Fulbright responded in the affirmative, adding later that, although the president had to that point consulted with Congress and had expressed no desire to escalate or widen the U.S. military commitment, under the terms of the resolution he could do so without returning to Congress for additional authorization.[12]

Fulbright shared Russell's disappointment and sense of betrayal when, after winning the 1964 election on a peace platform, Johnson decided to escalate U.S. operations beginning with Rolling Thunder in 1965. But where Russell chose to close ranks and support the flag, Fulbright resisted and donned the mantle of the "loyal opposition." He accused Johnson of violating the Senate's trust in failing to employ the Tonkin Gulf Resolution with "wisdom and restraint." In the end, he admitted, the Senate had only itself to blame. While he insisted that Johnson and Nixon wrongly interpreted the Senate's approval of the resolution as a sweeping endorsement of a large-scale land war in Southeast Asia, Fulbright held Congress equally culpable for granting so comprehensive an authorization with so little deliberation. He did not exclude himself from blame. "My role in the adoption of the resolution of August 7, 1964," he wrote in 1966, "is a source of neither pleasure nor pride to me today."[13]

In addition to leading the Senate opposition to the Vietnam War, Fulbright became one of the architects of the movement to restore congressional prerogatives that culminated in the passage of the War Powers Act in 1973. In urging the Senate to reassert its war-making authority, Fulbright attempted to deflate the crisis mentality that had contributed to its atrophy. He urged the Senate not to be swayed by "executive pleas for urgency and unanimity, or by allegations of 'aid and comfort' to the enemies. . . . We have gone too far in this respect," he argued, "to the point of confusing Presidential convenience with the national interest." The question, as he saw it, was not whether the "loyal opposition" had the right to debate administration policy, but whether it had the right *not* to.[14]

As one of the prime movers in the drafting of the Senate's war powers bill—a version with considerably more backbone than the watered down House-Senate compromise bill that eventually passed—Fulbright escalated his rhetoric. The "era of perpetual crisis," he charged, had rendered the United States a virtual "Presidential dictatorship" in the realm of foreign policy. But the president alone was not to blame. In Fulbright's view, "resolutions such as the Gulf of Tonkin Resolution amount[ed] to Congressional acquiescence in the exercise by the executive of a power which the Constitution vested in Congress and which the Congress ha[d] no authority to give away."[15]

Although its repeal in 1970 "remove[d] the frayed facade of constitutional legitimacy from the war," the constitutional crisis remained. Fulbright challenged Congress to take the lead in determining "how the constitutional vacuum should be filled."[16] Out of a well-intended but misconceived notion of what patriotism and responsibility require in a time of world crisis, Congress had permitted the president to usurp its constitutional powers to initiate war and to consent to, or withhold consent from, foreign commitments; in the process, Fulbright feared, a piece of democracy was lost.[17]

The sense of guilt in Fulbright's discourse is pervasive. Like Russell, he clearly agonized over the implications and consequences of decisions and actions he took during the Tonkin Gulf debate. Fulbright and Russell shared their regret at "the very great grant of power" with which the Senate empowered the president and the view that Johnson had abused that grant. Fulbright believed that the Senate, and the Senate alone, was accountable for its plight and faced the task not only of reasserting its powers but of reestablishing its good name. "Congress not only has to start using these powers again," he wrote, "it also has to reestablish its right to use them. After three decades of atrophy due to Congressional passivity, people in general—and Presidents in particular—have forgotten that it is Congress which is supposed to initiate wars, if wars are to be initiated, and the Senate which is supposed to approve treaties, if commitments are to be made at all."[18]

The War Powers Act establishes three procedures for the future commitment of U.S. forces to actual or potential hostilities: presidential consultation with Congress; presidential reports to Congress; and congressional termination of military action. Congress's termination authority under the War Powers Act was not voluntary. Military operations are to terminate after sixty days unless Congress takes one of the following actions: declaring war, enacting a specific authorization, or extending the sixty-day period by law. Finally, the act allows for automatic extension in the event that Congress is physically unable to meet as a result of an armed attack upon the United States. The act also states specifically that congressional approval cannot be inferred from any action other than a direct authorization specifically citing the War Powers Act. In so doing, the drafters of the War Powers Act aimed to preclude in the future arguments like the Nixon administration's contention that Congress gave tacit approval to the Vietnam War by continuing to pass defense authorization and appropriations bills.[19]

Fulbright was never sure that the war powers debate marked the beginning of a constitutional realignment rather than a temporary manifestation of anxiety over Vietnam. Time confirmed his doubts. The War Powers Act proved incapable of preventing executive wars, and may actually have expanded the president's power to commit U.S. forces abroad. American presidents have deployed American military forces into either actual or potential combat situations at least nine times since 1973—in the *Mayaguez* incident; the evacuation of Saigon; the Iran hostage rescue attempt; Lebanon; Grenada; El Salvador; Panama; the Persian Gulf; and Somalia. Not once has Congress invoked its authority under the act, and the White House has consistently complied only when it serves its purposes to do so. As the recent Persian Gulf crisis demonstrated once again, the implied presidential authority to introduce U.S. troops into actual or potential hostilities at his discretion effectively neutralizes the Senate's statutory authority. As both Russell and Fulbright acknowledged in 1964—and as numerous senators argued again in January 1991—once the president has committed national prestige, it becomes politically and, possibly, militarily impossible to reverse the operation. In such circumstances, legislators will tend to "rally 'round the flag" rather than subject the merits of the operation to a full independent debate.

In early 1990, the worldwide collapse of communism seemed to have brought the "era of perpetual crisis" to a close. Congress recognized that it faced a unique opportunity to implement a constitutional realignment that would spare its current and future members from the turmoil that Russell and Fulbright experienced. It was no longer necessary, it seemed, to close ranks against the enemy since—after four decades—America was finally demobilizing from the Cold War. In fact, if the United States was to avoid marching blindly into a new, post–Cold War world order that was very little different than the old world order, the reemergence of a loyal opposition seemed imperative. A new consensus concerning America's proper use of its new status as the premier superpower could only emerge through a full debate among all points of view—isolationists, interventionists, and internationalists.

Senator Sam Nunn took the lead in the peacetime realignment by energetically defending traditional Senate prerogatives and taking a place at the forefront of the "loyal opposition." In the winter and spring of 1990, he delivered a series of speeches in which he questioned administration defense policy and made it clear that the Senate, and the loyal opposition, fully intended to play an active role in determining the future direction of American strategy. He challenged the Bush administration to come up with a new strategy in response to a new threat environment. And he challenged Congress to stop relying on the War Powers Act—which, he said, has not and will not work—as an excuse not to play an active role. In the post–Cold War world, Nunn argued, Congress must exercise its constitutional authority—especially its power of the purse—to enforce its will, a process that he conceded would not be easy.[20]

Following Iraq's invasion of Kuwait in August 1990, Nunn openly supported the administration's initial deployment of U.S. forces to defend Saudi Arabia and enforce an international economic embargo against Iraq. Few in Congress challenged the president's authority or wisdom in committing American troops to what the administration repeatedly characterized as a defensive operation. The more heated constitutional debate began only after November 8, when President Bush announced his decision to build an ''offensive option'' in the Persian Gulf; but the decision to adopt an offensive stance was likely made as early as August 4, 1990 when the president vowed, to the surprise of both Congress and, apparently, his military commanders in charge of Operation Desert Shield, ''This will not stand, this aggression against Kuwait.''[21] In choosing not to exercise their prerogatives earlier in the crisis, Congress may have effectively preempted themselves from the important debate ahead.

Beginning in early November, Nunn took the lead in asserting the Senate's constitutional role in war making. Nunn argued that, lacking a state of imminent emergency, the president was obligated under the U.S. Constitution to seek congressional authorization before launching an offensive against Iraq.[22] In November 1990, no emergency confronted the nation, and there were no signs that the Iraqis had any intention of escalating the conflict by launching a military offensive of their own. Whatever defensive rationale had existed for the initial presidential *fait accompli* had expired, and Nunn and others began to urge Congress to take steps to exercise its proper authority.

In the weeks leading up to the January 15, 1991, United Nations's deadline for Iraq to withdraw from Kuwait, the Senate and House Armed Services committees held independent hearings on the Persian Gulf situation. In introductory remarks before the Senate Armed Services Committee, Nunn explained the committee's motives in holding its Persian Gulf hearings. The administration's announced intention to build an ''offensive option'' in the Gulf amounted, in Nunn's view, to ''a fundamental shift in the mission of our military forces,'' a shift that ''raise[d] a number of serious questions which these hearings will focus on.''

The questions that dominated the Armed Services Committee hearings were not intended to second-guess military strategy, but rather to clarify the administration's intentions and agenda to enable Congress to make a more informed decision concerning war and peace. Although praising the administration's effort to build and maintain an international coalition to resist Iraqi aggression, Nunn urged the president and Congress to remember that a UN resolution ''is not a substitute for fully informing the American people of our own nation's objectives and strategy. Those of us who represent the nation that will be doing most of the fighting, supplying most of the military forces, and taking the most casualties have the obligation to ask these fundamental questions.''[23]

When the Senate voted on the Nunn and Dole resolutions on January 13, 1991, its members were fully aware of the likely consequences of their action: A vote in favor of the administration's resolution amounted to a de facto declaration of war against Iraq. There are those who argue that the Senate acted too late; that the January 13 vote amounted to little more than a rubber-stamp approval of yet another presidential *fait accompli*.[24] But at worst, the vote still stands as a stop-gap measure that prevented Senate prerogatives from deteriorating even further. On the eve of war, both the Senate and the House of Representatives— despite administration pressure—fulfilled their obligation to debate administration policy and vote on whether to authorize war against Iraq.

The rhetoric about a vote for war to preserve peace notwithstanding, no one who participated in the Senate debate could claim surprise or betrayal when the allies began air raids on Baghdad on January 16. Sam Nunn and the forty-seven other senators who joined him in voting against the blanket authorization had fulfilled the responsibility that Russell and Fulbright had avoided to their later regret. In so doing, they have taken the first step in a process that Fulbright called for over twenty years ago: "The Senate as a whole," he wrote, "should undertake to revive and strengthen the deliberative function which it has permitted to atrophy in the course of twenty-five years of crisis. Acting on the premise that dissent is not disloyalty, that a true consensus is shaped by airing differences rather than suppressing them, the Senate should again become, as it used to be, an institution in which the great issues of American politics are contested with thoroughness, energy, and candor."[25] In the long run, the United States will face the world stronger from its having done so—surely stronger than it was in Vietnam.

NOTES

1. James Madison et al., *The Federalist Papers* (New York: Penguin, 1987), 97–98.

2. Ibid., 396.

3. Louis Fisher, *Constitutional Conflicts Between Congress and the President* (Princeton, NJ: Princeton Univ. Press, 1985), 299–307 [hereafter cited as *Constitutional Conflicts*].

4. See, for example, Jacob Javits, *Who Makes War?* (New York: Morrow, 1973), 223.

5. *Congressional Record*, 90th Congress, 1st Session, February 28, 1960, Vol. 113, part 4, 4715–17.

6. Senate Committees on Armed Services and Foreign Affairs, *The U.S. Government and the Vietnam War: Executive and Legislative Roles and Relationships*, by William C. Gibbons, Committee Print, Study 98–185, Part I: 1945–1961 (Washington, DC: U.S. Government Printing Office, 1984), 34.

7. Paul Kesaris, ed., *Vietnam: National Security Council Histories* (Frederick, MD: Univ. Publications of America, 1981), Reel 1: *Gulf of Tonkin*, McGeorge Bundy mem-

orandum for discussion, alternative public positions for the United States on Southeast Asia for the period of July 1–November 15; June 10, 1964, items 0743–0744.

8. *Congressional Record*, 88th Congress, 2nd Session, August 6, 1964, Vol. 110, part 16, 18411.

9. See, for example, *Congressional Record*, 89th Congress, 2nd Session, February 16, 1966, Vol. 112, part 3, 3135.

10. Joint Session of the Senate Committees of Foreign Relations and Armed Services, unpublished hearings, *The Dismissal of MacArthur and Far East Military Situation*, April 30–May 9, 1951, R.G. 46: Senate, 82A F7.9, National Archives, Washington, DC, Reel 2, frame 2150.

11. Stanley Karnow, *Vietnam: A History* (New York: Viking, 1983), 359.

12. *Congressional Record*, 88th Congress, 2nd Session, August 6, 1964, Vol. 110, part 16, 18406.

13. J. William Fulbright, *The Arrogance of Power* (New York: Random House, 1966), 51–52.

14. Ibid.

15. J. William Fulbright, *The Crippled Giant* (New York: Random House, 1972), 186–87.

16. Ibid., 189–90.

17. Ibid., 193–94.

18. Ibid., 200.

19. Fisher, *Constitutional Conflicts*, 310–12.

20. Remarks by Senator Sam Nunn, "After the Cold War: U.S. Defense Policy in Transition," Progressive Policy Institute Roundtable, September 14, 1990 (Washington, DC: Progressive Policy Institute, 1990), 3, 30.

21. Robert Woodward, *The Commanders* (New York: Simon and Schuster, 1991), 260.

22. Press Conference with Senator George J. Mitchell, Senator Sam Nunn, and Senator Claiborne Pell, "Deployment of Troops to the Persian Gulf," November 13, 1990.

23. "Prepared Statement of Senator Sam Nunn," United States Senate, Committee on Armed Services, U.S. Policy in the Persian Gulf, hearings before the Senate Armed Services Committee, November 27–30, 1990, 4.

24. For a particularly scholarly and effective exposition of this argument, see Michael J. Glennon, "The Gulf War and the Constitution," *Foreign Affairs* 70, no. 2 (Spring 1991), 84–101.

25. Fulbright, *The Arrogance of Power*, 54.

5

China and the Revisionist Thesis

John W. Garver

SALIENCE OF THE CHINA FACTOR

The central tenet of the revisionist critique of the United States's conduct of the Vietnam War is that gradual escalation of the war against North Vietnam and limitation of U.S. ground operations to South Vietnam (with the exception of the May 1970 Cambodian incursion) condemned the United States to fight a war of attrition on Hanoi's terms. Revisionist scholars propose that massive and quick application of U.S. military power against North Vietnam could have overwhelmed that small country's defenses, while extension of U.S. ground operations into the southern Laotian and North Vietnamese panhandles could have choked off the North Vietnamese infiltration which fed the insurgency in the South. In this way, North Vietnam's ability to prosecute the war would have been largely and quickly destroyed, while the Viet Cong insurgency, deprived of Northern cadre and arms, could have been handled by the Saigon government.

In advancing these propositions, revisionist scholars acknowledge that it was primarily American decision makers' fears of direct Chinese entry into the war that precluded such options. The most famous revisionist scholar, Colonel Harry Summers, for example, quotes General Dave Palmer's appraisal of the U.S. failure to launch a strategic offensive against North Vietnam at the end of 1965 after the U.S. 1st Cavalry Division defeated three regiments of the North Vietnamese army in a head-on battle in the Ia Drang Valley:

The Johnson administration had already barricaded the one sure route to victory—to take the strategic offensive against the source of the war. Memories of Mao Tse-tung's reaction when North Korea was overrun by United Nations troops in 1950 haunted the White House. America's fear of war with Red China protected North Vietnam from invasion more surely than any instrument of war Hanoi could have fielded.[1]

Summers does not directly say that such fears of Chinese intervention were ill-founded, but he strongly implies this. The United States, Summers writes, "allowed [itself] to be bluffed by China throughout most of the war. "[O]ur error was not that we were fearful of the dangers of nuclear war and of Chinese or Russian intervention in Vietnam. . . . The error was that we took counsel of these fears and in so doing paralyzed our strategic thinking." The closest Summers comes to addressing the question squarely is in a note in which he writes, "Whether the Soviets or the Chinese ever intended intervention is a matter of conjecture." Even here, however, the two events he cites (Mao's rejection of Moscow's 1965 proposal for united Sino-Soviet action in support of Hanoi, and Mao's suspicions that Moscow was trying to maneuver China into a war with the United States) both point toward the conclusion that Mao was already more afraid of the Soviet Union than of the United States and, by implication, that he was not serious about China's threats to intervene on behalf of Hanoi.[2]

The revisionists are quite correct in concluding that fear of Chinese intervention was a major factor underlying the U.S. strategy of graduated escalation. A basic purpose of that strategy was to prevent Chinese intervention by keeping the level of violence directed against North Vietnam controlled, precise, and below the threshold that would spark full-scale Chinese intervention. There is also no question that the China-induced U.S. strategy of gradual escalation was an immense boon to North Vietnam. It allowed Hanoi *time* to adjust to U.S. pressure and to find ways to circumvent U.S. moves. By helping to induce Washington to adopt this particular strategy, Beijing contributed substantially to Hanoi's eventual victory over the United States. The question, however, is this: Were Washington's fears of possible Chinese intervention well founded?

For us to accept the revisionist thesis, the question of the seriousness of China's threats to go to war with the United States in Indochina in the mid–1960s must be squarely addressed. The question is this: If the strategy advocated by the revisionists had been implemented, would China have sent armies to fight against the United States in Laos, Cambodia, Thailand, and Vietnam? Would the Vietnam War have escalated into a Sino-American war? It is, of course, impossible to definitively answer such a question regarding the "what ifs" of history. It is sometimes important to try, however, because we learn, and mislearn, so much from history.

CHINA'S STAKE IN HANOI

During the early 1960s, North Vietnam was one of Beijing's closest political and military allies. As the Sino-Soviet polemic escalated, and as the Soviet Union under Khrushchev inched toward disengagement from the mounting Indochina conflict, Hanoi increasingly lined up behind Beijing. By early 1964, Hanoi was virtually in China's camp of the bifurcated international Communist movement.[3] Hanoi moved back to a more balanced position after Khrushchev's fall and Moscow's adoption of a more interventionist policy under Kosygin and Brezhnev, but Hanoi-Beijing relations remained quite close. According to the later Vietnamese defector Hoang Van Hoan, until 1968 Hanoi always consulted with Beijing prior to deciding on any major move.[4] In short, the United States was making war on one of China's closest allies.

Beijing's alliance with North Vietnam served important national security and ideological objectives. From the standpoint of national security, China's support for Hanoi was Mao's way of rolling back U.S. containment in Asia. The "liberation" of South Vietnam would be a major blow to the South East Asian Treaty Organization and other U.S.–fostered anti-Chinese containment schemes in Asia. Conversely, were American control over South Vietnam consolidated, the American imperialists might be tempted to move even closer to China's borders. Ideologically, victory for Vietnam's war of national liberation with the support of the socialist camp would prove the political correctness of Mao Tse-tung's more militant strategy for dealing with U.S. imperialism and the incorrectness of Khrushchev's revisionist interpretation of peaceful coexistence. Once the correctness of Mao's line was demonstrated, the general line of the international Communist movement might be rectified and reoriented toward more militant struggle against U.S. imperialism.[5]

The gravity of Chinese interests in North Vietnam was reflected in the magnitude of Chinese support for Hanoi during its wars. According to Beijing, between 1950 and 1978 China provided over $20 billion worth of materiel to Vietnam. This included weapons, ammunition, and supplies sufficient to equip 2 million soldiers. In 1962 alone, China supplied 90,000 machine guns and rifles to the Viet Cong, substantially upgrading the latter's ability to counter U.S.–Saigon counterinsurgency efforts. As the United States–North Vietnam war unfolded, China provided vital support for Hanoi's logistical effort, supplying more than 30,000 trucks, 2 million tons of gasoline, and repairing 900 kilometers of railways. China also provided Hanoi with a large quantity of railway rails, locomotives, and wagons; fully equipped several hundred North Vietnamese factories; and provided 300 million square meters of cloth and 5 million tons of grain, along with large quantities of items needed by North Vietnam's populace for daily living. China also gave Hanoi several hundred millions of dollars in hard currency.[6]

As important as China's material support was, also important was its diplomatic-military support. One critical manifestation of this support came during the Laotian crisis and Geneva convention of 1961–1962. At Geneva, the United States eventually accepted a "neutralization" of Laos which tacitly allowed Hanoi to continue using the supply lines running through Pathet Lao–controlled areas of the Laotian panhandle.[7] Hanoi had begun using and expanding these Laotian supply lines in 1959 when it decided to renew armed struggle in the South. As the war escalated, those lines became increasingly vital to Hanoi's war effort. Revisionist analysts have assigned a large portion of responsibility for the U.S. defeat in Vietnam to Washington's acceptance of the particular type of "neutralization" of Laos agreed on at Geneva in 1962 and the limitation of the ground war to South Vietnam that followed from that decision.[8]

Chinese threats to intervene in Laos figured prominently in the U.S. decision in May 1962 to "neutralize" Laos. One of the key reasons why American leaders ruled out the use of U.S. troops to occupy the Laotian panhandle (this was the military alternative to the political solution of neutralization) was a belief that North Vietnam and China would strongly resist such a move. On May 19, 1962, for example, *Renmin ribao* (*People's Daily*, a newspaper published by the Central Committee of the Chinese Communist Party), had warned:

U.S. aggressive moves in Southeast Asia are a serious threat to the security of China. The Chinese people cannot remain indifferent to this. . . . The Chinese people firmly oppose U.S. imperialist armed intervention in Laos, and absolutely cannot tolerate the establishment by U.S. imperialism in areas close to China of any new military bridgeheads directed against this country. . . . We must serve a fresh warning to the Kennedy Administration that it shall be held fully responsible for all grave consequences arising from its policy of playing with fire.[9]

These were strong words. Not as hard or as blunt as those used by Beijing in the final weeks before its entry into the Korean conflict, but strong enough to convey Beijing's belief that China's own security was involved and that China was prepared for war to deal with these threats. As importantly, Beijing's verbal warnings were backed up by concentration of Chinese military forces in southern China adjacent to Laos.[10]

Confronted by the possibility of waging a land war with China in the interior of the Indochina peninsula, Washington retreated to "neutralization." In the face of possible Chinese counterintervention, the military option in Laos was simply unacceptable. According to Roger Hilsman, director of the State Department's Bureau of Intelligence and Research during the Laotian crisis, "What the United States would do if the Chinese Communists intervened was not spelled out, but the general impression was that the recommendation would be to retaliate on the mainland with nuclear weapons."[11]

Again in 1965–1967 China provided Hanoi with political-military support—support that, as the revisionists point out, figured prominently in shaping Washington's strategy of graduated escalation. In essence Beijing threatened to enter the war on Hanoi's side if the United States carried the war too far. Its purpose was to deter, limit, and defeat American attacks against its North Vietnamese ally.

There were five major dimensions to China's deterrent support for Hanoi in the mid–1960s.[12] First, it was sizable. By the spring of 1966, nearly 50,000 Chinese soldiers were in North Vietnam manning antiaircraft defenses, carrying out logistic work, and repairing bomb damage. According to official Chinese statistics, between October 1965 and March 1968 (when Chinese forces were withdrawn) a total of 320,000 Chinese troops served in North Vietnam with the annual maximum reaching 170,000.[13] North Vietnam's air force also operated out of bases in south China. An integrated radar grid including stations in south China and covering all of North Vietnam was established to provide intelligence about U.S. air operations to North Vietnam's air defense system. China's own air defenses in south China were also strengthened.

Second, Chinese deployments were not conducted under conditions of maximum security. Chinese People's Liberation Army (PLA) units deployed to North Vietnam retained their normal unit designations, wore regular uniforms, and used nonsecure methods of communications. This insured that Washington knew of China's moves and the seriousness of its intentions. To avoid locking itself into a situation that might escalate into a direct confrontation with the United States, however, Beijing did not officially acknowledge its military presence in North Vietnam.

Third, PLA units in North Vietnam did not remain in a passive, reserve role but actively engaged U.S. forces in combat. PLA aircraft based in China scrambled on occasion and engaged U.S. aircraft that penetrated Chinese airspace during combat operations against North Vietnam. Beijing claimed to have shot down nine U.S. aircraft and damaged two others in this fashion. Information is unavailable regarding the number of U.S. aircraft shot down by Chinese warplanes or by Chinese-piloted North Vietnamese warplanes over North Vietnam's airspace, but it is quite possible that this occurred. In any case, Chinese forces serving in North Vietnam suffered heavy casualties from U.S. bombing—possibly 20,000 dead and wounded according to later Chinese reports.

Fourth, Chinese units constructed a large, heavily fortified complex at Yen Bai some 140 kilometers northwest of Hanoi on the rail line running from Kunming to Hanoi along the Red River. This complex, replete with antiaircraft guns placed in caves and mounted on railway tracks plus a large runway, seemed designed to serve either as a North Vietnamese redoubt in the event that a U.S.–South Vietnamese invasion overran Hanoi, or to serve as a base for the PLA in the event of Chinese intervention.

The first four aspects of Chinese support for Hanoi were intended to convey to Washington the seriousness of China's intent to stand firm behind North Vietnam. The fifth and final characteristic of China's support for Hanoi was careful maneuvering to avoid an unnecessary war with the United States. While warning Washington not to go too far, Beijing also signaled that it hoped to avoid a Sino-American war.

As American bombing of North Vietnam escalated in 1965–1966, the Chinese and U.S. ambassadors to Poland discussed the Vietnam situation. (Ambassadorial talks in Warsaw began in 1965 and continued through 1971, and were the main conduit for Sino-American communication during that period.) At those talks, U.S. representatives assured China that American aims were limited to compelling Hanoi to forgo the conquest of South Vietnam and did not seek the destruction of the North Vietnamese regime. It is widely believed that by November 1965 the two sides had reached a tacit understanding that, as long as U.S. forces did not invade North Vietnam or attack China, China would not directly enter the war.[14]

Even if such an understanding was reached, however, it could have been undone by events. As long as China and the United States remained at sword points, leaders of both countries moved cautiously to avoid a second Sino-American war. Both sides sought to avoid a war by misperception and miscalculation, as had happened in Korea.

CHINA'S PREPARATION FOR WAR WITH THE UNITED STATES

Another indication of the seriousness of Beijing's threats to intervene on Hanoi's side was a massive, crash program to construct a large, self-sufficient industrial base deep in China's interior.[15] Begun in August 1964, as the United States initiated air attacks against North Vietnam in spite of Chinese warnings, the purpose of this industrial base was to sustain a war effort against the United States. The program was called the "Third Front." Under it, key industrial facilities from the coastal areas were completely or partially dismantled and moved to the provinces of Sichuan, Guizhou, western Hubei, Yunnan, Qinghai, and Hunnan.

In addition to relocation of existing factories, a very large percent of budgetary investment in new industry—perhaps as much as two-thirds—was concentrated in the Third Front region between 1965 and 1971. In 1965, the proportion of China's total industrial investment going to Sichuan and Guizhou provinces tripled. Within a few years hundreds of new mining, metallurgical, energy, chemical, and military machine-building and instrument factories appeared in the Third Front region. Rail lines were built to connect these plants, along with dams to provide electricity. In some cases, existing rail lines were torn up to provide rails for new lines into interior regions. The objective was to develop an integrated, comprehensive defense industrial base in China's interior.

To minimize their vulnerability to air attack, Third Front industrial plants were very widely dispersed, typically situated away from major urban areas, and often located in deep, narrow canyons or caves. This particular spatial arrangement was very costly, entailing great infrastructural spending to sustain the operations of these facilities. Often new towns, road and rail lines had to be built for the workers. Transport costs were greatly increased by having to move components long distances.

The Third Front program was premised on the assumption that in the event of war with the United States, China's established industrial centers along the coasts would be destroyed or occupied in the early stages of the conflict. The PLA's modernization during the 1950s meant that the PLA now needed a lot more supplies and logistical support than it had in the 1930s. Moreover, the breakdown of the Sino-Soviet alliance meant that the PLA could no longer obtain necessary supplies from the Soviet Union. Although the strategy of People's War included nationwide mobilization of guerrilla forces to diminish enemy strength, it also included preservation and utilization of PLA main force units. These main force units required a lot of steel, gasoline, instruments, chemicals, and so on. Third Front industry was intended to provide that materiel so that the PLA could continue to prosecute a large and modern war after the destruction of China's coastal industrial centers by U.S. forces.

The Third Front program was rushed forward under top secrecy and with little regard to costs or proper planning. The disruption it imposed on China's economic development was immense and it was very costly. Twenty-five years later, China's economic planners were still grappling with the costs of the program and struggling to recoup some of the immense capital invested in it. The decision to undertake this program can only be interpreted as an expression of serious intent to wage a war, if necessary, with the United States. The Third Front effort is powerful evidence of the seriousness of Beijing's warnings to the United States. These were not minor moves to signal messages to Washington. They were serious efforts to prepare China for a major war with America. Significantly, only in 1969 was the Third Front reconfigured to deal with a possible Soviet attack. Until that point, America was the hypothetical enemy.

Even if the Third Front effort is taken as convincing evidence that China's leaders seriously contemplated war with the United States, it does not necessarily follow that they would have committed China to war had the United States completely devastated North Vietnam, as the revisionists suggest should have been done. Indeed, during the period 1965–1967, Chinese leaders made statements indicating that they believed that the United States would *attack China*. Premier Chou En-lai elaborated Chinese perceptions in a December 1965 rally celebrating the fifth anniversary of the founding of the National Liberation Front of South Vietnam. If U.S. imperialism failed to achieve its aim of repressing the Vietnamese people's war of national liberation, Chou warned, "it is possible that in accordance with the objective laws governing the development of aggressive wars, U.S. imperialism will go a step further and extend its war of aggression to the whole of Indochina and to China."[16] These words implied that as long as the United States limited its attacks to North Vietnam's territory, China would have remained on the sidelines.

On the other hand, Chou made these comments a month *after* the U.S. ambassador to Warsaw had made it clear to his Chinese counterpart that the United States had no intention of invading China or crushing North Vietnam.[17] The fact that China declared its intention to remain nonbelligerent *after* the United States adopted its policy of graduated escalation cannot logically be taken as evidence that China would have followed the same policy had the United States adopted a very different policy. Indeed, the contrary is suggested by comments made by Chou En-lai to Algerian leader Ahmed Ben Bella and Cambodian leader Norodom Sihanouk in April 1965 to the effect that China would not intervene in the Vietnam conflict unless there was a U.S. invasion north of the 17th parallel.[18]

Most probably, China's policy toward the Vietnam War was not governed by hard and fast principles, but evolved in response to U.S. actions and other international developments. It may well be that China's leaders had not themselves decided precisely what circumstances short of a U.S. attack on China itself would lead to Chinese entry into the war on Hanoi's side. There is abundant evidence, however, that Beijing was deeply committed to Hanoi. There is also evidence indicating the seriousness of Chinese warnings to the United States. Taken together, these argue strongly in favor of the prudence of Washington's policy of limiting the conflict with Hanoi to avoid a broader war with China.

1972 WAS NOT 1965

Implicit in the revisionist argument is the notion that because China did not react strongly to the American naval blockade and heavy bombing of North Vietnam in 1972, it would have reacted in an equally relaxed fashion to comparable U.S. moves in 1965. Similarly, the revisionists imply that because Mao Tse-tung and Chou En-lai concluded in 1972 that China's interests would be best served by a several-year suspension of Hanoi's military campaign to conquer South Vietnam, Mao and Chou were not strongly committed to Hanoi in 1965.[19]

These propositions are non sequiturs. The world was very different in 1965 and in 1972. Chinese policy was very different. Chinese views of the world were very different. In the mid-1960s, Chinese global strategy was focused on defeating U.S. "containment." There were, of course, major disagreements between Moscow and Beijing, but the primary origin of those disagreements had to do with how to deal with U.S. imperialism. As noted earlier, Mao Tse-tung favored a much more militant, confrontational approach, whereas Khrushchev and Brezhnev generally favored avoidance of confrontation with the United States.

Virtually all of the studies of Sino-American rapprochement focus on the 1968–1969 period. The militarization of the Sino-Soviet border began in 1963 and threats of Soviet intervention in China were grave by 1967, but it was the 1968 Soviet intervention in Czechoslovakia and the 1969 Sino-Soviet border confrontation that boosted the Soviet threat over the American threat in the minds of China's leaders. Just as the Soviet threat was mounting, the United States was fundamentally altering its policies toward China. By the time of Henry Kissinger's secret July 1971 visit to Beijing, it was clear that Washington was willing to modify substantially the policy of isolating China that it had pursued since 1950. It was also clear that it intended to withdraw militarily from Indochina.[20]

By 1972–1973, Beijing was very concerned with the danger of Soviet attack or encirclement, and saw the United States as a partner in dealing with the Soviet threat. It is very wrong-headed, however, to read those views back to 1965–1966.

Another revisionist non sequitur is the proposition that Mao's determination to launch the Cultural Revolution and his purge of PLA Chief of Staff Lo Jui-ching in late 1965 indicate that Mao was primarily concerned with the internal purification of China's revolution and not prepared to undertake a war with the United States. It may be conceded that Mao gave defeat of China's domestic "revisionists," priority over the anti-imperialist struggle against the United States—as long as U.S. imperialism did not encroach on China's borders. The latter caveat is important. Had U.S. forces directly threatened China—for instance, by moving into Laos or waging an all-out war against North Vietnam—Mao might well have reordered his priorities.

Nor can we conclude that Mao Tse-tung believed his domestic antirevisionist struggle was contrary to preparation for war with the United States. Indeed, from Mao's perspective, the opposite may well have been the case. To Mao, Moscow was Washington's lackey while China's revisionists fawned after Moscow. The authoritative November 1965 statement rejecting Moscow's proposal of "united action" in support of Hanoi, for example, charged that "The U.S. imperialists urgently need to extinguish the roaring flames of the Vietnamese people's revolution. And so do the Khrushchev revisionists because they want to carry out their line of Soviet–U.S. collaboration for world domination."[21]

If Moscow was set on a course of collusion with Washington, purge of China's revisionists who had illusions about Moscow could well be necessary preparation for a final, cataclysmic struggle with the United States. Just as Stalin believed that elimination of internal opposition dovetailed with the forced industrialization of the Five-Year Plans to prepare the Soviet Union for war, Mao may well have believed that the purge of revisionists from China's leadership prepared China for battle. Mao, like Stalin, may have been mistaken about the military efficacy of his purges. That, however, is another matter. We are concerned here with whether Mao's initiation of purges can be taken as evidence of an expectation that war could or would be avoided. It seems to me that it cannot.

But surely Mao Tse-tung would not have thrown China into the chaos associated with the Red Guard rebellion had he anticipated war with America. But again, it cannot be taken as evidence that Mao was not prepared for war with the United States had Washington waged a much more violent and expanded war in Southeast Asia. First, Mao may well have underestimated the chaos that would result when he helped create the Red Guards. Second, Mao did not unleash the Red Guards until *after* China and the United States had come to the tacit understanding at Warsaw in November 1965. Mao's critical moves supporting the nascent Red Guards came only in mid–1966, well after the Sino-American understanding at Warsaw.[22] In fact Mao did not cross the Rubicon with the Cultural Revolution until October 1966.[23] In sum, Mao's support for the Red Guard upheaval may well have been premised on the Sino-American understanding at Warsaw. That support cannot, therefore, be taken as evidence that Mao was not prepared for war with the United States had such an understanding not been reached.

Nor did the chaos of the Cultural Revolution necessarily diminish the danger of Chinese intervention. The weakening of central command and control might have combined with radical Red Guard influence in certain military units to produce provocative moves or more forceful reactions to American moves. By 1967 there was a tremendous amount of frustration in China over the Vietnam

War. Washington had twice ignored China's warnings, once in August 1964 and again in 1965. From the Chinese perspective, the arrogant American imperialists were humiliating China and ravaging China's fraternal ally. The inflammatory nature of such emotions were probably kept in check by central organs. But American decision makers could not assume the effectiveness of central command and control after the Cultural Revolution gained steam. Even with the advantage of hindsight we have no way of knowing if Beijing could have maintained central control had U.S. escalation gone much further and faster, fanning emotional fervor and factional debate in China. Could Chinese frustration have combined with the chaos of the Cultural Revolution to produce tougher responses to American moves? Had greater assertiveness on the Chinese side been combined with a less cautious approach on the American side, an escalating spiral of response and counterresponse might have begun making it difficult for either side to back down.

Even with effective central control, there was no diminution of Chinese risk taking in support of Hanoi at the height of the Cultural Revolution's chaos in 1967. In that year the United States waged the most unrestricted war against North Vietnam until Linebacker I and II in 1972. All North Vietnamese air bases were destroyed, forcing North Vietnamese planes to operate out of bases in China. Select targets within Hanoi and Haiphong were bombed. By late 1967, the prohibited buffer along the Sino-Vietnamese border was squeezed down to only 5 kilometers. In response to this expanded U.S. bombing, China increased the number of Chinese antiaircraft divisions in North Vietnam from two to three.[24] I have not seen figures regarding yearly levels of Chinese forces in North Vietnam, but it is my impression that they peaked in 1967.

THE CONSEQUENCES OF A SINO-AMERICAN WAR

Since the revisionist critique is basically historical ''what-if-ism'' on a grand scale, it is perhaps fair that we engage in a comparable exercise and ask what might have been the consequences if American leaders had waged the war as the revisionists suggest and China had entered the war on Hanoi's side.

To stop and roll back a Chinese invasion of Indochina, the United States would probably have used nuclear weapons, either against Chinese forces in Indochina or against military and industrial centers in China. Even if we assume that this would have been militarily effective and that U.S. bombing could have preempted Chinese nuclear retaliation against U.S. bases or allies in Asia (China tested an A-bomb in 1964 and an H-bomb in 1967), the political costs would have been very heavy. What would have been the consequence of this U.S. resort to nuclear arms on public opinion in Japan and West European countries about their alliances with America? What would have been the impact on the global moral standing of the United States? As it was, American operations in Vietnam seriously tarnished the United States's moral reputation. How much more grievous would have been the political costs of a general Sino-American war involving nuclear weapons? Would the Atlantic alliance and/or the Japan–United States alliance have crumbled under the impact of a general Sino-American war?

A Sino-American war fought on the Indochinese peninsula would probably have facilitated the growth of Communist power in Thailand, Burma, the Philippines, and Malaysia. China would have spared no efforts to outflank the United States by supporting insurgencies elsewhere in Southeast Asia. As it was, Foreign Minister Chen I warned Bangkok not to allow the United States to use its bases in Thailand to support the war in Indochina, or face greater opposition within Thailand.[25] When Bangkok failed to heed Beijing's warning, Chen's prediction came true. In 1965 full-scale guerrilla war erupted in northeastern Thailand. Thai Communists began broadcasts from a radio station located in south China or North Vietnam. Two new Thai revolutionary organizations emerged, rapidly received Beijing's endorsement, and then merged with the older Thai Communist Party (CPT)–dominated revolutionary front.[26] By the late 1960s, the CPT-led insurgency was a serious threat. How much more serious would that threat have become if China and America had gone to war and China's support for the CPT and other Southeast Asian revolutionary movements had been much larger?

Would the successful economic development of Thailand, Malaysia, Singapore, and Indonesia have been aborted by war? We should not take the developmental success of most of the ASEAN countries for granted. Would that success have resulted if Southeast Asia had been the battlefield for a Sino-American war? A Sino-American war in the mid–1960s would have greatly strengthened the Soviet global position. Moscow could either have tilted toward Washington or Beijing. If it had tilted toward Washington, Moscow would have been in a good position to demand various concessions from the United States. American efforts to contain the Soviet Union might have been seriously relaxed as a result. If Moscow had tilted toward China by acceding to Chinese requests for assistance under the 1950 mutual security treaty (which was not abrogated by Beijing until August 1978), the Sino-Soviet alliance might have been restored. This would have represented the collapse of the U.S. strategy of "driving a wedge" between Moscow and Beijing that had informed U.S. policy throughout the 1970s.[27] Soviet support for China combined with the Chinese fear and hatred for America, which would certainly have issued from a Sino-American war in the 1960s, could have revitalized the Sino-Soviet alliance and sustained it well into the 1970s.

If Sino-Soviet rapprochement had occurred in the 1960s instead of Sino-American rapprochement in the 1970s, Moscow's global expansionist drive of the 1970s might have had Chinese support rather than opposition. How much further would Moscow's drive have gone without Chinese opposition, without Sino-American antihegemony cooperation, and without the two-front threat presented to Moscow by a hostile China? Or again, would the American people have rallied, as they ultimately did, to a reinvigoration of containment of Soviet expansionism in the 1970s, after a nuclear war with China in the 1960s?

Even if the United States had emerged militarily from such a war, would

American power have been enhanced if, say, the Sino-Soviet alliance was functioning, and the United States had lost major European and Japanese allies and bore the onus of large-scale use of nuclear weapons against Asian peoples, and was war-weary after a war with China? Could a United States thus weakened have stopped the Soviet expansionist drive of the 1970s? How much further might Moscow have advanced? Would American weakness have resulted in continued appeasement of Soviet expansion and, ultimately, a Soviet-American war when that appeasement was no longer tenable? In sum, the world could well have been a much darker place if the revisionist strategies had been tried and resulted in a Sino-American war.

NOTES

1. Brig. Gen. Dave Richard Palmer, *Summons of the Trumpet: U.S.–Vietnam In Perspective* (San Rafael, CA: Presidio Press, 1978), 110. Cited in Harry G. Summers, *On Strategy: A Critical Analysis of the Vietnam War* (New York: Dell, 1984), 127 [hereafter *On Strategy*].

2. Summers, *On Strategy*, 94, 96.

3. Brian Shaw, "China and North Vietnam: Two Revolutionary Paths," *Current Scene* (Hong Kong), Part I, vol. ix, no. 1 (November 7, 1971), Part II, vol. ix. no. 12 (December 7, 1971).

4. Hoang Van Hoan, "Yue Zhong youyi yu Le Duan de beipan" [Le Duan's betrayal of Vietnamese-Chinese friendship], (Beijing: Renmin chubanshe, 1982), 15.

5. See "Peaceful Coexistence: Two Diametrically Opposed Policies," in *The Polemic on the General Line of the International Communist Movement* (Beijing: Foreign Languages Press, 1965), 259–302.

6. Hoang Van Hoan, "Yue Zhong zhancheng youyi de shishi bu rong waichu" [It is impermissible to distort the facts of wartime Vietnamese-Chinese friendship], *Renmin ribao* (November 27, 1979): 1, 5.

7. Roger Hilsman provides a succinct analysis of the U.S. decision to "neutralize" Laos in *To Move a Nation* (New York: Delta, 1964), 105–55.

8. Norman B. Hannah, *The Key to Failure: Laos and the Vietnam War* (New York: Madison Books, 1987); Summers, *On Strategy*, 165–73.

9. *Peking Review*, no. 21 (May 25, 1962): 3.

10. Regarding Chinese policy, see Lee Chae Jin, "Chinese Communist Policy in Laos: 1954–1965" (Ph.D. dissertation, Political Science, Univ. of California, Los Angeles, 1966).

11. Hilsman, *To Move a Nation*, 147.

12. Unless otherwise indicated, this discussion of China's deterrent support for Hanoi in the mid–1960s is from Allen S. Whiting, *The Chinese Calculus of Deterrence* (Ann Arbor: Univ. of Michigan Press, 1975), 170–95.

13. *Renmin ribao* (November 21, 1979): 4.

14. Kenneth T. Young, *Negotiating with the Chinese Communists: The United States Experience, 1953–1967* (New York: McGraw-Hill, 1968), 268–75.

15. Barry Naughton, "The Third Front: Defense Industrialization in the Chinese Interior," *China Quarterly* 115 (September 1988): 351–86.

16. *Peking Review* 52 (December 24, 1965).

17. Young, *Negotiating with the Chinese Communists*, 270.

18. CIA Intelligence Information Cables, April 10 and 29, 1965, in *CIA Research Reports, China 1946–1976*, Reel II, frame 0245 and 0251, University Publications of America, 1982.

19. Regarding China's 1971–1972 efforts to pressure Hanoi to compromise with the United States and grant the latter a face-saving withdrawal, see John W. Garver, "Sino-Vietnamese Conflict and Sino-American Rapprochement," *Political Science Quarterly* 96, no. 3 (Fall 1981): 445–64.

20. Richard M. Nixon, *R.N.: The Memoirs of Richard Nixon*, vol. 2 (New York: Warner, 1978), 3–23.

21. Editorial departments of *Renmin ribao* and *Hong Qi* [Red Flag], November 11, 1965, in William E. Griffith, *Sino-Soviet Relations, 1964–1965* (Cambridge: MIT Press, 1967), 460.

22. The first Red Guard poster was broadcast nationwide, at Mao's personal decision, on June 1, 1966. The CCP Work Teams were withdrawn from universities on July 24, 1966. Mao publicly accepted an arm band from the Red Guards on August 31, 1966.

23. Jean Daubier, *A History of the Chinese Cultural Revolution* (New York: Vintage, 1974), 91–99. The title of Daubier's chapter dealing with the October-December 1966 period is "The Point of No Return. . . . The Rubicon Is Crossed." Also, Jean Esmein, *The Chinese Cultural Revolution* (New York: Anchor, 1973), 96–106.

24. Allen S. Whiting, correspondence with the author, April 9, 1991.

25. Ibid.

26. Peter Van Ness, *Revolution and Chinese Foreign Policy* (Berkeley: Univ. of California Press, 1971), 137–38.

27. See David A. Mayers, *Cracking the Monolith: U.S. Policy Against the Sino-Soviet Alliance, 1949–1955* (Baton Rouge: Louisiana State Univ. Press, 1986).

Part III

The Air War

The United States air campaigns during the Vietnam War began in early 1965 with the Flaming Dart reprisal raids against North Vietnam and soon expanded into the sustained Rolling Thunder campaign. Ultimately, major U.S. air action over Vietnam concluded with the Linebacker I and II campaigns of 1972, although some bombing shifted to Laos and Cambodia in 1973. It has been estimated that in all these U.S. air campaigns, which were finally terminated in August 1973, American aircraft dropped an estimated 8 million tons of bombs on enemy targets, possibly 4 million tons, or close to 50 percent, on targets inside South Vietnam, the country we were defending.

During the bombing, South Vietnam experienced a great population exodus from the countryside to the coastal cities, as the country became the most heavily bombed nation in history. About 3 million tons of bombs fell on Laotian targets. Only 1 million tons of bombs fell on North Vietnamese territory. Cambodia received a half-million tons. The United States lost over 2,200 aircraft in the Vietnam War, more than were deployed in the entire Desert Shield/Desert Storm operation.

Literature on the air war during Vietnam tends to group into five categories. First, there are the senior commanders, who believed that if the United States had bombed North Vietnam in 1965–1966, the way it bombed North Vietnam in 1972, the war would have ended in victory. Second, there are authors like Professor Earl H. Tilford, Jr., in his work *Setup*, who believe that air power advocates became overconfident about what military technology could actually do to guerrilla armies. He believes that both civilian misunderstanding of the nature of the air war and the failure of military leaders to correct these errors led to a fruitless, if not predictable, expenditure of men and material. Third, there are authors like Major Mark Clodfelter who, in his *The Limits of Airpower*, argues that the enemy in Vietnam did not present a homogeneous large-unit conventional target system until 1972 when the war did become more conventional in nature. Fourth, there are aviator-authors like Colonel Jack Broughton who, in *Thud Ridge* and *Going Down-*

town, shared the frustration and pain of trying to fly and fight effectively under the political and operational controls that characterized U.S. strategy. Finally, there are a growing number of fringe authors like J. William Gibson whose book *The Perfect War* seek sociological reasons to explain why superior U.S. mass military technology—especially in the air war—could never have defeated the North Vietnamese.

In this section, Professor Tilford appraises the U.S. air interdiction campaigns in Laos and Cambodia between early 1969 and early 1973 known as Commando Hunt. His study also includes the secret "Menu" bombing in Cambodia as well as overt bombing through December 1972 and the post-Vietnam ceasefire bombings of Cambodian targets until August 1973. Designed to cover the American military withdrawal begun under President Richard Nixon in June 1969, these special interdiction bombing campaigns, by the whole gamut of U.S. Air Force and U.S. Navy attack aircraft, went after Communist trucks, supplies, logistics trails, and antiaircraft guns. The broader goals of Commando Hunt and the other Cambodian operations sought to preempt Communist offensives and brace the Saigon and Phnom Penh governments, while convincing Hanoi of the high costs of continuing the war. Ultimately, of course, they failed.

Major Mark Clodfelter's assessment of air power in Vietnam is written, in part, with lessons in mind from the 1991 Desert Storm air campaign. Critical to Clodfelter's analysis of the Vietnam air campaigns is his juxtaposition of the Johnson and Nixon administrations' different goals and the different means both presidents used to gain them. The Johnson administration wanted to preserve a non-Communist South Vietnam, but allowed air power—particularly Rolling Thunder—to be stretched out year after year. President Nixon, however, had more limited goals but applied air power in much more concentrated fashion. Like Nixon, President George Bush in Desert Storm had limited goals for which air power was massively concentrated, in nonstop fashion, on key military, transportation, and industrial Iraqi targets. Moreover, Bush and Secretary of Defense Dick Cheney, like President Nixon and Admiral Moorer in Linebacker II, left the choice of targets to the military.

Unlike Rolling Thunder, air power in Desert Storm was not saddled with political, military, and operational restrictions, nor did it face a guerrilla enemy. Also unlike Rolling Thunder, Desert Storm concentrated on key centers of gravity from the start. North Vietnam's predicament after the 1972 Easter offensive was similar to Iraq's after it invaded Kuwait in 1990: Both armies were exposed and vulnerable to *conventional* air attack. North Vietnam, however, had the advantage of smart and realistic leadership, a united population, a disillusioned American public, and triple canopy jungle concealing much of its logistic network into the south. Finally, the merger of advanced precision-guided munitions with stealth technology allowed real devastation of the Iraqi war machine.

The final article in this section is by Douglas Pike, recognized Vietnam expert and director of the Indochina Institute at the University of California, Berkeley. Pike's contribution is particularly significant since, with the exception of his own work on the PAVN, little primary research or work has been done on the North Vietnamese military by Western or Vietnamese scholars. This is especially true with regard to the North's air defenses. Pike's treatment of North Vietnamese air defenses focuses on the differing perceptions of American and North Vietnamese officials toward airpower. Pike shows how Hanoi's leadership prepared the country to absorb the worst conventional air attack the Americans could muster. Hanoi bent to the task, erecting, with Soviet aid, one of the most extensive air defense networks in the world, including 300 SAM batteries, thousands of AAA guns, and 200 MiG fighters. American thinking, by contrast, was influenced by World War II and Korean War air campaigns in which emphasis was placed on interdiction and strategic bombing—both, in Pike's view, oversold to the U.S. public. During the Vietnam War there was considerable skepticism among U.S. civilian officials, especially in the Saigon embassy, regarding the utility of airpower; that contrasted with widespread confidence among the American military about the utility of bombing.

All three authors introduce new research and analysis to this vital aspect of the American war in Southeast Asia.

6

Bombing Our Way Back Home: The Commando Hunt and Menu Campaigns of 1969–1973

Earl H. Tilford, Jr.

As far as the U.S. Air Force is concerned, air power is offensive in nature. For seven decades strategic bombing has been the life blood of air power advocates because it provides the reason for being for a separate air force. U.S. Air Force doctrine has been wedded to the concept that air power, given its rein, can destroy virtually any enemy's warmaking capability—or—break that enemy's will. What air power as conceived by the U.S. Air Force does not do very well is to cover retreats; and for much of the American war in Vietnam, that is what it was asked to do.

When most of us who are so inclined think about the air war in Vietnam, the tendency is to think about bombs falling on North Vietnam. The primary air operations aimed at North Vietnam included the following: Operation Rolling Thunder, the bombing of North Vietnam from March 1965 through October 1968; Linebacker I, the air power response to the North Vietnamese spring offensive in 1972; and Linebacker II, the eleven-day aerial campaign in December 1972 to compel Hanoi to sign the Paris Accords. Although not necessarily "strategic" in nature, all were examples of offensive air power.[1]

Although the focus of the air war appeared to be on North Vietnam, only about 1 million tons of bombs, or 12 percent of the total tonnage fell there. By comparison, 3 million tons fell on Laos, 4 million tons on South Vietnam, and a half-million tons were dropped on Cambodia. Although uniformed air power advocates and civilian scholars will disagree on much, for a number of reasons they have shared this focus on bombing North Vietnam. First, records on bombing North Vietnam are generally more available. The bombings of Laos and Cambodia were shrouded in secrecy, and many of those records remain classified. Second, the Hanoi regime is the only government that existed during the years of the American involvement to remain in power, and some American scholars have gained limited access to its records. Third, the air war against North Vietnam still carries a great deal of ideological baggage. Air power advocates can point to the bombing, especially the Linebacker campaigns of 1972, to restate claims for air power's potential decisiveness. Those critical of American participation in the conflict characterize the bombing of the North as an example of a cruel technology unleashed on a peaceful and peace-loving people. Consequently, other than official histories published by the Office of Air Force History and the Naval Historical Office, few scholarly works have appeared on the air war over Laos, Cambodia, and South Vietnam.[2]

TRANSITION TO RETREAT

When President Lyndon B. Johnson ended Rolling Thunder on November 1, 1968, one effect was to limit President Richard M. Nixon's air power options in the first years of his presidency.

Nixon's bombing of Laos and Cambodia, as well as North Vietnam, can be divided into two periods: bombing during his first term, or Nixon ascending, and bombing during his truncated second term, or Nixon descending.

Following his inauguration in January 1969, President Nixon was politically constrained from restarting the bombing of North Vietnam which President Johnson has terminated on November 1, 1968. Other than the highly controversial "protective reaction strikes" directed at targets in North Vietnam's southern panhandle, and an occasional special operation like the Son Tay raid and Operation Proud Deep Alpha in December 1971, North Vietnam was essentially off limits to American air attack. The bombing, however, shifted to Laos and Cambodia and continued in South Vietnam. As a lame duck president, Lyndon Johnson authorized a new interdiction bombing campaign in Laos beginning on November 15, 1968. It was called "Commando Hunt" and President Nixon would continue it for nearly three and one-half years (see Figure 1).

By the spring of 1969, however, the U.S. Air Force had disengaged itself spiritually (but not physically) from the war. For example, on March 19, 1969, newly installed Secretary of the Air Force Robert C. Seamans, Jr., in his keynote address to the annual meeting of the Air Force Association, said:

There seems to be a trend toward viewing all national questions in the context of the frustrating struggle against aggression in Vietnam. . . . But there is no doubt that, however frustrated we are with the conflict in Vietnam, the cost of failure to provide adequate forces for our security could be infinitely higher than the cost of Southeast Asia.[3]

By March 1969, nearly a year had passed since Lyndon Johnson had curtailed bombing of North Vietnam. America's policy of Vietnamization had not yet been articulated, and the Air Force, like the other services, fought in somewhat of a strategic vacuum, even as the war shifted from what had been an unconventional war with increasingly conventional aspects, to a more conventional conflict, albeit one with considerable unconventional fighting.

In a sense, Secretary Seamans's speech to the Air Force Association, which

Figure 1
Indochina Air Campaigns, 1964–1973

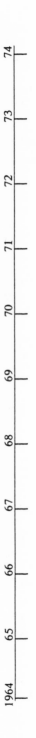

Linebacker II 18–29 Dec 72

Linebacker I 10 May 72 – 23 Oct 72

19 Mar 69 | Menu   15 Aug 73 |
          26 May 70 | Overt Bombing of Cambodia

10 May 72

10 Nov 68 | Operation Commando Hunt (I–VII)

1 Apr 65 | Operation Steel Tiger | 15 Nov 68

2 Mar 65 | Operation Rolling Thunder | 1 Nov 68

Dec 64 | Operation Barrel Roll & Steel Tiger (Bombing of Laos other than Commando Hunt) | May 73

1964   65   66   67   68   69   70   71   72   73   74

was entitled "Continuing Cooperation Between NASA and the DOD," represented a spiritual disengagement from the war. Despite the fact that the war still raged, the Air Force had refocused its attention on space and toward meeting the Soviet threat in Europe and elsewhere, in effect returning to where it had been in the 1950s and early 1960s. In Southeast Asia, the emphasis shifted to the introduction of new, technologically advanced weaponry and to tactics employed under an increasingly pervasive managerial approach to warfare that operated outside any coherent strategy.

COMMANDO HUNT: COVERING THE RETREAT

As the outlines of Vietnamization became clearer in late 1969 and actual withdrawals of American ground and air forces began, it was vitally important that what was left of the Viet Cong and the increasing numbers of North Vietnamese regulars (People's Army of Vietnam, or PAVN) not launch another attack on the scale of the 1968 Tet Offensive. To have done so could have derailed Vietnamization by making it politically unpalatable to the Republican right wing as well as to the Saigon regime which harbored fears of American abandonment. Commando Hunt, a series of interdiction campaigns aimed at reducing the flow of troops and supplies along the Ho Chi Minh Trail in Laos, was key to keeping Vietnamization on track.

Commando Hunt involved a series of seven air campaigns, each of approximately six months duration.[4] Air Force Manual (AFM) 1–1, *United States Air Force Basic Doctrine*—the officially sanctioned beliefs concerning how air operations should be conducted—in its 1964 edition stated: "Successful interdiction (using conventional weapons) requires large numbers of aircraft operating over the target areas. Sustained air strikes must be coordinated to reduce enemy logistics support below the high level necessary to sustain conventional operations."[5] This is what seven Commando Hunt campaigns endeavored to do.

Commando Hunt involved attacks against four target categories. First, there was the attack on trucks as they drove along the roads of the Ho Chi Minh Trail. Gunships, including large four-engine Lockheed AC–130s armed with an array of 20mm gatling guns, 40mm Bofors cannons, and—in some models—a computer-aimed 105mm howitzer, gradually took over the "war on trucks."[6]

Second, there was the attack on the Trail complex, the more than 200 miles of paved roads and up to 6,000 miles of dirt roads, tracks, pathways and waterways contained in the 250-square mile section of southeastern Laos that comprised Hanoi's logistical lifeline. It was estimated that up to 10,000 trucks at any one time could be shuttling troops and supplies along the Ho Chi Minh Trail.[7]

A third aspect of Commando Hunt was the attack on the terrain—the mountain passes, river fords, and the jungle itself. As a part of this effort the U.S. Air Force used laser-guided bombs to cause landslides. B–52 strikes—along with occasional Ranch Hand defoliation sorties—stripped away jungle canopy. Bombs rained down on rivers to alter their course. Finally, after the North Vietnamese moved large numbers of antiaircraft guns onto the Trail to defend it, the Air Force took them on. The 23mm and 37mm guns proved especially dangerous for slow, lumbering gunships. In fact, gunship development was, in large part, driven by a need to climb above North Vietnamese antiaircraft fire.

Virtually the entire gamut of Air Force and Navy attack aircraft took part in Commando Hunt. Jets as well as propeller-driven fighter-bombers bombed and strafed during the day. B–52s, in some models capable of carrying 105 500-pound bombs, hammered the passes leading from North Vietnam into Laos and from Laos into South Vietnam. In 1971, the 7th Air Force inaugurated an interdiction box campaign whereby approximately one-mile-square boxes, labeled "A," "B," "C," and "D," were established in the Ban Kari, Mu Gia, Ban Raving, and Nape passes, respectively, and around Tchepone, a key Laotian transhipment point along Route 9 leading into South Vietnam. Up to 27 B–52 sorties a day dumped bombs into these boxes. Fighter-bombers joined in; some were sent to the boxes and others dropped unused ordnance into them before returning to base. In 1971, during Commando Hunt V, a daily average of 27 B–52s and 125 fighter-bombers dropped bombs in the interdiction boxes.[8]

Igloo White made Commando Hunt work. The Igloo White sensor system predated Commando Hunt, being established in December 1967 under the auspices of Task Force Alpha at Nakhon Phanom Royal Thai Air Force Base (RTAFB), Thailand. Originally designated "Dutch Mill," the system was devised to facilitate targeting of PAVN units laying siege to Khe Sanh. Later, it was applied along the Ho Chi Minh Trail.[9]

The air war over the Trail had a rhythm that was synchronized with the movement of supplies along the ground. During the day, fighter-bombers attacked suspected truck parks and storage areas. Laser-guided bombs were used to destroy AAA guns and to cause road slides in the passes. At night, in an effort to deny the cover of darkness to the North Vietnamese, gunships roamed up and down the Trail using heat sensors and low-light-level television to seek out trucks, which were then attacked with their array of guns.

On the ground, the enemy moved with a pattern devised to avoid aerial attack. Peak traffic hours were between 4:00 A.M. and 8:00 A.M. and 4:00 P.M. and 8:00 P.M. These times coincided with shift changes at American bases and with changes in deployment of aircraft. Fighter-bombers usually arrived on station after dawn, at around 8:00 A.M. Pilots preferred to bomb after the sun had fully risen to avoid visual misperceptions more common in the half-light of dawn or dusk.

Additionally, if one were going to be shot down, it was better to be shot down earlier in the day rather than later to preclude having to spend the night on the ground. It was not until late in the war that rescue helicopters had even a modest nighttime recovery capability. Gunships, vulnerable to 23mm and 37mm antiaircraft fire, would not arrive on station until after dark, and needed to be out of the area by dawn. Furthermore, shift changes at the bases usually took place between 4:00 A.M. and 6:00 A.M. and 4:00 P.M. and 6:00 P.M. Senior officers came to work about 6:00 or 7:00 A.M. in the morning. The day shift began preparing for their arrival as much as two hours before, meaning that attention to current operations was curtailed. At the end of the day, senior officers departed between 4:00 P.M. and 6:00 P.M. to make late afternoon tennis matches or to catch "happy hours" at the officers' club. The enemy moved most of their supplies during those hours. Whether knowingly or unknowingly, the North Vietnamese got inside the Air Force's managerial loop.

But was it working? Progress was measured in the Vietnam War by statistics, and Commando Hunt lent itself well to that process. At the headquarters of the U.S. 7th/13th Air Force at Udorn RTAFB, Thailand, and at 7th Air Force headquarters in Saigon, the truck count (the Air Force's equivalent of the body count) was duly reported at briefings. The truck count was impressive, as the total number destroyed reached a high of 12,368 in Command Hunt IV in 1970.

When, in Commando Hunt V, the truck count rose to 16,266 destroyed and 4,700 damaged, the Central Intelligence Agency pointed out that this number of trucks more than doubled the total number estimated in all of North Vietnam and Laos! The Air Force was forced to revise its figures downward to a still whopping 11,000 trucks destroyed and 8,000 damaged.[10]

Whether or not Commando Hunt "succeeded" is an open question. Undoubtedly a good many trucks and their cargoes were destroyed. The North Vietnamese and what was left of the Viet Cong did not launch a major offensive between Tet of 1968 and the Spring Offensive of 1972. The PAVN, however, conducted sustained operations within the parameters of monsoonal weather cycles inside South Vietnam. Indeed, more Americans perished between mid–1968 and 1972 than died during the advisory years and buildup phases running from 1961 through 1968. Despite the lavish use of air power, in which nearly 3 million tons of bombs fell on Laos (making it the second most bombed country in the history of aerial warfare), each year American troops or South Vietnamese forces mounted significant ground operations either in Laos or Cambodia to prevent the enemy from launching a major offensive. In 1969, U.S. Marines went into the A-Shau Valley area near the Laotian border in the northern part of South Vietnam. In 1970, ARVN and American troops marched into the Cambodian border region to forestall enemy action around Saigon and in the IV Corps region of South Vietnam. Finally, in 1971, despite all the bombing of the Laotian logistical network, the ARVN attempted to cut the Trail on the ground in Operation Lam Son 719, which resulted in serious ARVN casualties.

Commando Hunt was significant for three reasons. First, Vietnamization continued and the majority of American troops were withdrawn from South Vietnam during this period. Second, since the results of Commando Hunt are debatable at best, one could make the point that except for either narrowly specified operations (like the Son Tay Raid) or an all-out strategic bombing campaign, air power must function within the context of a strategy inextricably connected to ground operations. Third, Commando Hunt reinforced the managerial ethos in what came to resemble "production line warfare" where success was determined based on statistics that became an end unto themselves. Statistics, however, proved to be no substitute for strategy, and all the perceived successes in the numbers game succeeded only in providing the illusion of victory and fooling air power leaders into thinking that Commando Hunt was working.

CAMBODIA I: NIXON ASCENDING—MENU BOMBING
MARCH 1969–MAY 1970

The secret bombing of Cambodia in 1969 and 1970—the so-called "Menu" bombing—was related to the war in Vietnam in three ways. First, the areas bombed were an integral part of the Viet Cong and PAVN logistical network supporting operations in the region and around Saigon.

Second, North Vietnam had shown little restraint in moving men and supplies southward through its panhandle and then into Laos and down the Ho Chi Minh Trail. The assumption had been that when President Johnson curtailed the bombing of North Vietnam on March 31, 1968, and then ended the bombing on November 1, Hanoi would reciprocate by reducing its support for the war in the South. The Military Assistance Command, Vietnam (MACV) estimates, however, not only showed an increase in traffic along the Laotian corridors, but also indicated that between October 1967 and September 1968, at least 10,000 tons of arms had moved from Sihanoukville along Friendship Highway into the border region and then on to Communist forces fighting inside South Vietnam. In 1969, the Nixon White House was convinced that the flow was continuing.[11]

The third factor was that the bombing was tied to Washington's strategy of Vietnamization and disengagement. Nixon knew, given the mood of the country, that he could not order a resumption of bombing over North Vietnam without risking a major escalation of the antiwar movement. *Bombing the Cambodian sanctuaries seemed to offer a way of sending Hanoi yet another message, and doing so without igniting passions at home.*[12]

Additionally, if Vietnamization was to succeed, the North Vietnamese and the Viet Cong could not be allowed another offensive like Tet 1968. The bombing of Cambodia, like the Commando Hunt campaigns, was aimed at giving Vietnamization a chance while covering the withdrawal of U.S. troops.

After considerable discussions, the first secret B–52 missions over Cambodia took place on March 18, 1969. The target was Base Area 353, a logistical storage network three miles inside Cambodia. The Pentagon assigned the code name "Breakfast" to the bombing. In May, Nixon ordered additional strikes in roughly the same region, dubbing these "Supper," "Lunch," "Dessert," and "Snack," according to the various base areas designated as targets. The whole series was called "Menu," and it continued until May 1970.[13]

For the U.S. Air Force, the secret bombings of Cambodia went beyond normal clandestine operations where secrecy and deception are expected and acceptable. In this case the duplicities involved deceiving Air Force officials and lying on official documents—court martial offenses. Deception to fool the enemy was one thing, but lying to Congress and key members of the government, including the chief of staff of the U.S. Air Force and the secretary of the U.S. Air Force, was something else.

The deception was revealed when a former Air Force major, Hal Knight, wrote a letter to Senator William Proxmire asking for "clarification" as to U.S. policy on bombing Cambodia. In his letter Knight admitted falsifying reports to indicate that B–52s that had bombed Cambodia had, instead, dropped their loads on South Vietnam.[14]

The deception went far beyond Hal Knight's pay grade, originating in the White House. Nixon and Kissinger believed secrecy was vital to the multifaceted diplomatic and military process of disengagement, and that revelation of the bombing could hinder that process. Accordingly, they did not inform the secretary of the U.S. Air Force or the Air Force chief of staff when a limited number of officers were incorporated into their scheme. Colonel Ray B. Sitton, an officer with a background in the Strategic Air Command (SAC), worked out a system for using Arc Light B–52 strikes in South Vietnam as a cover for cross-border missions. Radar bomb navigators were taken aside after their routine mission briefing and told that as they neared their drop points, they would receive a new set of coordinates from radar controllers inside South Vietnam. Poststrike reports were filed using the original regular target coordinates. Top secret "back channel" communications systems—those reserved for transmitting the most sensitive types of intelligence—were used to pass the real information to a very small number of military and civilian officials.[15]

The Menu bombing ended on May 26, 1970. It had lasted fourteen months, during which time B–52s flew 3,630 sorties into Cambodia to drop 100,000 tons of bombs. B–52 missions into Cambodia continued in the open in support of U.S. and South Vietnamese forces which had entered that country on May 1. The irony was that as the United States withdrew its forces, the war spread, and by 1970 the fighting ranged over a larger geographic area than before.

After Norodom Sihanouk was overthrown in March 1970, Cambodia's little air force, consisting of a handful of transports and MiG–17s, began supporting the burgeoning *Forces Armee Nationale Khmer* (FANK) in operations against the Viet Cong and North Vietnamese in the eastern provinces. The Chinese cut off shipments of spare parts to Phnom Penh and the MiGs were soon grounded. The 56th Special Operations Wing (SOW) at Udorn began training pilots for the Khmer air force, but in the meantime the U.S. Air Force, along with the South Vietnamese air force, carried the burden of the air war in Cambodia, flying in support of the FANK and bombing the southern extensions of the Ho Chi Minh Trail.[16]

The air war in Cambodia expanded along with the ground fighting. In 1970, 8 percent of the U.S. Air Force's total combat sorties went into Cambodia. The next year the figure jumped up 14 percent. Until the invading armies from North Vietnam forced a shift in sortie allocation back to South Vietnam to counter the

PAVN's massive invasion in the spring of 1972, that figure remained approximately the same. Meanwhile, B–52s began flying about 10 percent of their available sorties (around three per day) into Cambodia.[17]

The 1970 incursions into Cambodia and the bombing from 1969 to 1970 were, like Commando Hunt, linked to Vietnamization and, by extension, to America's retreat. Nearly two-thirds of South Vietnam's population lived in the Mekong Delta region and in the area just north and west of Saigon. If the Communists had launched another offensive of the scale of Tet in that area while substantial numbers of Americans were still serving in Vietnam, the process of withdrawal would have been hampered by the Republican and Democratic political right at home, and by President Nguyen Van Thieu in Saigon. The Cambodian bombing and the incursions had, if nothing else, prevented any large-scale action by the North that would have allowed the American political right or Thieu to block the continuing withdrawal.

WAR AS ANACHRONISM

By June 1970, Rolling Thunder had been over for nearly two years. Notwithstanding the "Protective Reaction" strikes—the unauthorized bombing of selected targets in the southern panhandle of North Vietnam ordered by 7th Air Force commander Gen. John D. Lavelle, occasional orders to "go north" were welcomed by many airmen as a meaningful diversion from jungle bashing in South Vietnam, Laos, and Cambodia.

Within the U.S. Air Force there was a sense that the war was over, although those airmen who fought in Southeast Asia during these years may not have felt that way. There, "war as an anachronism" had a deleterious effect on operations. By 1970, a pilot shortage and an experience gap were evident throughout the service. Many senior officers with combat experience in World War II, Korea, and Vietnam, had retired. These combat-seasoned officers, those most likely to serve as leaders within wings and squadrons, started retiring after reaching the twenty-year or thirty-year points in their careers. The airlines were hiring, and many younger airmen opted for the "friendly skies" rather than the possibility of a second tour in Southeast Asia.

To boost retention of experienced aircrews and enlisted personnel, the U.S. Air Force adopted a policy of no involuntary second Southeast Asia tours. The result was that by 1971 and early 1972, an ever-increasing number of newly trained pilots and navigators were assigned to combat units. Although this policy addressed retention and morale, it had major drawbacks.

Col. Stanley M. Umstead, Jr., commander of the 388th Tactical Fighter Wing (TFW), lamented that 25 percent of his F–4 aircraft commanders were recent graduates of pilot training classes. He added that although these aircrews were "highly motivated and [possessed] basic skills, they were deficient in formation flying and maneuvering."[18]

According to another wing commander, Col. Lyle E. Mann, "Aircrews graduating from UPT [undergraduate pilot training] need considerably more air-to-air training."[19]

Not only was the fighting force younger and more inexperienced than it had been during Rolling Thunder, it was also overworked. Despite the fact that men were flying, fighting, and dying, the United States was not officially at war. Thus, units in the Pacific Air Forces (PACAF) were manned at the same levels as those in Europe or the United States. Normally, the peacetime manning for the F–4 was 1.5 aircrew-per-seat-per aircraft and F–105 units were manned at 1.21 pilots per cockpit in that single-seat fighter-bomber.[20]

The realities of war seemed not to matter. Although aircrews operating in Indochina flew more often than those in Europe or the United States, the peacetime manning policy limited the ability of wings in Vietnam and Thailand to respond to surge efforts like Proud Deep Alpha, a five-day bombing of targets just north of the Demilitarized Zone (DMZ) in December 1971. The director of base medical services at Korat Royal Thai Air Force Base complained that "people were often changed from flying since . . . crewmembers are often called several times a night while they are asleep to notify them of a new schedule."[21]

If overwork was a problem, there were plenty of ways to unwind. At Udorn RTAFB in Thailand, all the snack bars on base, including the one by the Olympic-size swimming pool (where hamburgers and pizza were available twenty-four hours a day), were refurbished. The outdoor theater was expanded to accommodate 850 people, while the indoor theater was overhauled with a new air-conditioning system and rocking-chair seats. For those who wanted more exertion than flying combat missions over Laos or working on the flight line in twelve-hour shifts provided, newly resurfaced and expanded tennis courts, a new golf driving range, and an expanded archery range were available. Udorn was, to be sure, exceptional as bases in Southeast Asia went. Perhaps that is why this showcase base hosted the 1971 All-Thailand Slow Pitch Softball Tournament.[22]

MARKING TIME ALONG THE HO CHI MINH TRAIL

At the end of 1971, fighting during this period of bombing had declined to the point that the decreased effectiveness of the U.S. Air Force was not readily apparent. Since the end of Rolling Thunder on November 1, 1968, the Commando Hunt Laotian interdiction campaign had been the focus of the air war. The truck count reflected tactical successes, thus obscuring the strategic bankruptcy of the operation. Commando Hunt VII, from November 1971 to May 1972, was the final effort in this three-and-a-half-year campaign.

The plan for Commando Hunt VII was to bottle up the Communist transportation system in Laos, using B–52s to close the passes leading from North Vietnam into Laos and from Laos into South Vietnam and Cambodia, thus forcing the vehicles to congregate in truck parks where they could be attacked more profitably. Simultaneously, B–52s obliterated sections of some roads so that traffic would be diverted to specific routes where gunships and tactical bombers stalked them with increasingly predictable success. At least that was the official Air Force view of Commando Hunt.[23]

The Air Force's optimism was not justified. As an interdiction campaign, Commando Hunt was failing. The North Vietnamese shuttled men and supplies southward at a steady rate. In mid–1971, a major expansion program got under way along the Ho Chi Minh Trail. Several factors contributed to the North Vietnamese's continuing success in moving supplies to the PAVN units in the South. Keeping the Trail open was Hanoi's number-one priority. Thousands of young men and women lived in work camps throughout the Trail network. At night and in bad weather, when there was less danger from air attack, these workers repaired roads, bridges, and fords. They continuously were extending the bypass system—a web of small roads winding through the dense jungle underbrush. In part, this happened because Commando Hunt never successfully coupled the vast intelligence information emanating from Task Force Alpha with operations directed by 7th Air Force.

By 1971, the U.S. interdiction effort was fragmented into bureaucratic fiefdoms—the gunship program, the night-bombing effort with B–57Gs and A–26s, SAC's interdiction box program, and the intelligence gathering, assimilation, and collation effort at Task Force Alpha. It never came together under the aegis of a strategy devised to work toward a common end. Because each program seemed to have to validate its own existence, a truly coordinated effort never quite emerged.

Because of the bombing halt over North Vietnam, troops and trucks loaded with supplies had the advantage of getting into the 250-mile long Trail system before the Air Force had a chance to attack them. Essentially, this part of the air war was reactive, devolving into something analogous to trying to decrease the flow of water through a fire hose by inflicting thousands of tiny pinpricks (the war on trucks).

Finally, as 1971 ended, the scope of the air war had diminished as Vietnamization proceeded. The monthly average for fighter attack sorties during Command Hunt V, conducted between October 1970 and March 1971, was 14,000, about half what it had been for Commando Hunt I.[24]

As with Rolling Thunder and virtually every other operation conducted by the Air Force in Southeast Asia, the official view was that Commando Hunt was another in its unbroken string of unmitigated air power successes. After Commando Hunt VII, the U.S. Air Force Intelligence Service claimed 51,500 trucks and 3,400 antiaircraft guns had been destroyed or damaged throughout seven campaigns. Although "allowing an inflationary factor of 50 percent," the report continued, "the effectiveness of air power in finding and destroying these targets is unique in aerial warfare."[25]

Maj. Gen. Alton D. Slay, director of operations at 7th Air Force in Saigon during the final phases of the Commando Hunt campaign, had a view different from those shared by most high-ranking Air Force officers. Slay was convinced Commando Hunt had failed and that it had done so for two reasons. First, although the United States was expanding the air war to Cambodia and intensifying operations over northern Laos, the Air Force simultaneously was redeploying units to Europe and back to the United States. Second, since SAC was reluctant to use restriction meant that the passes leading from North Vietnam into Laos were off limits to B–52 strikes since the North Vietnamese began placing SAM sites in or near them in 1971.[26]

The strongest evidence against the reputed success of Commando Hunt was that North Vietnam launched a major invasion of South Vietnam in late March 1972. In scope, that invasion dwarfed anything since the Chinese had entered the Korean War in November 1950. That this offensive happened despite the fact that well over 2 million tons of bombs had fallen on the Ho Chi Minh Trail should have dampened the sanguinity of all but the most ardent air power enthusiasts. For the Air Force, however, Commando Hunt had become production line warfare, and the managers at the top of the corporation interpreted the figures to suit their own preconceived notions of victory.

The PAVN offensive, dubbed the "Nguyen Hue Offensive" by Hanoi, began on March 31, 1972. It prompted a massive air power response—Linebacker I. This bombing campaign directed at North Vietnam began on May 8 and ended on October 23, 1972. It was probably the most successful employment of air power during the Vietnam War. Its success was due to the fact that it operated under the aegis of a strategy appropriate to the war at that point. Linebacker I involved conventional air power used on North Vietnam to stop a conventional invasion by some fourteen divisions of PAVNs attacking South Vietnam. This bombing, along with significant changes in both the U.S. and North Vietnamese positions on a ceasefire agreement, brought Washington and Hanoi to the point where, as Henry Kissinger put it in early October 1972, "peace is at hand." But before the Paris Accords were finally signed on January 23, 1973, one more bombing campaign aimed at North Vietnam was required—Linebacker II. Dubbed "the Christmas bombing" by many of those critical of U.S. involvement and "the eleven-day war" by many airmen long anxious to be "let loose" on North Vietnam, this operation resulted in a signed agreement which allowed for the withdrawal of U.S. forces from South Vietnam, the return of American prisoners of war held in North and South Vietnam, and little else.

Contrary to what many believed and hoped, the fighting did not end with the signing of the cease-fire agreement in Paris on January 23, 1973. In South Vietnam, the fighting between the PAVN and the Viet Cong and the ARVN continued. Although the Americans stopped bombing in North and South Vietnam, the air war went on over Laos and Cambodia. Because the ceasefire in Vietnam released a large number of sorties, the bombing in the rest of Indochina increased accordingly.

BOMBING LAOS IN 1973: NIXON DESCENDING

The post-Vietnam cease-fire bombing in Laos took place during the period of crisis in the Nixon administration. With each passing day, U.S. policy unraveled due in large part to the mushrooming Watergate controversy. The power of the presidency, fundamental to the effective employment of air power during the period of Nixon ascending, was even more important to its effective employment in 1973, but Nixon was in trouble and his power and authority were on the wane. A Congress intent on disengagement from Vietnam, old political foes who sensed a wounded Nixon, and a public sapped of its will by years of frustration over the war combined to confound the direction of American policy in the months after the signing of the Paris Accords.

When a circle is drawn, it ends at the same point where it begins. Similarly, when the bombing stopped in Vietnam, American policy was where it had been a dozen years before—focused on Laos. As was the case during the Kennedy presidency and in the early months of the Johnson administration, the Air Force was bombing Laos and doing so to affect Hanoi's behavior. Interdiction had become, at best, a secondary objective since the United States had already agreed that Hanoi could maintain an army of at least 100,000 PAVN regulars *inside* South Vietnam.

The North Vietnamese, however, violated the Paris Accords by sending additional soldiers into South Vietnam. Meanwhile, in northern Laos the Pathet Lao and their PAVN ally moved west, gobbling up as much territory as possible in anticipation of a ceasefire. In Vientiane, Premier Souvanna Phouma searched for a way to keep Laos independent after the United States completed its withdrawal from Indochina. Despite a decade of fighting, the civil war in Laos had not changed in its dynamics—it had only become bloodier as a result of participation by the North Vietnamese, Thais, and Americans.

There were certainly valid reasons for the United States to continue bombing Laos in the early months of 1973. Hanoi blatantly violated Article 20 of the Paris Accords, which specified that all foreign troops be withdrawn from Laos and Cambodia and forbade the use of those countries as corridors of infiltration or staging areas for attacks on South Vietnam.[27]

U.S. Air Force B–52s and fighter-bombers stationed in Thailand, so recently engaged in Linebacker II, stood down for a few days after the signing of the Paris Accords. By mid-February, however, the sortie output was back at the level it had achieved during the "eleven-day war." Before the month was out, B–52s had flown 1,147 sorties in Laos, 308 more than had been directed at North Vietnam during Linebacker II. They struck 286 targets in northern Laos, including truck parks and storage areas. Along the Ho Chi Minh Trail and in areas west of the infiltration corridor, B–52 crews flew 948 Arc Light sorties to bomb 426 targets, including truck parks, storage areas, and staging bases from the Mu Gia Pass south to the Cambodian border. In addition, Air Force aircraft bombed PAVN and Pathet Lao units massing for an attack on Paksong, the Vientiane government's last stronghold on the Bolovens Plateau—the strategic high ground overlooking the Mekong River at the southern end of Laos.[28]

Although the fighting and the bombing of Laos continued, Henry Kissinger and Le Duc Tho, along with the various Lao parties, moved toward a ceasefire there. A cessation of hostilities in Laos, at least a temporary one, worked to Hanoi's advantage, as well as to that of the Pathet Lao, because it would require the United States to stop bombing. Given the weakened condition of the Nixon presidency, the North Vietnamese probably were savvy enough to figure out that once a major step had been undertaken, it would be nearly impossible for the beleaguered president to reverse it.

Additionally, they may have known that the American public was becoming more aware of the "secret war" in Laos. A sensational if flawed account of the narcotics trade in Indochina (*The Politics of Heroin in Southeast Asia* by Alfred G. McCoy, Cathleen B. Reed, and Leonard P. Adams), accused the Central Intelligence Agency (CIA), Air America, and the U.S. Air Force of working with Laotian drug lords and corrupt members of the Laotian and South Vietnamese governments and armed forces to produce and smuggle heroin from the Golden Triangle area of northwestern Laos. These revelations, however inaccurate or exaggerated, weakened the administration's already diminished credibility. All things considered, it was to Hanoi's advantage to compel their Pathet Lao clients to sign the cease-fire agreement, which took effect at noon Vientiane time on February 23, 1973.[29]

Two days after the ceasefire was signed, Pathet Lao and PAVN units occupied Paksong. Over the next two days, there were twenty-eight violations of the ceasefire, most of them initiated by the Communists. On February 24, B–52s and fighter-bombers returned to action over Laos for two days of bombing.[30] The bombing stopped again on February 26, after Hanoi halted the ground offensive and shifted its efforts to cramming as many troops and as much supplies as possible down the Ho Chi Minh Trail and into South Vietnam prior to the onset of the monsoonal rains in the spring. By mid-April they had moved an estimated 40,000 additional troops, 300 tanks, 150 heavy artillery pieces, 160 antiaircraft guns, and 300 trucks into South Vietnam.[31]

Henry Kissinger pushed for a renewed bombing of the Ho Chi Minh Trail. His efforts foundered when the Joint Chiefs of Staff insisted that any attack on targets in southeastern Laos would have to be coupled with bombing of adjacent areas in North and South Vietnam from which newly established SA–2 sites might menace B–52s flying over eastern Laos. Nixon did order the B–52s back into action April 16–17, but their targets were Pathet Lao and PAVN encampments in northern Laos around Ban Tha Vieng—a key town south of the Plain of Jars—and not the Ho Chi Minh Trail.[32] As it was, bombing northern Laos caused outcry enough from administration critics. Restarting the bombing of North or South Vietnam was politically infeasible, and Nixon demurred.

Although not of the proportions of the 1968 Tet Offensive or the spring offensive of 1972, April 1973 was another watershed in America's Vietnam experience. By not reacting forcefully to Hanoi's violations of the Paris Accords, Washington abdicated its role as guardian and guarantor of South Vietnam's independence. The deteriorating domestic political scene took away Nixon's ability to use bombing as an effective stick. Simultaneously, Congress withdrew the carrot by forbidding payment of some $3 billion in aid the administration had promised Hanoi so that it could rebuild its war-ravished economy and industries. Stories of torture related by returning American prisoners of war and Hanoi's disregard for the Paris Accords led Senator Harry Byrd to sponsor an amendment barring assistance to North Vietnam unless specifically authorized by Congress. It passed a vote of 83 to 3.[33]

Consequently, Nixon descending had neither the threat of bombing to compel—nor the promise of aid—to induce Hanoi into abiding by the accords. By April 1973 Hanoi, not Washington, had the initiative in Indochina and the fates of South Vietnam, Laos, and Cambodia were effectively sealed.

CAMBODIA II: THE OVERT BOMBING OF MAY 1970– AUGUST 1973—NIXON DESCENDING

While the North Vietnamese controlled events in Laos, and increasingly took charge of defining Saigon's future, their claim to have no influence over Cambodia's Khmer Rouge turned out to be true. From 1970 to 1972, the North Vietnamese army and the VC carried the brunt of the war against the Lon Nol government. Beginning in 1972, however, the Khmer Rouge took over the bulk of the fighting, and the conflict became much more of a civil war.[34]

Furthermore, the Khmer Rouge hated the Vietnamese Communists about as much as they hated any other Vietnamese, maybe more since matters of ideological interpretation were at stake. Reports of Khmer Rouge and Communist Vietnamese units clashing in the border regions increased in number. The ceasefires in South Vietnam and Laos did not lead to any decrease in the fighting in Cambodia. And when the bombs stopped falling elsewhere in Indochina, the air power of the United States focused all its efforts on Cambodia, and that country suffered accordingly. Despite the bombing in its behalf, the war was not going well for the Phnom Penh regime. The capital was, by early 1973, surrounded by the Khmer Rouge. The FANK had abandoned much of the countryside, holding onto only a few larger towns.[35] Air power probably saved the Lon Nol government in 1973, but by then the bombing was more the death rattle of a failed American policy than it was part of any coherent strategy to preserve the independence of Cambodia.

After the February 1973 ceasefire in Laos, fighter-bombers from Air Force units in Thailand began operating over Cambodia, many for the first time. Until then the 432d Tactical Reconnaisance Wing at Udorn had not sent planes as far south as Cambodia. However, between February 24 and August 15 (the latter the congressionally mandated halt to the bombing), the wing's F–4s and RF–4s flew 7,557 sorties over the Khmer Republic, a sortie rate approximated by other tactical wings based at Ubon and Korat.[36]

On February 25–26, 1973, sixty B–52s struck targets around the Chup rubber plantation in eastern Cambodia, marking the beginning of one of the more intense bombing campaigns in a war that had already produced record-setting bombing efforts. Air action over the Khmer Republic increased through mid-March, when Arc Light sorties averaged sixty per day. By April, B–52s were flying an average of eighty sorties a day.[37]

This bombing undoubtedly helped FANK units reopen major highways linking Phnom Penh to the provincial capital of Battambang in the north and the main port of Kompong Som in the south. B–52s and fighter-bombers also struck Khmer Rouge units entrenched along the Mekong River where they had been firing rockets and recoilless rifles at ships carrying supplies from Saigon to Phnom Penh.

Because there were no American advisers with the FANK, and because few Cambodians spoke English, close air support missions like those flown in South Vietnam, hardly ever occurred. Instead, the bombing focused on suspected troop concentrations and Khmer Rouge base camps identified by various American intelligence agencies. Furthermore, Cambodia presented unique problems for mission planners and targeteers.

Recall that the secret bombing missions conducted in Cambodia in 1969 and 1970 depended on Combat Skyspot radar stations located in South Vietnam. These stations were dismantled and the controllers withdrawn in early 1973. Combat Skyspot bombing had been an important technique because Cambodia's flat landscape rendered few distinct radar returns for the B–52 navigators to use as aiming points.

The U.S. Air Force devised two ways to remedy this situation. First, B–52s began using Loran bombing techniques previously employed by fighter-bombers, a form of bombing less accurate than that normally used by B–52s, but one not dependent on prominent radar returns. Second, radar beacons were placed in key towns and villages (for a while one was situated atop the U.S. embassy in Phnom Penh) for B–52 radar navigators to use in calculating their bomb release points.

The code names Pave Phantom and Pave Buff or "big ugly fat fellow" (informal term applied to B–52s), were given to the Loran missions over Cambodia. This kind of bombing involved a procedure that employed Loran systems in F–111s and F–4s, as well as those installed in a handful of B–52D models, to lead bombers and fighter-bombers not so equipped to their targets. In effect, the Pave Phantom (F–4s or F–111s) and Pave Buff (B–52D) aircraft were path-finders for other aircraft. Pave Buff operations were conducted primarily at night and continued with increasing frequency until the end of the campaign.[38]

The navigator-bombardier in the B–52 plotted the bomb release point off a radial from one of the beacons and fed that information into a computer which flew the plane to the appropriate place to drop its load. Otherwise, the computer, if tuned to a specific beacon, homed on it. As an unfortunate consequence of the "fog of war," on August 7, 1973, a navigator using the beacon placed in Neak Loung, a town on the Mekong River approximately fifty miles southeast of Phnom Penh, forgot to flip a switch that would have directed the computer to fly the bomber to the offset bombing point, and twenty tons of bombs fell on the town. More than 400 people were killed or wounded.[39] The "Neak Luong short round," as the incident was known within the Air Force, was a needless tragedy since only eight days of bombing remained before the congressionally mandated August 15 deadline ending all U.S. air operations in Indochina.

The mandated end of the bombing was the whimper with which America's longest war, and the most extravagant applications of aerial firepower in the history of warfare prior to Desert Storm, ended. The controversy generated by the bombing throughout Indochina contributed in no small measure to the ultimate fate of Cambodia, as well as the fates of Laos and South Vietnam. By the late spring of 1973, Congress only reflected the mood of the American people as it moved to halt further direct participation by American forces in Indochina. War weariness and pessimism concerning the way the war was fought and how the country was governed had taken a toll on the administration, inhibiting its ability to prevent Congress from ending the bombing. The compulsion to legislate the country out of the war manifested itself on May 10, 1973 when the House of Representatives voted 219 to 188 to block funds for a supplemental appropriations bill needed to fund the air war. President Nixon was so crippled by the revelations from the Watergate scandal that he could not muster the support needed to effect a compromise in the Senate that specified August 15 as a cutoff date. On June 29, 1973, the president signed the bill.[40]

IMPACT ON THE AIR FORCE

By 1973, many Americans were all too willing to view their soldiers, sailors, and airmen jaundicedly. Terms like "warmonger" and "baby-killer" were much in vogue. It seemed to many in uniform—this writer included—that the public failed to draw a distinction between a hated war and the warriors. Despite popular perceptions of a military marching in lockstep, the U.S. Air Force was never a monolith in support of the Vietnam War. Tensions tearing apart the larger society were also present in the Air Force.

By 1973, many people in uniform shared the same frustrations and disdain for the Vietnam War as the public at large. To be sure, Linebacker II—the "eleven-day war"—fostered a kind of high within the force. It was welcomed by many who were excited at being "turned loose" to "go downtown" to Hanoi and Haiphong "to end this thing." If going downtown (USAF slang for bombing of Hanoi/Haiphong) in a B–52 was dangerous, it was also purposeful. By comparison, paddy bashing in Cambodia seemed as pointless as jungle bashing in Vietnam and Laos had seemed a year or two before, especially to the B–52 crews who had so recently made the trip downtown.

According to an official SAC history, Col. James R. McCarthy, commander of the 43rd Strategic Wing, spent half his time meeting with different groups of aircrew members in efforts to address morale problems. He attended crew briefings and met both formally and informally with delegations of pilots, navigators, and gunners to discuss their concerns. He invited individual crew members to dine with him at virtually every meal to talk over factors affecting morale. McCarthy attended social functions—picnics and barbeques—to mingle with the troops. He also ordered a formal study of their grievances.

The study concluded that the B–52 crews, first and foremost, were tired of their indefinite status as members of a temporary but opened-ended redeployment of forces to Guam and Southeast Asia initiated by the Air Force in December 1971 and named Operation Bullet Shot. Now that the Paris Accords had been signed and America's war clearly was at an end, they wanted to know how long they would be remaining on Guam and if they might be forced into another temporary duty (TDY) assignment to U-Tapao RTAFB after other USAF units assigned to Thailand were withdrawn.

Because Bullet Shot deployments came up quickly, personal and family matters were left unsettled. Another irritant was the TDY assignments to Southeast Asia did not count as a remote or short tour, meaning that the personnel center in San Antonio, Texas, might send them back to Guam or to U-Tapao, to some other Thai base, or to a remote spot elsewhere in the world, for one of those one-year, unaccompanied tours. Furthermore, they were dissatisfied with the mission and the rigors of flying long hours across the Pacific to drop bombs on rice paddies or into "underwater storage areas" in the Tonle Sap (a large lake in Cambodia), targets hardly resembling anyone's concept of a vital center. The fact the U.S. Congress had already mandated an end to the bombing on August 15 did little to convince them that their mission had such relevance.

Then there were career considerations. SAC officers fretted that Arc Light TDYs hindered rather than aided their chances for promotion. Traditionally, SAC pilots—even navigators—enjoyed better promotion rates than their counterparts in the Tactical Air Command (TAC) or Military Airlift Command (MAC), but that was changing. Officers on a six-month TDY received a letter of evaluation (LOE) rather than an officer effectiveness report (OER) for their promotion folders. The LOEs seemingly did not carry the same weight with promotion boards as OERs, especially since they normally were not written nor endorsed by higher-ranking officers. Since the mid–1960s promotion rates for fighter pilots had gone ahead of those for bomber crews. Finally, airmen assigned to B–52D and G models were dispatched for Bullet Shot deployments, whereas those assigned to the B–52H, a model designated only for the nuclear mission, were not. Some believed that B–52H crew members, despite the fact that they spent long hours on nuclear alert, had an unfair advantage by being retained stateside where they could arrange future assignments more easily.[41]

Many of the same tensions that exacerbated the generation gap in the general population were present in the military. Throughout the Air Force, junior officers—men and women who had been in college in the mid–1960s—were far more likely to be morally opposed to the Vietnam War than were the more senior officers.

But it was not only the relatively junior officers, including those flying missions in Southeast Asia, who were concerned about bombing Cambodia. Colonels and generals at SAC Headquarters were worried as well, though their concerns were institutionally, and not necessarily morally, oriented. Those senior officers responsible for personnel matters were alarmed at the number of pilots leaving the Air Force for the airlines after their service commitments were completed. Officers who worked on the Single Integrated Operational Plan (SIOP)—the nuclear war plan—worried about accomplishing the nuclear mission with half the B–52 force deployed to Guam and Thailand. Maintenance specialists fretted about the wear and tear on the already aging B–52s caused by years of hauling large loads of 500-pound and 750-pound bombs on jungle and paddy-bashing missions.

A decade earlier, Secretary of Defense Robert McNamara had cancelled development and deployment of the XB–70. The projected follow-on for the B–52, the B–1A, was still in the early stages of development, and its future was far from certain. These officers worried that SAC would have to depend on an ever-aging fleet of B–52s well into the 1980s.

Additionally, those senior officers with an eye on doctrine and the future of the manned bomber (ergo, the future of SAC) were concerned about the ramifications and implications that might arise should the Khmer Rouge take Phnom Penh—in effect, win the war—while B–52s were bombing Cambodia. The future of the manned bomber, which seemed to be constantly under scrutiny in some quarters of Congress, might be less secure if critics asked what good such expensive and sophisticated airplanes were if they could not deny victory to a Third World guerrilla army. Most of these concerns dissipated after August 15, when a collective sigh of relief rose from SAC headquarters because Phnom Penh had held out for the duration of the aerial campaign. To be sure, aircrew morale improved when bomber crews began returning to their stateside bases.

Although Cambodia received less bomb tonnage than any of the other Indochinese states—some 539,129 tons between 1969 and 1973—it was still one of the most intensely bombed countries in the history of aerial warfare. One only has to consider that nearly half those bombs, some 257,465 tons, fell between February 24 and August 14, 1973. Even though much of this energy was wasted in paddy bashing or in bombing fictitious underwater storage areas in the Tonle Sap, it was still an imposing figure—the significance of which was magnified because it was divorced from a coherent strategy devised to secure the long-range security of Cambodia.[42]

AND THEN THE BOMBING STOPPED

Less than two years after the bombing of Cambodia came to an end, in April 1975, twenty PAVN divisions invaded and conquered South Vietnam. As the attack developed, columns of tanks and trucks were strung out along Route 1 and other major highways and roads leading to Saigon. A nearly perfect situation existed for the effective use of air power. Undoubtedly, Air Force and Navy fighter-bombers, along with those B–52s normally stationed on Guam, could have decimated those forces. The Republic of Vietnam might have survived, at least for a while longer.

However, President Gerald R. Ford did not order American planes back into action, except to cover the final withdrawal from Saigon. He understood that to have done so would have been political suicide. The fact that the United States had already dropped 8 million tons of bombs on Indochina had a great deal to do with Washington's seeming impotence in 1975. In the end, too many Americans believed too many bombs had already fallen, and Washington could do little to keep Saigon from becoming Ho Chi Minh City.

NOTES

1. Rolling Thunder was an unmitigated failure. Linebacker I was probably the most successful bombing campaign of the Vietnam War. Linebacker II, largely overrated by air power enthusiasts, especially within the U.S. Air Force, provided for the return of American prisoners of war and allowed for the withdrawal of U.S. military forces from South Vietnam.

2. Mark Clodfelter, *The Limits of Air Power: The American Bombing of North Vietnam* (New York: Free Press, 1989) is the best book on the bombing of North Vietnam. John Schlight, *The United States Air Force in Southeast Asia: The Years of the Offensive, 1965–1968* (Washington, DC: Office of Air Force History, 1989) is a comprehensive view of the air war over South Vietnam. Books on the air war in Laos and Cambodia tend to be specialized. Among these, Christopher Robbins, *Air America: The Story of The C.I.A.'s Secret Airlines* (New York: Putnam, 1979), and idem, *The Ravens* (New York: Crown, 1987), and John Clark Pratt, *Laotian Fragments: The Chief Raven's Story* (New York: Viking, 1974) are the best. For Cambodia, one is confined to a cautious reading of William Shawcross, *Sideshow: Kissinger, Nixon and the Destruction of Cambodia* (New York: Simon & Schuster, 1979) [hereafter *Sideshow*]. When reading Shawcross, try to keep in mind that the Khmer Rouge, Viet Cong, and North Vietnamese had at least as much to do with the demise of Cambodia as Richard Nixon and Henry Kissinger. Also useful is *Hearings Before the Committee on the Armed Services*, 93rd Congress, July 19–August 9, 1973.

3. Secretary of the Air Force Robert C. Seamans, Jr., Address to the 1969 Air Force Association Convention, March 19, 1969, Houston, Texas, "Continuing Cooperation Between NASA and DOD," *Air Force Magazine* (May 1969): 100.

4. The word "interdict" has Latin and Roman Catholic Church origins. In Roman law, an *interdict* was a prohibitory edict issued by a *praetor* forbidding or commanding an act. In the Catholic Church, to "interdict" was to punish the unfaithful by forbidding participation in the sacraments (*Random House Collegiate Dictionary*). The current issue of *Air Force Manual 1–1*, the Air Force's officially sanctioned body of beliefs and war-fighting principles, is more descriptive than definitive. It does, however, state that "air interdiction objectives are to delay, disrupt, divert, or destroy an enemy's military potential before it can be brought to bear effectively against enemy forces." *AFM 1–1, Basic Aerospace Doctrine of the United States Air Force* (March 16, 1984): 3–2.

5. *AFM 1–1, United States Air Force Basic Doctrine* (August 14, 1964): 5–2.

6. See Raphael Littauer and Norman Uphoff, eds., *The Air War in Indochina*, rev. ed., Air War Study Group, Cornell University (Boston: Beacon Press, 1971), 70–73

[hereafter *Air War in Indochina*]; Jack S. Ballard, *The United States Air Force in Southeast Asia: Development and Employment of Fixed-Wing Gunships, 1962–1972* (Washington, DC: Office of Air Force History, 1982), 45, 262 [hereafter *Fixed-Wing Gunships*].

7. See Edward Doyle, Samuel Lipsman, and Terrence Maitland, *The North* volume in Robert Manning, ed., *The Vietnam Experience* (Boston: Boston Publishing Co., 1986), 46; "Ho Chi Minh's Trail Revisited: Vietnam's Death March," *Washington Post* (April 26, 1990): 33.

8. *USAF Operations in Laos: 1 January 1970–30 June 1971* (Honolulu: HQ Pacific Air Forces, Corona Harvest Report, May 31, 1972): 27, in the U.S. Air Force (USAF) Historical Research Agency (HRA), Maxwell AFB, AL, File K717.0432–6 [hereafter *USAF Ops. in Laos*].

9. See John L. Frisbee, "Igloo White," *Air Force Magazine* (June 1971): 48–53; James William Gibson, *The Perfect War: Technowar in Vietnam* (Boston: Atlantic Monthly Press, 1986), 396–97.

10. See *USAF Ops. in Laos*, 76–79; Ballard, *Fixed-Wing Gunships*, 173. At the root of the problem was the faulty criteria for determining if a truck had, indeed, been destroyed or damaged. If a truck was peppered by 7.62mm minigun or 20mm gatling gun rounds, it was counted as damaged. However, if there was a secondary explosion caused by an ignited gas tank or ammunition in the cargo, the truck would be listed as destroyed. A direct hit by a 40mm Bofors gun or the 105mm howitzers placed on a limited number of Page Aegis AC–130s resulted in an automatic "truck destroyed" credited to the particular gunship. In 1971, tests conducted on a range at Bien Hoa AB, South Vietnam, indicated that trucks hit with 7.62mm and 20mm fire suffered only superficial damage. Even 40mm rounds, unless they hit the engine or gas tank, were not devastating, and while a direct hit by a 105mm howitzer round obliterated the truck, near misses at more than 5 meters quite often resulted in little or no substantive damage.

11. Henry A. Kissinger, *The White House Years* (Boston: Little, Brown, 1979), 241 [hereafter *White House Years*].

12. Ibid., 240.

13. See Gen. John Ryan, USAF Chief of Staff to Hon. John C. Stennis, Chairman, Senate Committee on the Armed Services, July 26, 1973, in *Hearings Before the Committee on Armed Services*, 93rd Congress, 1st Session, 121–22 [hereafter *Hearings on Bombing Cambodia*]; Kissinger, *White House Years*, 247.

14. Letter, Hal Knight to Senator William Proxmire, January 18, 1973, in *Hearings on Bombing in Cambodia*, 5.

15. John Morrocco, *Rain of Fire: Air War, 1969–1973* volume in Robert Manning, ed., *The Vietnam Experience* (Boston: Boston Publishing Co., 1986), 12.

16. Kissinger, *White House Years*, 240.

17. Shawcross, *Sideshow*, 64; Littauer and Uphoff, *Air War in Indochina*, 88.

18. Col. Stanley M. Umstead, Jr., commander, 388TFW, End-of-Tour Report, April 1971–August 1972, 6, in USAF HRA, File K717.131 [hereafter Umstead, EOTR].

19. Col. Lyle E. Mann, commander 432TFW, End-of-Tour Report, November 7, 1970–November 6, 1971, 15, in USAF HRA, File K717.131.

20. Umstead, EOTR, 6.

21. Maj. Edward W. Parker, Jr., director of base medical services, Korat RTAFB, End-of-Tour Report, July 1, 1971–July 1, 1972, 2, in USAF HRA, File K717.131.

22. Col. Theodore M. Katz, commander, 432CSG, Udorn RTAFB, End-of-Tour Report, April 28, 1970–May 2, 1971, 1–3, in USAF HRA, File K717.131.

23. Maj. Gen. Alton D. Slay, DCS, OPs, 7th AF, End-of-Tour Report, August 1971–August 1972, 20, in USAF HRA, File K717.131 [hereafter Slay, EOTR].

24. Ballard, *Fixed-Wing Gunships*, 111; "USAF Operations in Laos," 22–25.

25. *History, Air Force Intelligence Service: Fiscal Year 1973*, AFIN Linebacker II Summary file, vol. 3, Sup. Docs., 6, in USAF HRA, File K142.01.

26. Slay, EOTR, 20–30.

27. Henry Kissinger, *Years of Upheaval* (Boston: Little, Brown, 1982), 303 [hereafter *Upheaval*].

28. *History, 43d Strategic Wing (SW), 1 January–30 June 1973*, vol. 1, 65–67, in USAF HRA, File K-WG–43-HI [hereafter *His., 43SW*].

29. Arthur J. Dommen, *Laos: Keystone of Indochina* (Boulder, CO: Westview, 1985), 97.

30. See Kissinger, *Upheaval*, 316; *His., 43SW*, 67.

31. "A Trail Becomes a Turnpike," *Time* (March 26, 1973): 34.

32. Carl Berger, ed., *The United States Air Force in Southeast Asia, 1961–1973: An Illustrated Account* (Washington, DC: Office of Air Force History, 1984), 135 [hereafter *USAF in SEA*].

33. "The Secret Agony of the POWs," *Newsweek* April 19, 1973: 30.

34. Elizabeth Becker, *When the War Was Over: The Voices of Cambodia's Revolution and Its People* (New York: Simon & Schuster, 1986), 138–52.

35. Ibid., 59; *His., 43SW*, 38–39.

36. Col. Robert William Clements, commander, 432TRW, End-of-Tour Report, March 15, 1974, 2, USAF HRA, File K717.131 [hereafter Clements, EOTR].

37. *His., 43SW*, 70–71.

38. Ibid., 59; Clements, EOTR, 2.

39. See, Shawcross, *Sideshow*, 282–83; Berger, *USAF in SEA*, 147.

40. Kissinger, *Upheaval*, 359.

41. *His., 43SW*, 38–39.

42. As an intelligence officer at HQ SAC in 1973, the author briefed "underwater storage areas" in Cambodia as Arc Light targets. In discussing what was always a suspect target with Maj. William A. Buckingham, Jr., a colleague at the Office of Air Force History in 1979, Major Buckingham related a story told to him by a former targeteer in the U.S. Embassy in Phnom Penh. According to the targeteer, when SAC reached a sortie rate of 60 per day, there were not enough targets in Cambodia to justify that level of bombing. After several incidents when bombs fell on civilians rather than on legitimate military targets, the targeteer tried persuading SAC to reduce its allocated sorties. Neither 8th Air Force at Andersen AFB, Guam, nor HQ SAC would consider reducing the sortie rate, so the targeteer began submitting fictitious underwater storage areas as targets. In an interview on May 1, 1980, this author and Major Buckingham asked former U.S. Ambassador to Cambodia, Colby Swank if there was any truth to this allegation and our suspicions. Although Swank did not confirm the targeteer's remarks, he said these allegations had "an element of truth to them in that [General] John Vogt [7th Air Force commander] had these sorties to be used."

7

Of Demons, Storms, and Thunder: A Preliminary Look at Vietnam's Impact on the Persian Gulf Air Campaign

Mark Clodfelter

At a Pentagon briefing on March 15, 1991, U.S. Air Force Chief of Staff General Merrill A. McPeak summed up his service role in the recently concluded Persian Gulf war: "This is the first time in history that a field army has been defeated by air power."[1] General McPeak could indeed take a large measure of satisfaction from the Air Force's performance in the war. In less than forty days, a devastating display of aerial might had mauled Saddam Hussein's military machine, enabling a "hundred-hour blitzkrieg" to oust Iraqi forces from Kuwait.

President George Bush proclaimed that the totality of the triumph erased the stigma of an American defeat sixteen years earlier in the jungles of Southeast Asia. After announcing a ceasefire, he declared, "By God, we've kicked the Vietnam syndrome once and for all."[2] Bush had emphatically insisted that a war in the Persian Gulf would not be another Vietnam, and the specter of that debacle guided American military leaders—air commanders in particular—as they girded themselves for combat in the Middle East.

The Southeast Asian backdrop profoundly affected both the planning for and the conduct of the air campaign against Iraq. Yet to say that Operation Desert Storm's remarkably decisive air war exorcised the demons that had plagued the bombing campaigns against North Vietnam would be premature. Although the efforts to apply the perceived lessons of Vietnam contributed greatly to air power's success against Iraq, the unique circumstances of the Persian Gulf war were equally significant in making air power a decisive weapon. Moreover, an analysis of Vietnam's impact on the Desert Storm air war reveals that a few ghosts from Southeast Asia continue to haunt—and leaves the suspicion that in dispatching demons from Vietnam, the U.S. Air Force may have generated a phantom from the desert.

Against the North Vietnamese, the Air Force paid a steep price to accomplish meager results against a highly resourceful enemy. From 1964 to 1973, the service lost 617 fixed-wing aircraft over North Vietnam.[3] The United States also suffered economic costs from bombing that far exceeded those inflicted on the enemy. In early 1967, the Central Intelligence Agency estimated that rendering $1.00 worth of bomb damage on the North Vietnam cost American taxpayers $9.60.[4] North Vietnam's gross national product actually *increased* during the bombing, as Ho Chi Minh skillfully played off the Chinese against the Soviet Union to secure a vast amount of military and economic support from each.[5]

Few American civilian or military leaders had envisaged such dismal results when planning the air campaign eventually labeled Operation Rolling Thunder. President Lyndon Johnson's characterization of North Vietnam as a "raggedy ass little fourth rate country" typified the substance if not the style of most American views of the enemy.[6] Dean Rusk, Johnson's secretary of state, remembered, "I thought the North Vietnamese would reach a point, like the Chinese and North Koreans in Korea, and Stalin during the Berlin airlift, when they would finally give in."[7] Admiral U.S. Grant Sharp, commander of Pacific Command and the individual charged with the operational conduct of Rolling Thunder, initially shared Rusk's faith that limited air attacks would pay dividends. In early April 1965, one month after the sustained bombing of North Vietnam began, he notified the Joint Chiefs that "the damage inflicted by these attacks on LOCs [lines of communication] and military installations in North Vietnam will cause a diminution of the support being rendered to the Viet Cong. . . . Manpower and supplies will undoubtedly have to be diverted toward recovery and rebuilding processes."[8]

Convinced that the Viet Cong insurgency in South Vietnam could not continue without large doses of support from the North and that the threat of aerial destruction would persuade Ho Chi Minh to abandon that assistance, American civilian and military chiefs embarked upon this country's longest bombing campaign. They subconsciously assigned their enemy Western values and translated guerrilla war into a conventional conflict that they could better understand, only to discover that a preponderance of firepower could not overcome firmly entrenched tenacity. Not until the spring of 1972 did air power have a telling impact on the course of the war, and that impact was largely fortuitous. Hanoi's decision to mount a large-scale conventional invasion of the South, President Richard Nixon's detente with the Soviet Union and China, and Nixon's willingness to exit South Vietnam without a total victory for the South Vietnamese all combined to create conditions that favored bombing for limited ends.

The stark differences between the nature of the war during Johnson's Rolling Thunder (1965–1968) and during Nixon's 1972 Linebacker air offensives have gone unnoticed by many of the war's air commanders, who contend that a Linebacker-like assault against North Vietnam in early 1965 would have achieved victory in short order.[9] This assertion, however, ignores that Nixon's notion of "victory" differed from that of his predecessor. Johnson sought an independent, stable, non-Communist South Vietnam, capable of standing alone against future aggression. He also wanted to achieve that aim without undue cost to the United States. In particular, he did not want to run the risk of war with China or the

Soviet Union over Vietnam, nor would he permit Vietnam to eclipse his Great Society programs. Thus, the rapid aerial destruction of North Vietnam's war-making capability, which air commanders estimated they could achieve in sixteen days, was not a viable option.[10]

Moreover, destroying North Vietnam's capacity to fight was no guarantee that the insurgency in South Vietnam would stop. During the entire Johnson presidency, the vast bulk of the Communist army in South Vietnam consisted of Viet Cong who fought, along with their North Vietnamese allies, an average of one day a month.[11]

This infrequent combat produced a requirement for such a small amount of external supplies that *no* amount of bombing with conventional ordnance could have prevented their arrival. Nor did the Viet Cong need—or want—a large amount of North Vietnamese direction. As Larry Cable has convincingly shown in *Unholy Grail*, the Viet Cong sought to *minimize* northern influence in the National Liberation Front throughout the war.[12] In short, eliminating North Vietnam from the war in 1965 would likely have accomplished little toward achieving a stable, independent South. By the time that removing the North *would* have made a difference—after the 1968 Tet Offensive—the American public had lost its stomach for the war and the goal had changed to ''peace with honor.''

Such disparity between political goals and military objectives did not exist in the Persian Gulf, and the clear-cut nature of our announced aims heightened the possibility that air power could be a decisive instrument in a war against Iraq. In his January 16, 1991, announcement of hostilities, President Bush reaffirmed that the Iraqis must immediately and unconditionally withdraw from Kuwait, allowing the emir's government to return; they must fully accept the United Nations resolutions and they must release all prisoners of war, third-country nationals, and the remains of those who died in Iraqi hands.[13]

Bush also stated that American bombs were not aimed at Iraqi civilians, whom he urged to overthrow Saddam Hussein, although the president later acknowledged that Saddam himself was not a specific target.[14]

With very few exceptions, President Bush and Secretary of Defense Dick Cheney left the choice of targets to the military[15]—a notable difference from the ''Tuesday lunch approach'' of target selection employed by President Johnson during the Vietnam War. The unprecedented United Nations mandate permitted Bush to apply air power with minimal restraints; he did not have to worry about Soviet or Chinese intervention as had Johnson. Yet, like Nixon, Bush had to consider the potentially fragile nature of support from the American public, especially given the instantaneous reporting capability of television news agencies. The trauma of Vietnam suggested to him and his advisers that the American home front would not tolerate a conflict that was lengthy, bloody, or less than decisive.

Once the war started, an additional motive argued strongly for swiftly applying massive doses of American military power—Saddam Hussein's attack on Israel with Scud missiles. To avoid an expanded conflict that threatened the fabric of the coalition, Bush had to persuade the Israelis that he could eliminate the Iraqi menace to the Jewish state. An intensive air offensive offered him the means to do so. On the other hand, an air campaign devoting significant attention to Scud sites reduced the number of aircraft available to attack Iraq's key strategic targets, increasing the time needed to destroy them.[16]

Throughout the planning for the Desert Storm air campaign, American military and civilian leaders alike were conscious of Vietnam ghosts lurking in the background. "I measure everything in my life from Vietnam," observed Gen. H. Norman Schwarzkopf, the commander in chief of Central Command, who served two tours of duty in Southeast Asia.[17] President Bush noted in his war message on January 16, 1991: "I've told the American people before that this will not be another Vietnam and I repeat this here tonight. Our troops will have the best possible support in the entire world, and they will not be asked to fight with one hand tied behind their back."[18] Air Force Lt. Gen. Charles A. Horner, Desert Storm's air component commander, received full authority to direct virtually all air elements—Air Force, Army, Navy, Marine, and allied—as he saw fit.

No analogous position had existed in Vietnam. There, the individual services waged autonomous air wars over the South, rarely coordinating with the South Vietnamese air force. Over the North, the inability to gauge the precise effects of bombing on the enemy war effort yielded another method of measuring results—the sortie count. Competition developed between the U.S. Air Force and U.S. Navy for the highest daily sortie total, leading to missions with reduced ordnance to raise the count.[19] Both Horner and his chief air planner, Brig. Gen. Buster C. Glosson, had fought in Southeast Asia, and the experience colored their judgments regarding Desert Storm. "Chuck [Horner] and I remember flying in Vietnam with less than a full load of weapons," Glosson recounted. "You can bet we were not going to let *that* happen again."[20]

In trying to avoid the perceived mistakes of Vietnam, air commanders sought to destroy Iraq's war-fighting capability and its will to fight. Those two objectives had been goals of Rolling Thunder, as well as of American air campaigns in World War II and Korea. Air chiefs had believed that by attacking vital economic centers they could destroy an enemy's war-making capacity, which would in turn produce the loss of social cohesion and the will to resist. The logic proved flawed for Rolling Thunder. The multitude of political, military, and operational restrictions on bombing, multiplied by the guerrilla nature of the ground war in the South, emasculated the air campaign, enabling North Vietnamese leaders to use it to create popular support for the war at a minimum cost. During Linebackers I and II, the logic proved more suitable to the unique conditions that then existed. The relaxation of political controls, resulting from Nixon's detente; the development of precision-guided munitions; and the conventional nature of the 1972 North Vietnamese offensive, which required massive logistical backing and was exceedingly vulnerable to air power, all helped to make Nixon's bombing more effective than Johnson's.

Neither Rolling Thunder nor the two Linebacker operations aimed to kill enemy civilians, but air commanders did target civilian *morale* after attacks directed exclusively against the North's war-making capability failed to produce decisive results. This action meshed well with the conduct of past American air campaigns; air leaders in World War II and Korea had also resorted to attacks against civilian will after discovering that bombing aimed specifically at war-making capability did not yield quick victory.[21] During Rolling Thunder, attacks against morale occurred in early 1967 in concert with raids on North Vietnamese electric power facilities and industry, and the entire Linebacker II campaign targeted Northern resolve.[22] In both cases, air commanders bombed military facilities close to population centers (not the civilian populace) or structures such as electric power plants that were deemed essential to both the Communist war effort and the normal functioning of North Vietnamese society.

Against Iraq, airmen broke with tradition and designed an air offensive that targeted war-making capacity and enemy morale from the start. The rationale for the approach rested on two key considerations affected by the Vietnam experience: the perception of the enemy's "center of gravity" and the techno-logical prowess of American air power.

In his nineteenth-century magnum opus *On War*, the Prussian military theorist Carl von Clausewitz defined "center of gravity" as "the hub of all power and movement, on which everything depends . . . the point against which all our energies should be directed."[23] U.S. Air Force Col. John Warden focused on this concept in his own book, *The Air Campaign: Planning for Combat*, arguing that the center-of-gravity notion should guide target selection in offensive air operations.[24] A Pentagon staff officer and fighter pilot, Warden had flown 211 missions as a forward air controller in Vietnam, and his views significantly influenced the concept of air operations used in Desert Storm.[25]

Colonel Warden contended that an enemy nation's center of gravity con-sisted of five concentric, strategic rings. The center ring, the essence of an enemy's war effort, was its leadership. Surrounding this core was a second ring containing key production facilities such as oil and electricity. Next came a third ring of infrastructure consisting primarily of the means of trans-portation and communication. The civilian populace made up the fourth ring. While noting that air power should not be used to target an enemy population directly, Colonel Warden also maintained, "It's important that people [in the enemy nation] understand that a war is going on, and they put some pressure on their leadership to stop the war."[26] Surrounding the band of population was a fifth ring of fielded military forces. Warden insisted that fielded forces should not be the initial focal point of an air campaign, because those forces served only to shield the crux of an enemy's war effort, the internal rings, which contained the vital targets.[27]

In Rolling Thunder, air commanders had concentrated on severing North Vietnamese direction and support of the Viet Cong insurgency by attacking targets in the second, third, and ultimately fourth rings. The effort failed because of the nature of the war; North Vietnamese support and direction were not essential to the Viet Cong's war-making capacity. Colonel Warden observed, "Air [power] is of marginal value in a fight against self-sustaining guerrillas who merge with the population."[28] During the Linebacker campaigns, however, attacks against essentially the same targets as in Rolling Thunder paid dividends. The 1968 Tet Offensive had decimated the Viet Cong, and Hanoi's 1972 Easter invasion consisted of twelve North Vietnamese Army divisions backed by large numbers of tanks and heavy artillery. Linebacker, along with the aerial mining of Northern ports and massive doses of close air support in South Vietnam, wrecked Hanoi's capacity to wage offensive warfare and contributed to the willingness of North Vietnamese leaders to negotiate a peace ending American involvement in the war.

Air planners noted the similarity between Iraq's predicament following the invasion of Kuwait and North Vietnam's after the Easter offensive. Both nations possessed armies waging conventional war and sporting large amounts of Soviet equipment that needed heavy logistical support. Blockades limited the amount of imports available to the two countries. Yet planners noted that Iraq was even more vulnerable than North Vietnam to an aerial assault against the first, second, third, and fourth rings of Warden's model. Whereas a six-man Politburo led North Vietnam in 1972, Saddam Hussein was a monolithic force in Iraq whose approval was required in tactical as well as strategic decision making. The bulk of the North Vietnamese populace lived as rice farmers in the Red River Delta, whereas 70 percent of the Iraqi population lived in cities.[29] Iraq was also relatively industrialized, containing numerous modern oil refineries and the associated benefits of an oil glut, such as sophisticated transportation and communication facilities.[30] North Vietnam had to import all of its petroleum needs, boasted a single steel mill and one cement factory, and had only one railroad that ran the length of the country.

The North Vietnamese, however, possessed a key advantage that Iraq lacked— a unified populace. The fractured ethnic and religious backgrounds of the Iraqi people made Saddam Hussein more dependent than ever on the means of communication to exercise control, and ties to the army and his secret police were the primary methods of exercising that authority. Iraq's transportation and communication facilities were also more vulnerable than those of North Vietnam, which the Linebacker offensives had wrecked. By 1972, the North Vietnamese had constructed an oil pipeline through Cambodia and Laos to South Vietnam,[31] and the dense, triple-canopy foliage obscured the redundant multitude of roadways and paths merging to form the Ho Chi Minh Trail. The barren environment of the Iraqi desert stood in stark contrast to the Southeast Asian jungles. The vital road and rail links to Iraqi troops in Kuwait could not be concealed, nor could vehicles traveling on them be hidden.

The combination of these factors—an urban populace accustomed to many of the conveniences of twentieth-century industrialization and splintered in its support for the government, a dictator who depended on ties to his army and his police force to stay in power, an army that waged conventional war, and an almost complete isolation by the international community—made Iraq an ideal target for a strategic air campaign that simultaneously attacked war-making capacity and the will to resist.

An essential facet of General Horner's ability to attack Iraq's capability and will with devastating effect was another legacy of Vietnam—the widespread use of precision-guided munitions. The United States had first employed "smart" bombs in Southeast Asia in late 1967, but it was during Linebacker I that the ordnance achieved significant results. On May 10, 1972, thirty-two Air Force F–4 Phantoms dropped twenty-nine electro-optically and laser-guided bombs on Hanoi's key span across the Red River, the Paul Doumer Bridge.[32] The bridge collapsed the next day. On May 12, Phantoms from the U.S. Air Force's 8th Tactical Fighter Wing used smart bombs to wreck the defiant symbol of North Vietnam that had remained standing throughout the three and one-half years of Rolling Thunder—the infamous "Dragon's Jaw" bridge at Thanh Hoa.

After the Vietnam War, the accuracy of precision-guided munitions improved dramatically. Modern laser, electro-optical, and infrared targeting systems used against Iraq enabled U.S. Air Force pilots to bomb within one to two feet of a target even at night.[33] The combination of precision-guided munitions with another technological wonder—the F–117A stealth fighter—made the dream of an invulnerable precision bombing capability a reality. "Desert Storm was . . . a vindication of the old concept of precision bombing," commented former U.S. Air Force Chief of Staff Gen. Michael Dugan. "The technology finally caught up with the doctrine."[34] F–117As destroyed an estimated 95 percent of all key targets in Baghdad, and on one occasion a fighter guided a bomb through an air shaft in the roof of the Iraqi air defense headquarters.[35] The ability to achieve such amazing accuracy from unseen locations against military targets in densely populated areas permitted American air commanders to attack the will of a populace in a manner previously thought impossible. General Horner stated that he scheduled the middle-of-the-night raids against targets in Baghdad to remind Iraqis that a war was being fought and that Saddam was incapable of containing it, as well as to destroy the command and control network of the Iraqi military.[36] Given that Iraq was already vulnerable to air power, the merger of stealth and precision-guided munitions had a devastating impact on the Iraqi war effort. A captured senior Iraqi officer termed the air campaign shocking and listed its precision as a key reason for its impact. Many of his comrades shared his conviction.[37]

To guarantee that the air power had a maximum effect on the Iraqis, American military leaders, including General Schwarzkopf and the chairman of the Joint Chiefs of Staff, U.S. Army General Colin L. Powell, called for a massive, nonstop air campaign. Air planners initially dubbed the air offensive "Instant Thunder"—a conscious effort to eliminate any vestige of the gradual approach to bombing that had plagued Lyndon Johnson's air war against North Vietnam. General Horner also designed the air campaign to give the Iraqis no time to catch their breath. Rolling Thunder's bombing pauses had provided the North Vietnamese the chance to repair damage and move supplies in safety and American commanders during Desert Storm intended to deny Iraq the same opportunity. "The air part of the campaign will last until the whole campaign is over," General Powell declared during the war's first week.[38]

American military leaders were further determined not to underestimate Saddam Hussein's military machine. In contrast to the disdainful American attitude toward Ho Chin Minh's army following its victory over the French in the First Indochina War, Schwarzkopf and his lieutenants entered the Persian Gulf gravely concerned about Iraq's combat capability. With a population one-third the size of Iran's, Iraq had fought off repeated Iranian advances in the bitter 1980–1988 war and ultimately prevailed. In that conflict, Saddam Hussein used chemical weapons against Iranian troops and Iraq's Kurdish minority. After achieving complete air superiority, his air force provided over 200 close air support sorties a day in late 1982 and early 1983, when Iranian ground assaults threatened to score a major breakthrough, and then turned to attacking Iranian cities.[39] By the war's conclusion, Saddam possessed a million-man army backed by more than 5,500 tanks and an air force of more than 500 aircraft.[40] Moreover, in 1990 Iraq reportedly owned the largest supply of chemical weapons in the Third World, had developed the means to produce them, and had improved its ballistic missile force through modifications to its Soviet Scuds.[41]

To wreck Saddam's war-making capability, Horner attacked Iraq's vital components in methodical fashion. Memories of Southeast Asia produced the nuts and bolts of the Desert Storm air campaign—the air tasking order (ATO). Horner designated targets for all coalition air forces, as well as for the Navy's Tomahawk missiles, on a single air tasking order that often ran 700 pages a day and listed the sorties scheduled during a twenty-four-hour span.[42] Lt. Gen. Jimmie V. Adams, then U.S. Air Force deputy chief of staff for plans and operations observed: "We've got nine services singing off the same sheet of music—we didn't do that in Vietnam. There's one ATO for everyone who flies over Saudi Arabia."[43]

The air campaign itself was a multiphased effort. The first phase, scheduled to last seven to ten days, targeted Iraq's command and control facilities; airfields; Scud missile sites; nuclear, chemical, and biological warfare plants; and other war-making industries. Many of those targets were located in Iraqi cities, which guaranteed that the populace could not ignore the air campaign while precision-guided munitions kept civilian losses to a minimum. Phase 2 consisted of destroying enemy air defenses to permit allied air forces to fly unhindered over Kuwait. Phase 3 targeted supply lines, Iraqi troops in Kuwait, and the Republican Guard. Originally projected to occur in successive increments totaling about thirty days,[44] the three phases actually transpired simultaneously because of the abundance of coalition aircraft available. Phase 4, the final phase, focused on providing allied troops with air support once the ground offensive began. By that time, however, air power had substantially wrecked both Iraqi capability and will to resist. Saddam's command and control facilities were in shambles, and he could not resupply his battered army, whose units in Kuwait and along its border had suffered 50 percent attrition.[45] The Iraqi army had become an eggshell that cracked after it was tapped by advancing allied ground forces. David Hackworth, a Vietnam infantryman turned journalist, accompanied American troops into Kuwait and concluded, "Air power did a most impressive job and virtually won this war by itself."[46]

While the Vietnam legacy contributed enormously to air power's success in Desert Storm, one demon from Southeast Asia threatened to cast its evil eye on the air campaign. That ogre was the same Air Force mind-set that had been present on the eve of Rolling Thunder—a war-fighting doctrine geared to the policy of containment and stressing potential combat with the Soviet Union. Before the active involvement of the United States in Vietnam, this focus had led to the conviction that adequate preparation for general war with the Soviets would suffice to win any limited war. The 1959 edition of the U.S. Air Force's basic doctrinal manual, which guided the service through the initial stages of planning for Rolling Thunder, stated: "The best preparation for limited war is proper preparation for general war. The latter is the more important since there can be no guarantee that a limited war would not spread into general conflict."[47] Unfortunately, the guerrilla war waged by the North Vietnamese and the Viet Cong did not suit the mold, and Rolling Thunder was doomed to failure from the start.

A similar doctrinal void existed on the eve of Desert Storm. The unexpected end of the Cold War had left the Air Force with a basic doctrinal manual, dated August 13, 1984, little changed in substance from that of 1959. The belief of many air commanders in Southeast Asia that Linebacker II had single-handedly achieved the 1973 Paris Peace Agreement served to vindicate the pre-Vietnam doctrine emphasizing a potential war with the Soviets. As a result, Air Force planning following Vietnam had focused on fighting the Soviets where they were considered to be the greatest threat—Europe. Planners envisioned Strategic Air Command's bombers and missiles overlying the battle area to accomplish the independent mission of strategic bombing against the Soviet homeland with nuclear weapons. Meanwhile, Air Force fighters would support the ground defense of the continent.

Tactical Air Command (TAC) helped the Army design its AirLand Battle doctrine that outlined those fighters' specific tasks.[48] In tying bombers to the strategic nuclear mission and fighters to the mission of tactical air support, air planners neglected provisions for an independent air campaign using conventional weapons against a non-Soviet enemy. "The doctrinal paradigm since the 1950s has been an Air Force that separated strategic and tactical applications of air power institutionally, organizationally, intellectually, and culturally," noted Maj. Gen. Robert M. Alexander, the Air Force's director of plans, deputy chief of staff for plans and operations. "There was a need for an offensive, conventional, independent air campaign plan against Iraq. However, there was no provision in the paradigm."[49]

Doctrinal semantics contributed to the Air Force's difficulty in designing an independent air campaign against Iraq. Strategic Air Command had long equated "strategic" with "nuclear."[50] This emphasis on the nuclear mission resulted in B–52 crews arriving for duty during the Vietnam War "with only the barest introduction to conventional tactics" and using modified nuclear bombing procedures against enemy targets.[51] Yet with the exception of Linebacker II, the giant bomber's primary mission in Southeast Asia was battlefield interdiction or close air support. Meanwhile, fighter aircraft conducted most of the strategic missions—those aimed at North Vietnamese war-making potential rather than their deployed armed forces—during Rolling Thunder and Linebacker I. Despite the example of Southeast Asia, the perceived Soviet threat after Vietnam caused SAC's primary focus to return to the nuclear mission, while TAC, viewing its main role as assisting ground forces on the battlefield, focused on the AirLand Battle. TAC thus shunned planning for "strategic conventional" operations, even though, in terms of precisely delivering ordnance against such targets as factories or electric power stations, the capability of TAC's fighters had far outstripped that of SAC's bombers.

Rather than devising a makeshift air campaign against Iraq from strategies designed for war with the Soviets, air chiefs kept the Vietnam demon at bay by improvising. "There were no formalized procedures for the approval of the planning and execution of the conventional strike," General Alexander stated. "In response to this requirement, the Air Force headed an ad hoc joint working group under the auspices of the Joint Staff and provided the broad conceptual planning that was necessary."[52] Colonel Warden directed this diverse assembly, which comprised thirty to forty officers from the Air Force, Army, Navy, and Marines. Relying on many of the ideas articulated in his book, he developed a concept of operations emphasizing a conventional, strategic air assault as the fundamental underpinning of an air campaign. Generals Horner and Glosson took Warden's conceptual design, modified it to suit their views, and then hammered out the specifics of the Desert Storm air offensive.[53]

Many observers of the operation, however, have failed to note the emphasis placed on the air campaign's first phase—and that the phase 1 attacks were key to destroying Iraq's war-making capability. Instead, they focus on phases 3 and 4 of the air assault (which occurred simultaneously with phase 1), contending that Desert Storm vindicated AirLand Battle doctrine.[54] Yet air planners in the aftermath of Vietnam had envisioned AirLand Battle as a *tactical* concept to counter a Soviet thrust into Western Europe. The doctrine proved adaptable to guide an air offensive aimed at Iraqi forces in Kuwait and on the Kuwaiti border. AirLand Battle did not, however, provide for a *strategic* application of air power against the war-making capability and will to resist of an enemy nation. For that conceptual design, the Air Force had to rely on happenstance—and fortunately turned to a colonel with profound insight who was serving on the Air Staff when Iraq invaded Kuwait.

In contrast to air commanders after Vietnam, air leaders after Desert Storm must avoid the temptation to conclude that the air doctrine with which they entered the war was appropriate for it. Despite the spectacular success of the Desert Storm air campaign, the Persian Gulf war offers no blueprint guaranteeing a successful application of air power in the future. Linebacker II had helped achieve Nixon's goals in December 1972 because of unique circumstances, but many air chiefs ignored the changed nature of both the Vietnam War and American objectives in it to argue that such bombing would have achieved decisive results during Rolling Thunder. The situation in Iraq nineteen years after Nixon's Christmas bombing was also unique, and its uniqueness related directly to the magnitude of success achieved by air power. The combination of a fragmented, semi-industrialized, Third World enemy waging conventional war with Soviet equipment in a desert environment and led by an international pariah who personally made all key military decisions and relied on an intricate command and control network for their implementation, is unlikely to recur.

Nor is it likely that the United States will soon confront a commander as inept as Saddam. He granted the allied coalition five and a half months to refine planning and marshal forces, allowing its units to undergo extensive training in desert warfare. During that span (and throughout the war), his commanders suffered from a lack of intelligence data, whereas Generals Schwarzkopf and Horner received enormous quantities of information from satellites, reconnaissance aircraft, and remotely piloted vehicles.[55]

Saddam also failed to take any significant military action that might have affected the course of the war. Shunning an advance into Saudi Arabia after overrunning Kuwait, which would have denied coalition forces key staging areas, he did not seriously threaten the allied bases after the war began. "All you have to do is stand in Dhahran and look at the huge amounts of equipment we were bringing in there," General Schwarzkopf remarked. "If they [the Iraqis] had launched a persistent chemical attack that had denied the port of Damman to us, obviously this would have been a major setback."[56] The American commander further noted that an attack by Iraqi aircraft on Riyadh Air Base in Saudi Arabia could have caused tremendous damage. Saddam, however, chose to ground his air force in hardened shelters. Once those shelters proved vulnerable to American bombs, much of the remainder of his air force fled to Iran.

In the final analysis, Iraq's vulnerability to General Horner's air offensive could have stemmed as much from Saddam's attempt to apply the perceived lessons of Vietnam as it did from efforts by American civilian and military leaders to exorcise Southeast Asian ghosts. The Iraqi president believed that Vietnam permanently sapped American will to fight a long war abroad. "Yours is a society which cannot accept 10,000 dead in one battle," he told American ambassador April Glaspie before attacking Kuwait.[57] He likely thought that five months of waiting would cause the American public to reconsider the merits of combat, and that the high casualties he expected to inflict after war began would have the same impact on American will to fight as had the bloody 1968 Tet Offensive.

Apparently to goad General Schwarzkopf into a premature ground attack, Saddam lobbed Scuds at Israel and Saudi Arabia, launched assaults into Saudi Arabia (Khafji was one example), and dumped Kuwaiti oil into the Persian Gulf. These ventures failed to have a major impact on the war because of allied air power, a capability that Saddam dismissed from the start of the crisis. "The United States relies on the Air Force," he declared on August 30, 1990, "and the Air Force has never been the decisive factor in a battle in the history of wars."[58] Desert Storm proved otherwise.

Saddam Hussein was no Ho Chi Minh, and the next enemy is unlikely to be a Saddam Hussein. The relaxation of superpower tensions makes it probable that there will be a next enemy—sooner rather than later. The bipolar world of the Cold War tended to restrain regional conflicts, as the Soviet Union and the United States could use their leverage to keep client states in line. Now, however, uncertainty prevails on the world stage. Secretary of the Air Force Donald B. Rice highlighted this instability in the foreword to his white paper, *Global Reach—Global Power*, published a little over a month before Saddam's invasion of Kuwait. He noted: "Extraordinary international developments over the last few years have created the potential for a significantly different security environment as we approach the beginning of the twenty-first century. These changes demand fresh thinking about the role of military forces."[59]

Given the changing world scene, the Air Force needs a doctrine underscoring the flexible nature of air power. Air University's Center for Aerospace Doctrine, Research, and Education (AUCADRE) is currently putting the finishing touches on a new version of U.S. Air Force Manual 1–1 that will go far toward eliminating much of the dogma of the 1984 edition. In particular, the manual notes that no universal formula exists for the proper application of air power and that strategic operations are defined by their objective rather than by the weapon system used, type of munitions, or location of the target. General McPeak's call for composite air wings that combine fighters and bombers should also help eliminate the largely artificial distinction suggested by the titles *Strategic* and *Tactical* Air Commands.

The magnificent melding of technology, sophisticated planning, adroit leadership, and highly trained, courageous personnel in Desert Storm bodes well for the service's ability to respond to future contingencies. For over half a century, Air Force leaders have maintained that air power could be the decisive element in war, and Desert Storm has finally vindicated the claim. More importantly, however, air power again demonstrated that it is, above all else, a *flexible* instrument of national policy. If used inflexibly (as in Rolling Thunder), its application can be disastrous, but if unshackled from dogma, and applied with imagination and creativity (as during Desert Storm), it may be a decisive force.

Despite forthcoming cuts in both manpower and funding, the Air Force of the future can continue to play a significant role in American military operations by focusing on flexibility as the fundamental underpinning of service doctrine. The key to applying air power successfully is melding the appropriate amount of force to national objectives, which may or may not call for the Air Force to play the decisive role in combat. Now is an ideal time for the service to come to grips with its past by exorcising completely the demons of Vietnam. Yet in burying those phantoms, we must avoid creating a new specter that judges success or failure in future wars according to whether or not the Air Force was the most decisive factor. Given both a different foe and different circumstances from those encountered in the Persian Gulf war, the quest for air power's decisiveness may prove as bedeviled as Rolling Thunder.

NOTES

1. Quoted in Julie Bird, "McPeak: 'Brilliant . . . air deception,' " *Air Force Times* (March 25, 1991): 8 [hereafter "McPeak"]. Actually, air power had destroyed armies in both world wars. In a 1918 precursor of Desert Storm's air offensive, British general Edmund Allenby's five Royal Air Force squadrons wrecked two Turkish divisions in a narrow defile after the planes had previously destroyed the central Turkish telephone exchange and Turkish army headquarters. Twenty-six years later, during Lt. Gen. George Patton's dramatic dash across France, air power again destroyed an army. German Major General Eric Elster surrendered 20,000 troops on September 16, 1944, as a direct result of the punishment inflicted by the fighters of Brig. Gen. Otto P. Weyland's XIX Tactical Air Command. Weyland was requested to attend the surrender ceremony. See Robin Higham, *Air Power: A Concise History* (New York: St. Martin's, 1972), 41–43; Wesley Frank Craven and James Lea Cate, *The Army Air Forces in World War II*, Vol. 3, *Europe: Argument to V-E Day, January 1944 to May 1945* (Chicago: Univ. of Chicago Press, 1951; reprinted, Washington, DC: Office of Air Force History, 1983), 265–66.

2. Stanley W. Cloud, "Exorcising an Old Demon," *Time* (March 11, 1991): 52.

3. Michael M. McCrea, "U.S. Navy, Marine Corps, and Air Force Fixed-Wing Aircraft Losses and Damage in Southeast Asia (1962–1973)," Center for Naval Analyses Study, August 1976, 6–28.

4. *The Pentagon Papers: The Defense Department History of United States Decisionmaking on Vietnam*, Senator Gravel ed., Vol. 4 (Boston: Beacon Press, 1971), 136.

5. By January 1968, Hanoi had received almost $600 million in economic aid and $1 billion in military assistance. See Jason Summer, "Summary and Conclusions," August 30, 1966, *Pentagon Papers*, Gravel ed., Vol. 4, 116; Department of Defense Systems Analysis Report, January 1968, *Pentagon Papers*, Gravel ed., Vol. 4, 225–26.

6. Quoted in George C. Herring, *"Cold Blood": LBJ's Conduct of Limited War in Vietnam*, The Harmon Memorial Lectures in Military History, no. 33 (Colorado Springs, CO: United States Air Force Academy, 1990), 2.

7. Interview of Dean Rusk by the author, Athens, Georgia, July 15, 1985.

8. Message, CINCPAC to JCS, 040304Z April 1965, in *Commander-in-Chief, PACOM, Outgoing Messages, 22 January–28 June 1965*, K712.1623–2, USAF His. Res. Agency, Maxwell AFB, AL.

9. Air Force Generals Curtis LeMay and William Momyer, and Adm. U.S. Grant Sharp, among others, have argued that intensive bombing of North Vietnam could have proved decisive in Vietnam in 1965.

10. Senate, Committee on Armed Services, Preparedness Investigating Subcommittee, *Air War Against North Vietnam*, 90th Congress, 1st Session, pt. 3 (August 22–23, 1967), 212.

11. HQ USAF, *Analysis of Effectiveness of Interdiction in Southeast Asia, Second Progress Report* (May 1966), 7, K168.187–21, USAFHRA; Senate, *Air War Against North Vietnam* (August 25, 1967), pt. 4, 299.

12. Larry Cable, *Unholy Grail: The United States and the Wars in Vietnam, 1965–1968* (London: Routledge & Kegan Paul, 1991).

13. George Bush, "Address to the Nation Announcing Allied Military Action in the Persian Gulf," January 16, 1991, in *Weekly Compilation of Presidential Documents* (January 21, 1991): 51 [hereafter "Address to the Nation"].

14. "The President's News Conference on the Persian Gulf Conflict," January 18, 1991, in *Weekly Compilation of Presidential Documents* (January 21, 1991): 56.

15. Two targets that Cheney eliminated from the target list were a huge statue of Saddam Hussein and the Iraqi war memorial, both in Baghdad. See Tom Mathews, "The Secret History of the War," *Newsweek* (March 18, 1991): 30 [hereafter "Secret History"].

16. The hunt for Scuds ultimately diverted about 1,500 sorties originally designated for other strategic targets and increased the time required to finish the strategic campaign by three to five days. See Michael Dugan, "The Air War," *U.S. News & World Report* (February 11, 1991): 30 [hereafter "The Air War"].

17. Quoted in "General Admits Vietnam Body Counts Were Lies," *Detroit News* (March 11, 1991): 6.

18. Bush, "Address to the Nation," 51.

19. Oral History Interview, Lt. Gen. Joseph H. Moore, by Maj. Samuel E. Riddlebarger and Lt. Col. Valentino Castellina, November 22, 1969, 17–18, K239.0512–241, USAFHRA; Lt. Col. William H. Greenhalgh, interview with author, Maxwell AFB, AL, May 17, 1985; John Morrocco, *Thunder from Above* volume in Robert Manning, ed., *The Vietnam Experience* (Boston: Boston Publishing Co., 1984): 125.

20. Quoted in Mathews, "Secret History," 29.

21. Mark A. Clodfelter, *The Limits of Air Power: The American Bombing of North Vietnam* (New York: Free Press, 1989). This assertion is discussed in Ch. 1.

22. Ibid., 100–107, 177–85.

23. Carl von Clausewitz, *On War*, trans. and ed. Michael Howard and Peter Paret (Princeton, NJ: Princeton Univ. Press, 1976), 595–96.

24. John A. Warden III, *The Air Campaign: Planning for Combat* (Washington, DC: National Defense Univ. Press, 1988) [hereafter *Air Campaign*]. Warden first discusses "centers of gravity" on pp. 9–11 and refers to the concept throughout the book.

25. Richard Saltus, "Air Force Says It Might Have Won the War in 2 More Weeks," *Boston Globe* (April 5, 1991): 10. Lt. Gen. John B. Conaway, chief of the U.S. Air Force's National Guard Bureau, noted at an April 3, 1991, Conference on the U.S. Air Force at Tufts University that Colonel Warden was "one of the key individuals who put together the air campaign for Desert Storm."

26. John A. Warden III, "Airpower Employment in the Future World," paper presented at Conference on the USAF, Tufts Univ., Boston, Mass., April 3, 1991.

27. Ibid.

28. Warden, *Air Campaign*, 147.

29. Phebe Marr, *The Modern History of Iraq* (Boulder, CO: Westview, 1985), 270.

30. Ibid., 130, 248–58; David Segal, "The Iran–Iraq War: A Military Analysis," *Foreign Affairs* 66, no. 5 (Summer 1988): 952.

31. HQ PACAF, *Corona Harvest: The USAF in Southeast Asia, 1970–1973: Lessons Learned and Recommendations: A Compendium (16 June 1975)*, K717.0423–11, 82–83, USAFHRA.

32. HQ 7th AF, *7th Air Force History of Linebacker Operations, 10 May–23 October 1972*, n.d., K740.04–24, 7–10, USAFHRA.

33. William B. Scott, "Electro-Optic Targeting Tools Bolster Bombing Accuracy of Allied Aircraft," *Aviation Week & Space Technology* (January 25, 1991): 25; John D. Morrocco, "U.S. Tactics Exploit Advances in Avionics, Air-to-Surface Weapons," *Aviation Week & Space Technology* (February 18, 1991): 52.

34. Michael Dugan, "First Lessons of Victory," *U.S. News & World Report* (March 18, 1991): 36.

35. Jeffrey M. Lenorovitz, "F–117s Drop Laser-Guided Bombs in Destroying Most Baghdad Targets," *Aviation Week & Space Technology* (February 4, 1991): 30.

36. Julie Bird, "Horner: Further AF Role in Gulf Not Needed," *Air Force Times* (March 18, 1991): 8.

37. Donald B. Rice, Secretary of the USAF, "Global Change, Global Reach, and Global Power," address at Tufts Univ. Conference on the Air Force, April 3, 1991.

38. Quoted in John D. Morrocco, "Allies Attack Iraqi Targets; Scuds Strike Israeli Cities," *Aviation Week & Space Technology* (January 21, 1991): 22.

39. Efraim Karsh, "Military Lessons of the Iran-Iraq War," *Orbis* 33, no. 2 (Spring 1989): 217.

40. Phebe Marr, "Iraq's Uncertain Future," *Current History* 90, no. 552 (January 1991): 1.

41. Ibid., 1–2.

42. Dugan, "The Air War," 28.

43. Quoted in Bill Sweetman, "Learning Lessons of 'Desert Storm,' " *Jane's Defence Weekly* (March 9, 1991): 329. Subsequently a four-star general and commander of Pacific Air Forces (PACAF).

44. Bird, "McPeak," 8; Dugan, "The Air War," 26.

45. Schwarzkopf stated that air attacks left Iraqi units on the Kuwaiti border "at 50 per cent or below. The second level, basically that we had to face—and these were the real tough fighters that we were worried about—were attrited to some place between 50 and 75 per cent." See Ian Kemp, "100-Hour War to Free Kuwait," *Jane's Defence Weekly* 15, no. 10 (March 9, 1991): 326.

46. David H. Hackworth, "Lessons of a Lucky War," *Newsweek* (March 11, 1991): 49.

47. Air Force Manual 1–2, *United States Air Force Basic Doctrine* (December 1, 1959): 4.

48. For an analysis of the development of the "AirLand Battle" concept, and the Air Force's projected role in that doctrine, see John L. Rumjue, "The Evolution of the AirLand Battle Concept," *Air University Review* 35, no. 4 (May–June 1984): 4–15; James A. Machos, "TACAIR Support for AirLand Battle," *Air University Review* 35, no. 4 (May–June 1984): 16–24.

49. Robert M. Alexander, "World is Rapidly Changing and AF Must Keep Up," *Air Force Times* (February 11, 1991): 23 [hereafter "World"].

50. Thomas A. Keaney, *Strategic Bombers and Conventional Weapons: Airpower Options* (Washington, DC: National Defense University Press, 1984), 16.

51. Ibid., 29.

52. Alexander, "World," 23.

53. "Schwarzkopf: 'I Got a Lot of Guff,' " *Newsweek* (March 11, 1991): 34.

54. Three analysts who contend that AirLand Battle doctrine was a key reason for Desert Storm's success are retired Army officers Harry G. Summers, Jr., William E. Odom, and Trevor N. Dupuy. See Summers's "AirLand Doctrine Seems to Be on Target, So Far," *Air Force Times* (February 25, 1991): 25, 61; Odom's "Storming Past a New Threshold in Warfare," *Christian Science Monitor* (April 4, 1991): 19; Dupuy's "How the War Was Won," *National Review* (April 1, 1991): 29–31.

55. Barbara Starr, "Satellites Paved Way to Victory," *Jane's Defence Weekly* 15, no. 10 (March 9, 1991): 330.

56. Quoted in "Sayings of Stormin' Norman," *Time* (March 27, 1991), 27.

57. Quoted in Charles Lane, "Saddam's Endgame," *Newsweek* (January 7, 1991): 16.

58. "Excerpts from Interview with Hussein on Crisis in Gulf," *New York Times* (August 31, 1990): A–10.

59. Donald B. Rice, Secretary of USAF, *The Air Force and U.S. National Security: Global Reach—Global Power* (Washington, DC: Department of the Air Force, June 1990): i.

8

North Vietnamese Air Defenses During the Vietnam War

Douglas Pike

This chapter is divided into three parts. First, there is a general overview of the perception of air power during the Vietnam War held by officials in Saigon and Hanoi. Second, there is a brief description and discussion of the North Vietnamese high command's view of air power and air defense. Finally, some remarks are made on the historian's unresolved issues of air power in the Vietnam War. The focus is on the sociopsychological dimension of the subject, within the context of Vietnamese political culture.

OVERVIEW

To deal with this subject properly we first must examine how Hanoi viewed its enemy's perception of air power. It is an obvious but oft forgotten fact that Hanoi's leaders never regarded the war in Vietnam in general, nor air power in particular, in the same manner as did their counterparts in Saigon and Washington. Americans tended to define air war in impersonalized technical and highly specialized terms. Their concern chiefly was with types of aircraft, improved target acquisition methods, specialized ordnance, techniques to minimize bad weather, and so on.

In Hanoi, officials regarded air power largely as a political and psychological challenge—acquiring air defenses, of course—but equally important if not more so, employing various mobilizational and motivational devices that would allow the system to withstand any punishment that air power could deliver. They were less concerned with technology and more with recruiting soldiers and officers with correct personalities, who in effect were imbued with a nontechnological (or even antitechnological) view of life, and with strong ideological orientations. It was an attitude that air power did not matter very much one way or the other. Spirit was what counted in soldiering, not matters of material. This was the famed concept that it was better to be ''red'' than ''expert,'' all neatly encapsulated in Mao Tse-tung's dictum that China did not need the bomb (A-Bomb) because "man was a spiritual atom-bomb" (a line, incidentally, that Mao dropped once he got the bomb).

Most American strategists during the war, if they thought about it at all, did not seriously address this mind-set of the Hanoi leadership. It was for them an absurdity to maintain that being bombed and strafed was not very important. Yet this mind-set, and the associated indoctrination by Hanoi leaders, nullified much of the American air power's ability to achieve its strategic goals.

PAVN High Command strategy, in its parlance, required some new mix of the existing armed-political *dau tranh* (struggle) strategy to meet American intervention. General Vo Nguyen Giap, in *"Big Victory, Great Task,"* set forth a revised doctrine. In dealing with American forces in South Vietnam, he said, the chief problem was to meet the enemy's advantage in mass and movement, posed by its massive fire power and its great mobility, particularly provided by the helicopter. This meant, Giap wrote, (1) devising a new set of "fighting methods," which he set forth as his "Coordinated Fighting Methods" which were medium-size set-piece battles usually on remote or isolated battlefields, and (2) "Independent Fighting Methods" by which he meant numerous small-sized attacks launched simultaneously over a wide geographical area—as in the Tet offensive in late 1967–early 1968. These two methods were then to be combined into what was called a "continuous, comprehensive offensive."[1]

In the North, against the air war, Giap said, it was necessary to devise a two-fold dynamic and static defense against incoming American planes. To this end the USSR must deliver and install an air defense system of advanced weaponry and sophisticated control equipment. And it did; by the end of the war North Vietnam was employing the best weapons, both for ground and air war, that the USSR and the rest of the socialist bloc could manufacture.[2]

When in the spring of 1965 the air war against North Vietnam began in earnest, Hanoi's military and civilian officials made a series of confident sounding pronouncements. Later it was learned, and especially after the war, that Washington's dispatch of ground troops to South Vietnam and start of the air war against North Vietnam engendered enormous apprehension and even dismay among the Hanoi leadership.[3] The prospect, after all, was frightening: the most powerful military force in the world was on the attack.

However, after the initial round of air assaults had been absorbed by North Vietnam, PAVN High Command fears began to diminish. Its perception was that although the all-out American air war was destructive and punitive, it could be endured. As a matter of fact, these air attacks were not all-out but were sharply delimited, confined for the most part to North Vietnam's transportation and communication networks, facilities such as roads, bridges, railroad switching yards, freight trains, highway traffic, and communication centers which the American military referred to collectively as the LOC (lines of communication).[4]

Military targets were the second most common targets. These included air defense installations, troop encampments and military barracks, naval bases and supply depots. The third and numerically far smaller cluster of targets were industrial: the war-supporting industries, chiefly electric power plants and what the military called POL (petroleum, oil, lubricants) installations. A study by the author in mid–1966 that examined 10,000 after-action air-strike photos to determine what exactly had been hit, yielded this breakdown: communication-transportation matrix 90.4 percent; military targets 7.7 percent; other (including industrial installations, oil depots, etc.) 1.9 percent.[5]

A breakdown of the total number of air strikes in three years of air war, as tabulated by CINCPAC commander Admiral U.S. Grant Sharp in his *Report on the War in Vietnam* (1969), using this same classification yields: communication-transportation matrix 64,610; military targets 5,324; industrial targets (92 percent POL depots) 4,869; "buildings" (too vague to classify) 12,619.[6]

However, in Hanoi ruling circles the belief grew, then became entrenched, that North Vietnam was absorbing the worst the Americans could deliver, a view that persisted until the shock of the truly all-out Linebacker II bombing campaign of December 1972.[7]

U.S. CIVILIAN VIEW OF AIR POWER

A number of specific factors influenced the thinking of the U.S. Embassy in Saigon about air power—to the extent there was much systematic thinking. One factor was an institutional memory of the Korean War, a sense after the war that we civilian officials had been sold a bill of goods by the Air Force Association.[8]

Late in the Korean War, during the months leading up to the summer of 1953 ceasefire, a stalemate developed between the UN forces and the Chinese and North Korean armies. The positions of the two respective forces during this time had become stabilized at the main line of resistance (MLR)—roughly the 38th parallel—in civilian parlance, the front lines. Neither of the two armies facing each other across this MLR was able to dislodge the other or break through in a major offensive. Much of the day-to-day combat consisted of artillery exchanges and small arms fire, which required constant resupply of ammunition.

The United Nations forces had control of the air over the MLR and the approaches to it, most of which were long, narrow mountain passes. American civilians in Korea at the time were assured that air interdiction of these supply convoys was greatly reducing the amount of ammunition getting through to the MLR since vehicles were forced to pass through miles of "shooting galleries," thus highly vulnerable to air strikes. Yet after the war it was learned that at no time were either the Chinese or North Korean armies ever short of ammunition at the MLR. We had been misled and tended to blame, not the U.S. Air Force—and certainly not the fliers themselves—for overselling the prowess of air power, but rather the Washington-based U.S. Air Force Association, which was in effect a public relations agent for the Air Force in the United States and throughout the world. The association's intent was well meant—to convince Americans of the value of air power, but in overstating what air power could do, it set the stage for future disillusionment.

A second influence on official civilian thinking about air power was the residual attitudes left over from World War II, including what might be called revisionist thinking about air power in WW II. It is an old debate, this matter of the role of air power in modern warfare, as anyone familiar with military history is well aware.

In the United States it began with Brig. Gen. Billy Mitchell, the most glamorous American airman to come out of World War I, who in the 1920s advanced the doctrine that it was possible to win wars by bombing the enemy's homeland over the heads of battling armies. In the course of making his argument Mitchell, still in uniform, denounced U.S. Army and U.S. Navy leadership for its "incompetency, criminal negligence, and almost treasonable administration of U.S. national defense." For his trouble he was court-martialed and drummed out of the Army to become a classic case of prophet without honor in his own country. Mitchell's writings were carefully read by others, however, not the least of whom was Hermann Goering, father of the German Luftwaffe.

High-altitude bombing was raised to a strategic art during World War II. In the air campaigns, both sides demonstrated a previously unimaginable level of destructive power—in the form of saturation bombing that sometimes triggered firestorms with greater after-effects than the bombing itself. But in warfare, sheer destruction and military benefit are not necessarily the same. This was proven in the postwar bombing surveys by the Allied governments, especially those made by the British. These studies indicated that much of the late war strategic bombing, especially against the transportation matrix in eastern Germany, was unnecessary. However, later studies have tended to revise this judgment—particularly those based on German sources not available in the first study. Just one example is the fact that 90 percent of the Third Reich's energy supply depended on coal transported by rail. Allied bombing, it is now established, was well on its way to destroying not only this transport system and the power sector it supplied, but also the German economy itself at a time when the Allied bombers were tapering off the attack.[9]

At any event this great debate on the extent and/or limits of air power remains with us to this day. The subject is being discussed if not debated in the aftermath of the Persian Gulf war where air power advocates gained vast new prominence. The point to be made here is that there was in Vietnam throughout the war great uncertainty among American policy makers—in contradistinction to many American military strategists—as to the utility of air power, which is traceable to their institutional memory and the lessons they believed were learned in previous wars. Particularly in the early years of the Vietnam War there was doubt if not outright skepticism over the utility of air power given the kind of war being fought there. It was, of course, a revolutionary guerrilla war in which the enemy was nowhere and everywhere, seldom offering a target vulnerable either to strategic bombers or tactical air strike planes. Indeed, I can remember a U.S.

Embassy/Saigon staff meeting in 1965 at which a military briefer outlined plans to extend the B–52 bomber raids from North Vietnam to the Viet Cong guerrilla bases in South Vietnam, and he was greeted by outright laughter.

Sustained air strikes into North Vietnam, named Operation Rolling Thunder, began in March 1965. Earlier there had been reprisal raids. The first of these retaliations was the famed Tonkin Gulf incident of early August 1964 between DRV PT-boats and the American destroyers *Maddox* and *C. Turner Joy*. The PT-boat's home port bases were struck by American planes. In February 1965 came two additional reprisal raids—Operation Flaming Dart—against DRV military barracks and port facilities at Dong Hoi in retaliation for a mortar attack on the U.S. Army enlisted men's billet at Qui Nhon.[10]

The rationale for Rolling Thunder varied with time and place. The general view of the U.S. Embassy in Saigon in March 1965 was that it was a stop-gap measure, probably with little lasting effect but which could buy some badly needed time for South Vietnam. The strategic balance had shifted markedly toward the National Liberation Front (NLF), and air strikes might make a psychological contribution to restoring some balance. Further, the drama of taking the war to the North was a shot of adrenalin in the South Vietnamese vein which could, and did, boost morale.

The view from the White House was somewhat broader. It shared the Saigon Embassy's belief that the strikes might help stave off the collapse of the government of Vietnam (GVN). Also there was something of a consensus that punitive raids could raise the price of warfare beyond what Hanoi was willing to pay, and hence could lead it to cease support and direction of the war in South Vietnam, either agreeing to negotiate some sort of settlement or simply allowing the war to fade away. Later, another rationale was added by Washington, that the air strikes would curtail the flow of war material and men through North Vietnam and along the Ho Chi Minh Trail.

The thesis, offered in Vietnam by Secretary of Defense McNamara, was the "choke down" principle. The example used was squeezing a garden hose to reduce water flow, but acknowledging the flow could not be totally curtailed. The allied intelligence community in Vietnam generated vast amounts of data on this effort, all of which could be variously interpreted. Arguments continued without resolution throughout the war with pro- and antiair power debaters using the same sets of statistics to prove their respective cases. But, by this time the military uses of air power had become so technologically complex that the average civilian official was never sure what to think about the effectiveness of the air war.

HANOI'S VIEW OF AIR POWER

Among the many myths and historical fictions of the Vietnam War is the one ascribing a totally lop-sided character to American air war and North Vietnamese air defenses. Conjured up by reporting during the war was the image of North

Vietnam lying as helpless under incoming American airplanes as Ethiopia under Italian air attack in the 1930s. Actually it was a case of techno-airwar on both sides. The air defenses offered by North Vietnam were vastly superior to anything experienced previously, and far more sophisticated and effective than those used by the British defending London, the Germans in Berlin, or the Japanese in Tokyo. At the height of the war in the early 1970s these took the form of some 300 SAM batteries, 7,000 AAA (antiaircraft artillery) weapons, some 200 MiG fighter planes, and a modern ground-controlled intercept radar system.[11]

From my own research of PAVN documents the specific air defenses set up as follows:

During the Vietnam War, the Air Defense Force and the Air Defense Missile Force manned about 650 antiaircraft sites throughout North Vietnam, with a total of some 7,000 AAA weapons. The strategy was to use regular AAA weapons against low-flying aircraft and the SAMs against high-altitude attackers. Since the incoming planes often were at both high and low altitudes and the defenders were in two separate organizations, co-ordination problems never were satisfactorily solved. Nevertheless, PAVN air defenses in the Vietnam War were the most effective and sophisticated the world had ever seen in action—far surpassing the primitive defenses of London, Berlin, and Tokyo during World War II.[12]

After a detailed examination of the actual tactics and policies used by PAVN air defense leadership the following can also be said:

The Air Defense Force apparently does not employ the military-region structure but is organized by functional units: thirteen surface-to-air regiments of about 13,000 men each, defending some 60 sites using SA–2 and SA–3 missiles; four AA brigades of 1,500 men each, using 57mm and 100mm weapons; paramilitary AAA units at perhaps 1,000 sites, using 23mm and 37mm weapons.[13]

Hanoi was heavily defended. Mark Clodfelter in his book *Limits of Air Power* quotes a U.S. Air Force pilot as describing North Vietnam as the "center of Hell, with Hanoi as its hub."[14] Clodfelter also describes the enormous efforts made by North Vietnam to repair communication and transportation arteries quickly, often overnight, by massive use of labor—the red ant syndrome: thousands of people working nonstop. A half-million man and woman labor force was exclusively dedicated to keeping the transportation and communication systems operating. Repair crews would appear on the scene of damaged rail lines, roads, and bridges within minutes following an attack and in many instances have the system in sufficient repair to permit use within a matter of hours:

The North Vietnamese replaced destroyed bridges with fords, ferries, and pontoons. They constructed some bridges just below the water's surface, which prevented aerial observation of the structures. The Communists also restricted travel times and dispersed oil reserves. Men and supplies moved only [in] darkness or poor weather. Beginning in mid–

1965, the North Vietnamese placed oil storage tanks holding between 2,200 and 3,300 gallons near major highways. They supplemented those tanks with 55-gallon drums, which they deposited along roads and in cities, towns, and rice paddies. They placed large quantities near dikes as well, figuring that American raids against the structures were unlikely.[15]

North Vietnam may have been an unsophisticated "peasant society," but it was tightly organized and Hanoi was able to acquire a wide range of Soviet and Chinese air-defense weapons. When the war in the North began in 1964–1965, most of these were conventional 37mm and 57mm optically sighted weapons capable of reaching a restricted altitude—the "straight and level" attack—inevitably required moving into the killing zone, within range of rifles and machine guns in the hands of local peasants, organized into a countrywide militia. It took only a single bullet in a vulnerable spot to be able to down a jet fighter-bomber. With Soviet assistance as noted above, 100mm radar-guided AAA was added to the inventory, and proved to be deadly. Being mobile and difficult to spot from the air, this weapon had a range of 45,000 feet. By 1968, 80 percent of U.S. air losses were due to AAA. In addition, in July 1965, a number of Soviet-supplied surface-to-air missiles were acquired. Although the kill ratio of these SA–2s and SA–3s was comparatively low, it made the northern air war more dangerous.[16]

Beyond weapon acquisition, the Hanoi high command's view of air power centered on a great doctrinal debate that raged in North Vietnam military circles during the war—the so-called Red versus Expert argument, sometimes termed the spirit versus technology debate. In oversimplified terms it asked the question: In the proper conduct of war, which counts for more, men or weapons? Or is war itself defined as the "comprehensive test of all adversarial strengths; i.e. men, weapons, spirit, etc . . . ?"[17]

In the early years of the war—probably up to the final battles in 1975—the "Red" viewpoint dominated in Hanoi's perceptions of air power and air defenses. It held that air power could never be decisive in the kind of war being fought in Vietnam—that is, revolutionary war employing *dau tranh* (struggle) strategy. At the same time it was obvious to PAVN commanders that much could and should be done to reduce the punishment inflicted from the air, which of course required the services of the "Expert." Tactically it was more of a question of whether to confront or ignore air power, that is, whether to meet enemy air attacks head-on or to arrange that the threat be evaded. Both lines were pursued, by fielding a powerful and effective air defense system but at the same time relocating potential targets; also, by pressing ground offensives in the South, what was known as "attacking the beast in his lair," which meant guerrilla raids on airfields and airmen's quarters.

The overall DRVN strategy against air power, as expressed by its chief architect, General Vo Nguyen Giap, attempted to straddle the Red versus Expert debate, arguing for both by minimizing the significance of the air war:

We have strengthened our antiaircraft guns and other ordinary types of infantry weapons, while striving to develop the effectiveness of jet fighter planes and antiaircraft missiles in order to create thick and highly effective fire nets. While fighting, we have carried out training and drawn from our fighting experiences in order to improve the quality of antiaircraft defense of our armed forces. . . .

The principle of combat adopted by our armed forces in opposing the U.S. imperialists' air and naval war of destruction is: positively to annihilate the enemy; protect the targets the enemy wants to hit; and preserve and improve our forces. Only by succeeding in destroying the enemy can we protect our targets from him and preserve and improve our forces. Conversely, only by succeeding in protecting these targets and preserving and improving our forces can we create favorable conditions to annihilate the enemy. Judging concrete situations, sometimes we regard annihilating the enemy as the main task and sometimes protecting targets from him. Yet normally the principle of positively destroying the enemy is the most basic and most decisive content of our task.[18]

General Giap goes on to explain how actual events bear out his arguments made in the above declaration, by stating that defense measures had achieved great results from 1966–1968. The culture was, in spite of the extensive damage, surviving—economy, agriculture, communication, and education all remained stable and continued to develop.

It is obvious that the independent activities of an air force, even if it is the modern air force of the U.S. imperialists, cannot have the effect of deciding victory on the battlefield. The U.S. Air Force can cause certain damages to our people, but it surely cannot shake our people's rocklike determination to oppose the Americans for national salvation. It surely cannot save the U.S. imperialists from complete defeat in their aggressive war against the South. The North's big victories demonstrate the great power of the people's war and of the socialist system. This power has dealt and will deal heavy blows to the U.S. Air Force, smashing its so-called superiority.[19]

This illustrates in nearly complete form the general attitude of the North Vietnamese high command toward air power. Particularly, it highlights the dichotomy of the Red versus Expert argument. Clearly, it also suggests that this issue was one that cut across all considerations. It had to do with strategy, since it involved basic questions about how a war is to be fought, what sort of an armed force is to be created, and what tactics are to be used. It had much to do with leadership, with the *kind* of person recruited as officers. In subtle but important ways, it had to do with party-military relations by asserting the ideological issue of centrality in decision making by the party over the military. Finally, it involved foreign relations because of weapons requirements that were obtainable from abroad.[20]

Military science as it was taught in military schools in North Vietnam throughout the war stressed above all the doctrine of *dau tranh* (struggle), positing that there were two types, armed and political, on and off the battlefield. Certain key concepts were developed; these were applicable to air war as well as other forms of struggle:

1. There must be total mobilization of the people—"organizing millions to rush into battle"—a task only the Party is capable of handling.

2. The struggle must be geared to the broader world scene and to the direction history is taking. Harness "the Party's strength to the strength of the era and to the strength of international developments." Implicit in this instruction was the sense that there is need for outside support, psychic as well as material. In contradiction, the principle of self-reliance, of being dependent on no one, was stressed throughout.

3. The force of nationalism must be linked to the appeal of socialism-communism.

4. An aggressive mentality was required for all participants, and it must be manifested by continuing offensive actions even if insignificant. The great enemy was passivity.

5. The struggle, as they say in the theater, must build. Strategy should seek to deliver small defeats to the enemy, one after another, so that he is slowly reduced until the final *coup de grace* can be delivered. Struggle must come in stages.

6. The most important requirement is the proper blending and timing of armed struggle and political struggle, which seems in the final resolve to be a matter of intuitive judgement by the leaders. Time here is a mystic dimension.[21]

The political *dau tranh* arm of North Vietnamese grand strategy was also employed as a means of air defense. Throughout the war Hanoi officials and cadres sought to shape outside perception of the Vietnamese "struggle." A host of communicational, political, and psychological devices were employed to de-limit the American military response in Vietnam and to inhibit full use of Amer-ican military capability including air power. Inherent in this image projection was the idea that the Vietnamese "struggle" was political, that the use of massed military might was illegitimate (except "defensive measures" taken by "the People"), and that all force was, by definition, repression, terror, and war crime.

A campaign was generated and operated throughout called the *dich van* (action among the enemy) program; it involved nonmilitary action in the enemy camp, in Vietnam, and throughout the world. The program's first purpose was to shape perception, and its second to serve as a strategic weapon to subvert American war support at home, ruin American diplomacy abroad, and impede American war making in Vietnam. *Dich van* techniques were particularly useful to vilify American use of air power. During the 1965–1968 air war period and again during the so-called 1972 Christmas bombing, major *dich van* campaigns were launched to force cessation of the air attacks. Hanoi historians today generally believe, perhaps incorrectly, that the March 1968 halt in air strikes was the result of these efforts.[22]

Such activity of course was entirely legitimate and proper on the part of Hanoi. If the North Vietnamese could achieve a strategic goal with *dich van* techniques, if they and their agents of influence, and their unwitting allies, could pressure Lyndon Johnson into halting or curtailing the air war against them, who could say nay? Although we must not give this *dich van* program too much credit—many other influences were at work at the time—there can be little doubt that Hanoi's vilification of the American air war succeeded in the United States to the extent of causing many people to believe the air strikes somehow were more brutal and horrible than use of air power elsewhere—in Mid-East wars at the time, for example. It caused many to use the double standard proffered by the North Vietnamese: The demolition of a South Vietnamese bridge by the Viet Cong was acceptable, whereas the demolition of a North Vietnamese bridge by an American plane was not.

HISTORICAL CONCLUSIONS

Measuring the role and assessing the significance of air power in the Vietnam War probably is a historian's single most difficult task. Beyond raw tonnage and secondary explosion figures, the evidence is composed of imponderables, gross claims, emotionalized description, rationalized justification, interservice rivalries, and once again, of course, differing perceptions. The controversial assessments of the Vietnam air war were a straight line extension of the great air power debate that began in World War II. It has run through the Korean War and continues to this day. It is a debate between victory-through-air-power advocates and their military and civilian critics.

Regarding the Vietnam War, this much seems generally agreed upon: Air power played a minor role in the first years, the revolutionary guerrilla warfare state. Tactical air power, what there was of it, made a small but useful contribution; strategic airpower was virtually uninvolved. After 1965, the influence of air power—and the change it wrought—can hardly be exaggerated. Close air support saved the day in several key ground fights—for example, the crucial battle of Binh Gia in late 1964. Linebacker I also shattered much of the spring 1972 North Vietnamese invasion. North Vietnam's logistic buildup and troop movements were inhibited—although, of course, never halted—by air interdiction, and often air strikes were the only counter to enemy preparations for battle. The helicopter so changed the face of warfare that there can never be a return to prehelicopter tactics in future limited or revolutionary warfare.

However, historians of the Vietnam War are still at the starting gate as far as assessing its full historical meaning. It is now clear, from evidence developed since the end of the war in 1975, that few observers—military or civilian, American or Vietnamese, war supporter or antiwar activist—had the war very straight at the time. With a few exceptions, little of what was written at the time by way of historical critique or lessons learned has stood the test of time.

In attempting to make a historical judgment on airpower in the Vietnam War, we face the same general problem found throughout the conflict: no generally agreed on measurements. The yardsticks employed to date tend to be subjective. In truth, analysts have not yet reached agreement on how to really measure the war, or what criteria to employ.

An example of this problem of historical measure with respect to air power is found in evaluating the meaning of the December 1972 so-called Christmas bombing of Hanoi. That event stamped a huge question mark on most of what had been concluded earlier by American officials in Saigon and elsewhere. In the eleven-day air attack, Hanoi officials experienced true, all-out strategic air war for the first time. It had a profound effect, causing them to reverse virtually overnight their bargaining position at the Paris talks. This negotiational turn-around subsequently led to the thesis by some historians that if the United States had done in February 1965 what it did in December 1972, the Vietnam War, at least as the Americans knew it, would have been over by mid–1965. Other historians, challenging this thesis, argue that the two periods were not the same, that the stakes for North Vietnam were vastly different, and that U.S. policy and objectives were also different. Parenthetically, it should be noted that the problem of making historical conclusions also plagues historians in Hanoi. There is little agreement among *them* as to *how* they won the war; they divide the credit for victory between political *dau tranh* and armed *dau tranh*.[23]

This is not to say that historical judgments cannot be rendered. It seems well established now that one of the reasons for the outcome of the war, and the limited effects of U.S. air power, was the *nature* of North Vietnamese society and the singular qualities of those who led it. The Democratic Republic of Vietnam (DRVN) was deeply militaristic, not in outward appearance but in mind-set. Its leaders were used to warfare, and had been at it longer than any other ruling group in the world at the time. They were not stereotype militarists but "praetorians," men who thought only of campaigns, combat, victories. Thus, North Vietnam's culture was central to its wartime success. A second conclusion is that Hanoi had a highly effective strategy in the *dau tranh* (struggle) strategy. Its more important characteristics, with respect to air war, is what might be called its "power-nullification" abilities. As Hanoi applied it, it shunted off the foreign power—military, political, economic, and psychological power—that ranged against it. This also involved the Communists' skilled use of techniques of perceptional deception—in effect throwing sand in the eyes of the world as to what exactly was going on in North and South Vietnam and as to what the war actually involved. These are generalized kinds of conclusions. Still, they are forthright and essentially valid. On the other hand, fuller judgments of history are still to come.

NOTES

1. Vo Nguyen Giap, *"Big Victory, Great Task"* (New York: Praeger, 1968), 66–71 [hereafter *"Big Victory"*]. The original publication of this book was by Foreign Language Publishing House in Hanoi, 1967. Also see Vo Nguyen Giap, *People's War Against the United States Aeronaval War* (Hanoi: Foreign Language Publication House, 1975), 16–17.

2. Douglas Pike, *Vietnam and the USSR: Anatomy of an Alliance* (Boulder, CO: Westview, 1987), 116–29.

3. This information is based on interviews conducted by myself in the summer of 1968 among defectors and POWs who had been in Hanoi just prior to their defection and had seen the effects of the air war. Found in Douglas Pike, "Interviews Conducted in

South Vietnam: Notes and Transcripts," *General History of the Vietnam War: War Participants Interviews*, Indochina Archives, Unit III, Sec. 15, Univ. of California, Berkeley.

4. Ibid.

5. The information found in this and the following chart, as well as in Admiral Sharp's report, can be found in an unpublished study by Douglas Pike, *Assessment and Strategy of the Vietnam War: Retrospective on the War*, Unit I, Sec. 18.

6. Ibid.

7. For a graphic description of this campaign as viewed from those in Hanoi, see John Morrocco, *Rain of Fire: Air War, 1969–1973* volume in Robert Manning, ed., *The Vietnam Experience* (Boston: Boston Publishing Co., 1986), "The Christmas Bombings," Ch. 7.

8. For source materials on official U.S. civilian Saigon Embassy thinking of the use of air power, see cable traffic between the embassy and Washington in U.S. Department of State, *Foreign Relations of the United States, 1961–1963*, Vol. III, *Vietnam*, January– August 1963 (Washington, DC: Government Printing Office [GPO], 1991). The forth- coming volumes in this same series, particularly those covering the first few months of 1965, should contain a great deal of material on official civilian views of the air war (expected publication 1993).

9. Alfred C. Mierzejewski, *The Collapse of the German War Economy, 1944–1945: Allied Air Power and the German National Railway* (Chapel Hill: Univ. of North Carolina Press, 1987), Ch. 1.

10. Lester Sobel, ed., *United States–Communist Confrontation in Southeast Asia, 1961–1965, South Vietnam*, Vol. 1 (New York: Facts on File, 1966).

11. Douglas Pike, *PAVN: People's Army of North Vietnam* (Novato, CA: Presidio Press, 1986), 104 [hereafter *PAVN*].

12. Ibid.

13. Ibid.

14. Mark Clodfelter, *The Limits of Air Power: The American Bombing of North Vietnam* (New York: Free Press, 1989), Ch. 1.

15. Ibid., 132.

16. Ibid., Ch. 1.

17. Pike, *PAVN*, i.

18. Giap, *"Big Victory,"* Ch. 1.

19. Ibid.

20. Pike, *PAVN*, Ch. 2.

21. Ibid., Ch. 10.

22. Ibid., Ch. 11.

23. Ibid.

Part IV

The Ground War

The ground war in South Vietnam was the most violent and costly aspect of the Vietnam War. Eighty to 90 percent of U.S., South Vietnamese, and Communist forces' casualties occurred in conjunction with the ground war. Hundreds of thousands of South Vietnamese civilians were wounded or died in and around the ground fighting, associated air strikes and artillery fire. U.S. military deaths in the war were 58,000. Army of the Republic of Vietnam (ARVN) forces lost about 220,000. MACV estimated that Communist forces lost about 750,000 men. War-related hospital admissions in South Vietnam between 1965 and 1974 numbered about 475,000 people. They probably represented between 65 and 80 percent of those actually wounded, which would give a total range of 595,000 to 730,000 war-related wounded. Guenter Lewy has estimated the total South Vietnamese civilian war deaths from 1965 to 1974 to be 248,000 killed and 39,000 assassinated by Viet Cong (VC)/North Vietnamese Army (NVA) forces.[1]

While South Vietnamese military deaths over the same period were about 220,000, the total South Vietnamese casualty figure may well have been 1.2 million, or one out of every seventeen citizens of the republic. This would equate to about 13 million American casualties, 5 million of them dead, if populations were compared. In total, Vietnamese casualties—both North and South—compare forcefully with the 2 million (686,000 dead) American casualties from our own Civil War.

These South Vietnamese casualties were, in no small measure, a by-product of U.S. military search and destroy operations combined with lavish firepower from air, artillery, and armor. This U.S. munitions intensive firepower strategy that substituted firepower for manpower, when joined with the very questionable practice of H & I (harassment and interdiction) fire, produced operations that were mind-boggling in their lethality. For example, in the spring of 1968, the United States put $1 billion of ordnance into the Khe Sanh siege—which may have killed 10,000 PAVN. During the April 1972 offensive, U.S. forces averaged 250,000 rounds of ammunition *per day*.[2] During the years of this firepower holocaust, 40 percent of South

Vietnam's population left their homes and—as refugees—usually crammed into the RVN's coastal cities. One result was the severing of the tenuous political link between the Saigon government and its people.

In this part, John M. Gates and Larry Cable examine the ground war from conceptual and operational points of view, respectively, and come to reinforcing conclusions. Gates looks at the postwar defense of U.S. ground operations in Vietnam by senior U.S. commanders and conservative civilians, and their remark that the United States never lost a battle, and in light of the lost war, he asks "of what relevance is that?" He notes how revisionist writers answer the question "What went wrong in Vietnam?" with either "nothing" or "mistakes by civilians." In fact, as the collateral damage casualty figures attest for our South Vietnamese ally, plenty went wrong in the ground war. Moreover, U.S. ground commanders had *almost no* restrictions placed on them by civilian authorities as to where and how they could operate or with what kinds of tactics or firepower (as distinct from American pilots who were hemmed in by a host of restrictions in the air war over North Vietnam).

Gates notes how the American military command chose to "mirror image" the Communist threat, seizing upon the fact that since Hanoi and the VC made use, in part, of conventional forces, that justified U.S. officials' claims that the war was at heart conventional, and thus the United States should operate in an almost completely conventional mode. He also notes how U.S. military authorities downplayed or ignored the whole southern revolutionary situation and the critical role played by Viet Cong units and the Communist political infrastructure. For MACV, USARV, CINCPAC, the JCS, and the hawks in the Johnson administration, the war *had* to be conventional in nature in order to justify our huge, lavish firepower, munitions-intensive, conventional combat operations.

Finally, in analyzing the revisionists' mytho-history, and the "Ramboloney" depictions of the war, Gates weighs in with findings that other authors have also noted—the huge collateral damage to South Vietnam; the orphaning of the pacification effort in favor of big unit operations; the jealousy between the Army and the Marines and their very different approaches to contested villages; the six-month rotation policy that ruined unit cohesion; the military's self-indulgent base camps; the huge tail-to-tooth ratio; the fallacy of body counts; the irrelevance of the U.S. attrition strategy when the enemy controlled its losses; and so on. The net results: a strategic failure by the Army's leadership and by the highest Johnson administration officials, and an attempt to rewrite history.

Larry Cable's detailed discussion of ground operations in the period from 1965 to late 1967 notes how the flaws in Army doctrine and perceptions influenced the whole conduct of operations and, indeed, the vast decision-making and perceptual apparatus of the Johnson administration. Alternating his chronological appraisal of U.S. ground operations in South Vietnam with periodic reassessments by the Johnson administration, Cable notes how the administration, and the Army in particular, could not free itself of the big-unit, mobility and firepower first, body-count syndrome.

Operating from its presumption that the problem in South Vietnam was primarily military, not political, and conventional, not revolutionary, U.S. Army doctrine and conduct in Vietnam concentrated on multibattalion reconnaissance in force ("search and destroy") operations against Communist regular forces. Thus, the Army reached back to the Clausewitzian notion of closing on the enemy and destroying his forces through decisive, standup combat. Guerrillas, cadres, political infrastructure, and socioeconomic conditions were seen by the U.S. Army as secondary or superfluous. Superior U.S. firepower and mobility would win, regardless. Beginning in the fall of 1965, U.S. ground operations involved the 173rd Airborne Brigade and the 1st Infantry Division and then broadened to the 25th Infantry Division and the 1st Air Cavalry Division. Mid–1966 Johnson administration assessments, despite some prominent civilians' reservations, generally argued that these U.S. operations had forestalled a Viet Cong victory, braced the GVN, and—in CIA Director Richard Helms's remarkable view—had the additional *positive* effect of helping to generate over 800,000 South Vietnamese refugees: "liberty loving people" who were clearly "voting with their feet" by coming in under GVN control.

From April to mid-October 1966, the Army (and some Marine units) continued to take the initiative to the enemy in operations like Birmingham, Hollandia, El Paso II/III, Sante Fe, Yorktown, John Paul Jones, Sioux City, and Attleboro—involving the 1st and 25th Infantry Divisions, the 173rd Airborne Brigade, the 196th Light Infantry Brigade, the 101st Airborne Division, and various armored cavalry units. While racking up impressive body counts, these operations, in Cable's view, continued to illustrate the basic defects in American strategy. Concentrating on destroying material and disrupting enemy organizations, "neither of these [objectives] could be accomplished in a way which would permanently diminish either the will or the capacity of the Viet Cong or the PAVN to continue the war. . . . Search and destroy was something that could be done; not something that should be done." The enemy simply moved out of the way when big U.S. units came in or harassed them with snipers and mines.

As 1967 began, the Johnson administration was still unable to define its concept of victory in a clear and comprehensive form so as to build sufficient public and congressional support. The protests over the bombing and the war were growing. Moreover, Hanoi had concluded it could both continue to absorb the punishment from the air war and protract the violence in the South past the Americans' will to stay and South Vietnam's ability to effectively recover.

By mid–1967, with Secretary of Defense McNamara now publicly expressing doubts about U.S. strategy, the Johnson administration had hunkered down. The largest search and destroy operation of the war—Junction City I/II, a multidivisional campaign in War Zone C—had just concluded, but given the fixation with body counts, it did not destroy the Communist war effort in the III corps area around Saigon. Subsequent operations that fall, especially during the battle of Dak To in the highlands, again produced tactical results (while relying on a major air effort) but no strategic breakthrough. And then, in January 1968, came the Communist Tet Offensive. Although the Communist attack forces would ultimately be shattered, Tet broke the back of the Johnson administration's war policy, and in the process shattered the myths and measurements upon which the U.S. operational theory of victory had been based.

NOTES

1. Drawing on Guenter Lewy, *America in Vietnam* (New York: Oxford Univ. Press, 1978), 244, 451, as interpreted by Lawrence E. Grinter, "Vietnam: The Cost of Ignoring the Political Requirements," in Lawrence E. Grinter and Peter M. Dunn, eds., *The American War in Vietnam* (Westport, CT: Greenwood, 1987), 39.

2. See Andrew F. Krepinevich, Jr., *The Army and Vietnam* (Baltimore: Johns Hopkins Univ. Press, 1986), 170, 190–91, 196–205, 222, 224.

If at First You Don't Succeed, Try to Rewrite History: Revisionism and the Vietnam War

John M. Gates

Analyzing failure is never easy, but the United States military's analysis of the war in Vietnam has been made more difficult by the tendency of many military and political leaders to embrace an interpretation of the war, labeled revisionist by some historians, that inhibits rather than enhanced our understanding of the conflict.[1]

The revisionist interpretation gained prominence in military circles with the work of U.S. Army Col. Harry Summers, Jr. Although perhaps the best known of the revisionists coming from within the military, Summers is not the only publicist of the revisionist view. It is a widely held view, and it has dominated the image of the war found in most movies, the popular press, and the minds of many Americans for more than a decade.

In capsule form, the revisionist depiction of the war being passed along to the generations who were in the war, including many young military officers, is as follows: The Vietnam War was not a revolutionary conflict or a civil war, but a conventional war launched by North Vietnam against South Vietnam. The Americans might have won had they only recognized the war's true nature. The United States military was never defeated in Vietnam; it won every battle. It would have gained victory were it not for the inability of civilian leaders to define the objective, the limitations they placed on the use of American military power, and the failure of popular will at home, undermined by the media and the antiwar protesters.

Such revisionist views, familiar to any one studying the Vietnam War, constitute a historical interpretation that is as mythical as it is popular. Paying too little attention to the evidence before them, the revisionists have misperceived or misrepresented the actual nature of the Vietnam War, the identity of the enemy, the degree of American success, and the reasons for American failure. At its worst, revisionist writing is pure "Ramboloney," to use Stephen Pelz's

term, and the interpretation would hardly be deserving of scholarly attention if
it did not have such significant implications.[2]

In too many particulars, the revisionist answer to the question, "What went
wrong?" is either "nothing" or "something the civilians did." Thus, instead
of encouraging military leaders to look inward in evaluating the American failure
in Vietnam, the revisionist view shifts the focus and the blame to the nation's
political leaders, journalists, and antiwar protestors. If the conflict in Vietnam
was not a revolutionary war, or was lost because the United States did not direct
its power against the proper enemy, or because the American people and their
civilian leaders lacked sufficient courage or will, then the military need not
engage in major doctrinal or operational reform. If the Army and the other
services never lost a battle, then neither tactical nor strategic thinking need major
overhaul. However, at the very least the flawed interpretations of the revisionists
create a major stumbling block for officers attempting to understand why the
United States failed in Vietnam or trying to develop methods for countering
revolutionary warfare.

Unfortunately, one cannot hope to counter all of the flawed revisionist arguments in a single chapter, and thus a more limited goal is in order. The
argument that follows focuses on three of the more significant revisionist claims:
(1) that the Communists did not triumph in a revolutionary or people's war but
in a conventional one, (2) that the enemy was the North Vietnamese, and (3)
that the American military performed well in Vietnam.

CONVENTIONAL WAR OR REVOLUTIONARY WAR

At the heart of the revisionist argument is the view that the conflict in Vietnam
was first and foremost a conventional war and not a revolutionary or people's
war. Revisionists such as Norman Hannah have argued that the war "was not
a true insurgency but a thinly disguised aggression."[3] The successful Communist
attack in 1975, wrote Sir Robert Thompson, was "a straightforward conventional
invasion and conquest."[4] Others such as General Philip Davidson, Jr., have
characterized the war from 1964 onward as "an outright invasion of South
Vietnam by North Vietnam."[5]

According to other revisionists the Communists won the war "by purely
conventional means, using precisely the kind of warfare at which the American
army was best equipped to fight."[6] It was a style that Timothy Lomperis calls
"almost American."[7] To argue anything else, claims Colonel Summers, one
must accept "the North Vietnamese contention" that the Communist regular
forces "were an extension of the guerrilla effort, a point of view," Summers
asserts "not borne out by the facts."[8]

"The facts," of course, should determine the validity of any interpretation,
but in the case of Vietnam they do not support the revisionist view that the war
was a conventional conflict. Instead, considerable evidence exists to indicate
that from the start to finish the conflict was a revolutionary civil war.

The revisionist argument that the Communist use of conventional forces made the conflict a conventional war rests upon a misunderstanding of the theory and practice of revolutionary conflict. Revisionists often place undue emphasis on the importance of guerrilla warfare and assert that significant reliance on conventional operations represents either a failure or an abandonment of revolutionary warfare. The revisionist case, however, directly contradicts the views of the principal practitioners of people's war.

Mao Tse-tung, Vo Nguyen Giap, and Truong Chinh all stated that revolutionaries would move from guerrilla to mobile or conventional warfare as they gained strength. Mao saw regular forces as having "primary importance," and he deemed mobile warfare "essential."[9] In 1961, General Giap noted the importance of the progression in the war against the French from guerrilla warfare to "mobile warfare combined with partial entrenched camp warfare."[10] Even earlier, Truong Chinh wrote that in the final stage of a revolutionary conflict "positional warfare" would have a "paramount role."[11] Students of Asian revolutionary warfare such as Sir Robert Thompson recognized that the defeat of government forces by "*the regular forces of the insurgents . . . in conventional battle*" would be "a classical ending in accordance with the orthodox theory," although Thompson and others failed to recognize the "classical ending" for what it was when it came in 1975.[12]

Revolutionary war theory neither implied nor required that the Viet Cong guerrillas achieve victory on their own. Instead, in their attacks against the Republic of Vietnam and its American ally, the Communists used a variety of military forces, including "guerrilla, regional, and main-force units."[13] Resistance, wrote Truong Chinh, "must be carried out in every field: military, economic, political and cultural."[14] As Giap observed, "the fight against the enemy on all fronts—military, political, cultural, diplomatic, and so forth—is waged at the same time."[15]

If any single strategy element dominated in the Vietnamese view of people's or revolutionary war it was protraction of the conflict rather than the use of any particular military approach, guerrilla or conventional. As Ho Chi Minh observed in 1950, "in military affairs time is of prime importance." He placed it "first among the three factors for victory, before the terrain conditions and the people's support."[16] Giap also placed high value on "protracted resistance," calling it "an essential strategy of a people . . . determined to defeat an enemy and aggressor having large and well-armed forces."[17]

The image of Communist tanks moving through the streets of Saigon at the culmination of the successful spring 1975 offensive provides the cornerstone of the revisionist conventional war argument. A powerful image, quite reminiscent of World War II, it has helped to sustain the revisionist view. Despite all its seemingly conventional drama, however, even the final act of the war was an example of revolutionary warfare rather than a conventional invasion.

Although hurt during the Tet Offensive of 1968 and by operations such as the Phoenix program in subsequent years, the local Communist apparatus in the

South had not been destroyed, and estimates indicate that at the time of the 1973 cease-fire agreement local forces constituted a significant portion of Communist strength, particularly outside of Military Region I. Although the local units provided only 16.9 percent of total Communist combat strength, they contributed over 50 percent of the administrative and service personnel. In Military Region III, local forces supplied 20 percent of the combat troops and 68.8 percent of the administrative and service personnel. In Military Region IV, the percentages were much higher—40.7 percent and 92.3 percent, respectively.[18]

Such statistics, which do not appear to include the Communist political infrastructure, indicate that at the local levels Communist strength had recovered more than many revisionists would admit, particularly in the heavily populated Mekong Delta and the area surrounding Saigon. Although absent in the revisionist descriptions of the final offensive, local Communist forces do appear in other accounts of the attack.

Revisionists often cite General Van Tien Dung's memoir as evidence that the 1975 attack was purely conventional, but careful reading of Dung indicates something very different. He claimed that "regional forces" participated in the attacks that defeated the 4th and 5th regiments of the ARVN 2d Division on March 24 and 25. He also gave them credit, "in coordination with the masses," for the liberation of the northern part of Quan Ngai province and for success in Zone 5, including the attack on Danang.[19] He wrote that during the attack on Saigon local forces "tied down and drew off a number of enemy main-force units in IV Corps," while "special action and sapper units" attacked from inside the city.[20] Other Communist sources also contain references to the use of local forces and popular uprisings, including the observation that attacks by local forces on "outposts, subsectors, and district capitals" helped the regular forces stage their attacks.[21]

Interviews with RVN officials and military officers confirm the Communist claim that irregulars played an important role in the final offensive. According to the South Vietnamese who attempted to counter the Communist attack, ARVN forces in III and IV Corps were so "hard pressed and tied down by local Communist forces" that they "could not be disengaged from the north." Later, those same local forces moved in captured ARVN vehicles into Long An province to threaten Route 4 and support the attack on Saigon. The ARVN Chief of Staff for II Corps estimated that in 1975 Communist regular units made up no more than 46 percent of the forces he faced in his area.[22]

Describing their defeat, RVN officials and officers stressed their own failures in ways that emphasized the unconventional aspects of the war. Their stories of panic, disorder, demoralization, defeatism, paralysis, and incompetence confirm the Communist view that the war was won as much by political and diplomatic maneuvers as by military ones. The problems described were the result of years of protracted war, using all levels of forces and tactical repertoire, and not a function of the final Communist offensive. If one looks at "the facts," as revisionists such as Colonel Summers claim to do, one finds that the 1975 attack was the coup de grace of a successful people's war and not a conventional coup de main.[23]

THE ENEMY: NORTH VIETNAMESE ONLY?

To some degree the revisionist argument regarding the conventional nature of the war rests on the misidentification of the enemy. Revisionists tend to define the Communist movement in Vietnam as a North Vietnamese phenomenon, and they portray North Vietnam as a separate country bent on the conquest of its southern neighbor. But Vietnam's Communist leaders never recognized the partition that revisionists assume took place in 1954, and they were committed to the creation of a unified Communist Vietnam. In their view, the Democratic Republic of Vietnam (DRV) was not a complete state, but "the liberated half" of their country, "the revolutionary base" from which they would orchestrate and support the struggle to reunify the nation.[24]

Although for propaganda purposes Communist leaders sought to portray the war in the South as a conflict waged exclusively by the people of the south, the fiction could not be maintained, and in 1967 General Giap openly portrayed the war as a struggle involving the DRV.[25] The United States government was correct in its claim that the Communist guerrillas and cadres in the South, as well as the National Liberation Front, were operational elements of the DRV, but that does not mean that the South was being attacked by the North Vietnamese. America's enemy throughout the struggle was a Communist movement in which both leaders and followers came from *all* parts of Vietnam. The war in Vietnam was never a war of northerners against southerners, but of Communists against non-Communists.

Before World War II, members of the Vietnamese Communist party could be found throughout Vietnam, and Ho's August 1945 revolution was similarly nationwide.[26] In 1954, as northern nationalists such as Bui Diem and Nguyen Cao Ky cast their lot with the government in Saigon, southern Communists such as Pham Van Dong, Le Duan, and Pham Hung took up positions in the highest levels of the Communist government in Hanoi.

Although biographical information on Vietnam's Communist leaders is incomplete, the data that does exist indicates that the people who controlled the DRV and the war against the government in the South came from all regions of the country.[27] During most of the war four of eleven members of the politburo (36.4 percent) were southerners, and in 1973 a majority of the nine-member secretariat of the Vietnamese Workers' Party (VWP) came from the South. At the time of the Communist victory in 1975 six of fourteen members of the politburo (42.9 percent) were from the South, as were over half of the members elected to the council of ministers, whose place of birth can be determined (twenty of thirty-eight). To the extent that any region of Vietnam was overrepresented in the leadership of the Communist movement and the DRV, it was central Vietnam both north and south of the 17th parallel.[28]

The conclusion that seems inescapable directly contradicts the revisionists' interpretation. The war that ended in 1975 was not a conquest of the South Vietnamese by the North Vietnamese. Although the war clearly ended in a Communist victory, the leaders of Vietnam's Communist movement, like the anti-Communist nationalists they defeated, came from both sides of the 17th parallel.

U.S. BATTLEFIELD PERFORMANCE: HOW "MAGNIFICENT"?

For all its flaws, the revisionists' view of revolutionary warfare and the nature of the Vietnamese Communist movement looks almost scholarly compared to the revisionist Ramboloney regarding the American military's performance in Vietnam. In many respects, however, that element of the revisionist interpretation is most relevant to a discussion of the Army's Vietnam legacy.

Bill McCloud's interesting book, *"What Should We Tell Our Children About Vietnam?"* contains some very revealing passages. In it one finds General Westmoreland's chief of intelligence claiming that "American forces won every battle in, over, and around Vietnam." American forces, we are told, "conducted themselves . . . with great military effectiveness." According to an Air Force colonel, also an intelligence officer, "there is no record of any U.S. military unit of any size, down to companies and platoons, that was ever defeated or that did not achieve its goal or objective." In his view, "all American forces— Army, Navy, Marines, and Air Force—performed magnificently in Southeast Asia."General Westmoreland places the blame for the American failure in Vietnam squarely on the shoulders of Congress, saying "the military did not lose a single battle of consequence and did not lose the war."[29]

Assertions that U.S. forces "won every battle" or "performed magnificently," like the rest of the revisionists' mytho-history, do not stand up to scrutiny. Although Americans in and over Vietnam fought courageously, and large numbers of them also fought well, as an institution the American military did not perform effectively.

Although here we can give only a meager description of individual problems, numerous authors, military as well as civilian, have identified a variety of ways in which the military failed in Vietnam, and the problems they have noted are both extensive and significant. At virtually every turn high-ranking American officers made decisions that hurt the war effort and contributed to the defeat.[30]

One of the most important of the decisions made by the U.S. high command concerned the way in which the American military force assembled in Southeast Asia would be used. Although initially one finds command references to "counterinsurgency," the focus soon shifted to the large-scale operations that came to be known by the rubric "search and destroy." Although President Johnson restricted the American ground force to operating within the confines of the Republic of Vietnam, neither he nor any other civilian forced the Army to conduct operations as it did or compelled it to devote as little effort as it did to pacification operations.[31]

For General Wheeler, "the essence of the problem in Vietnam" was "military," and he believed that in the context of what was possible General Westmoreland's approach, using "superior American firepower . . . to find . . . fix . . . and defeat the enemy" gave "the best assurance of military victory in South Vietnam."[32] The firepower-intensive approach seemed equally acceptable to most of the corps and division commanders that served under Westmoreland.[33]

During and after the war few command decisions were subjected to such widespread criticism, even from revisionists such as Colonel Summers. General Dave Palmer later argued that the war of attrition was not a true strategy at all, only evidence of strategic bankruptcy.[34] Despite the criticism, however, the war proceeded as planned, although the planning was clearly not good.

When the Marines implemented their innovative Combined Action Program designed to protect the rural population in the I Corps area, they gained little praise at the Army-dominated MACV headquarters. General Westmoreland and his staff wanted the Marines to participate more actively in search and destroy operations. Criticizing them for involvement "in counterinsurgency of the deliberate, mild sort," General Depuy urged Westmoreland to direct them to launch large-unit operations, and another Army General, Harry O. Kinnard, was "absolutely disgusted" with the Marine approach.[35] Not wanting to "precipitate an interservice imbroglio" by dealing too abruptly with General Walt, Westmoreland "chose to issue orders for specific projects that as time passed would gradually get the Marines out of their beachheads," weakening one of the few American military approaches that made sense.[36]

The bad strategic choices of the U.S. high command were made worse by the equally bad managerial decision establishing the one-year tour of duty with a six-month rotation between staff and command positions for officers. The results of this policy were catastrophic. One major observed that everyone who talked to him "about the six-month-command, six-month-staff concept agreed that it was crap,"[37] and as Ronald Spector observed, "The system produced constant personnel turnovers, broke down unit cohesion, and ensured that, at any given movement, a platoon or company 'in the bush' would be made up largely of inexperienced newcomers."[38]

A good officer takes care of the troops, but American commanders in Vietnam confused care with indulgence. The result was a proliferation of elaborate bases with air-conditioned quarters, clubs, and PXs filled with luxury goods. Lt. General Joseph Heiser, who commanded the U.S. Army's 1st Logistical Command in Vietnam, complained that "too many luxuries burdened an already heavily taxed logistical system." After the war Gen. Hamilton Howze observed, "Our base camps became too elaborate, soaked up too much manpower, diverted our attention from the basic mission and lessened our operational flexibility."[39]

The military's self-indulgence, when combined with the emphasis on the use of firepower, also restricted operations in the field. As the logistical tail of a military force grows, the number of troops able to patrol and fight on the ground declines. It is a simple problem in mathematics; each soldier diverted to supervise a club, repair an air conditioner, or perform some other military unnecessary task is a soldier that might have been used in the field. Although the estimates vary, the number of combat troops available for deployment in sustained ground operations when the United States had 536,000 service personnel in Vietnam may have been as low as 80,000.[40]

In the realm of strategic decision making, personnel policies, and that most basic aspect of leadership, taking care of the troops, the high-ranking officers of the American military machine failed to exhibit wisdom. Even worse, perhaps, the military engaged in systematic self-deception that prevented the reevaluation of its bad decisions. The widespread evidence of the high command's stubborn commitment to error led Andrew Krepinevich, Jr., to conclude that the Army in Vietnam was "uninterested in information questioning its approach to the war."[41] Sadly, the military's self-deception not only exemplified bureaucratic wishful thinking, but also outright fabrication of information, as was the case in the statistical reporting of body counts.

In *On Strategy*, Colonel Summers claimed that "as far as logistics and tactics were concerned we succeeded in everything we set out to do," and "on the battlefield itself," he wrote, "the Army was unbeatable."[42] But a far different picture of the operational performance of American units appears in Shelby Stanton's very detailed work, *The Rise and Fall of an American Army*. In 1966, for example, the Army's own data indicate that "88 percent of all fights were being initiated by the NVA or the VC, and half of these (46%) began as ambushes." As Stanton observed, "The NVA and VC forces were able to seek or break off combat with relative freedom." The "battlefield initiative" was in their hands, and "green" American soldiers were "faring poorly as a result." Later in the war, although more successful, the Army was still fighting "well below its potential," and after the order to begin a withdrawal of American forces was issued, "morale and discipline caved in on an escalating basis, and combat performance declined."[43]

One finds a similarly dismal assessment of American battlefield performance in Dave Palmer's work on the war. Pointing to the American tendency to use its own troops as bait, he observed that "the time-honored technique of fire and maneuver had switched over to one of maneuver and fire." As a result, descriptions of military engagements in Vietnam are filled with references to American troops "pinned down" by "heavy fire," unable to "maneuver decisively." As Palmer observed, "The utter dependence on firepower represented a failure of the U.S. system of fighting in Vietnam."[44] Put another way, it represented a complete failure of American military leadership at the tactical as well as the strategic level. Of the Army generals who responded to Douglas Kinnard's questionnaire, 62 percent "thought that the tactics employed could have been improved in a major way."[45]

A problem of particular significance was what Edward Luttwak has termed the military's "tactical self-indulgence," in which "the grossly disproportionate use of firepower became the very theme of the war—and its imagery on television was by far the most powerful stimulus of antiwar sentiment."[46] Despite Colonel Summers's claim that the Communists were defeated "in every major engagement," American tactical decisions hardly seem better than the strategic ones, particularly given the disastrous impact of the firepower-intensive approach on the pacification program.[47]

Robert Komer, the civilian coordinator of the American pacification advisory program, focused much of his critique of the American effort in Vietnam on the tendency of bureaucracies to "play out" their institutional "repertories." As a result, wrote Komer, "Such institutional constraints as the very way our general-purpose forces were trained, equipped, and structured largely dictated our response."[48] In developing its doctrine, tactics, equipment, and tables of organization the American military focused on the problems of relatively large-scale, conventional war. Having developed their individual ideals of how a war should be fought, each service proceeded to act upon those ideas in Vietnam regardless of the actual nature of the war.

Finally, many military officers fell victim to their own individual ambition, and the evidence of opportunistic, careerist behavior described in the U.S. Army War College *Study on Military Professionalism*, completed in 1970, is truly shocking. According to the study, "the existing climate" within the officer corps was characterized by the

ambitious, transitory commander—marginally skilled in the complexities of his duties— engulfed in producing statistical results, fearful of personal failure, too busy to talk with or listen to his subordinates, and determined to submit acceptably optimistic reports which reflect faultless completion of a variety of tasks at the expense of the sweat and frustration of his subordinates.[49]

As one of the generals surveyed by Kinnard observed, "There were too many battalion and brigade commanders getting their tickets punched rather than trying to really lead."[50] One must overlook a lot of evidence to say that the Army performed "magnificently" in Vietnam, and except for its attack on the attrition strategy, the revisionist argument has little to offer anyone in the Army interested in learning from the Vietnam experience.

I am not so foolish as to think that the views I have presented in countering the revisionist argument represent the only interpretation that one can give to the existing data. However, much of what is commonly thought to be true about the Vietnam War rests on revisionist arguments that stand outside and in opposition to the facts. Although unsure about the final interpretation on some points, I am confident that I do have a good sense of what did *not* happen in Vietnam.

The war was not a case of aggression by North Vietnam against South Vietnam, nor was it a civil war indigenous to the South alone. It was also not solely a conventional war, nor were the conventional aspects of the war its most significant feature. Finally, the American military did not win every battle, and it certainly did not withdraw from Vietnam undefeated.

Assuming that the critique of the revisionist's view provided here is valid, what must the American military do to learn from the Vietnam experience? First and foremost, it must admit the fundamental truth of the American experience in Indochina: The United States lost the war; the Communists won. The United States went to Vietnam and stumbled into a revolutionary civil war. Unable to cope with the war as they found it, many Americans responded by redefining the nature of the conflict and, in defeat, creating a myth of success, in which the Americans won every battle. To learn from the experience, however, the military must reject the mytho-history and accept its fair share of responsibility for the defeat.

Second, in undertaking its assessment of the war, the U.S. military must make certain that the conclusions that replace the revisionist myths *fit the facts*. Little can be learned from Ramboloney parading as scholarship, and statements about the nature of the war, the enemy, and the American military's response to both must stand on the evidence and not outside it.

Whatever one calls the Communist approach in Vietnam (people's war, revolutionary war, or something else), it was a method of fighting that established the conditions for victory, and the United States and its South Vietnamese ally failed to counter it. Now, thanks in part to the revisionists and their highly persuasive rhetoric, the American military's misunderstanding of the nature of revolutionary warfare in the Third World may be even greater than it was during the Vietnam War. Has any loser in the history of human conflict ever learned less from defeat?

NOTES

1. The author has made similar arguments in "Peoples War in Vietnam," *The Journal of Military History* 54 (July 1990): 324–44; "American Military Leadership in the Vietnam War," from Henry S. Bausum, ed., *Military Leadership and Command: The John Biggs Cincinnati Lectures, 1987* (Lexington, VA: The VMI Foundation, 1987), 185–209.

2. Stephen Pelz, "Vietnam: Another Stroll Down Alibi Alley," *Diplomatic History* 14 (1990): 123.

3. Anthony T. Bouscaren, ed., *All Quiet on the Eastern Front: The Death of South Vietnam* (Old Greenwich, CT: Devin Press, 1977), 148–49.

4. Ibid., 119.

5. Bill McCloud, *"What Should We Tell Our Children About Vietnam?"* (Norman: Univ. of Oklahoma Press, 1989), 33 [hereafter *"What Should We Tell Our Children?"*].

6. W. Scott Thompson and Donaldson D. Frizzell, eds., *The Lessons of Vietnam* (New York: Crane, Russak, and Co., 1977), 279.

7. Timothy J. Lomperis, "Giap's Dream, Westmoreland's Nightmare," *Parameters* 18 (June 1988): 30.

8. Harry G. Summers, Jr., *On Strategy: A Critical Analysis of the Vietnam War* (New York: Dell, 1984), 121–22 [hereafter *On Strategy*].

9. Samuel B. Griffith, trans., *Mao Tse-Tung on Guerrilla Warfare* (New York: Praeger, 1961), 56, 113.

10. Vo Nguyen Giap, *People's War, People's Army: The Viet Cong Insurrection Manual for Underdeveloped Countries* (New York: Praeger, 1962), 103–4 [hereafter *People's War*].

11. Truong Chinh, *The Resistance Will Win in Primer for Revolt* (New York: Praeger, 1963), 116 [hereafter *Primer*].

12. Sir Robert Thompson, *Revolutionary War in World Strategy, 1945–1969* (New York: Taplinger, 1970), 11. Italics in original. For an overview of revolutionary war strategy and a summary of its strategic phases including mobile warfare, see John J. McCuen, *The Art of Counter-Revolutionary War* (Harrisburg, PA: Stockpole Books, 1966), ch. 2, 37–44 in particular.

13. Vo Nguyen Giap, *"Big Victory, Great Task"* (New York: Praeger, 1968), 74 [hereafter *"Big Victory"*].

14. Chinh, *Primer*, 11.

15. Giap, *"Big Victory,"* 52.

16. "Instructions Given at the Conference Reviewing the Second Le Hong Phong Military Campaign," in Bernard B. Fall, ed., *Ho Chi Minh on Revolution: Selected Writings, 1920–1966* (New York: Praeger, 1968), 188 [hereafter *Ho Chi Minh on Revolution*].

17. Giap, *"Big Victory,"* 55.

18. William E. LeGro, *Vietnam from Cease-Fire to Capitulation* (Washington, DC: Government Printing Office, 1985), 28.

19. Van Tien Dung, *Our Great Spring Victory* (New York: Monthly Review Press, 1977), 105.

20. Ibid., 249.

21. See Tran Van Tra, *Vietnam: History of the Bulwark B2 Theatre*, Vol. 5, *Concluding the 30-Years War* (Ho Chi Minh City: Van Nghe Publishing House, 1982, in JPRS 826783–2 February 1983), 132, 147, 151, 175–78, 182, 196; idem, *War Experiences Recapitulation Committee of the High-Level Military Institute, Vietnam: The Anti–U.S. Resistance War for National Salvation, 1954–1975: Military Events* (Hanoi: People's Republic of Vietnam, Foreign Ministry, 1980, in JPRS 80968–3 June 1982), 173, 176–77, 180 (quote), 182; Vo Nguyen Giap and Van Tien Dung, *How We Won the War* (Ypsilanti, MI: Reconstruction Publications, 1976), 41–42.

22. Stephen T. Hosmer, Konrad Kellen, and Brian M. Jenkins, *The Fall of South Vietnam: Statements by Vietnamese Military and Civilian Leaders* (New York: Crane, Russak, and Co., 1980), 168, 231, 232.

23. Ibid.

24. Giap, *People's War*, 49, 146. Ho Chi Minh expressed similar views; see, for example, "Letter to the Cadres from South Vietnam Regrouped in the North (June 19, 1956)," in Fall, *Ho Chin Minh on Revolution*, 272–74. Although the U.S. government denied the legitimacy of such views, it did recognize their existence, quoting passages from Giap and others in a section entitled "North Viet-Nam: Base for Conquest of the South," in Department of State Publication 7839, *Aggression from the North: The Record of North Viet-Nam's Campaign to Conquer South Viet-Nam* (Washington, DC: Government Printing Office, 1965), 20–21.

25. Giap, *"Big Victory,"* 28, 47.

26. See William J. Duiker, *The Communist Road to Power in Vietnam* (Boulder, CO: Westview, 1981), Chs. 1–5; Huynh Kim Khanh, *Vietnamese Communism, 1925–1945* (Ithaca, NY: Cornell Univ. Press, 1982).

27. Data compiled from Joint United States Public Affairs Office (JUSPAO), "VWP-DRV Leadership, 1960–1973," Document No. 114, *Viet-Nam Documents and Research Notes* (Saigon: Government of the Republic of Vietnam, 1973) [hereafter "VWP-DRV Leadership"]; Central Intelligence Agency, *Reference Aid: Council of Ministers of the Socialist Republic of Vietnam* (Washington, DC: Government Printing Office, 1977); Borys Lewytzkyj and Juliusz Stroynowski, eds., *Who's Who in the Socialist Countries* (New York: S. G. Sauer Publishers, 1978); P. J. Honey, *Communism in North Vietnam: Its Role in the Sino-Soviet Dispute* (Cambridge, MA: MIT Press, 1963).

28. JUSPAO, "VWP-DRV Leadership," 3–4.

29. McCloud, *"What Should We Tell Our Children?"* 79, 124, 137.

30. Only a representative sample can be given of the extensive secondary literature dealing with the failings of the military in Vietnam. See, for examples, Larry E. Cable, *Conflict of Myths: The Development of American Counterinsurgency Doctrine and the Vietnam War* (New York: New York Univ. Press, 1986); Cincinnatus (Cecil B. Currey), *Self-Destruction: The Destruction and Decay of the United States Army During the Vietnam Era* (New York: Norton, 1978) [hereafter *Self-Destruction*]; Andrew F. Krepinevich, Jr., *The Army and Vietnam* (Baltimore: Johns Hopkins Univ. Press, 1986) [hereafter *The Army and Vietnam*]; Guenter Lewy, *America in Vietnam* (New York: Oxford Univ. Press, 1978); Edward N. Luttwak, *The Pentagon and the Art of War* (New York: Touchstone, 1985) [hereafter *Art of War*]; Bruce Palmer, *The 25-Year War: America's Military Role in Vietnam* (Lexington: Univ. of Kentucky Press, 1984); Ronald H. Spector, *Advice and Support: The Early Years, 1941–1960* (Washington, DC: Government Printing Office, 1984); U.S. Army War College, *Study on Military Professionalism* (Carlisle Barracks, PA: U.S. Army, 1970) [hereafter *Military Professionalism*]. Among the available primary material, the oral history interviews with officers who were company and battalion commanders in Vietnam at the U.S. Army's Military History Institute Library, Carlisle Barracks, are particularly revealing.

31. General Westmoreland's justification for employing U.S. units in or near South Vietnam's "critical areas of high population density" is found in General William C. Westmoreland, USA, and Admiral U. S. Grant Sharp, USN, *Report on the War in Vietnam as of 30 June 1968* (Washington, DC: Government Printing Office, 1969), 99, 114, 132. As analyzed by Lawrence E. Grinter, "Vietnam: The Cost of Ignoring the Political Requirements," in Lawrence E. Grinter and Peter M. Dunn, eds., *The American War in Vietnam: Lessons, Legacies, and Implications for Future Conflicts* (Westport, CT: Greenwood, 1987), 36–37, 47 [hereafter *The American War in Vietnam*].

32. Krepinevich, *The Army and Vietnam*, 37, 166.

33. Resulting damage to the South Vietnamese population is presented in Grinter and Dunn, *The American War in Vietnam*, 37–39.

34. See David Richard Palmer, *Summons of the Trumpet: U.S.–Vietnam in Perspective* (San Rafael, CA: Presidio Press, 1978).

35. Krepinevich, *The Army and Vietnam*, 75.

36. Jack Shulimson, *U.S. Marines in Vietnam: An Expanding War, 1966* (Washington, DC: U.S. Marine Corps, 1982), 13.

37. Cincinnatus, *Self-Destruction*, 252.

38. Ronald H. Spector, "The Vietnam War and the Army's Self-Image," in John Schlight, ed., *Second Indochina War Symposium: Papers and Commentary* (Washington, DC: Army Center for Military History, 1986), 180.

39. Edward Doyle et al., *A Collision of Cultures* volume in Robert Manning, ed., *The Vietnam Experience* (Boston: Boston Publishing Co., 1984), 34.

40. Thomas C. Thayer, *War Without Fronts: The American Experience in Vietnam* (Boulder, CO: Westview, 1985), 94.

41. Krepinevich, *The Army and Vietnam*, 79.

42. Summers, *On Strategy*, 1.

43. Shelby L. Stanton, *The Rise and Fall of an American Army: U.S. Ground Forces in Vietnam, 1965–1973* (Novato, CA: Presidio Press, 1985), 86, 365.

44. Palmer, *Summons of the Trumpet*, 144–45.

45. Douglas Kinnard, *The War of Managers* (Hanover, NH: Univ. Press of New England, 1977), 44–45.

46. Luttwak, *Art of War*, 36.

47. Harry G. Summers, Jr., "The Army After Vietnam," in Kenneth J. Hagan and William R. Roberts, eds., *Against All Enemies* (Westport, CT: Greenwood, 1986), 367.

48. Robert W. Komer, *Bureaucracy at War: U.S. Performance in the Vietnam Conflict* (Boulder, CO: Westview, 1986), 48.

49. U.S. Army War College, *Military Professionalism*, 13–14.

50. Kinnard, *The War Managers*, 111.

10

Everything Is Perfect and Getting Better: The Myths and Measures of the American Ground War in Indochina, 1965–1968

Larry E. Cable

INTRODUCTION

Contrary to most interpretations of the American experience in the Vietnam War, the United States, by any meaningful definition, was losing the ground war prior to the Tet urban offensives of 1968.[1] The cause of the defeat was not the allegedly gradual nature of the American force deployment, but rather a failure on the part of American policy makers and military commanders alike to understand *the nature and character* of the war in which they involved the United States.

Plans and strategy more than troops, planes, and tanks are necessary for fighting a war. Plans that are relevant to the realities on the ground and employ the military instruments in a correct way as part of an overall program and strategy of political, social, economic, intelligence, psychological, and military measures are necessary for winning a war. The decision whether or not to go to war in Southeast Asia was not the central intellectual task confronting the Johnson administration and its military command structure. The central task, the most important intellectual process, was determining the purpose for which the war was to be waged, against whom it was to be fought, how it was to be conducted, and how the United States would know if it was winning or not.

Between spring 1964 and early fall 1965 the Johnson administration's policy makers, both civilian and military, had to ask and answer several interlocking and tough questions: What should be the purpose of fighting? Where should we fight? Against whom should we fight? How will we know if we are winning or losing? and How do we intend to win? It was necessary that all these questions be asked and answered in a way that was consistent, coherent, and reflected an accurate understanding of both the situation developing on the ground in Indochina and its implications for American national interests.

In any war to insure that military operations usefully serve a policy purpose as well as to assure that ground, air, and naval operations are effectively integrated, it is essential that the leadership establish the goal toward which all efforts are directed, define success or victory, and provide or approve an overall theory of victory.

A close scrutiny of military history argues powerfully that without the existence of a well-delineated goal, a definition of victory against which the progress of military operations can be assessed by decision makers, and a theory of victory predicated upon a candid and realistic appraisal of the strengths and weaknesses of all combatants, defeat is far more likely than victory. Unduly expansive goals, vague and overly elastic definitions or a "can do" theory of victory have usually resulted in failure. Fundamental intellectual failures in conceptualizing the war cannot be redeemed by the courage or blood of men. It cannot be rectified by the weight of munitions or prowess in the technologies of war.

An interventionary power usually enters a conflict not of its own making. It is therefore necessary to fully understand the goals and theories already at work in the war if the intervention is to have a real chance of success. In South Vietnam, the United States was acting as an interventionary power in support of a status quo regime threatened by domestic insurgency and the possibility of either conventional or guerrilla invasion. This was an uncomfortable role for Washington to play. It was a difficult role if the policy makers did not understand that the local belligerents had their own goals, priorities, and theories of victory. It was an untenable role if the policy makers failed to understand that these factors might or might not be compatible with those of the United States.

South Vietnam, the Viet Cong (VC)/National Liberation Front (NLF), and North Vietnam were the primary parties to the conflict; their definitions of victory or defeat and their goals served to constrain the freedom of the United States to impose its own power with any expectation of success. The Johnson adminis- tration was obliged to recognize that the complex and multiparty conflict in which it was immersing the United States arose from cultural, social, economic, and political factors that were indigenous to the region and were governed by strong local historical and cultural trajectories. This recognition must not simply be a matter of rhetorical genuflection; it must be *acted upon* as a central factor in policy formulation and execution. But the obligation was unmet. The rec- ognition was not made.

JOHNSON ADMINISTRATION PERCEPTIONS AND THE U.S. ARMY CONCEPT

The U.S. government had viewed the Vietnamese conflict for some time as a partisan war rather than an insurgency; it had assumed that the primary enemy was North Vietnam and that without support and direction from Hanoi, the Viet Cong would be reduced to the status of an annoyance readily handled by the police forces of the South. Thus, it had been presumed that Saigon's primary goal should be the deterrence of conventional cross-border invasion by North Vietnam with a subordinate goal of reducing the impact of guerrilla warfare. The definition of victory would be negative in nature—the absence of invasion and serious internal political violence. From the U.S. point of view the appropriate theory of victory for the South Vietnamese government coupled the development of an American-style general-purpose ground combat force, equally capable of suppressing guerrillas and defending the borders, with the implementation of reforms in land ownership, the development of efficient, honest government, and the creation of liberal, pluralistic, free market institutions.

Anticipating the escalation of U.S. forces in Southeast Asia, Joint Chief of Staff (JCS) Chairman General Earle Wheeler on July 2, 1965, had requested a special assessment regarding the "assurance the U.S. can have of winning in SVN [South Vietnam] if we do everything we can."[2] The execution of this assessment and the conclusions reached by the Ad Hoc Study Group constitute an excellent view of shared intellectual heritage operating in a military context as well as the policy ramifications of the process.

Placing the Ad Hoc Study Group's recommendations regarding a theory of victory into proper perspective requires an examination of what the group members knew about the way in which the American ground combat forces would prosecute operations within South Vietnam. It is not necessary to look for specific directives given to the Commander, U.S. Military Assistance Command, Vietnam (COMUSMACV) regarding operational conduct to gain this understanding. It is necessary simply to recall the doctrinal focus of the Army, and to a lesser extent the Marines, since it was this doctrine that formed the operational concepts upon which all significant ground combat would be planned and executed. Doctrine, not orders or directives, established the universe in which General William Westmoreland and his subordinates could function.

One item of command guidance can suffice to demonstrate the correctness of this contention. U.S. Army Chief of Staff Harold K. Johnson sent a memorandum to his colleagues on the JCS on April 12, 1965, concerning his view of the actions needed to be taken in South Vietnam now that the first U.S. ground forces had arrived in country.[3] General Johnson underscored the three "basic requirements involved in providing security."[4] They were: find the enemy, fix the enemy in place; fight and finish the enemy. Whether applied to Army of the Republic of Vietnam (ARVN) or U.S. ground combat elements the recipe remained the same. It represented with total fidelity the fundamentally Clausewitzian focus of Army doctrine.

Through all editions of FM 100–5, *Field Service Regulations–Operations*, published prior to the Vietnam War this focus was maintained. All U.S. Army officers were developed in the cult of battle with its single-minded focus upon closing on the enemy and destroying its forces in the field through decisive combat. Not even the introduction of nuclear war and the concomitant cautionary notes against allowing limited (nonnuclear) war to cross the nuclear threshold served to diminish the Clausewitzian tone or modify the focus of destroying the enemy's force in the field and thus its capability to conduct war.[5] The Clausewitzian approach was not limited to the higher operational levels, but extended to the conduct of tactics even at the company level.[6]

When considering guerrilla war, Army doctrine continued its basic concentration on destroying the enemy force in the field. Guerrillas might impose some modest changes in tactics or organization, but they were not immune to destruction through the application of superior mobility and firepower. Aggressiveness, mobility, and firepower represented the solution to the problems presented by the guerrillas.[7]

It was certain that COMUSMACV and his field commanders would use mobility and firepower to take the battle to the guerrillas either out in the bush or within what the enemy considered to be safe havens using superior air and ground mobility to fix him in place. The application of superior firepower, both ground and air delivered, would destroy him whether he attempted to stand or to run. It would be equally certain that U.S. forces would not attempt to hold the land they swept in offensive operations, for holding territory would be too demanding of scarce manpower resources and erosive of the offensive spirit held to be so important.[8]

The basic question confronting the Ad Hoc Study Group was simply that of making a strategic virtue out of an operational necessity. The solution arose from the group's assessment of the logistic requirements of North Vietnamese regular forces and the Viet Cong and the role played by North Vietnam in meeting these needs. The group accepted the argument that the VC were primarily indigenous southerners, led primarily by native southerners, who "produce most of their supplies in South Vietnam and are not solely dependent on an external supply system."[9] In support of this insurgent interpretation, it was noted that only 20 percent of the weapons recovered from the VC in 1964 were of PRC origin, whereas 34 percent were French and 31 percent had been made in America.[10] It was concluded that the entire VC main force of 125 battalion equivalents required only ten tons of supplies per day from North Vietnam given the level of combat intensity that had prevailed through mid–1965.[11] This requirement was too small to allow for easy interdiction by either ground or air attack. The addition of North Vietnamese regulars would increase the supply by only four tons per division.[12]

The small logistics requirements, not more than fourteen tons per day, coupled with the wide array of land and maritime infiltration routes explained why the aerial interdiction campaign had not impaired the ability of North Vietnam to supply its forces and assist the VC in the South.[13] The CIA agreed with group's assessments.[14]

In an excellent application of "if you can't raise the bridge, lower the water" logic, the group concluded that the way to make the lines of supply and the North Vietnamese infrastructure more vulnerable to air attack was to increase the demands placed upon them by the consumers in the South. If the level of combat could be intensified even to that of "a moderate combat situation as described in FM 101–10," Viet Cong requirements would leap from 10 to 125 tons per day and People's Army of Vietnam (PAVN) demands would increase from 12 to 100 tons per day for each full strength division.[15] At a sustained demand level of 225 tons per day, the logistic system would be far more susceptible to aerial interdiction and the North Vietnamese infrastructure far more vulnerable to Operation Rolling Thunder. The group developed a theory of victory that had three main components: ground combat operations against the VC main forces and any PAVN units that entered South Vietnam; interdiction of infiltration routes by air, sea, and ground efforts; and air attacks upon infrastructure and economic target systems in North Vietnam. The theory of victory focused upon the use of U.S. air power against infiltration routes and support facilities in North Vietnam with a secondary thrust on coercing Hanoi through air strikes. U.S. ground combat operations were relegated to the status of a force mutliplier backing the air effort.

In considering ground combat operations, the group made all the requisite genuflections before the Clausewitzian altar of "the destruction as effective fighting forces of a large percentage of the main force battalions" and "aggressive exploitation of superior military force to gain and keep the initiative," but, having done so, still saw the air war as the winning war.[16] Matters such as pacification, military civic action, regeneration of ARVN, or how the pace and scope of the air war might be modulated to facilitate diplomatic exchange were not considered.

The group was alone among military planners in accurately seeing the VC as an insurgent force with tenuous connections to the North. Having seen the situation in the South accurately, the group did not develop a theory of victory directed at countering an insurgency, but produced a theory based on the standard view of guerrilla war as partisan conflict with North Vietnam in the role of external sponsoring power and, therefore, the main enemy. Instead of asking the correct question, what does history show about the use of military force in the countering of insurgency; the group simply accepted the embedded misconceptions and designed a theory of victory for partisan war.

In a capsule form, the group's report reflected all that was going to be done anyway and all the assumptions that were to be made. General Westmoreland would have no alternative to massive search and destroy missions. The Air Force had no alternative to striking targets in North Vietnam. Given the shared intellectual heritage, the president and the senior policy makers like the military commanders had no option except to see the war as a partisan conflict in which the stakes were greater than a South that was non-Communist. The group reflected all the aspects of the heritage in one convenient package. There can be little doubt that General Wheeler and others read the report with a good degree of satisfaction for it contained the recipe for victory they were quite well prepared to cook.

IMPLEMENTING THE ARMY CONCEPT

At the end of August 1965, the JCS sent a memorandum to Secretary of Defense McNamara in which the chiefs laid out a general concept of operations for Vietnam. Working from the statement of goals contained in NSAM 288, they identified the major "problems to be dealt with in the conduct of the war" as being "the continued direction and support of the Viet Cong by the DRV . . . " and "the continued existence of a major Viet Cong infrastructure. . . . " They identified the basic tasks for the military as forcing the North to cease its direction and support of the VC; defeating the VC so as "to extend GVN control over all of the RVN," and deterring "Communist China from direct intervention. . . . " Their theory of victory was taken virtually intact from the Ad Hoc Study Group report. The emphasis was again on air power, on destroying the infrastructure, industrial base, and political will of the North. The chiefs agreed, at least implicitly, that the role of the American ground forces in the South was to act as a force mutliplier in support of the air war over Laos and North Vietnam. The secretary of defense accepted the JCS position.[17]

This made an advantage out of doctrinal necessity. All the troops had to do was increase the tempo and intensity of combat. The Army did not have to seize and hold ground. The troops did not even have to win battles, to kill the enemy, or capture his supplies, although it was expected that they would do all these things. The only thing that the ground forces had to do when they went out to bash the bush in the big battalions was to make the enemy increase its logistics requirements. If this could be done successfully, then air power over the North and the trails of Laos would win the real war. It is probably a very good thing that the Eleven Bravos, the grunts, did not know why they were really in the bush.

The White House was informed of the first major American ground operation of 1966 by a Special Situation Report at 11:27 P.M. on January 8. Twenty-two hours earlier, the 173rd Airborne Brigade and the 3rd Brigade of the 1st Infantry Division had launched a search and destroy operation, dubbed Crimp, in the Ho Bo Woods approximately twenty-five miles northwest of Saigon. The American movement was preceded by a massive air strike executed by B–52 strategic bombers.[18]

The after-action report filed by the 173rd enthusiastically spoke of the six-day operation as having been a complete success. The commander characterized Crimp as having been "one of the brigade's most successful" considering the "combined effects of VC killed or captured, weapons and materiel captured, installations destroyed and intelligence captured." The commander was satisfied with having successfully completed the major mission, "to smash the politico-military headquarters of the Viet Cong Military Region Four."[19]

Additionally he commented on the civilian population within the area of operations. He justified their removal on the basis of the long-term VC influence within the region which had resulted in the civilians having been thoroughly indoctrinated with Communist propaganda. After the evacuation of over 1,900 civilians, the lack of food and shelter prompted the Vietnamese provincial officials to stop the forced relocation.[20]

The evacuation provided an early demonstration of a conundrum never to be resolved satisfactorily—the effects on the civilian population of search and destroy operations. Sound military reasons might require the removal and relocation of civilians, but the relocation of South Vietnamese peasants caused disaffection and impaired the pacification, revolutionary development, and nation-building programs repeatedly urged by the United States. As the Herd's commander commented, it would take time to win over "thoroughly indoctrinated" civilians, but it might be doubted that forced relocation aided the process.[21]

The 3rd Brigade of the 1st Infantry Division had no sooner wrapped up its disappointing part of Crimp than it moved into another search and destroy operation, Buckskin, in conjunction with the recently arrived 3rd Brigade of the 25th Infantry Division. In the course of the fourteen-day operation, the brigade saw no significant combat as it executed sweeps designed to secure the area into which the 25th Infantry division was to move. Instead of conventional combat, the maneuver battalions of the 3rd Infantry came under repeated sniper fire and nighttime perimeter probes by VC sappers.

The course of Buckskin demonstrated some major points regarding battalion and larger search and destroy sweeps. The defender had the initiative. He could accept or reject battle essentially at will. He could refuse to become a lucrative target. This reality was reflected in a routine briefing memorandum sent to President Johnson from the White House Situation Room.

The Viet Cong are continuing to avoid South Vietnamese and Allied troops participating in large-scale search and destroy missions. They are, however, persisting in their aggressive campaign of terrorism, sabotage, and harassment of lightly defended and isolated outposts and villagers.[22]

By employing snipers, night probes, and passive mechanisms such as mines, booby traps, and punji stakes, the VC could inflict casualties in sufficient numbers to adversely affect the morale of the U.S. forces and, over time, the political will of the United States. Without accurate, timely intelligence and combat information, it was not possible to use effectively the superior American firepower in a way that would inflict either unacceptably heavy casualties or materiel damage upon the enemy. As a result, an operation such as Buckskin did not further a strategy of attrition; neither did it make progress toward the goals of eroding the enemy's material capacity to wage war and exhausting his morale and will to continue the war.

The same points were demonstrated in a division-sized search and destroy operation, Mastiff, undertaken by the 2nd and 3rd Brigades of the 1st Infantry Division between February 21 and 27, 1966, in an area of operation near the Michelin Rubber Plantation. The operational plan depended on two brigades exploiting their superior air and ground mobility to pin the large, well-established VC force within the Michelin Plantation against the Saigon River where it could be destroyed by firepower. The concept was taken directly from the counter-guerrilla field manual.

The effort involved in executing Mastiff was enormous. In return for a maximum division effort and the loss of seventeen killed, ninety-four wounded, and two M–16 rifles lost, the division could report sixty-one VC confirmed killed with six VC suspects, but no weapons captured and a large quantity of miscellaneous supplies destroyed. Although the commander characterized the operation as successful, his assertion must be questioned.[23]

From March 3–6, 1966, a battalion of the 3rd Brigade, 1st Infantry Division, conducted a search and destroy operation that worked exceptionally well.[24] This operation, Coca Beach, was one of five evaluated and used by a senior evaluation team to support the assessment that U.S. doctrine was proving itself correct for the war in South Vietnam.[25] There can be no doubt that the operation constituted a success.[26]

The reason for the success was quite obvious in the brigade's after-action report. The local VC commander used his initiative correctly. When VC preparations for an assault against the perimeter of the 2nd Company, 28th Infantry Battalion, were discovered by an American patrol, the guerrilla commander imprudently proceeded with his planned dawn attack. His decision assured that the VC regiment became a ''lucrative target'' for superior American firepower including the battalion's organic weapons, well-directed artillery fire, and air strikes. Despite the failure of a quickly inserted block force to finish the destruction of the rapidly withdrawing enemy, American firepower had done the job of finishing the enemy after it had found and fixed itself through an ill-considered attack.[27]

Coca Beach was not so much an American victory as it was a self-inflicted VC defeat. As such, it was quite misleading for an assessment team to have selected this operation instead of Mastiff or Buckskin which were far more accurate in their reflection of relative failure.

At the top of the chain of command, Coca Beach was seen as a success, being reported to the president on March 7, along with the USMC–South Vietnamese Operation Utah and the prolonged 1st Cavalry campaign in the Central Highlands, Masher, as significant victories.[28] As the first week of March came to an end, the news reaching the administration's senior members was quite encouraging. Viet Cong–initiated incidents were decreasing; ARVN morale was increasing.[29] The American forces were doing all that had been expected of them, and more.

Seen from close range, a picture that had appeared pleasing from a distance could become ugly. So it was with the picture of unrelieved success presented by the U.S. ground operations in early 1966. Fresh from the highly regarded, and publicized, success in operation Masher/White Wing, General Harry Kinnard ordered his 1st Air Cavalry brigades to commence Operation Jim Bowie on March 8.[30] The new campaign was to last three weeks and involve two brigades as well as several artillery batteries attached to the division for the duration. The target of the search and destroy sweeps was a presumed VC base area in the Vinh Tranh and An Tuc districts of Binh Dinh province on the sea coast of II CTZ (Central Zone).

Weather problems caused the start of the operation to be postponed from March 10 to 12. Citing a suspected VC captured on March 13, the after-action report concluded that the reason for light initial contact was a timely dispersal order given to the local guerrilla units.[31] Whether this was coincidence or the result of a VC intelligence coup cannot be determined, but the result was an operation frustrating in its execution and disappointing in its results.

The 1st Infantry Division was no more successful during the sixteen days of Operation Abilene between March 30 and April 15.[32] The concept was one of a massive search and destroy sweep through territory in Long Khanh and Phuoc Tuy provinces extending in from the coast in III CTZ. The area of operations was believed to contain significant VC base camps and some combat units. Beliefs did not bring results as there was only one significant contact between troops of the Big Red One and main force VC. On April 11, Charley or "C" Company, 2nd Battalion, 16th Infantry found itself in a meeting engagement with the D800 battalion. The divisional after-action report stated that the losses probably would not have any major adverse effects on future VC plans and operations.[33]

ASSESSING THE FIRST SIX MONTHS

The National Security Council met to consider the course of the war on May 10.[34] General Wheeler provided an optimistic briefing on American ground and air operations over the previous six months. The presumed importance of U.S. ground combat activities was underscored by the chronic political instability within South Vietnam. Secretary of Defense McNamara summarized the situation: "We hope that heavy pressure by U.S. forces will carry us over the present period." Ambassador Lodge asserted that despite the current political turmoil in Saigon, "military activity can go ahead and pacification proceed."

The only real dissenter was Robert Komer, who had recently been elevated to the rank of special assistant to the president with particular responsibilities for Vietnam and a distinctive interest in pacification and nation-building. He expressed grave concerns about the effects of the U.S. emphasis on search and destroy missions and on the progress of rural development and pacification. He believed the great and growing U.S. presence was also having a profoundly negative effect upon the stability of the South Vietnamese economy by stimulating inflation. The overall effect of U.S. operations was to increase anti-American attitudes with the concomitant potential of turning the political dynamic against the United States.[35] Little notice was evidently taken of Komer's reservations.

There was a definite tension between efficient employment of U.S. ground combat forces in South Vietnam and the need to develop more effective social, political, and economic institutions within that country. The high lethality of American weaponry and the emphasis placed on its employment in the doctrine governing the planning and execution of U.S. operations served to disrupt traditional patterns of rural life, to place the lives of civilians caught in an area of operations in jeopardy, and to force many to become rootless refugees or unwilling residents in the ''new life hamlets,'' as the refugee concentration centers were called.

The combination of extreme instability at the governmental center and social disruption under the pressure of rural war was recognized by the Johnson administration as being a real barrier to the achievement of American policy goals. The deterioration of the economy under the twin pressures of war and rampant inflation, both of which were largely the result of U.S. activities, was also a source of concern to some in the administration. The central conundrum was how to build a nation and win a war simultaneously without having the winning of the war destroy the nation under construction.

A related difficulty of virtually insoluble nature, not recognized by the administration, was that of gaining leverage on the South Vietnamese government. Any South Vietnamese regime, regardless of its composition, was immune to any unpleasant U.S. advice on social, economic, or political matters. This attitude was the expected result of the pervasive belief that the Americans were going to fight the VC and the North Vietnamese for reasons of their own. As long as the United States had no credible capacity to withdraw, the administration lacked effective leverage with the South Vietnamese government.

Key elements of U.S. military strategy were stated to be, in addition to the primary one of ''selective destruction of NVN war-supporting and war-making capability,'' the ''liberation of selected areas dominated by the Viet Cong,'' the destruction of enemy base areas, ''the defeat of the Viet Cong and PAVN forces in SVN, and the ''forced withdrawal of PAVN forces from SVN.'' The search and destroy operations conducted by U.S. troops and ARVN units operating under American guidance and advice had ''sought out and defeated, time after time, Viet Cong and PAVN main force units.'' The view shared by the Defense Department was that the U.S. theory of victory was succeeding and its implementation should be continued even though it had been ''at times costly in lives and equipment,'' lest the initiative be lost to the enemy.[36]

A similar conclusion was reflected in a memorandum sent to John McNaughton and others by Leonard Ungar in April 1966. This memorandum contended that U.S. military operations should ''continue in accordance with present concepts and at present levels aiming to destroy VC main force units and to clear and secure heavily populated areas in particular.''[37]

Ungar was wrong in one salient respect. It should be recognized that U.S. forces could not operate in heavily populated areas, and the attempt to do so would severely compromise their military strengths—firepower and air mobility. Further, American operations were aimed at searching and destroying, not clearing; even if the orientations were to be altered to one of clearing territory, the forces necessary to hold and defend the land cleared of major enemy units were not available.

George Carver, a senior CIA expert on Vietnam, viewed ground operations in a way quite similar to Ungar.[38] U.S. forces must be "aggressively and offensively employed" in order to harass the enemy and keep him from gaining the initiative.[39] Although Carver and Ungar both argued for implementing options with a higher reliance upon nonmilitary and diplomatic means of conflict termination, they both believed that the current American theory of victory on the ground was working.

Director of the CIA Richard Helms, in a long memorandum written to Senator Edmund Muskie shortly after the Honolulu Conference (of 1966), provided a summary of the apparent benefits of the increased U.S. ground combat operations.[40] One major effect of American operations had been a decrease in large-scale VC attacks "since the end of 1965," although this had been offset by "some increase in the total number of armed attacks." This recently observed change in VC behavior might be attributed to either the demoralization resulting from U.S. actions or a rationally calculated response meant to undercut the obvious American strengths in firepower and mobility, but Helms offered no analysis. A second positive effect of U.S. air and ground operations was that of spoiling VC and PAVN attacks so that tactical initiative was swinging to the U.S./GVN forces. Helms commented for several pages about the perceived enervation of VC and PAVN morale by U.S. ground attacks and the program of B–52 bombing in the South code-named Arc Light.[41]

Helms viewed the large number of refugees from the countryside as a clear indication that U.S. military operations were succeeding. The director portrayed the 800,000 refugees as liberty-loving people who were voting with their feet to leave areas of the country that were "insecure" and come under government control in "temporary shelters" rather than face life under the VC.[42] He chose to ignore the effect of the many refugees upon the plans for nation-building, rural development, and pacification. It would have been more accurate for the director to have argued that the massive American search and destroy operations along with air attacks transformed stable peasant communities into streams of refugees. From a military perspective, this might have been desirable, but for the "other war" it represented a major, perhaps insurmountable, obstacle.

Much of Helm's appreciation of the effectiveness of U.S. ground and air operations in the South focused upon the decline in VC morale and faith in eventual victory. His appreciation paralleled closely a widely circulated study of VC morale during the period of June to December 1965 done by Leon Goure of the Rand Corporation in January 1966.[43] On the basis of 450 interviews with VC prisoners and defectors of whom only 160 had come into government custody since the augmentation of U.S. forces started in June 1965, Goure attempted to draw general conclusions concerning the effect of the American presence on the guerrillas' will to fight and faith in victory as well as their psychological vulnerabilities.[44]

Goure believed that refugees constituted an overlooked weapon in the U.S. arsenal whose employment would do much to undercut the VC in manpower, resources, intelligence, and morale. At the same time the extent of effective population control would provide a meaningful and easily understood measurement of success. Victory could be demonstrated by counting full refugee camps and empty villages. Goure discounted the possibility that the VC could exploit the refugee streams for its own purpose with the facile assertion that it should be easier to identify active VC agents and political cadre in a camp than out in a village which was "undergoing pacification."[45] Although Goure might have been somewhat exuberant in his enthusiasm for a policy of converting peasants into refugees, the idea did have the virtue of capitalizing on the inevitable. The more the United States engaged in large-unit sweeps, the more villagers would be placed in the crossfire. It gave a new meaning to the concept search and destroy.

THE SECOND YEAR: MORE OF THE SAME

While these assessments gave no grounds for a belief that the ground combat operations would bring immediate success, the expectations of ultimate triumph on the ground remained strong since the American forces had been in the war less than a year and new divisions were arriving daily.

The 1st and 2nd Brigades of the 25th Infantry Division were among the recent arrivals with the last troops closing up in early April 1966. The relatively old hands of the 2nd Brigade who had arrived in South Vietnam in January went for a walk in the sun April 16–21 in a search and destroy operation called Kahala in honor of the Division's Hawaii home.[46] Two thousand infantrymen supported by tanks, armored personnel carriers, and artillery conducted an airmobile sweep in search of a seventy-man VC Local Force company and a platoon of "guerrillas."[47] While the Trang Bong Local Force Company went unlocated, the troops did encounter VC, primarily self-defense militiamen from the Quyet Chien Platoon #5 as well as scattered base areas with little meaningful effect. It was a learning experience for the 2nd Brigade but probably not a demoralizing nor destructive one for the VC.

A much larger operation was mounted between April 24 and May 17 by the 1st Infantry Division. Two brigades reinforced with supporting artillery and armor were employed in Operation Birmingham.[48] The target of the operation was War Zone C to the west of Saigon along the Cambodian border. War Zone C had long been a center of VC activities containing numerous base camps and logistics facilities as well as the Central Office for South Vietnam (COSVN), the political headquarters of the NLF. At the time of the operation, only two battalions of VC main forces were confirmed to be in the area of operations with the possibility that an additional two might be present.[49] Tay Ninh province was thoroughly penetrated by the VC and lay outside of South Vietnamese governmental control.

Birmingham was an important operation with the potential of severely crippling the VC in the politically and strategic significant areas. The 1st Infantry Division was experienced and aggressively commanded. If any unit could effectively apply the American theory of victory in a potentially pivotal battle, it was the Big Red One. It was acknowledged that the VC could exercise any one of several options including a withdrawal across the Cambodian border or the waging of diversionary attacks by a regimental size force in any of four provinces, but there was always the chance that "Mr. Charles" would be forced to defend his positions, offering battle on American terms.[50]

In concept, Birmingham consisted of a series of interlocking battalion-sized sweeps from temporary base camps established during the initial phase of the operation. As planned, the operation was to have consisted of five distinct phases. As executed, many changes in areas of operation and lines of advance were ordered to take advantage of the fluid tactical situation.

The operation terminated on D plus twenty-two days, or May 16, 1966, having had no major contact with the VC forces believed to be in the areas of operation. There had been repeated light contact as well as the discovery and seizure or destruction of much materiel and many facilities and structures. There was disappointment in the failure to locate the COSVN headquarters complex even though a long-range reconnaissance patrol had penetrated close to this objective.[51]

The division commander declared Birmingham to have been "another highly successful operation" and asserted, "possibly no other operation in Vietnam has accomplished such extensive damage to VC logistics and base systems."[52] There can be no doubt that a significant number of bunkers, caches, buildings, and trenches were destroyed, but their replacement required only labor and time. The VC had both.

The most experienced Army unit in South Vietnam was the 173rd Airborne Brigade. When it undertook operation Hollandia on June 9, 1966, it had been in-country just over a year. The brigade's eight-day visit to the Long Hai peninsula in Phuoc Tuy province on the seacoast in III CTZ east of Saigon was officially described as being both a search and destroy and a clear and secure operation.[53] The area of operation was believed to contain elements of the 860th Local Force Battalion. Over the course of the operation the brigade experienced sixty-six contacts with the VC, of which forty-seven were initiated by the enemy.

The brigade operated with its accustomed aggressiveness but without any positive results. The VC used their terrain familiarity with skill, choosing to initiate contact under favorable conditions and fading into the bush when the advantage lay with the Americans. By any standards the operation was completely unsuccessful. The brigade's commander commented that in difficult terrain, local knowledge was the key to success.[54] This commodity was possessed solely by the small, well-led VC force on the peninsula. The stranger making a sweep would find his blows landing on air and his units becoming large, noisy targets.

The 1st Infantry Division went back to War Zone C on June 2, 1966. It would stay for three months in an interlocking series of search and destroy operations called El Paso II/III.[55] The last time the Big Red One had fought in War Zone C in Operation Birmingham, the results had been unimpressive. Now, working with new intelligence, they hoped that the division and attached ARVN units would be able to verify the presence of several VC and PAVN formations and, in the process, find and destroy facilities, fortifications, and materiel.

The initial sweep by the 1st and 3rd Brigades resulted in fourteen significant engagements between June 8 and July 9. Of these, at least four were at VC initiative. The most important of these, the battle of Srok Dong on June 30, resulted in a major defeat for the 271st Main Force Regiment. The 3rd Battalion of that unit attempted to ambush an armored infantry task group at 9:30 A.M. on June 30. All four tanks were disabled by recoilless rifle fire during the first thirty minutes of the battle, but the defenders responded with heavy 50 caliber and personal weapons fire while calling in air strikes and artillery support. When the Americans were able to establish a defensive perimeter, the VC commander made a fatal mistake by not breaking off the failed ambush attempt and executing a withdrawal through the heavy brush that lined both sides of the road.

The ambushed unit was saved and the attacking VC were defeated by over-whelming American firepower. The VC had used their initiative to attempt the classic guerrilla coup, the ambush. The location was well chosen and the original results were good. The arrival of tactical aircraft and the success of the defenders in establishing a defensive perimeter should have cued the VC commander to execute a preplanned breaking of contact and withdrawal. His failure assured the defeat and virtual destruction of his unit.[56]

There were other significant engagements during the first several weeks of El Paso II/III. On June 8, an armored cavalry unit of the division spoiled an ambush plan by the 272nd Main Force Regiment when a forward air controller spotted the VC. In the course of a four-hour engagement, the armored unit reinforced by an infantry battalion and an ARVN mechanized unit, inflicted either 93 or 105 confirmed kills on the enemy and captured weapons including a 57mm recoilless rifle.[57]

On June 11, a heliborne sweep of the Loc Ninh rubber plantation resulted in contact with a battalion of the 273rd Main Force Regiment emplaced in heavily fortified bunkers and trenches. The encounter was developed in complete con-formity with the tactical principles laid out in the Field Manual on counterguerrilla operations. Additional infantry and reconnaissance elements were quickly air lifted to the site of contact and deployed to fix the VC in their positions. Air strikes were used as a blocking method. After a thorough artillery preparation culminating in a "sixteen volley bombardment," an infantry assault completely overran the VC position.

The action lasted a total of eight hours. The Americans lost thirty-three killed. There were ninety-eight confirmed VC dead. A 60mm mortar, one World War II German machine gun, and a Russian SKS carbine were captured.

The final significant action of El Paso II/III occurred on July 9, when the 272nd Main Force Regiment which had been roughly handled in the abortive ambush of June 8, was lured into attacking an armored cavalry task group on the Minh Tranh road. The 1st Brigade evolved a complex plan involving a simulated air assault and a B–52 Arc Light strike to induce the target VC unit, considered to be a road mobile unit operating in conjunction with the air assault.[58]

The ambush site was compromised to the oncoming American tanks when VC troops were observed crossing the road. An incorrect reading of the VC positions resulted in inaccurately aimed artillery fire, but with the assistance of air strikes, the armored column was able to defend itself as reinforcements were air lifted to a nearby landing zone. Around 1:30 P.M., approximately ninety minutes after first contact, the VC attempted to disengage, but their lines of withdrawal were bracketed by the reinforcement infantry units. Additional units were air lifted to join the running engagement which continued until dark. The next day the American forces took up the chase with minimal results. Ambassador Henry Cabot Lodge enthusiastically informed the president of the success along the Minh Tranh road and concluded that the battle constituted "a tremendously important development."[59] Lodge drastically overstated the case.

The 272nd Regiment had suffered a second major defeat with 239 confirmed dead and the seizure by U.S. forces of 13 crew served and 41 individual weapons.[60] Almost overlooked in the American euphoria of victory was the unpleasant reality that the regiment had apparently made good the casualties from its defeat a month earlier and that unit's will to fight had not been sapped by that setback. Although the American concept of operation had been well founded and carefully developed, it would not have worked if the VC were as demoralized by previous combat as might be assumed from the Goure reports.[61] It was unlikely that the second defeat served to destroy or demoralize the 272nd Regiment, even if it did complicate problems of manpower and materiel replacement.

Although the 1st Infantry Division was engaged in El Paso II/III, the 2nd Brigade of the 25th Infantry Division went out between June 13 and July 4, on Operation Sante Fe, a search and destroy mission in Hau Nghia province immediately west of Saigon.[62] The area of operation was believed to contain several small units of the local forces and the part-time militia. There were no main force units present, but the local force platoons had shown an aggressive predilection by planting mines, placing roadblocks, firing at ARVN units, and attacking American ambush teams. The local force guerrillas demonstrated the same degree of aggressiveness during Operation Sante Fe.

The American task force comprising a battalion of infantry and attached reconnaissance, supply, and artillery units was defeated by the local force guerrillas. The Wolfhound task force killed four VC and captured eighty-six suspected guerrillas. The Americans lost fourteen killed, thirty wounded, and fourteen weapons. The commander asserted that the task force "through balanced combination of tactical operations and civic action programs was able to dominate the terrain and population." This was not supportable by either the results or the daily record of the task force. If the VC would not accept the American way of war, they could not be brought to battle and defeated by it. The simple fact that villagers expressed appreciation for medical care and gifts of toothpaste and soap did not justify the comfortable assumption that they had become born again Saigon supporters or firm friends of the Americans.[63]

The peripatetic 173rd Airborne Brigade was busy in the bush, conducting a number of military nullities during July including Operations Yorktown, Aurora I, and Aurora II. All too typical, these operations inflicted little, if any, damage on the enemy while costing the United States little except time, energy and, ultimately, political will and military morale. Of course, the passage of the heliborne interlopers further ripped the precarious South Vietnamese social fabric and contributed freshets to the refugee stream.

The 1st Brigade of the 101st Airborne Division undertook a major set of interlocking search and destroy operations dubbed John Paul Jones in Phu Yen province on the seacoast of II CTZ not far from Qui Nhon city between July 21 and September 5, which had no more military success than those conducted by the "Herd."[64]

In addition to search and destroy sweeps, the brigade was to seize and hold vital terrain along National Route 1 near Vung Ro pass and to prepare to exploit opportunities developed by three Arc Light strikes by a total of 42 B–52s. The terrain seizure and consequent search and destroy sweeps occurred without incident or major contact. The Arc Light exploitation sweeps were likewise without major contact or result. Only after August 16 did the brigade sweeps yield any major contact with the VC forces believed to be in the area of operations. The intelligence catch during the operation had some significance. Not only had the presence of two PAVN units been confirmed, which in itself was noteworthy, but the observations showed that the VC and PAVN were both well motivated and equipped for the type of war they intended to fight. The enemy had deficiencies in medical supplies and were particularly vulnerable to malaria, but this did not materially cripple their combat capability.[65]

Of interest, although not commented upon in the after-action report, was the nature of many of the weapons captured—they were old! Their Mauser rifles dated back to at least World War II, while several of the others came from French forces of pre–1954 vintage. The implication that these weapons were captured in a cache or from second-line local forces is unavoidable as is the further ramification that the first-line PAVN and VC were well supplied with weapons of more recent vintage whether of Communist Bloc or American manufacture. It would have been impaired to any meaningful extent by either U.S. ground or air operations after eighteen months of escalation.

The Herd was back on the search and destroy trail on September 26, 1966, where it would stay until October 9. The results of Sioux City were impressive. Contact had been light and usually VC initiated; American fatalities were greater than those suffered by the VC. The guerrillas had made very effective use of mines and booby traps, whereas snipers had both slowed the tempo of American operations and caused the use of large volumes of fire on unimportant targets. Although the brigade listed a superficially impressive inventory of destroyed enemy materiel, the commander accurately surmised that "the VC will continue to use this area until it is saturated with permanent friendly military elements."[66]

SIOUX CITY, ATTLEBORO, AND OTHER OPERATIONS

Sioux City illustrates all the basic defects in the American theory of victory. The operational doctrine focused on the destruction of materiel and the disruption of enemy organizational integrity. Neither of these could be accomplished in a way that would permanently diminish either the will or the capacity of the VC and PAVN to continue the war. American doctrine capitalized on the inherent strengths of U.S. forces, mobility, and firepower, rather than seeking to identify and exploit intrinsic weaknesses of the enemy. Search and destroy was something that *could* be done, not something which *should* be done.

The VC or PAVN could neutralize the American proficiencies by proper use of their innate tactical initiative and by employing such simple expedients as snipers and mines. Snipers could slow combat sweeps to the pace of a crippled snail, and mines, as the 173rd's commander observed, could threaten tanks to the point that he considered their use inappropriate.[67]

Armored forces were employed in late 1966 on search and destroy missions despite their marginal utility in that role and their major irrelevance to an opponent whose tactical and operational doctrine made little use of roads and much use of trails impassable for tanks and armored personnel carriers. From October 7 to 15, the 3rd Squadron of the 11th Armored Cavalry Regiment conducted Operation Hickory, a search and destroy sweep near Bien Hoa north of Saigon.[68] The entire operation was slow in tempo and dubious as to merit. Contact had been light except for a VC ambush of a dismounted patrol.

American ground forces returned to War Zone C in fits and starts during the ten-week course of Operation Attleboro. This was an operation that grew as the illusion of opportunity presented itself between September 14 and the end of November. The major U.S. units employed were the 196th Light Infantry Brigade, which had arrived in South Vietnam the preceding month, the 2nd Brigade of the 25th Infantry Division, and the 173rd Airborne Brigade. The major opponent was the 9th VC Division whose three regiments, the 271st, 272nd, and 273rd had last seen combat in June and July against the U.S. 1st Infantry Division during Operation El Paso II/III.

Heavy losses were reported for the 9th VC Division. The inventory of supplies and facilities captured or destroyed made for impressive reading. The 196th Brigade reported a body count of 254 with six POWs, sixty suspected VC, and nineteen detainees. Thirty individual weapons were recovered. Eleven hundred tons of rice were captured or destroyed. The 2nd Brigade reported forty-three VC confirmed killed, one captured, and nine small arms recovered. Five hundred tons of rice were captured or destroyed. The 173rd Airborne Brigade reported seven VC killed and two weapons recovered with a total of 248,800 pounds of foodstuffs captured or destroyed. However, the enemy had already demonstrated a skill at rapid recovery.[69]

The 4th Battalion of the 503rd Infantry Regiment left the majority of the 173rd Airborne Brigade finishing Operations Sioux City and Waco and went north to Danang in I CTZ for a forty-eight-day search and destroy operation, Winchester, in cooperation with an armored element of the 1st Marine Division and a combined action company to provide an additional intelligence capability. For seven weeks the battalion conducted aggressive patrols in an area believed to be used by at least one VC main force battalion of 400 men plus two local force companies. In addition, a main force ''sapper'' battalion was believed to be located just south of the area of operations. There was ample theoretical justification for the expectation of significant results.

The reality was seven weeks of heat and dust, much movement, and little action—the boredom of endless tension which marked days and months in which the enemy refused to be found, fixed, and destroyed. The VC initiated sixty-nine incidents, virtually 100 percent of the contacts. The majority of the incidents were small arms and mortar sniping, followed by mines and booby traps. There were five small-scale attacks, or ambushes, and one serious mortar attack. It was the lowest of low-intensity guerrilla wars.

Operation Winchester demonstrated once again what happened when the VC or PAVN correctly used their inherent tactical initiative to evade major contact. A contemporaneous search and destroy operation, Atlanta, executed by the 11th Armored Cavalry Regiment, confirmed the overwhelming superiority of U.S. firepower when the enemy could be induced or forced to fight according to the American doctrine. The regiment was directed to open lines of communication in Bien Hoa, Long Khanh, and Phouc Tuy provinces using both search and destroy and Roadrunner missions. Intelligence estimates indicated the presence of three VC main force regiments as well as an artillery battalion and the 5th VC Division headquarters for a total of just over 5,000 men. Local force units with an additional 1,000 troops had also been identified as being within the areas of operation. The likelihood of significant contact was high, provided the enemy could be provoked or forced into battle. During Atlanta the VC read from the American script.[70]

If the enemy cooperated as it did during Operation Atlanta, there was nothing wrong with the American theory of victory in ground warfare. Highly concentrated firepower could and did decimate VC formations as occurred during the course of Atlanta. The only real difficulty was that the enemy cooperated so infrequently in 1966.

THE 1967 GOALS AND ASSESSMENTS

Secretary of Defense McNamara and Undersecretary of State Nicholas Katzenbach had lunch with the president on December 13, 1966. The third item on the agenda was a draft national security action memorandum setting forth American strategy for the Vietnam war for 1967.[71] The American goal in the war was now expressed in terms of achieving "a satisfactory outcome as soon as possible." The term "satisfactory outcome" was undefined. The definition of victory was now given as three separate alternatives: forcing Hanoi to negotiate, "weakening the VC/NVA [North Vietnamese Army] to a point where Hanoi will opt to fade away," and "at a minimum, making it patently clear to all that the war is demonstrably being won." The theory of victory was to continue "our anti-main force campaign and bombing offensive" and add increased efforts to "pacify the countryside and increase the attractive power of the GVN [Government of Vietnam]."[72]

National Security Advisor Walt Rostow reinforced these points in a memorandum to the president which reflected not only his thinking but that of Komer, Cyrus Vance, and Undersecretary of State Katzenbach. The familiar points of continuing the pressure on Hanoi, improving the efficiency of the interdiction effort and maintaining the pressure on the VC main force units in the south were all made. The necessity of significantly enhancing the pacification program was underscored. Rostow made another point, a point that was more salient than he perhaps recognized: the need to define victory in a clear and comprehensive form so that the public as well as the administration and Congress could assess the effectiveness of the United States's theory of victory. Without a definition of victory which was relevant to, and coherent with, the goal of the United States in the war, it was impossible to assess progress and evaluate the need for change of policy or means of implementation.[73]

On the military side in early 1967 there were mixed signs. General Westmoreland was going ahead with plans for offensive operations in II and III Corps Tactical Zones. He intended to follow on the reportedly successful Operation Junction City in War Zone C with a similar sweep through War Zone D. At the same time a new concern was emerging over the situation in I Corps. Westmoreland expressed apprehension about the region in mid-April. He believed that the forthcoming summer campaign in I CTZ "could be a decisive period of the war." An American success would not only improve the security in the northern portion of South Vietnam; it could have "a profound effect on the strategic thinking of the leadership in Hanoi."

It was possible that General Westmoreland saw the Clausewitzian conditions for decisive combat as emerging in the northern provinces and relished the potentials this implied. He had already formed Task Force Oregon as an operational reserve that could assist III MAF in countering the threat posed by the PAVN buildup or, preferably, be used offensively force to find, fix, and destroy North Vietnamese units in northern I Corps in June.[74]

A month later the CIA reported on the new North Vietnamese offensive in northern I Corps. The Agency concluded that the intention of Hanoi was to "keep the area insecure and to subject allied forces to substantial and sustained attrition." The analysts argued that by so doing the Communists could block any demonstrable U.S./SVN progress toward winning, and by so doing undercut the political will of the United States. The concentrations of enemy units and supplies had taken place despite the air campaign and earlier defeats inflicted upon PAVN forces by U.S. ground forces in I Corps during the first half of 1966. The new PAVN movements had provided both a north–south and an east–west axis of movement, thus enhancing North Vietnamese operational flexibility. The Agency noted that the twin lines allowed the enemy to mount "a sustained threat around the Khe Sanh area necessitating a continued protective deployment of the limited allied reaction elements." The PAVN presence and the Khe Sanh locus could have been interpreted by American command elements either as a threat or as an opportunity. The offensive-minded doctrinal thrust of the military would have predisposed all U.S. commanders in favor of the latter.[75]

The PAVN buildup in northern I Corps and the Demilitarized Zone (DMZ) was not new, having attracted CIA comment the previous November. At that time it was believed that the NVA intended to develop a stronghold in Quang Tri Province that would provide several military advantages including an enhanced ability to mount protracted conflict from relatively secure base camps conveniently close to both Laos and North Vietnam. To the CIA analysts, this suggested that a faction of the Hanoi Politburo led by Minister of Defense Vo Nguyen Giap had won out in a policy struggle.

If this was true, the use of protracted conflict by guerrilla and regular forces having the goal of exhausting American and SVN political will should have been expected. Additionally, the North Vietnamese force dispositions implied that the PAVN might have sought to fight a mini-Verdun campaign of attrition again directed toward the end of enervating American and SVN political will through the cumulative political and psychological effects of constant, purposeless bloodletting.

Left unsaid by the Agency analysts, but quite evident, the augmentation of PAVN strengths just south of the DMZ indicated that Hanoi had entered the war in its own right for its own ends. In a protracted guerrilla conflict, the VC would become expendable bullet-catchers, abrading their strengths and American political will simultaneously. An intact PAVN would then secure Hanoi's policy goal of forceful unification. Unfortunately, this possibility was not examined by the administration at the time. A close examination of the new North Vietnamese dispositions would have alerted the American decision makers that another change in the character of the war was underway.[76]

The JCS examined alternatives in May 1967. The major task undertaken by this study was the examination of two alternative force levels in South Vietnam. One prompted by General Westmoreland's request would have required the addition of 250,000 personnel to the forces in Southeast Asia. The other, prompted by Washington officials, would have called for an augmentation of only 70,000 men. The first option would have provided an additional four and two-thirds divisions and constituted an optimum, offensive capable force. It would also have required the mobilization of the reserves.

The second option did not bear that much heavy political freight, but would have added only one and one-third Army divisions to the ground combat force, much less than the optimum. The forces of the first option would have allowed a significant increase of troops in the threatened portion of I CTZ as part of Task Force Oregon while providing for a two-division exploitation reserve to be used in major operations such as Junction City. The smaller second option would have allowed for the reinforcement of Task Force Oregon but not provided for a mobile strategic reserve.

The Joint Chiefs believed that one result of selecting the second, smaller option would be the inability of American forces to participate in revolutionary development support activities without introducing a significant dilemma—endangering revolutionary development by reducing the level of military security provided to a pacified area or limiting new large-scale offensives meant to open new areas of pacification. A second result of restricting augmentation of ground forces to those available under the second option was adumbrated—without a politically risky major escalation in the forces committed to South Vietnam, PAVN and the VC would continue to enjoy the initiative since the enemy had by now gained escalation dominance. The Joint Chiefs were attempting to whipsaw the administration by holding revolutionary development hostage and hinting darkly at the consequences of allowing the enemy to maintain the initiative.

The Joint Chiefs and General Westmoreland understood attrition as one of the classic avenues to victory, the gradual destruction of the enemy's forces in the field until he was no longer militarily capable of continuing the war. Using this as a basis, it is easy to appreciate how the U.S. military high command welcomed the apparent blunder by Hanoi. In a contest of attrition against the United States, North Vietnam was at a decided disadvantage. Superiority in firepower and mobility together with the absolute air dominance enjoyed by the United States and its allies assured a bloody NVA failure. If the North did not share this classic, Clausewitzian understanding, but rather saw the correct avenue to victory as being enervation, the gradual exhaustion of the enemy's political will to continue the war, then the ability to inflict casualties was less important than the capacity to accept casualties. Further, if the North saw the NLF/VC not as allies but as rivals for power in a unified Vietnam, then losses inflicted on the VC by the allies would be a matter of sublime indifference to Hanoi.

The possibility that the North Vietnamese were in the process of trapping the United States in an insolvable dilemma was not considered by the U.S. military high command. The nature of the dilemma was easy to see and was even implied in the JCS draft presidential memo. By inveigling the United States into a continuation of the "big war" of search and destroy operations against PAVN and VC main force units, the North could assure continued social, political, and economic chaos within South Vietnam. This would impair efforts at pacification and nation-building and a continuation of U.S. losses without apparent useful result. Thus, political will within South Vietnam and the United States would be undercut.

The use of sanctuaries along the DMZ and Cambodian borders allowed PAVN and VC main forces to tie down a significant number of U.S. ground combat strength. By using the VC main forces as the primary offensive instrument, Hanoi could use southern blood to further deplete American will. If the United States diverted its ground resources to deal with pacification, the PAVN forces could threaten a spectacularly successful operation against a population center such as Quang Tri City, Hue, or Pleiku, again undercutting American and SVN political will. Hanoi could rely on the ongoing air war against the North to maintain and consolidate the popular support of its citizens for the war, particularly for the expansive goal of unification under northern control.

Whatever the U.S. forces did against the PAVN defensive locations would allow greater freedom of operation to the guerrillas; whatever the United States did against the guerrillas would invite a PAVN spectacular. Whatever the United States did to expand the scope of the big war hurt efforts at pacification and nation-building. Whatever the United States did from the sky over the North would further consolidate political will in the North. More fundamentally, the JCS and General Westmoreland sought victory through the attrition of the enemy forces in the field and the erosion of the enemy's material capacity to continue the war. Arguably, Hanoi sought victory through the exhaustion of U.S. and SVN political will. As a result, whatever the allies did to further their course helped the North further theirs.

The JCS preferred the first option but did acknowledge that the second had merits, as their comparative assessment of the options demonstrated. The JCS expressed their criticism of the second course as a question: How long could this course be followed if progress was slow and the NVA failed to move toward a settlement?[77]

The first course had risks, but it also had the best chance of success in a reasonable length of time. As a result, the JCS clearly preferred this course, although, as General Wheeler wrote on May 29, they had "not recommended the deployment of COMUSMACV's optimum force or adoption of Course A."[78] Later, most of the members of the JCS protested that they had never been proponents of "Course A." That might have been correct in some narrow sense, but the tone and thrust of both the "Alternatives" study and the draft presidential memos showed a marked predilection for that option including both the force level augmentation and air war escalation.[79]

DOUBTS, SKEPTICISM, AND PROPOSALS FOR DISENGAGEMENT

Cyrus Vance, the successor to John McNaughton, was not so inclined. He recommended against the large augmentation. Instead, he proposed a seven-stage operational concept to the VNCC which would start the process of American disengagement. He based the process on a redefinition of goal and victory. For Vance the goal was "to permit the people of South Vietnam to determine their own future."[80] Victory could be declared at any time after the September 1967

South Vietnamese elections, provided that the United States had not further escalated by that time. Vance believed that the process of politically coopting the VC could be commenced under a policy of national reconciliation after September. He was quite optimistic about the possibility of disengagement. He was in the dark concerning the North's goals and how the character of the war had changed. He stood at the antipodes from the JCS regarding the course of the war. He stood with them in his lack of understanding of its nature and character.

Secretary of Defense McNamara was closer to Vance than to the JCS. His initial reaction to the JCS recommendation and Vance's proposal was to order another reevaluation of the air war and to take a closer look at the situation in I Corps. As he and the CIA went about the assessment, the new U.S. ambassador, Ellsworth Bunker, arrived in Saigon amongst the ongoing political turmoil. Bunker's first report emphasized the ongoing village elections which had been long seen by the United States as a critical component of nation-building and the continued rivalry at the center between Nguyen Cao Ky and Nguyen Van Thieu.

Bunker expressed alarm over the military situation in northern I CTZ where the PAVN buildup continued. He believed that the enemy's intentions were unclear but cited a number of reports that held "the enemy may calculate that a spectacular victory of some sort in the First Corps area is needed either to bolster enemy morale or as the prelude to negotiations." Bunker stressed the unspoken reality that the initiative lay with PAVN when he reported that the attack may come in the western highlands rather than against I Corps.[81]

Had the administration been able to view closely the progress of ground operations through 1967 some of these cracks would have been evident. It should be recalled that the senior decision makers of the Johnson administration did not follow the course of ground combat in any except the most cursory manner, unless a particular engagement was unusually blood
captured a high degree of media attention. It should be noted also that the after-action reports filed several weeks or months after an operation by the units involved were not available nor used as sources of information concerning the rate of advance toward victory. As the conclusions of the reports were unrelentingly positive, it is doubtful that their availability would have altered in any significant way the perceptions of the administration and senior military commanders. Only close examination would have facilitated the hoisting of cautionary flags regarding the success of American doctrine and policy on the battlefield or the relevance of apparent combat success to the accomplishment of policy goals.

FROM JUNCTION CITY TO DAK TO: REINFORCING THE BODY COUNT DECEPTION

In War Zone C of II CTZ, Operation Gadsden conducted in four phases February 2–21, 1967, by two brigades of the 25th Infantry Division, the 3rd

Brigade of the 4th Infantry Division and the 196th Light Infantry Brigade, demonstrated the persistence of the search and destroy focus and the still inconclusive nature of this type of operation. This multibrigade sweep against an old advisory, the 9th VC Main Force Division, resulted in an impressive list of facilities, material, and food destroyed, a less imposing body count and a commander's conclusion that the enemy had been ''forced to abandon a major base area and exfiltrate to another safe area'' thus making him resort to a lengthy period of reorganization. The question of initiative was never discussed. The assumption that the operation had forced the VC to withdraw for a prolonged period of reorganization was never examined.[82]

It was, however, immediately shown to have been wrong by one of the largest and best reported search and destroy operations of the early 1967 Junction City I/II. More a campaign than an operation, Junction City was a multidivision sweep in War Zone C conducted between February 22 and April 15, 1967. The two phase operational concept sought to block routes of withdrawal from War Zone C into Cambodia through the insertion of major forces by ground and air, including the first battalion-sized parachute assault since the Korean War, following which pressure would be applied from three sides on the 9th VC Main Force Division. The concept and plan had been drawn directly from the Army's basic doctrine. Its execution demonstrated American competence at mobility, logistics, engineering, and communications.[83]

In terms of assessing American success in the war generally, Operation Junction City might have been taken either as a very positive sign or a dark indicator. A focus on the body count or an unquestioning acceptance of the statement made in the 1st Infantry Division's after-action report that all four regiments of the 9th VC Division, which then included the 101st PAVN regiment, had been defeated would have supported the positive interpretation. There was no doubt that when the enemy incorrectly used his initiative to attack American defensive positions, he was routed. The overwhelming quantity of U.S. firepower, the weight of the half-million artillery rounds fired during the operation and the volume of air strikes insured his tactical defeat.

An appraisal based on less dramatic and attention-riveting factors other than body counts and failed night assaults did not allow such an optimistic perspective. When the enemy used his initiative correctly, when he exploited his strengths and U.S. weaknesses rather than playing to the strengths of U.S. forces, he could evade contact and employ a growing array of countersweep tactics to vex, frustrate, exhaust, and inflict casualties. The mere fact that the components of the 9th VC Division remained so active, aggressive, and well equipped despite previous setbacks at the hands of American search and destroy sweeps in War Zone C should have been seen as reason to doubt the apparent success of the American theory of victory.

Even the distinction between the U.S. and North Vietnamese theories of victory might have been inferred from a close examination of Junction City. The United States focused on attrition of combat strength and erosion of material capacity to continue the war. This was evident in the attention paid in the assessment process to the destruction of enemy formations and facilities. The North Vietnamese sought victory through the exhaustion of political will, and this was visible in the ability of Hanoi and PAVN to accept the appearance of defeat while supporting the substance of prolonging the war.

The nature of the enemy theory of victory and the fundamental irrelevance of American suppositions were evident in a number of search and destroy operations occurring in the first half of 1967. Skillful exploitation of the terrain and the judicious use of snipers, surveillance units, and ambushes marked the PAVN tactical doctrine. It was difficult to find the enemy units and even more difficult to employ supporting firepower with full effectiveness. The NVA had obviously learned much regarding American strengths and weaknesses and were now operating to limit the former and to exploit the latter.

The differences between operations against the NVA and VC established in early 1967 held true through the year. In September, the 1st Brigade, 101st Airborne Division, started a ten-week search and destroy campaign in Quang Tin Province at the southern edge of I Corps. Their target was the 2nd PAVN Division which was believed to be in the western portion of the area of operation. Contact with the PAVN force was made after a preliminary period of skirmishing with local force VC. The PAVN Division was characterized as well trained and very well equipped with the latest Soviet Bloc weaponry. The NVA were aggressive and operated not only at night but also by day. Combat was heavy as were losses. The brigade commander stated, ''Operation Wheeler produced the largest number of enemy killed [by body count] of any single operation conducted by the brigade since its arrival in Vietnam twenty-eight months ago.'' Interestingly, even though the major combat was against the 2nd PAVN Division, more than twice as many VC, 793, than NVA regulars, 312, were included in the confirmed killed category.[84]

If Hanoi leadership was pursuing victory against the United States by seeking the exhaustion of political will and was seeking victory against the VC through attrition, and if Hanoi sought to deflate American will with southern blood, then Operation Wheeler was a success from the NVA perspective. In that it did little to reduce PAVN's capacity to continue domination of western Quang Tin Province, the operation did little, if anything to advance U.S. hopes for victory. Fundamentally, Wheeler constituted a misleading indicator of success if viewed through the myopic lens used to count bodies.

Further south, in the May Tao Secret Zone, the 9th Infantry Division undertook a two-month, three-phase search and destroy offensive against the 5th VC Division. The commander declared the operation to have been ''an overall success although it failed to locate, fix, and destroy'' the targeted division. The absence of contact, the lack of material captured or destroyed, the apparent age of bunkers and other structures along with the lack of signs indicating recent use, combined to furnish convincing proof that the intelligence on which the operation had been planned and executed was wrong.[85]

In operations against the VC throughout 1967, there had been a pattern of intelligence failure. Even when intelligence had been accurate, the VC had often been able to evade engagement while using guerrilla tactics to vex and inflict casualties on the Americans. The absence of significant contact and the willingness of the VC to evade combat should not have been taken automatically to be a sign of American success without any consideration of alternative explanations for the enemy's behavior. The CIA, as previously noted, had raised the cautionary flag against the simple assumption that evasion meant a lack of will and capacity to fight, but the warning had been too low key. As a result it was lost in the noise of bodies falling to be counted.

The overall pattern of operations had never been made available to policy level personnel in the administration. The small hints of a pattern that might have impinged on the policy consciousness were obliterated by the din of big battle, particularly the biggest battle of the year, the battle for Dak To. The series of engagements that stretched through November 1967, which collectively constitute the battle of Dak To, occurred within the context of a major search and destroy operation directed against PAVN forces in the highlands of Pleiku Province. The 4th Infantry Division was responding to an upsurge in NVA-initiated incidents near the junction of the Laotian, Cambodian, and South Vietnamese borders which started in early October following three months of relative quiescence.

The interlocking series of sweeps and engagements were too complex to fully describe, but the essential features can be outlined. Accurate information regarding the PAVN plans and dispositions concerning forthcoming attacks were provided to the division by a NVA defector on November 2. Rapid movement by U.S. forces preempted the attacks and the PAVN regiments withdrew to prepare positions apparently in the hope of provoking the United States into costly assaults against ready defenses. Elements of the 4th Infantry Division and the 173rd Airborne Brigade accepted the challenge. Over the next three weeks numerous battles occurred around each of the fortified PAVN bases in which casualties ranged from moderate to heavy. Despite the superior American firepower and repeated air strikes, the PAVN formations held their positions. As an example, the 174th PAVN Regiment slugged it out with the 173rd Airborne Brigade at Hill 875 from November 12 to 23, when the position finally fell to the Herd.

In addition to effective and tenacious positional warfare, the NVA employed diversionary attacks delivered by VC main force units. Heavy fire from 122mm rockets and 120mm mortars were employed directly against U.S. forces and against diversionary targets such as Kontum City. The lack of coordination, fatally compromised by the defection of Sergeant Vu Hon, was not apparent when the North Vietnamese went on the tactical defensive. Their effective change of plans and dispositions in the face of the U.S. preemption was a mark of high professionalism and unusual command flexibility. Their willingness to use the tactical defensive to further a strategic offensive demonstrated that the overall northern theory of victory was not dependent upon spectacular successes in either the capture of territory or the destruction of forces.

The territory selected by the PAVN was well suited for defense as it was mountainous, heavily covered with dense vegetation, and well provided with caves. The PAVN engineers had improved on the terrain, so it constituted an even more formidable obstacle for the U.S. and ARVN troops who attacked. American and ARVN forces used artillery liberally with nearly 152,000 rounds of 150mm and larger-caliber munitions being fired during the course of the Dak To campaign. Air strikes were employed heavily, with over 2,000 tactical and 305 B–52 sorties flown. In all, the aircraft delivered over 6,000 tons of ordnance. Maximum use of helicopter mobility enabled the Americans to move artillery, large masses of supplies, and quantities of men quickly around the rugged terrain. The reported figure of 1,644 PAVN dead was believed to be low due to the enemy's policy of emphasizing the recovery of dead and wounded personnel from the battlefield, which was facilitated by the nature of the terrain. American forces lost 290 KIA with the ARVN units losing 56 or 73 more.

The commander of the 4th Infantry Division, Gen. William R. Peers, thought "the battle for Dak To might well become the turning point of the war in the Central Highlands." He was too optimistic, but his view was echoed up the chain of command. The competent and courageous performance of the U.S. forces and the large number of PAVN bodies counted obscured the less pleasant realities. The battle developed as it did in large measure because of one defector's information, and good luck of this magnitude was not a commodity one can generally count on. The NVA had broken contact on their own initiative and withdrawn in good order, probably to sanctuaries across the Laotian or Cambodian borders. The performance of the PAVN on the defense had been excellent, the leadership quite professional, and troop morale high as indicated by the small number of NVA defectors—five in addition to the talkative Sergeant Vu. The 314 individuals and 96 crew-served weapons captured did not seriously affect the capability of the PAVN 1st Division to fight on.[86]

The commander of the 173rd Airborne Brigade, the unit that had suffered the most fatalities at Dak To, was sober in his assessment, commenting on the enemy's determination, fighting qualities, and material strengths.[87] Dak To looked like a real victory to both the administration and to the public alike, having been reported as such by the legion of journalists who landed in the combat zone.[88] Dak To was interpreted a milestone on the road to overall success in South Vietnam. This was an interpretation that was not justifiable. The will, capability, integrity, and initiative of the PAVN had not been eroded or seriously affected by the battle or the larger Operation McArthur. There had been no turning point in the Central Highlands.

CONCLUSION: RESULTS OF CUMULATIVE DECEPTIONS

If the Johnson administration had been able to closely examine the after-action reports during 1967, and if it had been possible to abandon the body count fixation, the picture of U.S. success which was being painted so ardently in November could not have been accepted so easily. It was true that the American operations were killing an impressive number of people, capturing an imposing quantity of supplies, equipment and weapons, and destroying a large number of structures and facilities. But were these relevant indicators of real progress on the battlefield, and were they winning against Communist policy?

The debate over the Communists order of battle and rates of replacement had resulted in sterile statistics of dubious relevance. The enemy had shown no difficulty in replacing losses. The CIA had confirmed in August 1967 that the war was "becoming an increasing North Vietnamese show."[89] This would reduce VC manpower requirements and the difficulties of maintaining morale within the guerrilla forces. The operational and tactical concepts employed by the VC during 1967 were assisting in the process of conserving manpower while buying time during which remedial actions could be taken to improve morale. In any event, despite losses and an increase in the number of low-level, local force defections, "VC troops continue to fight well and there have been no mass or unit defections."[90] American ground and air actions had not broken the morale or will to fight of either the VC or PAVN troops.

American forces had killed a lot of enemy soldiers, but it did not seem possible to kill our way to victory. The losses so eagerly counted by field commanders and Washington decision makers alike had not translated into a denial of initiative or political will to the enemy. In short, below the appearance of success, the military situation was, at best, a battlefield stalemate in which neither side could obtain a quick or decisive advantage. Rather, the military balance resembled the almost motionless embrace of two equally matched sumo wrestlers, a dynamics stasis awaiting some small slip or hesitation.

The change in the character of the war that occurred in 1967 with the introduction of major PAVN regular units was not recognized. Also unacknowledged was the change in the relationship between Hanoi and the NLF/VC. The NVA ended their brief period as "external sponsor" of the southern guerrillas through late 1966 and were now seeking to unify Vietnam and its Communist forces under Hanoi's domination. The NLF/VC had become potential rivals for power with Hanoi and, thus, were now expendable tools.

The presence of the North Vietnamese regulars in I Corps and the Central Highlands of II Corps complemented the VC forces and presented the United States and South Vietnam with an operational dilemma. Actions against the PAVN forces facilitated the guerrilla activities of the VC; concentrations of force against the VC, whether in big battalion sweeps or pacification support missions, laid I and II Corps open to a PAVN spectacular. In any case the prolongation of the war, the infliction of casualties, and the increase of chaos in the South had the strong potential of gutting the political will of the United States and Saigon to continue the war.

The American planners assumed that Hanoi not only was continuing as an external sponsoring power but was pursuing a strategy of attrition. As the United

States was following a strategy that mixed attrition with the erosion of the North's material capacity to continue the war, this constituted an exercise in mirror imaging. It was also wishful thinking. The assumptions were not correct. Despite the rhetoric issuing from Hanoi regarding the role of the NLF as the sole legitimate representative of the South Vietnamese people, there was a strong reason to assess the role of Hanoi as a rival rather than a patron of the NLF/VC. There was no reason to see the strategic avenue of attrition as the one pursued by Hanoi. On many occasions individual policy makers made reference to a perception that Hanoi hoped to triumph by exhausting the political will of the United States.

As it was, the misunderstandings and confusion regarding the changing character of the war as well as U.S. goals and definitions of victory were so pervasive and pernicious that it was impossible to establish realistic and meaningful measurements of progress toward victory. By default the focus upon statistics emerged. Numbers pretended to be facts and statistics were seen as realities. The real accomplishments of 1967, such as the village and national elections and the improvements of ARVN, floated in an amorphous mass of irrelevant or dangerously misleading statistics, real progress overwhelmed by the quantified appearance of success. In fact, the enemy maintained the initiative and controlled escalation dominance. Real pacification and revolutionary development progress was difficult to establish. The "other war" was undercut by the destabilizing effects of the big battalion sweeps and free fire zones. The generation of refugees, an approach urged by MACV, was incompatible with the establishment of a secure South Vietnamese rural economy, polity, or society.

The cross-currents and cross-purposes that lurked beneath the statistics of success could have been seen if the administration had the wit and intellectual courage to look for them. The numbers that promised progress toward victory were repeatedly belied by events on the ground. That dichotomy should have rivaled the administration with corresponding adjustments of goals, strategy, and means. It did not, and that stands as a clear indictment of the administration at its middle and upper levels. The February 1968 Communist Tet Offensive would shatter most of the myths and mismeasurements upon which the Johnson administration strategy and commitments had been built.

NOTES

1. The best-known works advancing the thesis of an American military victory undercut by politicians and press are Harry G. Summers, *On Strategy: A Critical Analysis of the Vietnam War* (Novato, CA: Presidio Press, 1982) [hereafter *On Strategy*]; Bruce Palmer, *The 25-Year War: America's Military Role in Vietnam* (Lexington: Univ. of Kentucky Press, 1984).

2. Summers, *On Strategy*, i.

3. Lyndon B. Johnson File (LBJ), National Security File (NSF), Country File (CF), Vietnam (VN), No. 16, M32, 213, 213a, Lyndon B. Johnson Library, Austin, Texas. All Johnson File material located at LBJ Library.

4. Ibid., 213a, 1.

5. Field Manual (FM) 100–5, *Field Service Regulations-Operations* (Washington, DC: Department of the Army [DA], 1962), 4–5.

6. FM 7–10, *Rifle Company, Infantry and Airborne Battlegroups* (Washington, DC: DA, 1962), 3–4.

7. Special Warfare Board [Lt. Gen. Hamilton Howze, chair], *Final Report* (Ft. Monroe, VA: HQ USCONARC, January 28, 1962), 140.

8. This was explicitly recognized and accepted by the Ad Hoc Study Group. See their "Summary Report," v.

9. LBJ, NSF, CF, VN, No. 20, M37, 413a, p. F–4. Secretary of Defense Robert J. McNamara had accepted this contention as early as May 1964; see LBJ, NSF, National Security Council (NSC), No. 1, T4, 2, p. 5.

10. LBJ, NSF, CF, VN, No. 20, M37, 413a, p. F–5.

11. Ibid., pp. F–6, G–28.

12. Ibid., pp. F–6, F–18.

13. Ibid., pp. G–25–28.

14. LBJ, NSF, CF, VN, Nos. 78, 79, 3C, North Vietnamese (NVN) Infiltration into South Vietnam (SVN), No. 7, June 24, 1965.

15. LBJ, NSF, CF, VN, No. 20, M37, 413a, pp. G–28, G–29.

16. Ibid., pp. I–1, I–3, Summary Report III.

17. LBJ, NSF, NSCH No. 42, VII, T436, 36a, pp. 1–2.

18. LBJ, NSF, CF, VN, Nos. 26, 27, C45, 74, (declassified [decl.] July 1989).

19. 173rd Airborne Brigade [Separate], Combat After Action Report [hereafter CAAR], Operation Crimp, February 23, 1966, pp. 16–17.

20. LBJ, Papers of William C. Westmoreland (WCW), No. 7, V.3, 42, 173rd Airborne Brig., Commander's Note No. 91, January 22, 1966, p. 4.

21. Ibid., p. 6.

22. LBJ, NSF, CF, VN, Nos. 26, 27, M45b, 118.

23. 1st Inf. Div., CAAR, Operation Mastiff, December 21, 1966. This report includes the second-echelon reports from the brigades and division artillery; written in March, see pp. 15–18.

24. 3rd Brig., 1st Inf. Div., CAAR, Operation Coca Beach, April 3, 1966 [hereafter Coca Beach CAAR].

25. ARCOV, *Summary Report*, Enclosure (Encl.) 1, pp. 20–28.

26. Coca Beach CAAR, p. 7.

27. The artillery employed in support of the operation delivered 2,334 rounds aggregating 590 tons while the USAF provided 73 close air support sorties. See Coca Beach CAAR, pp. 2, 6.

28. LBJ, NSF, CF, VN, Nos. 26, 27, M48, 155.

29. LBJ, NSF, CF, VN, Nos. 26, 27, M48, 153.

30. 1st Cav. Div. (Airmobile), CAAR, Operation Jim Bowie, May 8, 1966.

31. Ibid., p. 5.

32. 1st Inf. Div., CAAR, Operation Abilene, April 27, 1966—includes CAAR from 2nd and 3rd Brigades.

33. Ibid., p. 3.

34. LBJ, NSF, NSC Meetings, No. 2, T2, 2.

35. Ibid., pp. 2–3.

36. LBJ, Papers of McGeorge Bundy, No. 12, Basic Political Position 6, pp. 2–4.

37. LBJ, PPW-JMF, 1, McNaughton Drafts 1966, I, II, 61, p. 1.

38. LBJ, PPW-JMF, 1, McNaughton Drafts 1966, I, II, 62 (decl. February 1988).

39. Ibid., p. 4.

40. LBJ, NSF, Agency, Nos. 8, 9, 10, CIA II, 22. Helms stated that the memorandum was not a "formal coordinated paper" but that it represented a joint effort between the CIA and the Defense Intelligence Agency.

41. Ibid., pp. 4–7.

42. Ibid., p. 9.

43. LBJ, Papers of McGeorge Bundy, Nos. 15, 16, Vietnam Intell., No. 3.

44. Ibid., p. 1.

45. Ibid., p. 11.

46. 2nd Brig., 25th Inf. Div., CAAR, Operation Kahala, May 14, 1966.

47. Ibid., p. 4.

48. 1st Inf. Div., CAAR, Operation Birmingham, June 15, 1966.

49. Ibid., p. 3.

50. For a detailed intelligence appreciation of VC options, see ibid., p. 4.

51. Ibid., pp. 4, 6, 10–21.

52. Ibid., p. 37.

53. 173rd Airborne Brig. (Separate), CAAR, Operation Hollandia, September 15, 1966.

54. Ibid., pp. 2–11.

55. 1st Inf. Div., CAAR, Operation El Paso II/III, December 8, 1966.

56. Ibid., pp. 3–5, 57–65.

57. Ibid., p. 3, gives the figure as 93 killed in action (KIA), whereas on p. 57 the KIA figure is given as 105.

58. Ibid., pp. 89–96, 101–8.

59. LBJ, NSF, Memos to the President, No. 8, W. W. Rostow (WWR), V.6, 21a, Transcript of Saigon 879 dated July 13, 1966, p. 1 (decl. July 1988).

60. Ibid., p. 106.

61. Besides previously cited reports, see Goure, Rpt., August 1, 1966, LBJ, NSF, CF, VN, No. 35, M57, 163a, especially p. 4, which went to WWR and was marked for presidential reading.

62. 2nd Brig., 25th Inf. Div., CAAR, Operation Sante Fe, July 20, 1966.

63. Ibid., pp. 8–17; quote on p. 18.

64. 1st Brig., 101st Airborne Div., CAAR, Operation John Paul Jones, September 28, 1966.

65. Ibid., pp. 4, 9.

66. 173rd Airborne Brig. (Separate), CAAR, Operation Sioux City, December 15, 1966, pp. 2–5, 19, 22–24; quote on p. 23.

67. Ibid., p. 23.

68. 3rd Squadron, 11th Armored Cav. Reg., CAAR, Operation Hickory, October 26, 1966.

69. 196th Light Inf. Brig., CAAR, Operation Attleboro, n.d., pp. 18–20; 2nd Brig., 25th Inf. Div., CAAR, Operation Attleboro, n.d., p. 14; 2nd Bat., 27th Inf. (the Wolfhounds), CAAR, Operation Attleboro, April 28, 1967; 173rd Airborne Brig. (Separate), CAAR, Operation Attleboro, December 30, 1966, p. 14.

70. 4th Bat., 503rd Inf. Reg., 173rd Airborne Brig., CAAR, Operation Winchester, n.d., pp. 2, 23, 53.

71. LBJ, NSF, NSC Meetings No. 2, Meetings with the President No. 2.

72. LBJ, NSF, NSC Meetings No. 2, Meetings with the President, No. 2b, p. 1 (decl. May 1987).

73. LBJ, NSF, Memos to the President, No. 11, WWR, No. 15, 8, 8a, p. 21 (decl. February 1990).

74. LBJ, Papers of WCW, No. 11, V. No. 15 (1), 48, Telex, Commanding Gen., II FFORCEV to COMUSMACV, "Visit by COMUSMACV to II FFORCEV," April 16, 1966; ibid., April 14, 1967, especially pp. 4–5; No. 15, 44, Telex, WCW to Adm. Sharp and Gen. Wheeler, "Situation in I Corps," April 12, 1967 (decl. January 1989), especially pp. 2, 3.

75. LBJ, NSF, CF, VN, No. 66, 2a(1), 49c, Intell. Memo., "The Communist Build-up in South Vietnam's Northern I Corps," May 11, 1967, especially pp. 2, 9, 11.

76. LBJ, NSF, CF, VN, No. 66, 2a(1), 54, Intell. Memo., "The Communist Build-up in Northern South Vietnam," November 22, 1966, especially pp. 7, 9.

77. LBJ, Papers of Paul Warnke, John McNaughton Files, No. 5, McNaughton V. XIII, 19, JCS Study, "Alternative Courses of Action for Southeast Asia,"May 1967, pp. 2, 18b, 18c, 18d, 36, 42, 43.

78. LBJ, NSF, CF, VN, Nos. 81–84, 3e(1), Future Military Operations, No. 17, Memo Gen. Wheeler to Secy of Def., "Future Actions in Vietnam," May 29, 1967, p. 2 (decl. June 1989).

79. For the disclaimer of advocacy, see ibid., no. 17a, Appendix, "Portions of Draft DPM with Factual Corrections," p. 10 (note).

80. Ibid., No. 18a, Draft Memo for the President, "Future Actions in Vietnam,"May 19, 1967, p. 18a (decl. June 1989). This draft was sent by Cyrus Vance OSD/ISA to Katzenbach and the VNCC.

81. LBJ, NSF, Memos to the President, No. 14, WWR V. No. 27, 147a, Transcript of Saigon 24624, Ellsworth Bunker to LBJ, May 3, 1967, especially p. 5.

82. 25th Inf. Div., CAAR, Operation Gadsden including report of 196th Inf. Brig., March 22, 1967, especially pp. 52–53; 3rd Brig., 4th Inf. Div., CAAR, Operation Gadsden, March 10, 1967.

83. 1st Inf. Div., CAAR, Operation Junction City, May 8, 1967, including Brig. Div. Artillery, Aviation, Engineer and Support Services A. A. Rpts.; 173rd Airborne Brig., CAAR, Operation Junction City, June 15, 1967; 11th Armored Cav. Reg., CAAR, Operation Junction City, n.d.; 3rd Brig., 4th Inf. Div., CAAR, Operation Junction City, May 12, 1967; 1st Brig., 9th Inf. Div., CAAR, Operation Junction City, n.d.

84. 1st Brig., 101st Airborne Div., CAAR, Operation Wheeler, December 11, 1967, especially pp. 1–4; quote on p. 12.

85. 9th Inf. Div., CAAR, Operation Sante Fe I/II/III, January 20, 1968; quote on p. 38.

86. 4th Inf. Div., Special CAAR, "The Battle for Dak To," January 3, 1968, especially pp. 19, 21, 24, 31, 34, 35, 46–47; quote on p. 66. Page 35 gives the lower number for both U.S. and ARVN KIAs while p. 16 gives the higher number.

87. 173rd Airborne Brig., CAAR, "The Battle of Dak To," December 10, 1967, p. 41.

88. Eighty-eight journalists and cameramen covered the 173rd Airborne Brigade alone, including four teams from CBS News and two from ABC News. See ibid., Encl. No. 7.

89. LBJ, NSF, National Intelligence Estimates, No. 5, 14.3, North Vietnam, No. 4, SNIE 14.3–1–67, ''Problem of Viet Cong Recruitment and Morale,'' August 3, 1967, p. 4 (decl. March 1990).

90. Ibid., p. 3.

Part V

Legacies

The Vietnam War left crucial and difficult legacies for the United States. The death of over 58,000 Americans and the wounding of 300,000 more in a lost war was the most obvious and tragic legacy. The related wounds in the larger U.S. body politic were also fundamental as evident, for example, in the Vietnam Veterans War Memorial in Washington, and the public reactions to it. The war also produced a constitutional crisis in this country between the executive and congressional branches regarding which body would have the ultimate authority to authorize undeclared wars. Another legacy was the crisis of legitimacy about government in general, provoked by charges of government deception and years of optimistic official reporting in the face of contrasting battlefield realities. And, of course, the war produced a fundamental rethinking about U.S. interests abroad: What are "vital" interests? When do they come into play? When are they worth fighting for?

The Vietnam War coincided with, and obviously exacerbated, a traumatic reevaluation within American society about this country's purposes and morality. The year 1968—the year of the King and Kennedy assassinations, the Chicago Democratic Convention, the Watts and Detroit riots, the Weathermen "Days of Rage," the Tet Offensive, and President Johnson's abdication, all instantaneously televised—nearly produced a nervous breakdown in the United States. Finally, in the years between 1975 and 1981–1982 the United States temporarily lost its leadership role in world affairs. The Soviets and their clients laid siege to the Third World, taking advantage of American introspection and loss of nerve. And our military services, deliberately sought to forget everything about their Vietnam experiences as fast as possible. Fortunately, they were not entirely successful.

The Vietnam War left extraordinary legacies for Southeast Asia as well. South Vietnam collapsed and came under Hanoi's Communist rule. Between 1975 and 1985, about 1.5 million South Vietnamese escaped or bribed their way out of Vietnam—possibly one-third of them dying at sea in the attempt. About 750,000 Indochinese refugees ultimately made their way to the United

States. Inside Vietnam nearly 1 million former ARVN soldiers, policemen, officials, and other people associated with the United States or from wealthy or educated backgrounds were swept into the Communist gulag. Untold tens of thousands, including southern Communists and radicals who "knew too much," perished in these camps.[1] Vietnam's economy collapsed under the weight of Communist rule, corruption, and the U.S. trade embargo. In Cambodia, an even more hideous "social purification" campaign was executed by Pol Pot's Khmer Rouge resulting in the death of about 1.5 million Khmer citizens out of 7 million.[2] In Laos, the Communist gulag was smaller and less efficient but ruthless enough.

In this section we examine just two of the many legacies of the Vietnam war: the American public's moods regarding Vietnam and Iraq, and the often difficult relationship between Saigon and Washington during the war.

Lorenzo Crowell's "The Lessons and Ghosts of Vietnam" examines how the many lingering, and often contradictory, perceptions and lessons of the Vietnam War, and what went wrong there, continue to influence the current public mood about war and peace. Certainly, the American military did not like the gradual application of force in Vietnam, nor did the complex and micromanaged chain of command prove popular. In post-Vietnam actions like Operations Just Cause and Desert Storm these problems were not repeated. But post-Vietnam Army assessments of what went wrong in Vietnam have come to contradictory conclusions. Some argue the war was conventional from start to finish and that the insurgency was simply a "smoke screen." Others contend the war was revolutionary and the U.S. big-unit operations contributed to the eventual loss by the collateral damage they caused and the public outrage in the United States, which they provoked.

Crowell also surveys media coverage of the Persian Gulf crisis and notes how Vietnamese images, analogies, and messages kept influencing the Middle East news. Gradualism was rejected in favor of a "decisive" victory over Iraq; President Bush's assurances to the American public before Desert Storm proved popular. Fighting without restrictions was also generally favored by the U.S. public. Control of media coverage of the Gulf also, naturally, came in for debate. The inevitable antagonism between the military and the media made itself felt throughout Desert Shield and Desert Storm. Finally, domestic dissent played a role in the Gulf crisis but, in spite of the troops' concern over it, the war ended too quickly for it to become a real factor.

The next chapter here is by Bui Diem, the former South Vietnamese minister-at-large to the United States. Ambassador Diem was not only a key government official for the Republic of Vietnam but is also a scholar, teaching today for the Indochina Institute at George Mason University. In his analytical essay entitled "Reflections on the Vietnam War: The Views of a Vietnamese on Vietnamese-American Misconceptions," not only does he provide his personal observations of the war, but he also explains the misunderstandings between the South Vietnamese and the Americans which, in his opinion, contributed to the debacle in Vietnam.

The ambassador's essay reiterates his long-held view that, in spite of America's best intentions to support and preserve the South, American usurpation of much of the actual fighting of the war in early 1965 did more harm than good. It expanded the war by increasing Communist involvement from North Vietnam, China, and the USSR. Worst of all, it harmed the viability of the southern government and left its leaders incapable of standing on their own. His arguments are an expansion of those first made in his book *In the Jaws of History*. Using the perspectives he has gained over the past seventeen years, Diem examines the troubled days of the sixties and seventies and provides an ardent reconsideration of the misconceptions that existed between the two allies as an explanation for the ultimate collapse of South Vietnam.

Ultimately, perhaps Bui Diem's greatest contribution is the fact that he has not become an embittered expatriate but remains a committed scholar whose search for the truth about the war in Vietnam has allowed him to change his mind and to accommodate new theories and arguments. By himself, he is a valuable resource who provides us all with a powerful witness to the sincere efforts of many in the South Vietnamese government and to the virtue of the Vietnamese people, especially those millions who died in that war.

NOTES

1. See, for example, the eyewitness accounts in David Chanoff and Van Toai Doan, *The Vietnamese Gulag* (New York: Simon & Schuster, 1986).

2. Two important sources are: Michael Vickery, *Kampuchea: Politics, Economics, and Society* (London: Frances Pinter, 1986), 184–88 and Craig Etcheson, *The Rise and Demise of Democratic Kampuchea* (Boulder, CO: Westview, 1984), 143–49.

11

The Lessons and Ghosts of Vietnam

Lorenzo M. Crowell

Americans have been unable to lay to rest the ghosts of Vietnam, apparitions that haunt the American military, policy-making community, media, and general public alike. These apparitions may be based on facts or on myths, but they are apparitions that haunt us nonetheless. These ghosts, lessons that we have learned or at least think that we have learned, are an important part of the legacy of Vietnam.

In exploring the lessons of Vietnam, this chapter looks at three issues. The first issue is how we learn from history; how we draw lessons. The second issue, briefly covered, is the military lessons of Vietnam. The final issue is the use of the lessons of Vietnam during the public debate about Operation Desert Shield between August 1990 and January 1991.

Most Americans agree with the slogan "no more Vietnams." We agree that we do not want to repeat "the Vietnam Experience." The problem is *which* Vietnam. Because we do not agree about what we mean by the Vietnam we do not want to repeat, we cannot agree what the lessons of Vietnam have been.

In January 1991, Ellen Goodman of the *Boston Globe* made this point in a syndicated column entitled "Which Vietnam Will This Not Be?"[1] In her title, "This" refers to Desert Shield which became Operation Desert Storm. She was not the only one to make this point; the same issue had been raised in the *Economist* in December 1990 in an editorial asking, "Which Vietnam Was That Exactly?"[2]

The answer to the question "Which Vietnam Will This Not Be?" varied widely. For General Colin Powell, chairman of the Joint Chiefs of Staff, "this" would not be the Vietnam of gradual escalation. For Dr. Howard (Dan) Embree, Associate Professor of English at Mississippi State University who served as an artillery officer in Vietnam after graduating from West Point and who later became a founding member of Service Academy Graduates Against the War, "this" would not be a war into which an administration led an unsuspecting

American public.[3] Many in the Congress were determined that "this" would not be a war fought on a blank check from the Congress. The central point here is that each of us in the Vietnam generation had a different experience and drew different conclusions—consciously or unconsciously.

Those who lived through Vietnam are every bit as much a generation marked by a shared experience as the World War I generation. Richard E. Neustadt and Ernest R. May in their important book *Thinking in Time: The Uses of History for Decision Makers* analyzed at length how we learn by experience and deal with the present, using analogies that become the lessons of such an event as Vietnam. This learning is not restricted to participants or contemporary observers. People born long after an event learn the lessons from books, from films, and from their parents, among other sources.[4]

Historical theories of generations shaped by a particular experience which create apparent cyclic patterns in history go in and out of fashion (perhaps a cyclic pattern itself). This author received a serious introduction to these from Theodore Ropp, whose thoughts on generational cycles in political and military affairs were published in *History and War*.[5] Although historians generally are skeptical, as they should be, about cycles in history, the performance of European and American political decision makers and senior military commanders in the 1930s reflected their experiences as the World War I generation.

In attempting to understand European political and military developments between World War I and World War II, it is essential to recognize that, although almost everybody agreed that World War I had been a disaster, different conclusions were drawn by different individuals depending on their perspective. Some concluded that they should never fight any war again. Others concluded that they should never fight a war that way again. Those who concluded "never that way again" split into at least two camps—offensive and defensive—about how to fight next time. Thus, we see the signing of the Kellogg–Briand Pact outlawing war, the development of strategic bombing and blitzkrieg, and the building of the Maginot Line—all more or less based on the lessons of World War I.

It is important to remember that World War II was fought by senior officers and policy makers who had lived through World War I. Chamberlain, MacArthur, Eisenhower, Montgomery, Guderian, Churchill, Roosevelt, and so on, had all participated at some level in World War I. Japanese leaders certainly had the least direct combat experience, but they at least watched. All of them and the peoples of their countries who followed these leaders and fought in World War II either learned from, or suffered under, the lessons of World War I. In the same vein, U.S. leaders and people have learned from, or suffer under, the lessons of Vietnam.

One of the most vehemently debated of the military lessons of Vietnam is the impact of the gradual application of force. This author, in an analysis of Operation Just Cause, concluded that:

The calculation that hitting all the major PDF [Panama Defense Force] units simultaneously with overwhelming force would destroy their combat capability and prompt all concerned to accept the United States' replacement of the Noriega regime with the Endara government was correct. The use of overwhelming numbers was a departure from previous thinking concerning economy of force. The planners in this operation defined economy of force as the number of troops necessary to accomplish the mission expeditiously but without either running the risk of having inadequate forces or so many forces that they interfered with one another. Thus, U.S. forces were able to accept losses and meet unexpectedly strong resistance without facing disaster. Soldiers, not bureaucrats, planned this operation.[6]

The unstated lesson of Vietnam here is that the gradual escalation of the application of force in Vietnam by the United States was a mistake.

This lesson of Vietnam is widely shared by professional line officers who served in Vietnam, such as Generals Powell and Maxwell R. Thurmon who bear primary responsibility for the planning and execution of Operation Just Cause. As a group they are convinced that gradualism and escalation as advocated by sophisticated analysts of whatever sort—systems or otherwise—simply does not work. It gets more of our people killed.[7]

Analysts of Vietnam routinely point to the complex chain of command and to civilian interference in military tactical decisions—epitomized by Lyndon Johnson's control in the White House of target selection for Operation Rolling Thunder—as lessons of how *not* to conduct a war. In part as a consequence of these lessons during Operation Just Cause in December 1989, General Thurmon, as Commander of U.S. Southern Command, had complete tactical authority and his simple and direct chain of command ran through the chairman of the Joint Chiefs of Staff (JCS) to the secretary of defense and hence to the president. The secretary apparently issued political objectives, reviewed and approved plans, but let his commanders command. This lesson was institutionalized in the Nichols–Goldwater Act which brought the chairman of the JCS directly into the chain of command and increased his authority relative to the service chiefs.

There were other apparent lessons of Vietnam in Operation Just Cause. One can point, for instance, to the effective use of night vision devices by both aircrews and ground troops as a lesson of Vietnam. One can also point to the effective use of AC–130 gunships in particular, and special operations forces in general, as lessons of Vietnam.

There are other lessons of Vietnam at the micro-, or anecdotal, level. In December 1982, Brigadier General Robin Olds spoke to cadets studying military history at the U.S. Air Force Academy. He told them that after the Korean War he had agitated in the air staff for a new fighter to use in the next conventional war. He was dressed down and told to get it through his head that the Air Force would never fight another conventional war. With irony in his voice, General Olds explained that he consequently fought in Vietnam in a Navy airplane with Navy weapons.

After he left the classroom, Olds looked at a picture of the F–15 and remarked that, when he returned from Vietnam, Air Force leaders asked him what the next-generation fighter needed. His answer was that the pilot must be able to see out in all directions, and they therefore put the bubble canopy on the F–15.[8] Whether the bubble canopy was a direct result of his debrief or not, his story represents a lesson of Vietnam. The microlesson was the shape of the canopy, but the macrolesson for the Air Force was to prepare to fight some future conventional war in the nuclear age.

Are these examples of the lessons of Vietnam, or are they simply the results of the normal evolution of military technology and doctrine? In dealing with the issue of the military lessons of Vietnam, there is the possibility of a logical fallacy. This issue is in the realm of intellectual history with the inherent difficulties of proving causal relationships between ideas and actions. The possibility of this logical fallacy, however, is almost ludicrous. This is a professional military that has been routinely criticized for preparing to fight the last war by learning its lessons too well.

The United States military establishment is a professional military force whose staff systems are designed to produce lessons through systematic debriefings, after-action reports, and other staff analyses. One of the key elements of modern professional militaries, developed in the nineteenth century, is the systematic distillation and application of lessons learned in combat and in exercises to change military weapons, organizations, doctrines, tactics, and strategies in a deliberate attempt to improve military effectiveness.[9] This professional military search for lessons is one of the roots of the tension between academic historians and war college military history. The academicians know that each historical circumstance and event is unique and will never recur, whereas the professional military, who also recognize that precisely the same situation will not recur, must analyze past events in an attempt to learn how to improve their performance in a future analogous situation. The very idea of the lessons of Vietnam makes academicians nervous, but it is a vital professional issue for the U.S. military.

Two scholarly studies sponsored by the Army demonstrate institutional attempts to define the lessons of Vietnam and thereby improve the Army's performance in future wars. In reading Colonel Harry G. Summers's splendid book *On Strategy: The Vietnam War in Context*,[10] among the lessons of Vietnam one learns is that the U.S. Army was seduced by the trendy idea of unconventional warfare. Summers's critique appears to be that the Army should have fought the conventional war it was trained and organized to fight. On the other hand, reading Major Andrew F. Krepinevich, Jr.'s, equally splendid book *The Army and Vietnam*,[11] one learns that the Army's fundamental problem in Vietnam was its underlying doctrine: the "Army Concept" was a commitment to fighting in Vietnam with an army patterned after Patton's and Bradley's armies of World War II, even though the enemy was waging an insurgency. In short, Krepinevich's lesson and Summers's lesson apparently are complete opposites.

Moving from the military's professional lessons of Vietnam to the use of the lessons by public policy makers and the general public, the question is, how were the lessons of Vietnam used in the debate about Desert Shield between August 1990 and January 1991? A review of newspapers and television news generally available in a small Mississippi city reveals the debate as seen and heard far from the seats of power. From this perspective, a noteworthy aspect of the debate was the recurring references to the lessons of Vietnam used to justify policies and actions or to argue against the same policies and actions. The use of the lessons of Munich and other historical events were also noteworthy but are beyond the scope of this chapter, as are also the lessons of Vietnam in Operation Desert Storm.

One of the most widely acclaimed of the lessons of Vietnam was that gradual escalation in the application of military force was a mistake. On December 21, 1990, General Powell told troops in Saudi Arabia that "When we launch it, we will make it decisive so we can get it over as quickly as possible and there's no question who won."[12] This rejection of gradualism as a military lesson of Vietnam demonstrated in Operation Just Cause has been discussed above.

This lesson of Vietnam was expressed by civilian commentators as well as by military officers. Paul Greenberg of the *Pine Bluff Commercial* in a nationally syndicated column spoke out against restraints. In December, Greenberg complained that, "The object of war, as American generals used to know, is not to die for one's country but to make the other fellow die for his. Now, instead of Shermans and Pattons and MacArthurs, we seem at home with ideas like protracted conflict, rules of engagement, graduated escalation . . . and all the other euphemisms for a land war in Asia." After voicing this complaint Greenberg asked us to "Imagine: a war without privileged sanctuaries this time. And no restrictions on the kind of weapons used, including the nuclear variety. . . . Once the decision to use force is made it should be *used* [emphasis in the original]— without pause or equivocation, jabber, and hesitation." He then asserted that "there is no lack of firepower available to assure swift and certain victory in the Persian Gulf, but where is the willpower? That is the key ingredient."[13]

This lesson of Vietnam—that military force should be used without restrictions—was challenged in the Operation Desert Shield debate. In a letter to the editor of the *Jackson Clarion-Ledger*, Jim Waide, who identified himself as "a Marine Forward Observer" in Vietnam in 1969 and 1970, took exception to the promise that a war in the Persian Gulf would not be like the Vietnam War:

One way the war in Vietnam and the proposed war in Iraq are very similar is in civilian deaths. With our air power and artillery, we killed, maimed, and rendered homeless thousands of civilians in Vietnam. . . .

This use of massive air power and artillery assured that the rural Vietnamese civilian population would hate us, and resulted in their booby-trapping every trail near a Vietnamese village.

Now, Bush proposes a massive use of air power in Iraq. He promises that we will use even more air power and artillery in Iraq and Kuwait than was used in Vietnam.

This will ensure that the people of Kuwait who survive will abhor Americans and be our eternal enemies.

People who have been liberated by being destroyed are not really free.[14]

Waide's last statement apparently was a reference to the incident at Ben Tre during Tet of 1968 where a U.S. Army officer commented, "We had to destroy the town to save it."[15]

This lesson, that military force should be applied massively and without restrictions, reflects an assumption that the unsatisfactory Vietnam experience might have been satisfactory without gradualism. The assumption is that the war could have been ended quicker, perhaps even with victory. In December 1990, President George Bush said, "Let me assure you, should military action be required, this will not be another Vietnam. . . . This will not be a protracted, drawn-out war."[16]

Secretary of Defense Cheney on "The MacNeil–Lehrer News Hour" on January 11, 1991, when asked to say how long a war in the Gulf would last, dodged the question with comments about not wanting to arouse false expectations and pointing out that nobody could know precisely how a war would unfold. When pressed, Cheney said it could last as long as four or five months.[17]

The assumption that fighting without restrictions would bring a quick decision was not shared by everyone. Columnist Robert Maynard of the *Oakland Tribune* pointed out in a syndicated column:

Small wars always look easier to win on paper than in reality. Another president thought a few advisers and superior air power made his military opponents in the jungles of Vietnam a pushover. Lyndon Johnson left office wistfully wishing he had examined more carefully a peaceful path not taken.[18]

Christopher Layne and Ted Galen Carpenter, in a Cato Institute report, said the following: "Instead of dismissing the lessons of Vietnam, Americans must remember them. Superpowers are not omnipotent. The United States lacks the material, psychological, and spiritual resources to reshape, or impose order on, a fractious and unruly world."[19] Here Layne and Carpenter expressed the lesson of Vietnam that U.S. power, despite our enormous resources, has limits—we cannot control the entire world.

In the Operation Desert Shield debate, the individuals making war and peace decisions on behalf of the United States clearly were justifying their plans based on the lesson of Vietnam that gradual application of military force contributed to our long agony and defeat in Vietnam. Despite the conviction of those in power, others were not convinced that immediate and unrestricted application of military force in Vietnam would have produced victory. In the short run of Operation Desert Storm, the advocates of the immediate application of massive force appear to have been correct this time. In the long run, just when the United

States will be clear of the Kurdish refugees and other residual problems from Operation Desert Storm and how satisfied the American public will be with the overall results remain to be seen.

The debate over Desert Shield revealed that the American military and the American media drew opposing lessons from the news coverage of Vietnam. In response to the Pentagon announcement that in the interest of security in a Persian Gulf war officers would review news reports and only reporters in the approved pool with military escorts would be permitted to report on combat, Anna Quindlen of the *New York Times* flew to the defense of a free press invoking lessons of Vietnam. She remembered JFK's, "anger at David Halberstam who won a Pulitzer Prize by reporting not what the government said, but what was really happening in Vietnam. 'Don't you think he's too close to the story?' complained the president."

In Quindlen's view, reporters must get "too close" to fulfill their role in American society. She also remembered that:

Vietnam taught us that when the press and the military make a bargain, the press to be cautious and the military to tell the truth, those with the notebooks keep their end better than those with the guns.

But it also taught us that telling the truth about war can shift public opinion toward peace.[20]

Quindlen's shift of public opinion toward peace is the military's negative reporting that undermined support at home.

Another view was provided by Liz Trotta in the *Wall Street Journal* when she wrote:

The front ranks of American journalism are thick with those who got their first break covering Vietnam, righteously deciding that victory wasn't worth dying for—and, anyway, the fall of Goliath was a far better story. During the Tet Offensive of 1968, for example, the televised pictures of Viet Cong on the embassy lawn never caught up with the reality—that the enemy was severely punished and dispersed, a fact even Hanoi's commanders would admit years later. . . .

Nothing suggests that information will flow from the Middle East as once did Kuwaiti crude. Indeed, the hapless Pentagon media pool . . . represented an effort to dispel suspicion that the brass still remembered the enthusiasm with which Vietnam's debacles had been aired. Never again would they let the press "lose" a war. . . . Military men cannot forget those humiliations and, despite revisionist assertions that the reporting from Southeast Asia had negligible effect on public opinion, they still taste the gall. They provided access—and got a bonus set of battle scars for their trouble. Such memories have become a legacy. Ask any cadet at West Point, any raw recruit, what he thinks of newspeople. What's more, they no doubt reflect the attitude of their commander-in-chief, George Bush. . . .

There are demonstrably authentic grounds for secrecy—the risks to our side—but they also mask the "fog of war," the catalog of blunders that is war's companion—and so often the red meat of news.

Media executives insist they understand why "sensitive strategies" must not be revealed, yet they demand the "facts"—names, numbers, places and plans—all of which collides with that admirable summary of the military attitude offered by a British intelligence chief during World War I: "Say what you like, old man. But don't mention any places or people."[21]

The debate over responsible media coverage of Desert Shield reflects antithetical assumptions: the media's news is the military's intelligence data or at least bad for morale. The experiences of both sides in Vietnam have left too many with the lesson that the other is not to be trusted. Those in authority clearly believed the lesson of Vietnam that failure to restrict the flow of news contributed to our defeat.

Another lesson of Vietnam debated during Desert Shield was the impact of domestic dissent. Some were convinced that domestic dissent had led our government to recognize the error of its ways and pursue peace, and therefore must be repeated. Others were equally convinced that it had led us to defeat in Vietnam and should not be repeated. Two subthemes in this debate were the credibility of the American government and making the troops scapegoats for the government's policies.

On December 19, 1990, a young student from the University of Michigan, Karima Benoune, organizing resistance to the Bush administration's policies in the Gulf, appeared on "The McNeil–Lehrer News Hour." She sincerely asserted that we all knew the resistance had to start immediately before hostilities opened so that it could succeed. When asked how one who was a little child when the United States withdrew from Vietnam and who had not experienced that war and its resistance could be so sure, she simply replied that we all knew the antiwar movement played a role in ending the war in Vietnam.[22]

Another example of that same lesson learned by a generation not directly involved, perhaps not even alive, during Vietnam appeared on January 15, 1991, as the United Nations deadline for Iraqi withdrawal from Kuwait expired. The Associated Press provided a photograph of students from George Washington Junior High School in Alexandria, Virginia, demonstrating against the possibility of war. Prominently displayed in the picture was a poster with the message, "Remember Vietnam? Don't make the same mistake twice." On the poster also was the peace sign of the sixties antiwar movement.[23]

Charley Reese of the *Orlando Sentinel* weighed in on the side of dissent as a positive force in a syndicated column on August 17, 1990:

"Lyndon Baines" Bush ought to be impeached. He has made his Gulf of Tonkin speech and like the original, it's a big fat fib.

Where are the antiwar protesters when you need them? Where is the Congress? Is the collective IQ of the American people so low that we learned nothing from the Vietnam War?

Bush said Iraq threatens our oil supply and that's a lie. Bush said Iraq threatened to invade Saudi Arabia, and I suspect that's a lie, too. As you recall, Lyndon Johnson claimed American ships had been attacked by North Vietnamese in the Tonkin Gulf but it turned out—thousands of American lives later—that there had been no attack. [Author's Note: Not all historians agree with Reese's account of the Gulf of Tonkin incident.]

If there are satellite photos that show an Iraqi invasion force poised on the border of Saudi Arabia, then, Mr. Bush, let's see them. We've been lied to too often for us to take your word for it. Read my lips: your word is no good.[24]

Charley Reese believed that one of the lessons of Vietnam is that protests in the Congress and on the streets of this country were essential to changing the policies of a deceitful government.

Reese wrote other columns critical of Desert Shield and on January 5, 1991, the *Jackson Clarion-Ledger* printed a letter to the editor taking issue with Resse's position:

We are now in a crisis situation. It is ironic that the Charley Reeses of the world scream that they don't want another Vietnam, yet they do their best to create one by stirring up public sentiment against the actions taken by the president. It is high time that the people of this nation realized this and pledged our support not only for our president, but for our soldiers and their families.[25]

The lesson of Vietnam for this reader was clear—dissent brought defeat and undermined our troops.

The *Jackson Clarion-Ledger* in its editorial position took the antidissent side of the debate. On November 14, 1990, the editor announced his idea of what the rules should be if Desert Shield led to war. He wrote:

We cannot allow another Vietnam. If there is war, we must be in it to win. If we commit troops to military conflict, it should be the stated intent of Congress to fight. The president cannot have his hands tied with a bunch of military arm-chair quarterbacks if military action is required. Anything less is to invite defeat.[26]

For the editor of the *Jackson Clarion-Ledger*, a lesson of Vietnam was clearly that domestic dissent contributed to American defeat.

In a story datelined "In Eastern Saudi Arabia," the Associated Press articulated the position that dissent undermines the troops.

Vietnam was long ago and far away, but the conflict is on soldiers' minds in Saudi Arabia. Word of antiwar demonstrations back home has trickled back to the troops here, who are the tip of the military spear pointed at Saddam Hussein's forces. They are mindful of the hostile reception that greeted veterans a generation ago when they came home from an unpopular war. . . . Maj. John Bates, 44, of Little Rock, an executive officer for a Marine battalion, was wounded in the [the Vietnam] conflict. . . . From his standpoint, the American people misdirected their anger at the fighting men in Southeast Asia, instead of targeting the politicians who sent them there.[27]

The debate over the role of dissent during the Vietnam War as a lesson reflected the role of assumptions in historical analysis. Both sides agreed that domestic dissent played an important role in our unpleasant Vietnam experience. Those who started with the assumption that the most unpleasant aspect of the Vietnam War was our defeat drew the lesson that, by undermining the president and the armed forces, domestic dissent bore responsibility for that defeat. Those who started from the position that the very participation of the United States in the war was wrong and that the government misled the American people drew the lesson that dissent was essential to inform and arouse the American people to save us from that self-destructive and immoral war.

In the debate over Desert Shield some commentators pointed to the failure of the United States to stop an aggressor in Vietnam as the democracies had failed to stop Hitler at Munich. Paul Greenberg provided an example in a column entitled " 'Never Again' the Most Important Words to Remember in Middle East" where he wrote, "Never again. That's what some of us said after Vietnam. . . . Never again would an aggressor be allowed to wage war on his terms—and mainly on his victim's soil."[28] This lesson too was not universally accepted.

No more liberal a commentator than Paul Harvey took exception. He wrote, "I guess the arguments 'we must stop the tyrant' and 'the dominos will fall' leave me unconvinced because I have so recently watched our nation pay a terrible price in Korea and Vietnam."[29] Harvey's lesson of Vietnam was a rejection of preventive war, that is, that stopping current aggression with a limited war now was justified and necessary to prevent a predicted worse situation in the future. He would rather wait and deal with the future as it unfolded. Both Harvey and Greenberg in these columns were also firmly in the antigradualism camp.

What does all this mean? It means we use the lessons of our past constantly— we have nothing else to use. It means the Vietnam War was clearly one of those shared traumatic events in the history of a country which becomes a reference point. We have taken military and foreign policy decisions ever since with our understanding of current issues shaped by the lessons of Vietnam. It means our problem has been and remains, "Which Vietnam?" The Vietnam War was so complex, as any major war is, that analysts can find evidence to support any lesson their assumptions lead toward. Vietnam is as useful as the Bible or Carl von Clausewitz's *On War* to those who want to buttress an argument. They are all rich sources for conscientious scholars, rascals, or true believers of whatever sect. The use and abuse of the lessons of Vietnam will continue to be a legacy of Vietnam.

The last word goes to B.D. of the "Doonesbury" comic strip. In a bull session with young troops in Saudi Arabia who were awestruck at discovering that he was a Vietnam veteran, B.D. told them, "The number one lesson was: no matter how frustrating, it's better to be *sitting* on your butt than having it *shot* at!" [emphasis in the original]. His number two lesson was, "Always check your underpants for scorpions."[30]

NOTES

1. Ellen Goodman, "Which Vietnam Will This Not Be?" *Jackson* (MS) *Clarion-Ledger* (January 7, 1991): 9A.

2. "Which Vietnam Was That Exactly," *Economist* (December 22, 1990): 27.

3. Telephone conversation, Dr. Embree with the author, November 28, 1990.

4. Richard E. Neustadt and Ernest R. May, *Thinking in Time: The Uses of History for Decision Makers* (New York: The Free Press, 1986). See particularly chapter 9, "Placing Strangers," 157–80.

5. Theodore Ropp, *History and War* (Augusta, GA: The Hamburg Press, 1984).

6. Lorenzo M. Crowell, "The Anatomy of *Just Cause*: The Forces Involved, the Adequacy of Intelligence, and Its Success as a Joint Operation," in Bruce W. Watson and Peter G. Tsouras, eds., *Operation Just Cause: The U.S. Intervention in Panama* (Boulder, CO: Westview, 1991), 96.

7. I have no formal documentation to support this point, only twenty-three years of service as an Air Force officer which includes two and one-half years flying in Southeast Asia and four years on the faculty of the Air War College working with faculty and students who were largely fellow Vietnam veterans. In my experience, the professional officer Vietnam veteran who believes that the gradual application of military force in Vietnam was the correct policy is not just a rare exception. The fact is, I have never met one.

8. The author escorted General Olds on his visit to the USAF Academy on December 1, 1982.

9. See Lorenzo M. Crowell, "Military Professionalism in a Colonial Context: The Madras Army, *circa* 1832," *Modern Asian Studies* 24, 2 (1990): 249–74.

10. Harry G. Summers, *On Strategy: The Vietnam War in Context* (Carlisle Barracks, PA: Army War College, 1981).

11. Andrew F. Krepinevich, Jr., *The Army and Vietnam* (Baltimore: Johns Hopkins Univ. Press, 1986).

12. "Cheney, Powell Give Tough Pep Talks, Say War More Likely," *Starkville* (MS) *Daily News* (December 22, 1990): 12.

13. Paul Greenberg, "Let's Say It Again: No Land War in Asia, Since We Learned from Korea, Vietnam: Speculation Is So Thick that the Simplest, Surest Guide from the Past Is Being Overlooked," *Jackson* (MS) *Clarion-Ledger* (December 31, 1991). See also Paul Greenberg, " 'Never Again' the Most Important Words to Remember in Middle East," *Jackson* (MS) *Clarion-Ledger* (August 27, 1990): 7A.

14. Jim Waide, "Letter to the Editor," *Jackson* (MS) *Clarion-Ledger* (January 11, 1991): 8A.

15. George C. Herring, *America's Longest War: The United States and Vietnam, 1950–1975*, rev. ed. (New York: Knopf, 1986), 192.

16. Walter R. Mears, "More Parallels Between Vietnam and the Gulf: AP News Analysis," *Starkville* (MS) *Daily News* (December 10, 1990): 4.

17. "The McNeil–Lehrer Newshour," January 11, 1991.

18. Robert Maynard, "Will Bush Soon Be Facing an 'Elephantine' Decision in the Middle East?" *The Oakland Tribune* (September 19, 1990): 7A.

19. Christopher Layne and Ted Galen Carpenter, "Arabian Nightmares: Washington's Persian Gulf Entanglement," *Policy Analysis*, no. 142 (November 9, 1990): 13.

20. Anna Quindlen, "What U.S. Citizens Demand Is More 'Coverage' of Gulf Action, Not Less," *Jackson* (MS) *Clarion-Ledger* (January 11, 1991): 9A.

21. Liz Trotta, "Press vs. Army: Front Action in an Old Battle," *Wall Street Journal* (September 13, 1990): A18.

22. "The McNeil-Lehrer News Hour," December 19, 1990.

23. "American, Iraqi Emotions Beginning to Boil Over," *Jackson* (MS) *Clarion-Ledger* (January 16, 1991): 2A.

24. Charley Reese, "You Read My Lips, Mr. President," *Jackson* (MS) *Clarion-Ledger* (August 17, 1990): 11A.

25. Christopher A. Broaddrick, " 'Charley Reeses Could Lead Us Into War," *Jackson* (MS) *Clarion-Ledger* (January 5, 1991): 6A.

26. "War: If It Comes, We Must Be in It to Win," *Jackson* (MS) *Clarion-Ledger* (November 14, 1990): 16A.

27. "Specter of Vietnam Haunts Operation Desert Shield," *Jackson* (MS) *Clarion-Ledger* (October 29, 1990): 5A.

28. Greenberg, " 'Never Again,' " 7A.

29. Paul Harvey, "News Commentary: Embroiled in Another Faraway War," *Starkville* (MS) *Daily News* (January 11, 1991): 4.

30. Garry Trudeau, "Doonesbury," *Jackson* (MS) *Clarion-Ledger* (December, 27, 1990): 13A.

12

Reflections on the Vietnam War: The Views of a Vietnamese on Vietnamese-American Misconceptions

Bui Diem

INTRODUCTION

During the past few years, we have been exposed to a myriad of discussions and reevaluations of Vietnam in dozens of magazines, newspapers, and television programs. In colleges and universities around the country there are hundreds of courses dealing with the American experience in the Vietnam War. It appears as if, after a long period of recoil and amnesia during which nobody wanted to hear or think about the divisive war, the citizens of the United States are now catching up with the study of this tragic event. Thus has begun the earnest process of making a serious and objective assessment of the lessons of Vietnam.

There is no longer any doubt that the war in Vietnam was a watershed in American history. Based on the available abundance of materials on Vietnam, there is clear evidence that the war is still much in the subconscious of the American people and that, denial notwithstanding, the Vietnam syndrome remains like a ghost, lurking in their minds. This is true whether or not time has tempered our judgments on the war and the way it was conducted.

History may never render a clear and final verdict as to what went wrong during the war and why American and South Vietnamese forces failed to prevent North Vietnam from achieving its conquest of South Vietnam. Many of the so-called ''doves'' who opposed the war at that time continue to condemn U.S. intervention as wrong and immoral. Many maintain that for these reasons alone it was doomed to failure from the very beginning. By the same token, many of those we dubbed ''hawks'' who supported the war, continue to believe that it could have been won if only the United States had had the stomach to see it through to the end. Historian Robert Schulzinger of the University of Colorado noted in this respect that: ''As the war itself was divisive, its memory is divisive.''[1] So the arguments will probably continue as long as there are different views, opinions, and perspectives, not only on Vietnam but also on larger issues such as those pertaining to the U.S. role in the world, the use of U.S. military forces overseas or, in general terms, the advisability of U.S. intervention abroad on any level or in any fashion.

It would be futile in this chapter to attempt to address all of these issues. As a Vietnamese who happened, by the hazards of his assignment in Saigon and Washington, to be an eyewitness watching American and Vietnamese leaders at work during the peak of the U.S. intervention in the midsixties as well as at the end in 1975, I simply offer a few of my personal reflections on the war. It is my sincere hope that these reflections will contribute to "the quest for wisdom" that, according to Henry Kissinger, "America owed to itself if Vietnam is to leave any useful legacy."[2]

ONE MAN'S VIEW OF THE TWO VIETNAMS

The Geneva Agreements of 1954 divided Vietnam into two states at the 17th parallel: The Democratic Republic of Vietnam (North Vietnam) and the State of Vietnam (South Vietnam), later changed to the Republic of Vietnam. For the great majority of those in South Vietnam all they asked for was to be left alone so they could devote their energies to rebuilding their homes and families after the destruction of eight years of war. They did not take pleasure in the partition of the country imposed upon them by the big powers but, while protesting against it, they saw in it their only real opportunity for getting rid of the French.[3]

South Vietnamese citizens also hoped to regain their national independence as well as peace, albeit a temporary one, and the chance to carve out a prosperous territory from the richer half of Vietnam, one without Communist influence. As to the unity of the country, an ultimate goal for all Vietnamese, it would have to be a matter for future generations to decide. These later generations would have to decide when the moment was right for a *peaceful* solution to this problem.[4]

Southerners willingly waited for the reunification of their country. Vietnam had been occupied and divided many times throughout its long history, and all Vietnamese accepted the de facto and temporary partition of the country as a partial solution comparable to the situations in Germany and Korea. In a sense, ours was basically a defensive posture, a passive attitude, and our wish to be left alone contrasted vividly with the North Vietnamese Communists' aggressive determination to try to reunify the country immediately and at any cost. This was best demonstrated by Hanoi's decision in 1959 to support the creation of the National Liberation Front of South Vietnam and begin a war of subversion to take the South.[5]

AMERICAN INVOLVEMENT: THE VIETNAMESE VIEW

The United States became deeply involved in the Vietnam War in the midsixties but, as everyone knows, the roots of the involvement can be traced back to the midfifties when, following the French defeat at Dien Bien Phu and the resultant

Geneva Peace Agreement of 1954, the United States decided to shore up the government of Ngo Dinh Diem and transform South Vietnam into an anti-Communist bastion.

Counting the years from the 1950s to the fall of Saigon, it was no less than two full decades that America was immersed in the Indochina conflict. In terms of coexistence and joint efforts between two peoples who shared the same goal of defeating communism, this was indeed a long period of time. Yet, strangely enough, the way I saw it, the degree of understanding between the two sides was such that at times, for many Americans and South Vietnamese, it looked as if there were two separate wars—one fought by the Americans and another fought by the South Vietnamese. In my opinion, that was one of the main reasons for the tragic outcome in Vietnam.

In looking back at this period one cannot help being impressed by the fact that, at the onset, the United States and Vietnam had nothing in common and that if it were not for the fortuitous geopolitical events and international circumstances of the post–World War II era these two peoples would never have come together. Indeed, two nationalities, quite apart in terms of geographical location, international status, civilization, culture, and conceptualization, were thrown together at a time when the Vietnamese knew almost nothing about America and Americans knew even less about Vietnam.

I still remember those days in the fifties and the early sixties. The few vague notions that we had about the United States involved the generous Marshall Plan in Europe, the prestigious Gen. Douglas MacArthur in the war in Korea, the decisive and moralistic anti-Communist stands of John Foster Dulles, and especially the idealistic inaugural address of John F. Kennedy: "We shall pay any price, bear any burden, meet any hardship, support any friend, oppose any foe, in order to assure the survival and the success of liberty."[6]

Vietnamese knowledge and understanding of the United States was, to be sure, limited, but the attraction to what America represented in the world was irresistible and that was the reason why, in their fight for freedom against both the French and the Communists, the South Vietnamese looked on the Americans as their natural friends and allies. They did not even question the virtue, or the right and wrong, of the American intervention. They considered it a logical continuation of the American salvation of South Korea. South Vietnamese faith in the United States was unshakable simply because, in the trusting, and perhaps naive, minds of the masses of South Vietnamese citizens they believed that such a powerful and seemingly omnipotent nation as the United States of America could not be wrong. Besides, they reasoned, the United States had never lost a war in its illustrious history.

But if the faith of the South Vietnamese in American power was total, their ignorance about America's people, culture, and politics, was equally profound. The great majority of the Vietnamese—including the southern leadership and intellectual elites—did not understand the American political process or the power of American public opinion. Having lived too long under one authoritarian regime or another, southern Vietnamese could not evaluate the influence of public opinion on the U.S. Congress, or understand the influence that the Congress could have over a president and his administration in terms of budget and foreign policy. In fact, during my tenure in Washington, I spent a great deal of time dealing with this matter. Each time I was called home for consultations or my colleagues came to the United States on their fact-finding tours, I briefed these South Vietnamese legislators, military men, journalists, professors, and dozens of others. I tried to describe to them what I saw from my observation post in Washington. I tried to convey to them the changing mood of Americans during the tumultuous days of the late 1960s, the spreading antiwar feelings, the emerging conflict between the executive and legislative branches of the U.S. government which made access to foreign aid more and more difficult.

With their fixed ideas about the United States, they nevertheless regarded as inconceivable the possibility of a reduced American role in international affairs, and particularly in Vietnam, since they themselves had witnessed the huge U.S. investment and involvement in the midsixties. This inflexible vision was even more deeply rooted in the minds of the South Vietnamese military leaders who practically ruled the country during the last ten years of South Vietnam's existence. These leaders, having had close contacts for many years with their U.S. military counterparts and, to a large degree, having been conditioned by the generally conservative ideas of the U.S. military establishment, could not and would not believe that America would be compelled to withdraw in 1973. In fact, many South Vietnamese generals believed until the final days before the collapse of Saigon that the U.S. B–52s would return and wipe out the Communist offensive.

The innocence and naivete of the South Vietnamese can perhaps best be illustrated by my own experiences. In 1964, as a journalist, I made an initiation trip of three months to the United States. After that trip, I wrote some articles about life in the United States and what I had seen in San Francisco at the Republican National Convention of 1964. From that time forward, I was seen by those in South Vietnam as somewhat of an expert on American affairs. Thinking of it now, I cannot help but be a little embarrassed because there is a mountain of differences between even the little that I know now about America— American policies and politics, after three decades of painful and costly lessons— and what I knew then in the 1960s.

In politics, perception quite often counts more than facts. In this respect, the Americans were perceived by the Vietnamese as having a contingency plan for every situation, and of course the CIA was believed to be behind every move by the United States Embassy in Saigon. These misconceptions gradually led to an abdication of judgments on the part of South Vietnamese leaders and to increased reliance on the Americans. The American buildup in 1965 reinforced these beliefs among the South Vietnamese. Many in fact, were awestruck by scenes such as American helicopters ferrying, in some cases, hot meals to U.S. troops—even during the fighting. The Vietnamese marveled at the scores of gadgets piled high in huge post exchanges (PXs) for the use of the American GIs. Many Vietnamese whispered among themselves that "the men of the affluent society have brought here a new sort of war," an "affluent war" that they had never seen or even thought of before. They witnessed the generous, perhaps excessive, use of bombs and strafings by American aircraft which lasted for hours and hours. In many cases these attacks were undertaken where U.S. forces had only encountered enemy sniper fire. Of course, the South Vietnamese were not then aware of the fact that hundreds of millions and even billions of U.S. taxpayers dollars were being spent to pay for the hot meals, PXs, and bombs. When protests later began in the United States most people in South Vietnam attributed America's growing desire to withdraw to the antiwar critics who believed, unfairly and wrongly, that all the billions of dollars being spent in Vietnam were on the South Vietnamese. Indeed, both sides misunderstood each other.

The South Vietnamese, in fact, failed to understand the real nature of the U.S. intervention, making erroneous assumptions about the staying power of America and, in the process, abdicated their own role in the war. This resignation which, in retrospect appears to be one of the most fatal mistakes made by my countrymen, was somewhat facilitated by their partners, the Americans, who either out of impatience or overconfidence, tried to do everything themselves. In the end, North Vietnam's control of their own destiny contrasted to South Vietnam's failure to create viable local leadership and was one of the most fundamental and important differences between the two factions. It may well have been why the South lost the war.

AMERICAN MISCONCEPTIONS

These are only a few examples which illustrate the innocence or, to put it more accurately, the ignorance of the South Vietnamese about America, and South Vietnam's basically defensive sociopolitical posture and military objectives during the war. The Americans, for their part, did not have any better understanding of Vietnam, its culture, or its people. To quote Allan E. Goodman, of the School of Foreign Service at Georgetown University:

A basic point must be made about the American ignorance of the Vietnamese. U.S. policy planners never had the kind of anthropological and sociological analyses of South Vietnamese behavior and customs that the French had of the North Vietnamese, for example. The classic work from the French era—Paul Mus's *Sociologie d'une Guerre* (1952)—was never translated into English. . . . In the years during which our commitment to Vietnam was in the process of gathering momentum, there were no academic programs of language study research in Vietnamese available in any U.S. university. Between 1965 and 1970 only twenty Ph.D. theses were done on Vietnam, out of some five thousand in the field of modern history and international relations. Throughout this period, moreover, Vietnamese studies were orphans in American academia. And when, in early 1970,

AID [Agency for International Development] offered $1 million to create a Vietnamese Study Center there was only one taker.[7]

The Americans came to Vietnam with good intentions, and at least in the midsixties the power of U.S. military forces was so overwhelming that for many Americans it seemed not to matter much whether or not they should understand the Vietnamese. It was believed that there was no problem that could not be solved if America set its mind to do it, so the mood was "let's do it." Unfortunately, the war dragged on inconclusively, and in the end the contradictions were precisely those that stemmed from the American failure to understand not only the nature of the war, but also the mentality of both their friends and enemies.[8]

Together these mutual misunderstandings added fuel to the fire of Communist insurrection. For example, after encouraging the overthrow of South Vietnam's authoritarian leader Ngo Dinh Diem and putting ashore more than a half-million men and bombing targets in the country from north to south, the United States continued to claim that "it is not proper for the United States to intervene into the internal affairs of South Vietnam." After repeating over and over again President Kennedy's last public words about Vietnam, "In the final analysis it is their war and they are the ones who have to win or lose it," the United States *took over the war* and tried to do everything the American way with almost no consideration as to whether or not such a strategy would meet the complexities or local conditions of the war.[9]

Undoubtedly, Americans and Vietnamese had different habits and different ways of thinking; therefore, it was not easy for Americans to understand and evaluate the South Vietnamese. But the Americans made things all the more difficult for themselves by the rotation system under which they came into South Vietnam for a short period of time and then went home, making room for others to follow. With such a system, millions of Americans came to Vietnam, at a cost of billions of dollars, but few had the time, or the desire, to really get acquainted with the people they came to help, and especially with the very special nature of this war.

One of the many difficulties of the war in Vietnam that the Americans had to cope with was its complex nature. The good, the bad, and the ugly—you could find it all in Vietnam, depending on where you chose to look. Stereotype images and misperceptions characterized many Americans' judgments. To be sure, American misunderstanding of the South Vietnamese was one thing, but misunderstanding of the North Vietnamese Communists was another, and that was what hurt the most.

The whole concept of gradual escalation was, in this context, a vivid example of misunderstanding. It was based on the assumption that at some point the Communists would have to accept a compromise because the cost would be too high for them to go on fighting. The truth of the matter was, after having been assured publicly that their territory would never be invaded, the Communists found that if they could extend the war indefinitely they could win simply by not losing. Their own heartland, despite massive, but often sporadic air attacks, would not be invaded. By the same token, the search and destroy operations in the South ultimately became a hide and seek war game in which the Communists controlled not only the place, but also the tempo of the fighting when and where they were strong. In turn, when they were not strong they could hide in their sanctuaries in North Vietnam, Laos, and Cambodia. Thus, they only had to survive, no matter what the cost, and wait for America to tire of the war, no matter how long that might take.[10]

CONCLUSION

The list of mistakes and oversights by both allies is a long one, but the more I have reflected on the Vietnam War, the more I come to the conclusion that a very powerful explanation for what went wrong in Vietnam can be found in the lack of understanding between the United States and South Vietnam. American military and diplomatic strategy was shaped by a profound misunderstanding of the Vietnamese—both friends and foes—of their culture as well as their view of the fundamental issues of war and peace. The tragedy did not come in one day, but was an accumulation of years of errors and mistakes the biggest of all, it seems to me, being the lack of effort from Americans and South Vietnamese to better understand each other.

It has been said that America lost its innocence and arrogance in Vietnam. As a Vietnamese, I would complete the remark by saying that South Vietnam had no arrogance to lose but instead lost its innocence and, ultimately, its existence as a free nation.

NOTES

1. See Robert Schulzinger, *The Wise Men of Foreign Affairs: The History of the Council on Foreign Relations* (New York: Columbia Univ. Press, 1984) and idem, *American Diplomacy in the Twentieth Century* (New York: Oxford Univ. Press, 1984).

2. For the attitudes and opinions of Dr. Kissinger, see Henry Kissinger, *Memoirs*, Vol. II, *Years of Upheaval* (Boston: Little, Brown, 1982), 9–43, 302–73.

3. In fact, most people in South Vietnam called the day the Geneva Accords were signed "National Shame Day." For details, see Robert F. Randle, *Geneva, 1954: The Settlement of the Indochinese War* (New York: Harper & Row, 1969), 569–72.

4. South Vietnam Foreign Minister Tran Van Do, "Four Points Speech," June 22, 1965.

5. Statements by General Vu Ban to French newspaper interviewers, 1983; remarks by Le Duan, Secretary General of the Vietnamese Communist Party (VCP), "Victory Day Speech," 1975.

6. *Public Papers of the Presidents of the United States: John F. Kennedy, Containing the Public Messages, Speeches and Statements of the President*, Vol. I, January 20–December 31, 1961 (Washington, DC: Government Printing Office, 1962), 1. The entire

inaugural speech can be found on pp. 1–3. Also see Arthur M. Schlesinger, Jr., *A Thousand Days: John F. Kennedy in the White House* (Cambridge, MA: Houghton Mifflin, 1965), 1–5. For details of Kennedy's attitudes regarding America's role concerning South Vietnam, see *The Pentagon Papers: The Defense Department History of United States Decision Making in Vietnam*, Vol. II U.S. Senator Gravel Ed. (Boston: Beacon Press, 1971), 735, 738–39, 751–66, 827; Johnathan R. Adelman, ed., *Superpowers and Revolution* (New York: Praeger, 1986), 126.

7. Allan E. Goodman, "Discussion of the Vietnam War," *Conference on the Vietnam War*, sponsored by the Woodrow Wilson Center, January 8, 1983.

8. For strong and convincing arguments supporting this, see Douglas Pike, *Vietcong: The Organization and Techniques of the National Liberation Front of South Vietnam* (Cambridge, MA: MIT Press, 1966); Douglas Pike, *PAVN: People's Army of North Vietnam* (Novato, CA: Presidio Press, 1986).

9. This quote as well as the events surrounding the overthrow of Diem can be found in Neil Sheehan et al., *The Pentagon Papers (New York Times)* (New York: Bantam, 1971), 158–232.

10. For a more complete discussion of these issues of American misunderstanding, see Bui Diem and David Chanoff, *In the Jaws of History* (Boston: Houghton Mifflin, 1987).

Selected Bibliography

The following is a composite of the major works and sources used by the various authors in their individual chapters.

PRIMARY SOURCES

Some of the collections from which the authors took primary materials included: presidential papers, U.S. Army records and after-action-reports, National Security Council meeting minutes, Westmoreland papers, George Ball papers, papers of Lady Bird Johnson, various diaries, oral history interviews, etc., from the *Lyndon Baines Johnson Presidential Library*, Austin, Texas; CBS litigation files and various other files from the *Federal Records Center*, Suitland, Maryland; various files and documents from the *Marine Corps Historical Center*, Washington, DC; various files and documents from the *U.S. Naval Institute Library*, Annapolis, MD; private papers of General William Westmoreland in the personal possession of Dr. George Herring; various files and documents from the *U.S. Army Military History Institute*, Carlisle Barracks, PA; various files and documents from the main depository of the *National Archives*, Washington, DC; official papers, end-of-tour reports, and various other papers and documents from the *U.S. Air Force Historical Research Agency*, Maxwell AFB, AL; various files and documents from the *Indochina Archives*, University of California, Berkeley; and microfilm from *University Publications of America* on the CIA, Indochina, Southeast Asia, and the U.S. military's operations in the Indochina War, all from 1946 to 1976.

GOVERNMENT PUBLICATIONS

The authors also used primary sources published or unpublished by various agencies of the U.S. federal government and other governments including: *Congressional Record*, congressional sessions 1946–1991; *Foreign Relation Papers* of the U.S. State Department, 1941–1962; hearings and official publications of the Senate Armed Services and Foreign Relations Committee and other various Senate and House committees, special committees, and subcommittees dealing with the war in Southeast Asia; official U.S. Air Force, U.S.

Army, U.S. Navy, and U.S. Marine Corps service, operations, personnel, and indoctrination manuals; official U.S. Air Force, U.S. Army, U.S. Navy, and U.S. Marine Corps annual, unit, and official histories; published presidential, senatorial, and congressional news conferences; published public papers of presidents Dwight David Eisenhower, John Fitzgerald Kennedy, Lyndon Baines Johnson, and Richard Milhous Nixon; annual *Defense Department Reports*; end-of-year reports from the Military Airlift Command, Tactical Air Command, and Strategic Air Command; and published reports and document collections from the People's Republic of Vietnam, People's Republic of China, and the former Union of Soviet Socialist Republics.

SECONDARY SOURCES: JOURNALS, MAGAZINES, AND NEWSPAPERS

The authors used the following journals, magazines, and newspapers in the writing of their articles.

Journals and Magazines

ABA Journal, *Air Force Journal of Logistics*, *Air Force Magazine*, *Air Force Times*, *Air Power History*, *Air University Review* (today *Air Power Journal*), *Airman*, *Aviation Week and Space Technology*, *China Quarterly*, *Commentary*, *Current Scene*, *Diplomatic History*, *Economist*, *Facts on File*, *History Today*, *Indochina Chronicle*, *International Security*, *Jane's Defence Weekly*, *Journal of Asian Studies*, *Journal of Military History*, *National Review*, *Newsweek*, *Orbis*, *Pacific Affairs*, *Parameters*, *Peking Review*, *Political Science Quarterly*, *Review of Politics*, *Studies on the Soviet Union*, *Time*, *U.S. News & World Report*, *Vietnam Generation*, and *World Press Review*.

Newspapers

Atlanta Constitution and Journal, *Boston Globe*, *Christian Science Monitor*, *Herald-Tribune* (New York), *International Herald-Tribune* (New York), *Jackson Clarion-Ledger* (Mississippi), *Lexington Herald-Leader* (Kentucky), *New York Times*, *New York Times Magazine*, *Starkville Daily News* (Mississippi), *USA Today*, *Wall Street Journal*, *Washington Post*, and *Washington Post Magazine*.

BOOKS

The following are selected works from the authors' footnotes. They are works directly or indirectly dealing with Southeast Asia and/or U.S. involvement. For other sources, see the Notes following each chapter.

Ball, George W. *The Past Has Another Pattern*. New York: Norton, 1982.

Ballard, Jack S. *The United States Air Force in Southeast Asia: Development and Employment of Fixed-Wing Gunships, 1962–1972*. Washington, DC: Office of Air Force History, 1982.

Baskin, Lawrence, and William A. Strauss. *Chance and Circumstance: The Draft, the War, and the Vietnam Generation*. New York: Vintage, 1978.

Bell, Dana. *Air War Over Vietnam*. Harrisburg, PA: Arms and Armour Press, 1982.

Berger, Carl, ed. *The United States Air Force in Southeast Asia, 1961–1973: An Illustrated Account*. Washington, DC: Office of Air Force History, 1984.

Berman, Larry. *Planning A Tragedy: The Americanization of the War in Vietnam*. New York: Norton, 1982.

———. *Lyndon Johnson's War: The Road to Stalemate in Vietnam*. New York: Norton, 1989.

Boettcher, Thomas D. *Vietnam: The Valor and the Sorrow*. Boston: Little, Brown, 1985.

Bouscaren, Anthony T., ed. *All Quiet on the Eastern Front: The Death of South Vietnam*. Old Greenwich, CT: Devin Press, 1977.

Braestrup, Peter, ed. *Vietnam as History: Ten Years After the Paris Peace Accords*. Washington, DC: Univ. Press of America, 1984.

Brandon, Henry. *Anatomy of Error: The Inside Story of the Asian War on the Potomac, 1954–1969*. Boston: Gambit Press, 1969.

Brown, Dale E., ed. *Assessing the Vietnam War*. McLean, VA: Pergamon-Brassey, 1987.

Buttinger, Joseph. *A Dragon Embattled: A History of Colonial and Post-Colonial Vietnam*, 2 vols. New York: Praeger, 1967.

Cable, Larry. *Conflict of Myths: The Development of American Counterinsurgency Doctrine and the Vietnam War*. New York: New York Univ. Press, 1986.

———. *Unholy Grail: The United States and the Wars in Vietnam, 1965–1968*. London: Routledge & Kegan Paul, 1991.

Cady, John F. *The Roots of French Imperialism in Asia*. Ithaca, NY: Cornell Univ. Press, 1954.

Caputo, Philip. *A Rumor of War*. New York: Ballantine, 1977.

Chanoff, David, and Van Toai Doan. *Portrait of the Enemy*. New York: Random House, 1986.

———. *The Vietnamese Gulag: A Revolution Betrayed*. New York: Simon & Schuster, 1986.

Charlton, Michael, and Anthony Moncrief. *Many Reasons Why: The American Involvement in Vietnam*, 2nd. ed. New York: Hill & Wang, 1989.

Chen, King C. *China and Vietnam, 1938–1954*. Princeton, NJ: Princeton Univ. Press, 1969.

Chinh, Truong. *The Resistance Will Win in Primer for Revolt*. New York: Praeger, 1963.

Cincinnatus (Cecil B. Currey). *Self-Destruction: The Destruction and Decay of the United States Army During the Vietnam War*. New York: Norton, 1978.

Clodfelter, Mark. *The Limits of Air Power: The American Bombing of North Vietnam*. New York: Free Press, 1989.

Currey, Cecil. *Edward Lansdale: The Unquiet American*. Boston: Houghton Mifflin, 1988.

DeBenedetti, Charles. *An American Ordeal: The Antiwar Movement of the Vietnam Era*. Syracuse, NY: Syracuse Univ. Press, 1990.

Diem, Bui, and David Chanoff. *In the Jaws of History*. Boston: Houghton Mifflin, 1987.

Dommen, Arthur J. *Laos: Keystone of Indochina*. Boulder, CO: Westview, 1985.

Doyle, Edward, Samuel Lipsman, and Terrence Maitland. *A Collision of Cultures* volume in Robert Manning, ed., *The Vietnam Experience*. Boston: Boston Publishing Co., 1984.

———. *The North* volume in Robert Manning, ed., *The Vietnam Experience*. Boston: Boston Publishing Co., 1986.

Duiker, William J. *The Rise of Nationalism in Vietnam*. Ithaca, NY: Cornell Univ. Press, 1976.

———. *The Communist Road to Power in Vietnam*. Boulder, CO: Westview, 1981.

———. *China and Vietnam: The Roots of Conflict*. Berkeley, CA: Institute of East Asian Studies, Univ. of California, 1986.

———. *Vietnam: Nation in Revolution*. Boulder, CO: Westview, 1983.

Dung, Van Tien. *Our Great Spring Victory*. New York: Monthly Review Press, 1977.

Errington, Elizabeth Jane, and B.J.C. McKercher, eds. *The Vietnam War as History*. New York: Praeger, 1990.

Etcheson, Craig. *The Rise and Demise of Democratic Kampuchea*. Boulder, CO: Westview, 1984.

Falk, Richard. *The Vietnam War and International War*, 4 vols. Princeton, NJ: Princeton Univ. Press, 1968–1976.

Fall, Bernard B., ed. *Ho Chi Minh on Revolution: Selected Writings, 1920–1966*. New York: Praeger, 1968.

FitzGerald, Frances. *Fire in the Lake*. New York: Vintage, 1972.

Flacks, Richard. *Making History: The American Left and the American Mind*. New York: Beacon, 1988.

Gallucci, Robert L. *Neither Peace Nor Honor: The Politics of American Military Policy in Vietnam*. Baltimore: Penguin, 1975.

Gates, John. *Schoolbooks and Krags*. Westport, CT: Greenwood, 1973.

Giap, Vo Nguyen. *People's War, People's Army*. Hanoi: Foreign Language Publication House, 1962.

———. *People's War, People's Army: The Viet Cong Insurrection Manual for Underdeveloped Countries*. New York: Praeger, 1962.

———. "*Big Victory, Great Task*." New York: Praeger, 1968.

———. *People's War Against the United States Aeronaval War*. Hanoi: Foreign Language Publication House, 1975.

Giap, Vo Nguyen, and Van Tien Dung. *How We Won the War*. Ypsilanti, MI: Reconstruction Publications, 1976.

Gibson, James William. *The Perfect War: Technowar in Vietnam*. Boston: Atlantic Monthly Press, 1986.

Gilbert, Marc Jason, ed. *The Vietnam War: Teaching Approaches and Resources*. Westport, CT: Greenwood, 1991.

Gitlin, Todd. *The Sixties: Years of Hope, Days of Rage*. New York: Bantam, 1987.

Graff, Henry. *The Tuesday Cabinet*. Englewood Cliffs, NJ: Prentice-Hall, 1970.

Grant, Zalin. *Over the Beach: The Air War in Vietnam*. New York: Norton, 1986.

Grinter, Lawrence E. *Realities of Revolutionary Violence in Southeast Asia: Challenges and Responses*. Maxwell AFB, AL: Cadre Paper Series, Air Univ. Press, 1990.

Grinter, Lawrence E. and Peter M. Dunn, eds. *The American War in Vietnam: Lessons, Legacies, and Implications for Future Conflicts*. Westport, CT: Greenwood Press, 1987.

Hagan, Kenneth J., and William R. Roberts, eds. *Against All Enemies*. Westport, CT: Greenwood Press, 1986.

Haines, David, ed. *Refugees as Immigrants: Cambodians, Laotians and Vietnamese in America*. Totowa, NJ: Rowman and Littlefield, 1989.

Halberstam, David. *The Best and the Brightest*. New York: Random House, 1972.

Hammer, Ellen. *The Struggle for Indochina, 1940–1955*. Stanford, CA: Stanford Univ. Press, 1966.

Hanh, Thich Nhat, and Vo-Dinh. *The Cry of Vietnam*. Santa Barbara, CA: Unicorn, 1968.

Hannah, Norman B. *The Key to Failure: Laos, and the Vietnam War*. New York: Madison, 1987.

Herring, George. *America's Longest War: The United States and Vietnam, 1950–1975*. New York: Wiley, 1979.

———. *America's Longest War: The United States and Vietnam, 1950–1975*, rev. ed. New York: Knopf, 1986.

Hewes, James E., Jr. *From Root to McNamara: Army Organization and Administration, 1900–1963*. Washington, DC: Center for Military History, 1975.

Hilsman, Roger. *To Move a Nation*. New York: Delta, 1964.

Hodgkin, Thomas. *Vietnam: The Revolutionary Path*. New York: St. Martin's, 1981.

Holsti, Ole R., and James N. Rosenau. *American Leadership in World Affairs: Vietnam and the Breakdown of Consensus*. Winchester, MA: Unwin Hyman, 1984.

Honey, P. J. *Communism in North Vietnam: Its Role in the Sino-Soviet Dispute*. Cambridge, MA: MIT Press, 1963.

Horne, A. D., ed. *The Wounded Generation: America After Vietnam*. Englewood Cliffs, NJ: Prentice-Hall, 1981.

Hosmer, Stephen T., Konrad Kellen, and Brian M. Jenkins. *The Fall of South Vietnam: Statements by Vietnamese Military and Civilian Leaders*. New York: Crane, Russak, and Co., 1980.

Jeffords, Susan. *The Remasculinization of America: Gender and the War*. Bloomington: Indiana Univ. Press, 1989.

Johnson, Lady Bird. *A White House Diary*. New York: Holt, Rinehart, and Winston, 1970.

Johnson, Lyndon B. *The Vantage Point: Perspectives of the Presidency, 1963–1969*. New York: Holt, Rinehart, and Winston, 1971.

Kahin, George McTurnan, and John W. Lewis. *The United States in Vietnam*. New York: Dial, 1967; rev. ed., Dell, 1969.

Karnow, Stanley. *Vietnam: A History*. New York: Viking, 1983.

Kearns, Doris. *Lyndon Johnson and the American Dream*. New York: Harper & Row, 1976.

Khanh, Huynh Kim. *Vietnamese Communism, 1925–1945*. Ithaca, NY: Cornell Univ. Press, 1982.

Kiernan, Ben. *How Pol Pot Came to Power: The Rise and Demise of Democratic Kampuchea*. London: Verso, 1985.

Kimball, Jeffrey. *To Reason Why: The Debate About the Causes of the U.S. Involvement in the Vietnam War*. New York: McGraw-Hill, 1990.

Kinnard, Douglas. *The War of Managers*. Hanover, NH: Univ. Press of New England, 1977.

Kissinger, Henry. *The White House Years*. Boston: Little, Brown, 1979.

———. *Years of Upheaval*. Boston: Little, Brown, 1982.

Komer, Robert W. *Bureaucracy at War: U.S. Performance in the Vietnam Conflict*. Boulder, CO: Westview, 1986.

Krepinevich, Andrew F., Jr. *The Army and Vietnam*. Baltimore: Johns Hopkins Univ. Press, 1986.

Lacouture, Jean. *Ho Chi Minh: A Political Biography*, trans. by Peter Wiles. New York: Vintage, 1968.

Lake, Anthony. *The Legacy of Vietnam: The War, American Society and the Future of American Foreign Policy*. New York: Council on Foreign Relations, 1976.

Lam, Troung Buu. *Patterns of Vietnamese Response to Foreign Intervention, 1858–1900*. New Haven, CT: Southeast Asia Studies, Yale Univ. Press, 1967.

Lattenberg, Paul M. *The Vietnam Trauma in American Foreign Policy, 1945–1975*. Boston: Beacon, 1980.

LeGro, William E. *Vietnam from Cease-Fire to Capitulation*. Washington, DC: Government Printing Office, 1985.

Levinson, Jeffrey L. *Alpha Strike Vietnam: The Navy's Air War 1964 to 1973*. Novato, CA: Presidio Press, 1989.

Lewy, Guenter. *America in Vietnam*. New York: Oxford Univ. Press, 1978.

Long, Ngo Vinh. *Before the Revolution: The Vietnamese Peasants under the French*. Cambridge, MA: Harvard Univ. Press, 1973.

Luttwak, Edward N. *The Pentagon and the Art of War*. New York: Touchstone, 1985.

McAlister, John T., Jr. *Vietnam: The Origins of Revolution*. New York: Knopf, 1969.

McCarthy, James R., and George B. Allison. *Linebacker II: A View from the Rock*. Washington, DC: Office of Air Force History, 1979.

McCloud, Bill. *"What Should We Tell Our Children About Vietnam?"* Norman: Univ. of Oklahoma Press, 1989.

Marr, David G., and A. C. Milner, eds. *Vietnamese Anti-Colonialism on Trial*. Berkeley: Univ. of California Press, 1971.

———. *Vietnamese Nationalism on Trial*. Berkeley: Univ. of California Press, 1981.

———. *Southeast Asia in the Ninth to Fourteen Centuries*. Canberra, Australia: Research School of Pacific Studies, The Australian National Univ., 1986.

Maurer, Harry. *Strange Ground: An Oral History of Americans in Vietnam, 1945–1975*. New York: Avon, 1989.

May, Someth. *Cambodian Witness: The Autobiography of Someth May*. London: Faber and Faber, 1986.

Mersky, Peter B., and Norman Polmar. *The Naval Air War in Vietnam*. Annapolis, MD: Nautical and Aviation Publications Company of America, 1981.

Mesko, James. *VNAF: South Vietnamese Air Force, 1945–1975*. Carrollton, TX: Squadron & Signal Publications, 1987.

Morrocco, John. *Thunder from Above* volume in Robert Manning, ed., *The Vietnam Experience*. Boston: Boston Publishing Co., 1984.

———. *Rain of Fire: Air War, 1969–1973* volume in Robert Manning, ed., *The Vietnam Experience*. Boston: Boston Publishing Co., 1986.

Moss, George Donaldson. *Vietnam: An American Ordeal*. Englewood Cliffs, NJ: Prentice-Hall, 1990.

Mrozek, Donald J. *Air Power and the Ground War in Vietnam: Ideas and Actions*. Maxwell AFB, AL: Air University Press, 1988.

Nixon, Richard M. *R.N.: The Memoirs of Richard M. Nixon*, vol. 1. New York: Grosset & Dunlap, 1978. Vol. 2, New York: Warner, 1978.

Oberdorfer, Donald. *Tet!* Garden City, NY: Doubleday, 1971.

O'Brien, Tim. *Going After Cacciato*. New York: Delacorte, 1978.

O'Conner, Valerie. *The Indochina Refugee Dilemma*. Baton Rouge: Louisiana State Univ. Press, 1990.

Olson, James, and Randy Roberts. *Where the Domino Fell: America and Vietnam, 1945–1990*. New York: St. Martin's, 1990.

Osborne, Milton E. *The French Presence in Cochin China and Cambodia: Rule and Response, 1859–1905*. Ithaca, NY: Cornell Univ. Press, 1969.

Palmer, Bruce. *The 25-Year War: America's Military Role in Vietnam*. Lexington: Univ. of Kentucky Press, 1984.

Palmer, Dave Richard. *Summons of the Trumpet: U.S.–Vietnam in Perspective*. San Rafael, CA: Presidio Press, 1978.

Papp, Daniel. *Vietnam: The View from Moscow, Peking and Washington*. Jefferson, NC: McFarland Press, 1981.

Pentagon Papers: The Defense Department History of United States Decision Making in Vietnam, U.S. Senator Gravel ed. Boston: Beacon, 1971.

Perry, Mark. *Four Stars*. Boston: Houghton Mifflin, 1989.

Pfeffer, Richard N., ed. *No More Vietnams? The War and the Future of American Foreign Policy*. New York: Adlai Stevenson Institute of International Affairs, 1968.

Pike, Douglas. *Vietcong: The Organization and Techniques of the National Liberation Front of South Vietnam*. Cambridge, MA: MIT Press, 1966.

———. *PAVN: People's Army of North Vietnam*. Novato, CA: Presidio Press, 1986.

———. *Vietnam and the USSR: Anatomy of an Alliance*. Boulder, CO: Westview, 1987.

Pisor, Robert. *The End of the Line: The Siege of Khe Sanh*. New York: Norton, 1982.

Pluvier, J. M. *Southeast Asia from Colonialism to Independence*. New York: Oxford Univ. Press, 1974.

Pratt, John Clark. *Laotian Fragments: The Chief Raven's Story*. New York: Viking, 1974.

Raffel, Burton. *From the Vietnamese: Ten Centuries of Vietnamese Poetry*. New York: October House, 1968.

Randle, Robert F. *Geneva, 1954: The Settlement of the Indochinese War*. New York: Harper & Row, 1969.

Reid, Anthony. *Southeast Asia in the Age of Commerce, Vol. 1, The Lands Below the Winds*. New Haven, CT: Yale Univ. Press, 1988.

Robbins, Christopher. *Air America: The Story of the C.I.A.'s Secret Airlines*. New York: Putnam, 1979.

———. *The Ravens*. New York: Crown, 1987.

Rosenberger, Lief. *The Soviet Union and Vietnam*. Boulder, CO: Westview, 1986.

Salisbury, Harrison E., ed. *Vietnam Reconsidered: Lessons from a War*. New York: Harper & Row, 1984.

SarDesai, Damodar R. *Vietnam: Struggle for National Identity*, 2nd ed. Boulder, CO: Westview, 1991.

Schalk, David L. *War and the Ivory Tower: Algeria and Vietnam*. New York: Oxford Univ. Press, 1991.

Schandler, Herbert Y. *The Unmaking of a President: Lyndon Johnson and Vietnam*. Princeton, NJ: Princeton Univ. Press, 1977.

Schlesinger, Arthur M., Jr. *A Thousand Days: John F. Kennedy in the White House*. Cambridge, MA: Houghton Mifflin, 1965.

———. *The Bitter Heritage: Vietnam and American Democracy, 1941–1966*. Greenwich, CT: Fawcett, 1967.

Schlight, John. *The War in South Vietnam: The Years of Offensive, 1965–1968*. Washington, DC: Office of Air Force History, 1988.

————, ed. *Second Indochina War Symposium: Papers and Commentary*. Washington, DC: Army Center for Military History, 1986.

Scott, James. *The Moral Economy of the Peasant: Rebellion and Subsistence in Southeast Asia*. New Haven, CT: Yale Univ. Press, 1976.

Shaplen, Robert. *The Lost Revolution: The United States in Vietnam, 1946–1966*. New York: Harper & Row, 1966.

Sharp, Ulysses Simpson Grant. *Strategy for Defeat: Vietnam in Retrospect*. Novato, CA: Presidio Press, 1986.

Sharp, Ulysses Simpson Grant, and General William C. Westmoreland. *Report on the War in Vietnam*. Washington, DC: Government Printing Office, 1969.

Shawcross, William. *Sideshow: Kissinger, Nixon and the Destruction of Cambodia*. New York: Simon & Schuster, 1979.

Sheehan, Neil, Hedrick Smith, E. W. Kenworthy, and Fox Butterworth. *The Pentagon Papers* (*New York Times* version). New York: Bantam, 1971.

Shulimson, Jack. *U.S. Marines in Vietnam: An Expanding War, 1966*. Washington, DC: History and Museum Division, U.S. Marine Corps, 1982.

Small, Melvin. *Johnson, Nixon and the Doves*. New Brunswick, NJ: Rutgers Univ. Press, 1988.

Smith, Ralph. *Vietnam and the West*. London: Heineman, 1971.

————. *An International History of the Vietnam War*, 4 vols. London: Macmillan, 1983–1990.

Smyser, W. R. *The Independent Vietnamese: Vietnamese Communism Between Russia and China, 1956–1969*. Athens: Ohio Univ. Center for International Studies, 1980.

Spector, Ronald H. *Advice and Support: The Early Years, 1941–1960*. Washington, DC: Government Printing Office, 1984.

Stanton, Shelby L. *The Rise and Fall of an American Army: U.S. Ground Forces in Vietnam, 1965–1973*. Novato, CA: Presidio Press, 1985.

Stevens, Robert Warren. *Vain Hopes, Grim Realities: The Economic Consequences of the Vietnam War*. New York: New Viewpoints, 1976.

Summers, Harry G., Jr. *On Strategy: The Vietnam War in Context*. Carlisle Barracks, PA: Army War College, 1981.

————. *On Strategy: A Critical Analysis of the Vietnam War*. Novato, CA: Presidio Press, 1982.

————. *On Strategy: A Critical Analysis of the Vietnam War*. New York: Dell, 1984.

Taylor, Keith W. *The Birth of Vietnam*. Berkeley, CA: Univ. of California Press, 1983.

Thayer, Thomas C. *War Without Fronts: The American Experience in Vietnam*. Boulder, CO: Westview, 1985.

Thompson, Sir Robert. *Revolutionary War in World Strategy, 1945–1969*. New York: Taplinger, 1970.

Thompson, W. Scott, and Donaldson D. Frizzell, eds. *The Lessons of Vietnam*. New York: Crane, Russak, and Co., 1977.

Tilford, Earl H., Jr. *Setup: What the Air Force Did in Vietnam and Why*. Maxwell AFB, AL: Air Univ. Press, 1991.

Tra, Tran Van. *War Experiences Recapitulation Committee of the High-Level Military Institute, Vietnam: The Anti–U.S. Resistance War for National Salvation, 1954–1975: Military Events*. Hanoi: People's Republic of Vietnam, Foreign Ministry, 1980.

———. *Vietnam: History of the Bulwark B2 Theatre*, vol. 5, *Concluding the 30-Years War*. Ho Chi Minh City: Van Nghe Publishing House, 1982.

Trooboff, Peter D., ed. *Law and Responsibility in Warfare: The Vietnam Experience*. Chapel Hill: Univ. of North Carolina Press, 1975.

Tuchman, Barbara. *The March of Folly*. New York: Knopf, 1984.

Turley, William S., ed. *Vietnamese Communism in Comparative Perspective*. Boulder, CO: Westview, 1980.

Turner, Kathleen J. *Lyndon Johnson's Dual War: Vietnam and the Press*. Chicago: Univ. of Chicago Press, 1985.

Veninga, James, and Harry A. Wilmer, eds. *Vietnam in Remission*. College Station: Texas A&M Univ. Press, 1985.

Vickery, Michael. *Cambodia: 1975–82*. Boston: South End, 1984.

———. *Kampuchea: Politics, Economics, and Society*. London: Frances Pinter, 1986.

Warden, John A., III. *The Air Campaign: Planning for Combat*. Washington, DC: National Defense Univ. Press, 1988.

Westmoreland, William. *A Soldier Reports*. New York: Doubleday, 1976.

Wheeler, John. *Touched with Fire: The Future of the Vietnam Generation*. New York: Avon, 1985.

Woodside, Alexander. *Vietnam and the Chinese Model*. Cambridge, MA: Harvard Univ. Press, 1971.

Zagoria, Donald S. *Vietnam Triangle*. New York: Pegasus, 1967.

Zasloff, Joseph J. *The Pathet Lao: Leadership and Organization*. Lexington, MA: D.C. Heath, 1973.

———. ed. *Postwar Indochina: Old Enemies, New Allies*. Washington, DC: Foreign Service Institute, U.S. Department of State, 1988.

Zasloff, Joseph Jr., and Paul Langer. *North Vietnam and the Pathet Lao*. Cambridge, MA: Harvard Univ. Press, 1970.

Zasloff, Joseph Jr., and McAlister Brown. *Apprentice Revolutionaries: The Communist Movement in Laos, 1930–1985*. Palo Alto, CA: Stanford Univ. Press, 1986.

Index

Abilene, Operation, 199
Abrams, Creighton, 30, 82
Adams, Jimmie V., 152
Adams, Leonard P., 136
Afghanistan, 60–61, 64
Agent Orange, 28
Air America, 136
Air Campaign, The: Planning for Combat (Warden), 149, 154
Alexander, Robert M., 153–54
Algeria, 56, 111
American Friends of Vietnam, 87
American Soldiers, The (film), 67
America's Longest War: The United States and Vietnam, 1950–1975 (Herring), 5, 19, 42
Amin, Hafizullah, 60
An, Chfong-hyo, 67
Anderson Platoon, The (film), 67
Apocalypse Now (film), 1
Arab-Israeli wars, Vietnam War compared to, 5
Army and Vietnam, The (Krepinevich), 232
Aronson, Bernard W., 65
ARVN (Army of the Republic of Vietnam), 25, 128, 134, 180, 195, 198, 219; casualty figures, 173, 217; Dak To and, 217; El Paso II/III and, 203–4; Khe Sanh and, 34; operational con-

cepts of, 193, 200; Saigon's fall and, 40; Vietnamization and, 37
ASEAN (Association of Southeast Asian Nations), 55, 115
Associated Press, 236, 237
Atlanta, Operation, 208
Attleboro, Operation, 175, 207
Aurora I/II, Operation, 206
Australia, 22; Vietnam War and, 55, 67

Ball, George, 82, 83, 85
Bao Dai, 19, 20, 22, 23
Bates, John, 237
Bat–21 (film), 65–66
Beers, Burton, 19
Ben Bella, Ahmed, 111
Benoune, Karima, 236
Bernstein, Carl, 39–40
Binh Gia, battle of, 170
Binh Xuyen, 24
Birmingham, Operation, 175, 202–3
Boomer, Walter E., 2
Borodin, Michael, 18
Bose, Subhas Chandra, 53
Boston Globe, 229
Bradley, Omar, 87, 232
Brezhnev, Leonid, 38, 39, 106, 112
Britain, 17, 54, 57, 58, 96, 164, 166; Indochina/Vietnam wars and, 20, 22, 67
Bru, 34, 42

Buchanan, John, 59
Buchwald, Art, 35
Buckskin, Operation, 197, 198
Buddhist faction, South Vietnamese, 26, 53
Bui Tinh, 55
Bundy, McGeorge, 35, 80, 85, 88
Bundy, William, 90
Bunker, Ellsworth, 213
Burdick, Eugene, 67
Burma, 9, 23, 53; Vietnam War and, 115
Burns, Ken, 68
Busby, Horace, 86
Bush, George, 8, 60, 65, 101–3, 147–48, 235, 236–37; on Vietnam War, 2, 6, 51, 64, 145, 234
Byrd, Harry, 137

Cable, Larry E., 6, 9–10, 30, 57, 147, 174, 175
Calley, William, 37
Cambodia, 52, 58; Indochina/Vietnam wars and, 22, 28, 35, 37–41, 54, 56, 67, 105, 106, 111, 123, 124, 128–35, 137–41, 150, 202, 203, 211–12, 214, 216, 217, 247; Khmer Rouge in, 40–41, 62, 64, 137–38, 141; *Mayaguez* incident, 41, 101; U.S. bombing of, 28, 123, 124, 128–35, 137–41; U.S./ South Vietnamese incursions, 37–39, 105, 128, 130–31
Canada, 55
Cao Dai, 24, 53
Caputo, Philip, 28, 67
Carpenter, Ted Galen, 234
Carver, George, 200–201
Catholic faction, South Vietnamese, 24
Cato Institute, 234
Ceylon, 23
Chamberlain, Neville, 230
Cheney, Dick, 147, 234
Chen I, 115
Chiang Kai-shek, 18
Chile, 67
China, People's Republic of (PRC), 25, 38, 39, 41, 63, 134, 162, 163; Cultural Revolution, 112–14; formation of, 20, 41, 54; Indochina/Vietnam wars and, 3, 9, 20, 22, 29, 54–56, 59, 86, 105–16, 146–47, 167, 194, 196; North Vietnam, aid to, 20, 29, 54, 55, 106–16, 146, 167, 194; People's Liberation Army (PLA), 109–12; Red Guards, 113
China, pre-Communist, 17, 18, 20, 52, 53
Ch'ing Dynasty, 17
Chou En-lai, 38, 111, 112
Churchill, Winston, 31, 80, 86, 230
CIA (Central Intelligence Agency), 30–31, 128, 146, 175, 194, 200–201, 209–10, 213, 216, 218, 244; Diem's overthrow and, 26; Laos and, 136
Civil War (U.S.), Vietnam War compared to, 88, 96, 173
Civil War, The (film), 68
Clausewitz, Carl von, 60, 149, 175, 193, 195, 209, 211, 238
Clifford, Clark, 35, 36
Clodfelter, Mark, 4, 166–67
Clyde, Paul, 19
CNN, 3, 60
Coca Beach, Operation, 198
Collins, "Lightning Joe," 87
Commanders, The (Woodward), 8
Commando Hunt, Operation, 28, 131; details of, 124, 126–29, 132–34
Conflict of Myths (Cable), 30
Constitution of the United States, 96, 98, 100–102
Cooper, John Sherman, 99
Cornell Law Quarterly, 99
Crimp, Operation, 196–97
Cronkite, Walter, 35
Crowell, Lorenzo M., 10, 16
Cuba, 80–81
Czechoslovakia, 112

Dabney, Bill, 33, 34
Dai Viet, 53
Dak To, battle of, 175, 216–17
Da Nang Air Base, 28, 180
Davidson, Philip, Jr., 178
Debre, Michel, 36
Depuy, William, 183

Desert Shield/Desert Storm, Operations. *See* Persian Gulf War
Dewey, Peter, 19
Diem, Bui, 6, 9, 10, 181
Diem, Ngo Dinh, 60; assassination of, 13, 16, 26; opposition to, 13, 16, 24, 26, 62–63; overthrow of, 26; rise to power, 24; U.S. aid to, 16, 22–24, 26, 62–63, 243; U.S. opposition to, 246
Dien Bien Phu, battle of, 25, 33, 242–43; details of, 21–22
Dog Soldiers, The (Hasford), 67
Dole, Robert, 103
Domier, Paul, 52–53
Dominican Republic, 56
"Doonesbury," 238
Dugan, Michael, 151
Dulles, John Foster, 20, 22–23, 243
Dung, Van Tien, 180
Duras, Marguerite, 67

Economist, 229
Egypt, 54
Eisenhower, Dwight D., 20, 62, 97, 230; Diem, formal commitment to, 23; on Indochina War, 21
Ellsberg, Daniel J., 38
El Paso II/III, Operation, 175, 203–5, 207
El Salvador, 54, 58, 62, 101
Embree, Howard (Dan), 229–30
Endara, Guillermo, 231
End of the Line, The: The Siege of Khe Sanh (Pisor), 33
Ethiopia, 6, 166

Far East, The (Clyde and Beers), 19
Federalist, The, 96
Ferry, Jules, 52–53
Fire in the Lake (FitzGerald), 15–16
FitzGerald, Frances, 15–16, 25, 30, 35, 36
Flaming Dart, Operation, 165
Ford, Gerald R., 40; *Mayaguez* incident and, 41; Saigon's fall and, 142
France, 6, 17–19, 95; Dien Bien Phu and, 21–22, 242–43; Indochina/Vietnam wars and, 9, 13, 15–16, 19–22,

36, 52–54, 62, 63, 67, 152, 194, 206, 242–43, 245
Fulbright, J. William, 27, 95, 97–101, 103
Full Metal Jacket (film), 1, 67

Gadsden, Operation, 213–14
Gandhi, Mohandas K., 53
Garver, John W., 9
Gates, John M., 6, 9–10, 30, 57, 174
Geneva Convention of 1954, 13, 16, 21–22, 242, 243
Geneva Convention of 1961–62, 107
Germany, 6, 20, 31, 62, 164, 166, 238, 242; Vietnam War and, 67
Giap, Vo Nguyen, 19, 181, 210; Dien Bien Phu and, 21; Khe Sanh and, 32, 33; strategy/tactics detailed, 162, 167–68, 179
Gilbert, Marc Jason, 13
Glaspie, April, 155
Global Reach—Global Power (Rice), 156
Glosson, Buster C., 148, 154
Goering, Hermann, 164
Going After Cacciato (O'Brien), 67
Goldberg, Arthur, 34
Goldwater, Barry, 26
Goodman, Allan E., 245
Goodman, Ellen, 229
Gorbachev, Mikhail, 55
Goure, Leon, 201–2, 205
Greenberg, Paul, 233, 238
Greene, Graham, 57, 67
Greene, Wallace, 83, 85
Grenada, U.S. invasion of, 41, 101
Gruning, Ernest, 27
Guderian, Heinz, 230

Hackworth, David, 153
Haiti, 64
Halberstam, David, 83, 235
Hamilton, Alexander, 96
Hannah, Norman, 178
Harvey, Paul, 238
Hasford, Gustav, 67
Haslip, Le Ly, 66
Head, William, 13
Heffron, Richard T., 67

Heiser, Joseph, 183
Helms, Richard, 175, 201
Herring, George C., 5–6, 8, 16, 19, 31, 34, 35, 42
Hickory, Operation, 207
Hilsman, Roger, 108
History and War (Ropp), 230
Hitler, Adolf, 6, 31, 63, 238
Hmong, 42
Hoagland, Paul, 19
Hoa Hao, 24, 53
Hoang Van Hoan, 106–7
Ho Chi Minh, 6, 16, 53, 54, 63, 146, 152, 156, 179; background of, 18; death of, 38; formation of Democratic Republic of Vietnam, 19, 20, 181; Geneva Convention of 1954 and, 22; NLF and, 24
Ho Chi Minh: A Political Biography (Lacouture), 16
Ho Chi Minh Trail, 35, 38, 150; U.S. bombing of, 28, 126–28, 130, 132–35, 165
Hollandia, Operation, 175, 203
Horner, Charles A., 148, 151, 152, 154, 155
Howze, Hamilton, 183
Hue, battle of, 32
Humphrey, Hubert, 36, 37

In Country (film), 67
India, 23, 53, 56, 63; Vietnam War and, 55
Indonesia, 23, 53, 54, 56, 58; Vietnam War and, 115
Iran, 101; -Iraq War, 152; Persian Gulf War and, 155
Iraq. *See* Persian Gulf War
Ireland, 56
Israel, 147–48, 156
Italy, 6, 166

Jackson Clarion-Ledger, 233–34, 237
Jackson State University antiwar protest, 39
Japan, 15, 17–19, 54, 166, 230; Vietnam War and, 55, 67, 114–16
Jay, John, 96

Jim Bowie, Operation, 198–99
John Paul Jones, Operation, 175, 206
Johnson, Hansford T., 8
Johnson, Harold K., 82–83, 87, 193
Johnson, Lady Bird, 87, 90
Johnson, Lyndon B., 2, 5, 8, 27–28, 30–32, 60, 62, 174, 176, 182–83, 191, 197, 234; air power, use of, 17, 28, 36, 82, 83, 88, 99, 124, 129, 135, 146, 146–49, 152, 169, 175, 196, 231; antiwar movement and, 36–37, 86–88, 175; failure of, analyzed, 79–90; invasion of North Vietnam considered by, 9, 26, 105; JCS and, 81–82, 84, 88, 211; Khe Sanh and, 33, 79; 1964 presidential election and, 99; reelection, decision not to run for, 17, 36; Tet Offensive and, 35–36, 88, 219; Tonkin Gulf incident/Resolution and, 27, 38, 97–100, 236–37; on Vietnam War, 26–27, 79, 86, 87, 146; war goals of his administration, 192–93, 200, 208–9, 212–15, 217–19
Joint Chiefs of Staff (JCS), 2, 30, 61, 146, 174, 210–13, 229; Ad Hoc Study Group recommendations, 193–96; Johnson and, 81–82, 84, 88, 211; lessons from Vietnam, 151–52, 154, 231; Nichols-Goldwater Act and, 231; Nixon and, 136
Junction City I/II, Operation, 175, 209, 211, 214–15
Just Cause, Operation. *See* Panama, U.S. invasion of

Kahala, Operation, 202
Karnow, Stanley, 15–16, 19, 24
Katzenbach, Nicholas, 87, 88, 208–9
Keeva, Steven, 61, 62
Kelso, Frank B. II, 2
Kennedy, Edward "Ted," 87
Kennedy, John F., 5, 25–26, 62, 80, 108, 235, 243, 246; air power, use of, 135; assassination of, 16, 26
Kennedy, Paul, 63–64
Kennedy, Robert, 35, 36, 87
Kent State University antiwar protest, 39

Kenya, 53
Khe Sanh, battle of, 17, 31, 79, 127, 173; details of, 32–34
Khmer Rouge, 40–41, 62, 64, 137–38, 141
Khrushchev, Nikita, 81, 106, 107, 112, 113
Kinnard, Douglas, 184, 185
Kinnard, Harry, 183, 198
Kissinger, Henry, 112; Cambodia and, 130; Paris peace talks and, 38, 40, 63, 134–36; on Vietnam War, 242
Knight, Hal, 130
Komer, Robert, 185, 199, 209
Korean War, 20, 131, 238, 243; Vietnam War compared to, 4, 5, 9, 35, 57, 83, 85, 86, 89, 105, 108, 110, 134, 146, 148, 149, 163, 170, 214, 231
Kosygin, Aleksei, 106
Krepinevich, Andrew F., Jr., 184, 232
Krulak, Victor "Brute," 82
Kubrick, Stanley, 67
Kuwait. See Persian Gulf War
Ky, Nguyen Cao, 181; rise to power, 29; Thieu rivalry, 213

Lacouture, Jean, 16
Laniel, Joseph, 9, 21, 22
Lansdale, Edward, 57
Lao Dong (Communist Party of the North), 23, 24
Laos, 42, 58; Geneva Convention of 1961–62 and, 107; Indochina/Vietnam wars and, 22, 28, 33, 41, 54, 56, 105–8, 113, 123, 124, 126–29, 131–37, 139, 150, 210, 216, 217, 247; Pathet Lao in, 41, 107, 135–36; U.S. bombing of, 28, 123, 124, 126–28, 131–37, 139, 196
Lavalle, John D., 131
Layne, Christopher, 234
League for the Independence of Vietnam. See Vietminh
Lebanon, 101
Lederer, William J., 67
Le Duan, 181
Le Duc Tho, 38, 40, 135–36
Libya, 60

Limits of Air Power, The: The American Bombing of North Vietnam (Clodfelter), 4, 166–67
Lincoln, Abraham, 79–80, 88
Linebacker I/II, Operation, 4, 28, 29, 39, 40, 58–60, 114, 123, 124, 134, 135, 139, 146, 148–51, 153–55, 163, 170
Lippmann, Walter, 87
Live for Life (film), 67
Lodge, Henry Cabot, 26, 83, 199, 205
Lo Jui-ching, 112
Lomperis, Timothy, 178
Lon Nol, 38, 64, 137
Luttwak, Edward, 184–85

MacArthur, Douglas, 83, 84, 87, 89, 98, 230, 233, 243
McArthur, Operation, 217
McCarthy, Eugene, 35
McCarthy, James R., 139–40
McCloud, Bill, 182
McCoy, Alfred G., 136
McGovern, George, 39
McNamara, Robert, 30, 141, 199, 213; failure of, analyzed, 80, 83–84; as opponent of the war, 83–84, 87–88, 175; as supporter of the war, 9, 26, 80–83, 86, 165, 195–96, 208–9
McNaughton, John, 200, 212
"MacNeil-Lehrer News Hour," 234, 236
McPeak, Merrill A., 145, 156
McPherson, Harry, 88, 90
Maddox, U.S.S., 27, 165
Malaya, 56, 57
Malaysia, 54; Vietnam War and, 115
Mann, Lyle E., 131–32
Mao Tse-tung, 20, 105–7, 112–13, 162, 179
Masher, Operation, 198
Mastiff, Operation, 197–98
May, Ernest R., 230
Mayaguez incident, 41, 101
Maynard, Robert, 234
Mendes-France, Pierre, 22
Mexican War, Vietnam War compared to, 95
Mexico, 95
Mitchell, Billy, 164

Montagnard, 34, 42
Montgomery, Bernard, 230
Morse, Wayne, 27
Morton, Thurston, 97
Moyers, Bill, 86
Mus, Paul, 245
Muskie, Edmund, 201
Mussolini, Benito, 6
My Lai massacre, 37, 61

Napoleon III, 17
National Endowment for the Humanities,
   Vietnam War symposium of, 66
National Liberation Front (NLF), 17, 25,
   30, 111, 147, 165, 181, 202, 211,
   218, 219; Ho Chi Minh and, 24; inde-
   pendence of, 9; official recognition of,
   24, 242; Tet Offensive and, 9, 32, 34–
   35; war goals, 192
National Public Radio, 65
National Security Council (NSC), 27,
   199
NATO (North Atlantic Treaty Organiza-
   tion), 5, 22, 23
Netherlands, 54
Neustadt, Richard E., 230
Nevarre, Henri, 21
'' 'Never Again' the Most Important
   Words to Remember in Middle East''
   (Greenberg), 238
New Caledonia, 53
Newsday, 2
New York Times, 37–38, 235
New Zealand, 22
Nguyen Du, 66
Nguyen Dynasty, 17–19, 53
Nguyen Huu Tho, 25
Nguyen Khac Vien, 55
Nhan Dan, 55
Nhu, Ngo Dinh, 24, 26
Nichols-Goldwater Act, 231
Nixon, Richard M., 2, 60, 98, 99, 101,
   147; air power, use of, 37, 39, 40,
   124, 129–41, 146, 148–49, 155; anti-
   war movement and, 39; Cambodia and,
   37–39, 129–35, 137–41; Haiphong
   harbor, U.S. mining of, 39; JCS and,

136; 1968 presidential election and,
   36, 37; 1972 presidential election and,
   39; Paris peace talks and, 38–40, 63,
   137; Vietnamization policy, 37, 38,
   124, 126, 128–31, 134, 146; Watergate, 39–40, 135, 139
Noriega, Manuel Antonio, 231
North Korea, 55, 242. See also Korean
   War
North Vietnam, 6, 177, 178, 181, 185,
   200, 209, 235, 245; air defenses detailed, 161–71; Chinese aid to, 20, 29,
   54, 55, 106–16, 146, 167, 194; formation of Democratic Republic of Vietnam, 19, 20, 54, 181, 242; Geneva
   Convention of 1954 and, 22, 242; Haiphong harbor, U.S. mining of, 39;
   Paris peace talks/Accords and, 13, 17,
   38–40, 58–59, 123, 134–37, 171; possible U.S. invasion of, 9, 17, 26, 105,
   109, 111; Soviet aid to, 3, 5, 20, 29,
   54, 146, 150, 162, 167; U.S. aid to,
   withdrawal of promised, 136–37; U.S.
   bombing of, 4–5, 17, 27–29, 36, 37,
   39, 40, 58–60, 82, 83, 88, 99, 108–
   12, 114, 123–24, 127–29, 131–34,
   136, 139, 145–57, 161–71, 174, 175,
   194–96, 212, 231, 246; U.S. POWs/
   MIAs, 42, 134, 137; war goals, 192,
   210–15, 218–19, 241, 242, 246–47.
   See also Vietnam; individual leaders,
   groups, battles/incidents
North Vietnamese Army (NVA), 6, 173,
   184, 209–12; Dak To and, 216–17;
   morale, 217; strategy/tactics detailed,
   215–18
Nunn, Sam, 8, 95, 101–3

Oakland Tribune, 234
O'Brien, Tim, 67
Ochs, Phil, 65
Odd Angry Shot, The (film), 67
Olds, Robin, 231–32
On Strategy: A Critical Analysis of the
   Vietnam War (Summers), 184
On Strategy: The Vietnam War in Context
   (Summers), 232

On War (Clausewitz), 149, 238
Orlando Sentinel, 236–37

Pakistan, 22
Palestine, 56, 62
Palmer, Dave, 105, 183, 184
Panama, U.S. invasion of (Operation Just
  Cause), 66; Vietnam War compared to,
  41, 101, 230–31, 233
Paris peace talks, 38–40, 58–59, 63, 171;
  Accords (1973), 13, 17, 40, 59, 123,
  134–37, 140, 153
Pathet Lao, 41, 107, 135–36
Patraeus, David, 59
Patti, Archimedes, 19
Patton, George S., 232, 233
PAVN (People's Army of North Viet-
  nam), 4, 5, 16, 38–39, 129, 133, 135,
  136, 175, 200, 201, 204, 206, 208–10,
  213, 214; Dak To and, 216–17; Hue
  and, 32; Khe Sanh and, 31–34, 127,
  173; logistics requirements, 194–95;
  morale, 217, 218; Pleiku and, 216;
  Saigon's fall and, 40, 141–42; Spring
  Offensive of 1972 and, 128, 131, 134;
  strategy/tactics detailed, 162, 166, 167,
  207, 211–12, 215, 217; Tet Offensive
  and, 31, 34, 35, 126, 128
PAVN: People's Army of North Vietnam
  (Pike), 16
PBS, 15
Peers, William R., 217
Pelz, Stephen, 177–78
Pentagon Papers, 37–38, 82
People's Army of North Vietnam. *See*
  PAVN
People's Liberation Army (PLA), Chi-
  nese, 109–12
Perry, Mark, 84
Persian Gulf War (Operations Desert
  Shield/Desert Storm), 31, 41, 51, 95;
  Vietnam War compared to, 2–9, 16,
  59–66, 101–3, 139, 145–57, 164, 229–
  30, 233–38
Peru, 62, 64–65
Pham Hung, 181
Pham Van Dong, 23, 181

Phan Boi Chau, 18
Philippines, 22, 54, 56–58, 62; Vietnam
  War and, 115
Phoenix program, 179–80
Pike, Douglas, 4–6, 16, 24–25, 30, 57
Pine Bluff Commercial, 233
Pisor, Robert, 33, 34
Platoon (film), 1, 67
Pleiku infiltration, 27–28, 216
Poland, 6, 109, 111, 113
Politics of Heroin in Southeast Asia, The
  (McCoy, Reed, and Adams), 136
Polk, James K., 79
Pol Pot, 41
Powell, Colin, 2–3, 30, 61, 151–52, 229,
  231, 233
Proud Deep Alpha, Operation, 124, 132
Proxmire, William, 130

Quiet American, The (Graham Greene),
  57, 67
Quindlen, Anna, 235
Quinhon infiltration, 27–28

Rambo (film), 1
Rambo: First Blood, Part II (film), 67
Rand Corporation study of VC morale,
  201–2
Rayburn, Sam, 80
Reagan, Ronald, 87
Red Guards, 113
Reed, Cathleen B., 136
Reese, Charley, 236–37
Renmin ribao (People's Daily), 108
Report on the War in Vietnam (Sharp and
  Westmoreland), 163
Resor, Stanley, 85
Rice, Donald B., 156
Ridgway, Matthew, 87
*Rise and Fall of an American Army, The:
  U.S. Ground Forces in Vietnam,
  1965–1973* (Stanton), 184
Rolling Thunder, Operation, 28–29, 59,
  99, 123, 124, 131–33, 146–57, 165,
  195, 231
Roosevelt, Franklin D., 79–80, 96, 97,
  230

Ropp, Theodore, 230
Rosen, Peter, 80, 89, 90
Rostow, Walt, 209
Roy, M. N., 53
Rumor of War, A (Caputo), 28, 67
Rumor of War, A (film), 67
Rupert, Raymond, 62
Rusk, Dean, 35, 83, 86, 90, 146
Russell, Richard B., 8, 95, 97–101, 103
Russia, pre-Soviet, 17
Rutan, Dick, 59

Saddam Hussein, 3, 6, 8, 63, 64, 145, 147–48, 150–53, 155–56, 237
Safer, Morley, 27–28, 30, 31
Safire, William, 63
Saigon, fall of, 17, 29, 40, 101, 141–42, 243, 244
Sainteny, Jean, 38
Salisbury, Harrison E., 15
Sante Fe, Operation, 175, 205–6
Saudi Arabia. *See* Persian Gulf War
Schanberg, Sydney, 2
Schlesinger, Arthur, 20–21, 23, 25, 29
Schulzinger, Robert, 241
Schwarzkopf, H. Norman, 6, 62, 151–52, 155, 156; on Vietnam War, 148
Seamans, Robert C., Jr., 124, 126
SEATO (Southeast Asia Treaty Organization), 22–23, 99, 107
Sea Wall, The (Duras), 67
Self-Portrait (film), 67
Service Academy Graduates Against the War, 229–30
Setup: What the Air Force Did in Vietnam and Why (Tilford), 7, 28–29
Sharp, U.S. Grant, 6, 29–30, 146, 163
Sherman, William Tecumseh, 233
Shining Path *(Sendero Luminoso)*, 62, 64–65
Sihanouk, Norodom, 38, 111, 130
Singapore, 31–32; Vietnam War and, 115
Sioux City, Operation, 175, 206–8
Sitton, Ray B., 130
Slay, Alton D., 133–34
Sociologie d'une Guerre (Mus), 245
Soldier Reports, A (Westmoreland), 29–30
Somalia, 101

Son Tay raid, 124, 128
South Africa, 56
South Korea, 61, 242; Vietnam War and, 55, 67. *See also* Korean War
South Vietnam, 6, 9, 107, 112, 137, 139, 148, 162, 171, 175, 177–86, 194–99, 202, 207, 209–13, 218, 219; casualty figures, 173–74; Geneva Convention of 1954 and, 22, 242, 243; leadership struggles, 23–24, 213, 246; misconceptions, U.S./South Vietnamese, 243–47; 1950s and 1960s U.S. aid to, 16, 20, 22–24, 26, 62–63, 243; Paris peace talks/Accords and, 40, 136; Saigon, fall of, 17, 29, 40, 101, 141–42, 243, 244; SEATO and, 22–23; U.S. bombing of, 123, 124, 127, 130, 131, 134, 136, 138, 165, 201, 204–6, 217, 233–34, 245; Vietnamization/withdrawal, 37, 38, 40, 57, 124, 126, 128–31, 134, 146, 184, 186, 244; war goals, 192–93, 241
Souvanna Phouma, 135
Soviet Union, 6–7, 18, 20, 23, 38, 39, 55, 60–61, 63, 64, 80–81, 107, 110–13, 126, 152–56; Indochina/Vietnam wars and, 3, 5, 9, 20, 22, 29, 39, 54, 56, 59, 63, 86, 106, 115–16, 146–47, 150, 162, 167; North Vietnam, aid to, 3, 5, 20, 29, 54, 146, 150, 162, 167. *See also* Vietnam; *individual leaders, groups, battles/incidents*
Spain, 17–18, 57, 95
Spanish-American War, 57; Vietnam War compared to, 95
Spector, Ronald, 183
Spring Offensive of 1972, 128, 131, 134, 136, 146, 148–50, 173
Sri Lanka, 53
Stalin, Joseph, 63, 113, 146
Stanton, Shelby, 184
Stennis, John, 84
Strategy for Defeat: Vietnam in Retrospect (Sharp), 29–30
Stubbe, Ray W., 34
Study on Military Professionalism (U.S. Army War College), 185
Summers, Harry, Jr., 105–6, 177, 178, 180–81, 183–85, 232

Summer Soldiers (film), 67
Sun Tzu, 60

Tale of Kieu (Nguyen Du), 66
Taylor, Maxwell, 31
Tell Me Lies (film), 67
Tet Offensive, 9, 13, 17, 31, 37, 62, 88, 126, 128, 129, 131, 136, 147, 150, 156, 175–76, 179–80, 191, 219, 234, 235; details of, 32–36
Thailand, 9, 141; Indochina/Vietnam wars and, 106, 115, 127, 132, 135, 137, 140
Thieu, Nguyen Van, 39, 40, 131; Ky rivalry, 213; rise to power, 29
Thinking in Time: The Uses of History for Decision Makers (Neustadt and May), 230
Thompson, Robert, 57, 178, 179
Thurmon, Maxwell R., 231
Ticonderoga, U.S.S., 27
Tilford, Earl H., Jr., 4, 6, 7, 28–29, 58, 59
Tonkin Gulf incident, 16, 27, 38, 97–98, 165, 236–37
Tonkin Gulf Resolution, 8, 16, 27, 97–100
Torricelli, Robert C., 65
Tranh Van Dinh, 67
Tran Xuan Bach, 55
Trotta, Liz, 235–36
Truman, Harry S., 20, 62, 80, 89
Truong Chinh, 23, 179
Turkey, 58
Turner Joy, C., U.S.S., 27, 165

Ugly American, The (Lederer and Burdick), 67
Umstead, Stanley M., Jr., 131
Ungar, Leonard, 200, 201
Unholy Grail: The United States and the Wars in Vietnam, 1965–1968 (Cable), 147
United Nations, 3, 22, 63, 102, 147, 163, 236
U.S. Agency for International Development (AID), 245
U.S. Air Force, 7, 8, 28, 29, 163–64, 166, 168, 182, 195; Air Force Academy, 231–32; Air University's Center for Aerospace Doctrine, Research, and Education (AUCADRE), 156; lessons from Vietnam, 58–60, 123, 124, 126, 139–42, 145–46, 148, 149, 151–57, 231–32; manpower constraints, 131–32. *See also individual operations*
U.S. Air Force Association, 124, 126, 163–64
U.S. Army, 28, 57, 105, 164, 182, 234; Khe Sanh and, 33, 34; lessons from Vietnam, 58, 59, 148, 151–52, 154, 174–75, 183–85, 207, 231, 232; My Lai and, 37; operational concepts of, 193–96, 200, 207, 208, 214; Special Forces (Green Berets), 33, 34; War College, 185; Westmoreland's strategy opposed by, 82–83. *See also individual operations*
U.S. Congress, 31, 41, 65, 81, 85, 86, 90, 135, 141, 175, 209, 230, 236, 237; Cambodia and, 130, 140; North Vietnam, withdrawal of aid promised to, 136–37; Senate's warmaking role analyzed, 95–103; Stennis committee hearings on the war, 84; Tet Offensive and, 35; Tonkin Gulf Resolution, 8, 16, 27, 97–100; War Powers Act, 9, 99–102; Watergate and, 39–40, 139
U.S. Department of Defense, 35–36, 58, 87–88, 129; lessons from Vietnam, 61–62, 149, 231, 235; *Pentagon Papers*, 37–38, 82. *See also* Joint Chiefs of Staff; *individual secretaries of defense and branches of the Armed Forces*
U.S. Department of Justice, 39–40
U.S. Department of State, 65, 87–88, 97, 108, 208–9
U.S. Marines, 28, 29, 85, 128, 174, 175, 182, 233, 237; Khe Sanh and, 32–34; lessons from Vietnam, 59, 148, 154, 183; *Mayaguez* incident and, 41; operational concepts of, 193; opposition to strategy of, 183; Westmoreland's strategy opposed by, 82, 83. *See also individual operations*
U.S. Navy, 28, 29, 124, 152, 164, 182,

231; lessons from Vietnam, 148, 154.
See also individual operations
U.S. News & World Report, 2
Utah, Operation, 198

Vance, Cyrus, 209, 212–13
Viet Cong (VC), 1, 4–6, 16, 17, 56,
  105, 129, 130, 134, 137, 146, 147,
  153, 165, 170, 173–75, 184, 196,
  198–200, 202–10, 213–15, 219; Dak
  To and, 216–17; development of, 24–
  25; Hue and, 32; Khe Sanh and, 31,
  34; logistics requirements, 194–95;
  morale, 201–2, 218; Pleiku infiltration
  and, 27–28; Quinhon infiltration and,
  27–28; Spring Offensive of 1972 and,
  128; strategy/tactics detailed, 179, 197,
  207, 208, 211–12, 216–18; Tet Offensive and, 31, 32, 34, 35, 126, 128,
  129, 150, 235; war goals, 192
Vietcong: The Organization and Tech-
  niques of the National Liberation Front
  of South Vietnam (Pike), 16
Vietminh (League for the Independence
  of Vietnam), 6, 16, 24, 60, 62; background of, 19; Chinese aid to, 20;
  Dien Bien Phu and, 21; Geneva Convention of 1954 and, 22
Vietnam, postwar, future of, 55; reunification of, 24, 41–42, 181–82, 241
Vietnam: A History (Karnow), 15–16
Vietnam Reconsidered: Lessons from a
  War (Salisbury), 15
Vietnam Veterans Leadership Program,
  61
Vu Hon, 216, 217
Vuono, Carl E., 2

Waco, Operation, 208
Waide, Jim, 233–34
Wallace, George, 37
Wall Street Journal, 235–36
Walsh, Paul, 30–31

Walt, Lewis W., 183
Warden, John, 149, 150, 154–55
War of 1812, Vietnam War compared to,
  95
War Powers Act, 9, 99–102
Washington Post, 39–40
Watergate, 39–40, 135, 139
Westmoreland, William, 26, 28–31, 36,
  195, 209–12; Ho Chi Minh trail and,
  35; Khe Sanh and, 33, 34; opposition
  to strategy of, 82–83, 88; on responsi-
  bility for American failure in Vietnam,
  182; support for strategy of, 183; Tet
  Offensive and, 35
What Should We Tell Our Children About
  Vietnam? (McCloud), 182
Wheeler, Earle, 82–84, 183, 193, 195,
  199, 212
Wheeler, John, 61
Wheeler, Operation, 215
When Heaven and Earth Changed Places
  (Haslip), 66
"Which Vietnam Will This Not Be?"
  (Ellen Goodman), 229
White Badge (film), 67
White Badge: A Novel of Korea (An), 67
White Tiger: A Tet Story (Tranh Van
  Dinh), 67
White Wing, Operation, 198
Wilson, Woodrow, 19
Winchester, Operation, 208
Woodward, Robert, 8, 39–40
World War I, 6, 54, 164; Vietnam War
  compared to, 95, 96, 210, 230, 236
World War II, 18–19, 54, 58, 131, 181,
  243; Vietnam War compared to, 4–6,
  31, 62–63, 95–97, 148, 149, 164, 166,
  170, 179, 230, 232, 238

Xuan Thuy, 38

Yorktown, Operation, 175, 206

Ziemke, Caroline F., 8–9

About the Editors and Contributors

LARRY E. CABLE is Associate Professor of History at the University of North Carolina at Wilmington. He served in, and is now an acknowledged academic expert on, Vietnam-era military intelligence and unconventional warfare. His recent books, *Conflict of Myths: The Development of American Counterinsurgency Doctrine and the Vietnam War* (1986) and *Unholy Grail: The United States and the Wars in Vietnam, 1965–1968* (1991) are major contributions to this field.

MARK CLODFELTER is an Air Force major and Professor of Airpower History at the School of Advanced Airpower Studies, Maxwell Air Force Base, Alabama. He served on the faculty of the Department of History at the Air Force Academy for over five years during the 1980s, culminating his career there as director of military history. He is the author of *The Limits of Air Power: The American Bombing of North Vietnam* (1989), and is currently writing a comprehensive history of American strategic bombing.

LORENZO M. CROWELL is Associate Professor of History at Mississippi State University. He was an officer in the Air Force from 1965 to 1988, retiring as a lieutenant colonel. He taught at the Air Force Academy from 1974–1976 and again from 1981–1983. He taught at the Air War College from 1983 to 1987 and was Chief of the Oral History Program in 1988. Among his publications are: "Military Professionalism in a Colonial Context: The Madras Army, 1832" (*Modern Asian Studies* 1990); "The Anatomy of 'Just Cause': The Forces Involved, the Adequacy of Intelligence, and Its Success as a Joint Operation," in *Operation Just Cause*, ed. B. W. Watson and P. G. Tsouras (1991).

BUI DIEM, former Ambassador of South Vietnam to the United States, is presently Associate Director of the Indochina Institute at George Mason University in Fairfax, Virginia, and also President of the National Congress of Vietnamese (NCVA) in America. He is the coauthor of *In the Jaws of History* (1987), recognized as one of the most important and illuminating books written about the U.S. experience in Vietnam. He is presently writing another book that analyzes negotiations between the United States and the Democratic Republic of Vietnam between 1965 and 1975.

JOHN W. GARVER is a specialist in Chinese foreign policy and Asian international relations and teaches international relations in the School of International Affairs of Georgia Institute of Technology. He has authored many articles and three books on Chinese foreign relations. The latter include: *China's Decision for Rapprochement with the United States, 1968–1971* (1982), *Chinese-Soviet Relations, 1937–1945: The Diplomacy of Chinese Nationalism* (1988), and *The Foreign Relations of the People's Republic of China* (1993). He is currently working on studies of the geopolitics of Sino-Indian relations and the dynamics of the U.S.–Nationalist alliance.

JOHN M. GATES is a Professor of History at The College of Wooster in Wooster, Ohio, where he teaches military, American, and Latin American history. Professor Gates is the author of *Schoolbooks and Krags: The United States Army in the Philippines, 1898–1902* (Greenwood, 1973), and one of his articles, "The Alleged Isolation of U.S. Army Officers in the Late 19th Century" (*Parameters*, 1980), received the first Harold L. Peterson Award for work in American military history.

MARC JASON GILBERT is Professor of History at North Georgia College. A specialist in South and Southeast Asian history who received his doctorate from UCLA in 1978, Professor Gilbert has participated in many regional and national conferences on the study and teaching of the Vietnam War, including a symposium at the Air Force Academy and an institute sponsored by the National Endowment for the Humanities. He is the editor and chief contributing author of *The Vietnam War: Teaching Approaches and Resources* (Greenwood, 1991).

LAWRENCE E. GRINTER is Professor of International Security Affairs at the Air War College. Dr. Grinter is the coeditor of four books and author of thirty-one scholarly articles and reviews, and a dozen government studies on Asian security problems. He worked in South Vietnam on the pacification programs in 1966–1967. He teaches Asian security topics and international security affairs at the Air University, Maxwell Air Force Base, Alabama.

WILLIAM HEAD is Deputy Center Historian, Warner Robins Air Logistics Center, Robins Air Force Base, Georgia. He was the coorganizer of the conference "The Vietnam War: Impact and Legacies," held at Georgia Tech in 1991. He has written many books and articles including *Yenan: Col. Wilbur J.*